# KINGSHIP IN INDIAN HISTORY

## The Japanese Association for South Asian Studies

Established in 1988

- **Office Bearers as of 1 July 1999**

  *President*
  Noboru Karashima, Taisho University
  *General Secretary*
  Yoshihiro Matsunami, Taisho University
  *Members of the Board of Executive Directors*
  Gen'ichi Yamazaki, Kokugakuin University
  Haruka Yanagisawa, University of Tokyo
  Hiroshi Yamashita, Tohoku University
  Masaichi Tanaka, Kyoto University
  Michio Yano, Kyoto Sangyo University
  Nariaki Nakazato, University of Tokyo
  Takako Hirose, Daito University
  Takanobu Takahashi, University of Tokyo
  Teiji Sakata, Takushoku University
  Yasumasa Sekine, Japan Women's University

- **Head Office** (untill September 2000)

  c/o Department of Indian Culture, Taisho University
  3-20-1 Nishi-Sugamo, Toshima-ku, Tokyo, Japan 170-8470
  Tel. +81-3-3918-7311 (ex. 541)
  Fax. +81-3-5394-3037
  E-mail. jasas@mail.tais.ac.jp

- **Publications in English**

  1 *JJASAS* (*Journal of the Japanese Association for South Asian Studies*), (annual publication in Japanese and English, the current issue: No. 10)
  2 Newsletter (annual publication, the current issue: No. 7)
  3 Japanese Studies on South Asia Series
    No. 1 H. Kotani ed., *Caste System, Untouchability and the Depressed*, Manohar, New Delhi, 1997.
    No. 2 N. Karashima ed., *Kingship in Indian History*, Manohar, New Delhi, 1999.

*Japanese Studies on South Asia No. 2*

# KINGSHIP IN INDIAN HISTORY

*Edited by*

NOBORU KARASHIMA

MANOHAR
2004

First published 1999
Paperback edition 2004



ISBN 81-7304-544-5

*Published by*
Ajay Kumar Jain for
Manohar Publishers & Distributors
4753/23 Ansari Road, Daryaganj
New Delhi 110002

*Printed at*
Lordson Publishers Pvt. Ltd.
Delhi 110007

# Contents

| | | |
|---|---|---|
| | *Preface* | vii |
| | *Contributors* | ix |
| | Introduction<br>NOBORU KARASHIMA | 1 |
| 1 | Kingship in Ancient India as Described in Literary Sources and Inscriptions<br>GEN'ICHI YAMAZAKI | 17 |
| 2 | The Treatment of King and State in the *Tirukkuṟaḷ*<br>TAKANOBU TAKAHASHI | 37 |
| 3 | God as Warrior King: Images of God in Late Classical Tamil Literature<br>HIROSHI YAMASHITA | 63 |
| 4 | Polity and Kingship of Early Medieval Rajasthan: an Analysis of the Nadol Cāhamāna Inscriptions<br>MASAHIKO MITA | 89 |
| 5 | The Changing Concept of Kingship in the Cōḷa Period: Royal Temple Constructions, c. A.D. 850–1279<br>YASUSHI OGURA | 119 |

6 Vijayanagar Nāyakas in Tamil Nadu and the King
NOBORU KARASHIMA 143

7 Bēḍa Nāyakas and their Historical Narratives in Karnataka during the Post-Vijayanagara Period
NOBUHIRO OTA 163

8 Kingship, Community and Commerce in Late Pre-colonial Khurda
AKIO TANABE 195

9 Kingship, State and Local Society in the Seventeenth-to-Nineteenth Century Deccan with Special Reference to Ritual Functions
HIROYUKI KOTANI 237

# Preface

For the past twenty years, the issue of Indian kingship has attracted the attention of many historians and anthropologists, generating the recent lively polemic on it. My intention in editing this volume is to open the way for Japanese scholars also to join this polemic by providing empirical studies on this key issue as well as constructive criticism of some of the tendencies arising in the recent research. More detailed discussion on this point is presented in the Introduction.

In 1998 I edited with this same intention in mind an issue of *Acta Asiatica* entitled 'Kingship in South Indian History.' Since the work remained preliminary and therefore not as supportive of the purpose as we would have liked, I have undertaken to again edit this book, as it were, as a revised and much enlarged version. The specific relationship between these two volumes is also explained in the Introduction.

This book is the second volume in the series called 'Japanese Studies on South Asia,' the publication of which began in 1997 for the purpose of introducing in English important works on South Asia written by Japanese scholars. This has been done under the general editorship of the Japanese Association for South Asian Studies for the benefit of the international academic community as many of the Japanese researchers have customarily been publishing their works only in the Japanese language. This volume is to be followed by the publication of *Studies in the Pratiṣṭhā* (ed. Shingo Einoo) and others in due course of time.

Prof. Hiroyuki Kotani of Tokyo Metropolitan University, who has had previous experience as the editor of the first volume in this series, and Ms Sae Nakasone, Research Student assisting him, have helped me greatly in preparing the camera-ready copy for this volume. I am grateful to both of them for their painstaking service.

In this volume considerable effort has been made to give uniformity to the spelling of terms in the Indian languages. Unfortunately, some differences have remained, however, since the writers have chosen to adhere to the different spelling style customarily prescribed by their respective disciplines.

*12 July 1999* Noboru Karashima

# Contributors

NOBORU KARASHIMA: Professor, Taisho University. *South Indian History and Society: Studies from Inscriptions A.D. 850-1800*, Oxford University Press, New Delhi, 1984. *Towards a New Formation: South Indian Society under Vijayanagar Rule*, Oxford University Press, New Delhi, 1992.

GEN'ICHI YAMAZAKI: Professor, Kokugakuin University. *The Legend of Aśoka: A Critical Study*, (in Japanese), Tokyo, 1979. *Society in Ancient India: The Social Structure and Middle/Low Classes*, (in Japanese), Tokyo, 1986.

TAKANOBU TAKAHASHI: Associate Professor, University of Tokyo. *Tamil Love Poetry and Poetics*, E.J. Brill, Leiden/New York/Köln, 1995. 'The Breast Price: The Bride Price in Ancient Tamil,' *Tohogaku Ronshu, Eastern Studies Fiftieth Anniversary Volume*, (in Japanese), Toho Gakkai (Institute of Eastern Culture), Tokyo, 1997.

HIROSHI YAMASHITA: Associate Professor, Tohoku University. 'The Forms and Functions of the Aiyanar Temple Complex: A Preliminary Study on the Cult of the Male Godlings in Rural Tamil Nadu,' Y. Ikari and Y. Nagano eds., *From Vedic Altar to Village Shrine: Towards an Interface between Indology and Anthropology*, Senri Ethnological Studies Series 36, Osaka, 1993. 'Some Remarks on the Tirumal/Vishnu Cult in Early Tamil Religion and Literature with Special Reference to the Tirumal Odes of the Paripatal,' *The Memoirs of the Institute of Oriental Culture* 126, Tokyo, 1995.

MASAHIKO MITA: Research Associate, Nagoya University. 'Land Distribution and Kinship of the Nadol Cāhamāna: Structure of Rajput Polity in 12th-Century Rajasthan,' *Journal of the Japanese Association for South Asian Studies* 8, Tokyo, 1996. 'Paddy Production in the Middle Gangetic Basin: c. 600 B.C. to A.D. 300,' (in Japanese), *Journal of Oriental History* 16, Nagoya University, 1992.

YASUSHI OGURA: The Late Associate Professor, University of Tokyo. 'Formation of the Tālamāna System: Iconometry of South Indian Sculpture,' *The Memoirs of the Institute of Oriental Culture* 124, Tokyo, 1994. *Spatial Structure in the Hindu World: Symbolism of Hindu Temples*, (in Japanese), the Institute of Oriental Culture, Tokyo, 1998.

NOBUHIRO OTA: Research Fellow, University of Tokyo. 'A Case Study of the Local Political System under the Tuluva Dynasty of Vijayanagara,' (in Japanese), *Kyoai Ronshu* 12, Tokyo, 1999. 'British Perceptions of South Indian Villages and the Formation of the Ryatwari System,' (in Japanese), N. Karashima ed., *The Dravidian World*, (in Japanese), Tokyo, 1994.

AKIO TANABE: Associate Professor, Kyoto University. 'Ethnohistory of Land and Identity in Khurda, Orissa: From Pre-colonial Past to Post-colonial Present,' *Journal of Asian and African Studies* 56, Tokyo, 1998. 'Kingship and Caste: the Relationship between King/Dominant Caste and Brahman Reconsidered,' H. Kotani ed., *Rituals as Popular Culture: Towards Historico-Anthropological Understanding of Modern Indian Society*, Tokyo, 1999.

HIROYUKI KOTANI: Professor, Tokyo Metropolitan University. *Caste System, Untouchability and the Depressed* (ed.), Manohar, New Delhi, 1997. *Rituals as Popular Culture: Towards Historico-Anthropological Understanding of Modern Indian Society* (ed.), Tokyo, 1999.

# Introduction

NOBORU KARASHIMA

The past twenty years have witnessed the focusing of attention by many historians and anthropologists on the issue of Indian kingship. Notably, the historians who have actively participated in this intensifying study include Burton Stein, Hermann Kulke and B. Chattopadhyaya[1] and the anthropologists Nicholas Dirks, Gloria Raheja and Declan Quigley,[2] whose primary concern has been to elucidate the relations between the king and Brahmins or the position of the king in the caste hierarchy. The main thrust of their study seems to revolve around a criticism of Louis Dumont for his subordinating the king to Brahmins in terms of the pure/impure opposition and, instead, a revival and appreciation of A.M. Hocart for his placing of the king at the pinnacle of society in terms of the gift-giving and -receiving system, though this Hocartian idea is not so conspicuous in the case of Kulke and Chattopadhyaya. Significantly, the interaction among these scholars of differing disciplines has greatly advanced the study of Indian kingship for fostering better understanding of Indian society as a whole.

At the same time, however, a number of problems have also emerged from these studies, urging us toward further and more careful investigation of the issue. Principal among these seems to be the blurring or loosing of the historical perspective in these studies with changes in the meaning and function of kingship having been ignored. With a view toward contributing to this investigation, I edited in 1998 *Acta Asiatica* 74 entitled 'Kingship in South Indian History' by compiling five essays of prominent Japanese scholars working in the area of ancient and medieval south Indian kingship.[3] At that time, however, as these five scholars did not share the same interest in the historico-anthropological or ethno-historical studies of Indian kingship I briefly explored above, the investigation remained insufficient and I described our work as an 'interim report' in its Introduction. Though still preliminary in many senses, the present publication, which I am again privileged to edit, is intended to serve as a review, I sincerely hope, of our deeper exploration of the noted issue.

In this collection I have added to the works of the former five contributors four more essays of other notable scholars in order to extend the scope of our study more broadly to all of India proper. Three of the former essays (those by Takanobu Takahashi, Hiroshi Yamashita and Noboru Karashima) have been revised for this collection. I am saddened, however, to record here the death of Yasushi Ogura, one of our former contributors, who unfortunately met with a fatal car accident in 1998 at the young age of 38. His essay on the Chola kingship, therefore, has been reproduced here in its original entirety except for the change in the noting system and a few corrections of somewhat obvious errors. For a different reason, Nobuhiro Ota, another former contributor, has not altered the text of his previous essay except for some changes in the last two paragraphs. I am grateful to the Institute of Eastern Culture, the publisher of *Acta Asiatica*, for their permission granted to us for reproducing these articles in this publication.

Before discussing the problems studied in this book, I shall give a quick overview of each of the papers. To begin with, Yamazaki's paper examines north Indian kingship as described in the three different kinds of Sanskrit sources dealing with kingship, specifically, the Hindu *Dharmaśāstras*, Buddhist texts and the Kauṭilya's *Arthaśāstra* to ascertain what points (aspects or attributes) of kingship are commonly and necessarily mentioned in all three sources. Of the 18 points thus discovered in them, 12 are stressed as being commonly accepted as necessary by all three sources in recognising the attributes of kingship. However, the three sources differ from each other in their treatment of the remaining six points. Interestingly, while the 12 points accepted by all sources concern mostly secular matters such as the protection of subjects and the collection of taxes, the six points, acceptance of which differs according to the source, concern religious matters such as the divinity and purity of the king. The use of force by the king in ruling also differs according to source, and while Hindu texts accept its use, the Buddhist texts do not.

Following his analysis of the three sources, Yamazaki examines four principal inscriptions to clarify how the concepts of kingship determined through the above analysis were followed or practised by certain kings. In his clarification, Yamazaki selected Aśoka, Khāravela, Rudradāman and Samudragupta for examination, as they left particular inscriptions that enable us to comprehend their idea of kingship. Importantly, all of them accept most of the 12 points as the items they should follow or practise, but they differ considerably in the treatment of the remaining 6. Aśoka, who followed Buddhism, stands at one extreme and Samudragupta, following Vaishnavism, stands at the other, while Khāravela and Rudradāman occupy the middle position. Yamazaki's study thus confirms the relevancy of analysing the issues of Indian kingship by dividing it into the two broad aspects of 'secular' and 'religious,' suggesting also how we might best interpret the difference between the two.

Takahashi's essay examines kingship as revealed from *Tirukkuṟaḷ*, a didactic Tamil classic of the fifth century. This work is often referred to as the south Indian (Dravidian) counterpart of Kauṭilya's *Arthaśāstra*, as it treats *artha* in addition to *dharma* and *kāma*. According to Takahashi, however, *Tirukkuṟaḷ* neither provides us with any prescription for the duties and rights of the king as we see them in the *Arthaśāstra* nor presents us with the often-supposed ferocious image of early south Indian kings as being a brave warrior. It presents, instead, a vague image of the king as an ideal and righteous man. Takahashi's main concern in this essay is to ascertain the reason for this discrepancy as is evidenced between the insufficient and somewhat naïve treatment of kingship and the expectations held by scholars of its more detailed treatment in this work. He attributes this to the author's unique idea concerning the composition of this work as well as to the formal way in which commentators have interpreted the hymns.

As to the historical interpretation of the king's image, Burton Stein assumes that this image of king as a righteous man reflects the influence of Jainism brought from the north. Takahashi throws doubt, however, on the change in the king's image from that of the ferocious warrior to righteous man by claiming that no poems of the Sangam classics can be dated with any degree of certainty. He is also skeptical about the interpretation of the early Tamil kings merely as fierce warriors on the same and on other grounds as well, and suggests the undertaking of more prudent study of the problem based on the more well-supported chronology.

Yamashita's essay again examines the works of the later Sangam period, namely *Tirumurgāṟṟupaḍai* and *Paripāḍal* of the fifth century. The purpose of his study, however, is to examine the assumption of George Hart and other scholars that the concept of the Tamil devotional gods was formed on the basis of the conception of ancient Tamil kings. His study clarifies that Tirumāl and Chevvēḷ, two important dieties praised in the hymns of these two works composed at the dawn of the devotional (*bhakti*) movement, have already assumed the images of Vishṇu and Kārtikeya respectively, popular deities that both appear in north Indian Brahmanical texts. There are, however, some points which suggest a close relation with the ancient Tamil kings who are supposed to have been brave warriors. Yamashita cites, as examples, Chevvēḷ's possession of a long lance, the typical weapon of ancient Tamil kings, and the association of Tirumāl's discus with a particular ancient sacred power called *aṇaṅgu*.

As Yamashita does not take up for examination the texts of the earlier centuries, his criticism against Hart and others, who try to attribute the origin of the devotional god to the king of the earlier centuries, is not as convincing as it might otherwise be, but he is successful in proving the established north Indian Brahmanical influence on fifth-century south India. Notably, therefore, his study together with that of Takahashi, urges us to reexamine the early Sangam texts before we can readily accept Stein's assumption that the earlier image of the Tamil kings as being ferocious warriors was replaced later by that of them being righteous men under the Jain influence. In a similar vein, we have yet to verify Hart's suggestion that the remarkable notion of the concept of Tamil gods of a devotional nature is greatly indebted to that of ancient Tamil kings.

To emphasise briefly here, both examinations made by Takahashi and Yamashita concern the question of what changed and what remained unchanged with regard to the conceptions of god and king, or what change, if any, actually occurred in the relations between the two in ancient south India. Ogura's essay examines this point carefully. He emphasises the change which seemingly occurred in the middle Chola period relating to temple construction. The main trend in temple construction seen during the early Chola period was to build the sepulchral temple (*paḷḷippaḍais*), which implies the practise of hero worship carried down from the Sangam period. During the middle Chola period, however, Rājar̄aja I introduced a new policy of temple construction, in which, though hero worship is discernible in the form of the apotheosis of even the living king in the form of a *liṅga*, another aspect of the king as the supreme priest/devotee of the god (Śiva) also emerged.

Ogura attributes the emergence of this new aspect of kingship to the rise of the Śaivasiddhānta sect of Brahmins in the Chola court. He thus deals with the change in the conceptions of the king in two ways: on the one hand, in terms of the relation between 'king and god,' and on the other, that between 'king and Brahmins.' According to him, the apotheosis of king tended to disappear during the later Chola period and instead king-Brahmin relations began to assume greater importance. This latter point has been discussed by Stein and others in their study of Indian kingship and connects Ogura's essay to those of Karashima and others presented below.

Mita's essay examines Sanskrit inscriptions of the Nadol Chahamana dynasty flourishing in Rajasthan during the twelfth century when the Chola dynasty was still ruling in the south. He first studies the titleholders who were given certain villages or performed important roles in state administrations. This study finds that the ranking system adopted by Nadol Chahamanas was designed and functioned to maintain the political superiority of the royal kinsmen such as the king's heir apparent (usually the eldest son) and other sons, though the members of other clans also participated in the state administration as titleholders. Interestingly, however, the study of village assignments and local administration reveals that once the king changed, almost all of the titleholders also changed according to their relations with the new king.

From this finding, Mita concludes that the ruling system of Nadol Chahamanas did not depend on the clannish relations as often presumed by many scholars, but on the kindred relations of the reigning king. The functioning of the *sāmanta* system, which depends on the local chiefs, is also negated for this kingdom. Consequently, the editor hopes that the following two points will be studied in future: one, in the situation where the intermediaries between the king and the locality were often-transferred royal officers and not local chiefs or magnates, how the kingship could penetrate into localities, or what relations the king had with the local people; and the other, how the so-called clannish ruling system of the Rajiput kingdoms of the later period developed from this kindred-based ruling system. Though Mita does not use the word 'patrimony' for the regime he has described, the application of this concept to it may also deserve examination.

Karashima combines in his essay his recent study of Vijayanagar *nāyakas* in the inscriptions of South Arcot, Tiruchirappalli and Thanjavur districts with the previous ones on those in North Arcot and Chingleput districts, and discusses their rule as local rulers by ascertaining for the first time their numerical strength during the Vijayanagar period. Examining the relations which these *nāyakas* had with the Vijayanagar king, Karashima points out the conspicuous political relations existing between the *nāyakas* and the king. Conversely, Stein denies the existence of political relations between *nāyakas*, who were, according to him, magnates in the locality (segment), and the king, who integrated all of the localities only 'ritually.' Karashima's conclusion is thus to criticise Stein's 'segmentary state' interpretation of pre-modern south Indian states, though in the final stage of his study Stein was inclined to abandon the idea of denying the king's exercise of political sovereignty over the whole kingdom.

Karashima, examining Chola inscriptions as well, points out that the king's deeds of collecting or exempting taxes from the locality by giving orders to the intermediaries responsible in the local administration always occupy the chief position among the matters recorded in inscriptions. According to him, however, the relations between the king and local people assume different forms in accordance with the change of social formation, particularly with the change of the intermediary between the king and locality, such as *nāṭṭārs* in the Chola period and *nāyakas* in the Vijayanagar period, and also with the change of ideology in the rule.

In his essay, Ota examines the ideology of the king's rule by taking up the ancestor legends in inscriptions and family histories for the legitimation of their political authority by Beda Nayakas, or Karnataka 'little kings,' in the seventeenth and eighteenth centuries. He finds in them two rather contradictory points of logic concerning legitimation, namely, their recognition as *nāyakas* by the Vijayanagar king through his grants of land and honour, and their claims of authentic descent in their caste geneologies. Ota explains this dual identity of the Beda Nayakas by stating that after the decline of the Vijayanagar universal kingship, Beda Nayakas had to seek some other legitimation for the basis of their rule than on their position in the royal *dāna* system of the universal king.

According to Ota, the new logic they employed was descent-based caste identity as Bedas. This explanation of the change from an achieved *nāyaka* identity to an ascribed Beda caste identity during the seventeenth and eighteenth centuries is quite interesting, though the latter identity may only be relevant to and effective for mustering the Beda community by their leaders, or in the area where this community was dominant. If we situate this phenomenon in the broader context of social change in India after the disappearance of universal kingship, Ota's essay affords a point for comparison with, or in contrast to, Dirk's interpretation of the continuation of the *dāna* system in Pudukkottai and the somewhat similar situation suggested by Tanabe to have existed in Orissa, both of which were little kingdoms active in the same period as studied by Ota.

Tanabe examines the palm leaf documents preserved by a family in the Khurda region in Orissa recording the account of the Fort Manitri area, an important locality of the Khurda kingdom during the seventeenth and eighteenth centuries. The purpose of his examination is to ascertain the relations the king had with the local community by analysing the accounts pertaining to revenue collection and distribution. According to Tanabe, the previous studies undertaken on Indian kingship featured such flaws as separating the king from local polities by assigning ritual function to the former and administrative function to the latter, or admitting the king's management in the affairs of the locality in his capacity as the pinnacle of the caste hierarchy. Tanabe suggests, instead, the 'interaction' between the king and the local community for the purpose of reproduction of the local community as well as the state. He proposes to understand this interaction in terms of that between 'sacrificer state' and 'sacrificial community,' regarding the king as 'sacrificer' in the local community organised under the 'system of entitlements' which defines the division of labour and distribution of resources in a locality.

In relation to the huge amount of money spent for waging wars during the period, he argues for the king's dependence for that purpose on the monetary economy boosted by the cotton textile production in the hinterland and also by the supply of surplus rice held by the entitlement holders. In this argument, however, he conspicuously excludes the commodity producers and merchants from the interactive relations of the king and locality, which he assumes to have functioned as a logical connection between the kingship and locality in the first half of his essay. The editor would like to see the study of these interactive relations in the form which also includes commodity producers and merchants.

According to the classical law books existing in India such as *Manusmṛti*, the king's prime duty is the protection of his subjects. For fulfilling this aim, he is allowed to inflict punishment (*daṇḍa*) on those individuals who commit social crimes. Besides the punishment by the king (*rājadaṇḍa*), however, there are two other kinds of punishment, one exercised by the assembly of learned men (*pariṣaddaṇḍa*), and the other, by the community itself (*jātidaṇḍa*). Kotani examines a number of Maratha judicial documents from the seventeenth and eighteenth centuries to ascertain what sorts of punishment were exercised in the Maratha kingdom. *Rājadaṇḍa*, *brahmadaṇḍa* and *jātidaṇḍa* described in those documents appear to correspond more or less to the aforementioned three kinds of punishments, though their meanings seem to have changed to some extent in pace with the changes witnessed by society.

Through the examination of the cases in the documents, Kotani distinguishes the punishment exercised impersonally by the state and that exercised for ethical purposes by the king. Further, in relation to this distinction, he draws our attention to the existence of an official called *dharmadhikārī* who performed rituals for purifying the sinner to maintain the social order in the locality. Significantly, the *dharmadhikārī* is not a state official but rather the functionary sustained by the locality. From these elucidated factors, Kotani criticises the recent study of Indian kingship pursued by anthropologists and historians for not taking cognizance of the importance of the king's role as the state head who inflicted punishment impersonally independent of ideology and also for their arguing for the penetration of kingship into the local community through the performance of rituals. According to him, the locality has its own ritualistic apparatus for maintaining social order as revealed by the existence of *dharmadhikārīs*.

We shall now discuss the salient points of the Indian kingship studies emerging from the examinations made in the aforenoted essays. The first point concerns Kotani's suggestion for distinguishing the two aspects of kingship: one, the king's authority which he exercised impersonally and secularly as the head of the state, and the other, that which he exercised personally and ethically as the supreme follower and guardian of a certain creed or ideology. This distinction may well be said to correspond to a considerable degree with the well-known dichotomy of the Indian kingship into 'secular' and 'religious' or into 'political' and 'ritual' as maintained by many scholars and supported also by Yamazaki's analysis in this volume. However, Kotani gives more importance to the 'secular' and 'political' aspect of the kingship than to the 'religious' and 'ritual' aspect, thus criticising the tendency of giving more significance to the latter in recent anthropological studies. Karashima is also explicit on this point by saying that 'the purpose of this [his] essay is to review the political aspect of kingship from the perspective of the historical development of the state and society, specifically to swing purposefully the pendulum to the opposite end in an endeavour to reinfuse the historicity into the study of Indian kingship.' Thus the standpoint of Kotani and Karashima is rather close to that of, among the scholars who actively participated in the recent polemics, Chattopadhyaya and Kulke who argue for the combined exercise of the two aspects of the king's authority [Chattopadhyaya 1983 ; Kulke 1985].

The second point regards the relations between the king and the locality, that is to say, questions whether or not the kingship permeated into the local community, and if it did, how it was realised. There seems to be two factors to be considered in this relation. The first one concerns the 'size' of the kingdom. Though Tanabe criticises Dirks for his giving the highest authority to the king even in local affairs ignoring the institutional or systemic power of the local community, he also admits the permeation into the locality of the authority of king as the 'sacrificer.' It is interesting to note here, however, that both the Pudukkottai kingdom in Tamil Nadu studied by Dirks [1987] and the Khurda kingdom in Orissa taken up by Tanabe are so-called 'little kingdoms' characterised by limited area and population. Though we do not know the precise situation in the Beda Nayakas' area, another 'little kingdom' in Karnataka of the same period examined by Ota, we may raise the question here as to whether or not the permeation of the kingship into the locality was possible and realised only in those 'little kingdoms.'

In the examination of this point, however, we must relate the problem necessarily with the division of kingship into the two aspects of 'political' and 'ritual.' Tanabe's suggestion for the permeation of kingship into localities in the 'little kingdom' may be acceptable, as he argues for the combination of the two aspects working together as a 'cultural paradigm' in such kingdoms. If we accept the penetration of kingship into localities in that way in the 'little kingdom,' we must ask how it relates to the 'great kingdom' in general or in the 'early medieval' chieftaincy. This point will be considered below coupled with the historical aspect of the problem, as it relates inseparably to the issues of the *sāmanta* system, feudalism, *bhakti* ideology and other matters, which can be properly analysed only in the historical perspective.

As the second factor, therefore, we shall now consider the historical stage in which the permeation of the kingship into localities was realised. Tanabe states that the interaction of the kingship and the local community and the subsequent permeation of the kingship into the latter were made possible only under the historical circumstances generating the state formation in Orissa during the sixteenth through eighteenth centuries. This interpretation may be acceptable for the later medieval Orissa, but it immediately raises the question of whether or not it is applicable to the early medieval kingdoms in general. There, according to Chattopadhyaya [1983], a similar process was under way in the form of expansion of the *sāmanta* kingdoms, whereas, according to some other scholars [Jha 1979; Sharma 1985], feudalism was the prevailing social formation. Concerning the early medieval kingdoms, however, neither Ogura, who studied the kingship of the Cholas ruling in the south from the ninth to thirteenth centuries, nor Mita, who studied that of the Nadol Chahamanas of the twelfth century, have discussed the problem of the permeation of the kingship into localities in the manner Tanabe has done. Though their silence on this point seems to derive from the non-availability of information on the matter in their sources, i.e., Chola temple structures and Chahamana Sanskrit inscriptions, Karashima, who discussed the kingship of the Chola and Vijayanagar kingdoms, both of which were 'great kingdoms,' argues for the penetration of the king's authority into localities. He does so by referring, for example, to the king's name recorded in the temple-wall inscriptions and to the swearing of allegiance by the local leaders to the king for their remission of the tax in their locality. He thus argues for the penetration of the 'secular' and 'political' authority of the king into localities in the 'great kingdoms.'[4]

It would then serve us to ask a pertinent question about the ideological or ritualistic aspect of the kingship, specifically whether it also permeated into the locality. Kotani is rather unsupportive of this point in his delineating the salient role which *dharmadhikārīs*, sustained by the local society, played in the area of religious matters. He distinguishes the king's ritual from that instituted and maintained by the local community. Karashima and Ogura, however, point out the use of Brahmins and the Brahmanical ideology by the Chola kings in their state administration. The interdependent relations between the king and Brahmins warrant further study notwithstanding the present popularity of Hocartian views in recent studies. Many scholars seem to believe, however, that there occurred a change at a certain stage in the medieval period from the king-Brahmin relations to the king-temple relations in the sphere of politico-religious interdependence [Appadurai 1977: 49]. *Bhakti* worship, given importance by M.G.S. Narayanan and Kesavan Veluthat in their study of south Indian early medieval kingdoms [Narayanan & Veluthat 1978], seems to have constituted the ideology fusing both the centre and the locality. All of these points should be clarified in relation to the issue of permeation of kingship into localities.

As a final point, we should discuss here the relation between the king and the state. As for the study of states, however, we have at hand a vast accumulation of studies. As examples, while Romila Thapar [1984] discussed the ancient state formation as the process of transformation from lineage to state, Kulke [1985] and Chattopadhyaya [1983] examined the process of state formation for later periods. R.S. Sharma and other scholars have studied the early medieval state and society by applying the concept of feudalism to them.[5] Contrarily, Harbans Mukhia [1981] was opposed to this application of feudal theory to Indian states, and Kathleen Gough [1980] applied the concept of Asiatic Mode of Production to south Indian history. Meanwhile Burton Stein [1977; 1980] introduced a thought-provoking new theory of the 'segmentary state' into the study of south Indian states, and Karashima [1984; 1992] argued for the change in the state and society between the Chola and the Vijayanagar periods, suggesting the appearance of a new formation during the latter period. R. Champakalakshmi [1996] and others have clarified mainly the urban economy of the state.[6] Among the studies of the Mughal and other later medieval states,[7] the 'patrimonial' interpretation presented by Stephen Blake [1979] deserves special mention. The polemics generated by this variety of stimulating research has greatly enriched our knowledge of Indian history and advanced its study.

There is no doubt, however, that the segmentary state theory put forward by Stein was one of the most stimulating of these new interpretations. This is because it opened the way for introducing anthropological analysis into the state studies through taking up the ritual sovereignty, or the religious aspect of the kingship, for discussion, though the importance of religion in Indian state administration had been well recognised by many scholars in the past.[8] Nonetheless, considerable criticism arose against this segmentary state theory of Stein's.[9] Some of the principal points of its criticism are the 'ignoring of the class character of the state' [Sharma 1993], 'negation of king's exercise of political sovereignty over the kingdom' [Chattopadhyaya 1983], 'lack of viewpoint of historical change or development of society' [Karashima 1984: xxvii] and 'misunderstanding or ignoring of certain fundamental facts' [Subbarayalu 1982; Jha 1984]. Though the separation of the ritual sovereignty from the political one and the denial of the king's exercise of the latter over the whole kingdom constituted the crucial points of his theory, he abandoned the second point in the final stage of his study [Stein 1991].[10] However, his discussion about the ritual sovereignty has measurably enlarged the scope of Indian state studies, with many anthropologists subsequently joining the historians or *vice versa* in the study as stated earlier. In this process of having the study proliferate through the expanding group of participating anthropologists and historians, however, 'the lack of viewpoint of historical change or development of society' seen in Stein's theory has remained uncorrected in some cases or rather has been enhanced by certain scholars. Thus, our efforts made toward correcting this tendency is evidenced in the studies collected in this volume.

Kingship is certainly one of the most important issues in the study of the Indian state and society, and its recent research has greatly increased our knowledge. But it is also certain that we must engage in a great many more empirical studies on the functioning of kingship in terms of the various pre-modern Indian states in existence by examining contemporary source materials such as inscriptions, village accounts and family histories. In the course of such studies, the relevancy of the dichotomy of kingship into 'political' and 'ritual,' or that of the state into 'little' and 'great,' should also further be examined. Kingship in the ancient Tamil kingdoms additionally should be explored through the more prudent examination of the Saṅgam classics. Moreover, we must relate the issue of kingship with the economic development of the society in order to better understand the historical perspective in its study as Tanabe attempted in his essay.

In the past studies most scholars have tended to focus their research on some particular period by employing a specific analytical concept. Essential to any such study, however, is the placing of the issue of kingship in the larger historical perspective which will enable us to discuss pertinent changes in the kingship's concept and function in pace with the changes witnessed in the overall socio-economic formation. Toward this endeavour I sincerely hope that this collection of essays will contribute notably through its provision of empirical explorations in conjunction with added stimulus for impelling inquiry into the recent polemics concerning the Indian kingship.

## Notes

1 Their representative works are [Stein 1980], [Kulke 1993] and [Chattopadhyaya 1994].

2 Their representative works are [Dirks 1987], [Raheja 1988] and [Quigley 1993].

3 The five scholars are T. Takahashi, H. Yamashita, Y. Ogura, N. Karashima and N. Ota.

4 In this relation it may not be irrelevant to recall the presence of a king's agent at the assembly of a Brahmin village on the occasion of its deliberation on some important local affair, the fact, to which due attention was first paid by Nilakanta Sastri more than fifty years ago in his study of Chola inscriptions [Sastri1955: 496]. P. Shanmugam and James Heitzman have clarified the establishment and activities of the land revenue department of the Chola state [Shanmugam 1987: 121-38; Heitzman 1997: 156-61].

5 Sharma's magnum opus is [1965]. For another of his works and those by others, see [Jha (ed.) 1987] and [Jha 1993].

6 Their works include [Hall 1980], [Spencer 1983] and [Subrahmanyam (ed.) 1990].

7 Some of the important works are referred to or included in [Subrahmanyam 1986] and [Habib (ed.) 1992].

8 Karashima's paper [1972], read at the Second International Conference-Seminar of Tamil Studies-1968, also discusses the use of Brahmins for the state rule by the Chola kings.

9 The most recent and representative criticism against Stein is [Sharam 1993], though it takes the form of criticism against Southall.

10 As he began to argue in [1991] for the combined exercise of the two aspects of the sovereignty, the demarcation between his interpretation and that held by Kulke, Chattopadhyaya and others who argued for the combined exercise of the two in the *sāmanta* system has been blurred or lost.

## References

Appadurai, Arjun

1977 'Kings, Sects and Temples in South India,' *The Indian Economic and Social History Review*, vol. XIV, no. 1.

Blake, Stephan P.

1979 'The Patrimonial-Bureaucratic Empire of the Mughals,' *Journal of Asian Studies*, vol. 39, pp. 77-94.

Byres, T.J. and Mukhia, Harbans, eds.

1985 *Feudalism and Non-European Societies*, Frank Cass, London.

Champakalakshmi, R.

1996 *Trade, Ideology and Urbanization: South India 300 BC to AD 1300*, Oxford University Press, Delhi.

Chattopadhyaya, Brajadulal

1983 'Political Process and the Structure of Polity in Early Medieval India: Problems of Perspective,' Presidential Address, Ancient India Section, *Proceedings of the Indian History Congress*, 44th Session, Burdwan, and reprinted in [Chattopadhyaya 1994] and [Kulke 1995].

1994 *The Making of Early Medieval India*, Oxford University Press, Delhi.

Dirks, Nicholas B.

1987 *The Hollow Crown: Ethnohistory of an Indian Kingdom*, Cambridge University Press, Cambridge.

Fox, Richard G. (ed.)

1977 *Realm and Region in Traditional India*, Vikas Publishing House, New Delhi.

Gough, Kathreen

1980 'Mode of Production in Southern India,' *Economic and Political Weekly*, Annual Number, February.

Habib, Irfan (ed.)

1992 *Medieval India 1: Researches in the History of India 1200-1750*, Oxford University Press, New Delhi.

Hall, Kenneth R.

1980 *Trade and State Craft in the Age of the Colas*, Abhinav Publications, New Delhi.

Heitzman, James

1997 *Gifts of Power: Lordship in Early Indian State*, Oxford University Press, Delhi.

Jha, D.N.

1979 'Early Indian Feudalism: A Historiographic Critique,' Presidential Address, Ancient India Section, *Proceedings of the Indian History Congress*, 40th Session, Waltair.

1984 'Validity of the "Brahmana-Peasant Alliance" and the "Segmentary State" in Early Medieval India,' *Social Science Probings*, vol. 1, no. 2.

1993 *Economy and Society in Early India: Issues and Paradigms*, Munshiram Manoharlal, New Delhi.

Jha, D.N. (ed.)

1987 *Feudal Social Formation in Early India*, Chanakya Publications, Delhi.

Karashima, Noboru

1972 'The Power Structure of the Chola Rule,' *Proceedings of the Second International Conference-Seminar of Tamil Studies–1968*, vol. II, Madras, and reprinted in [Karashima 1984].

1984 *South Indian History and Society: Studies from Inscriptions A.D. 850-1800*, Oxford University Press, New Delhi.

1992 *Towards a New Formation: South Indian Society Under Vijayanagar Rule*, Oxford University Press, New Delhi.

1998a 'Vijayanagar Nayaka and King: An Examination of Nayakas in North Arcot District Inscriptions' in [Karashima 1998b: 59-99].

Karashima, Noboru (ed.)

1998b *Kingship in South Indian History* (*Acta Asiatica* 74), Institute of Eastern Culture, Tokyo.

Kulke, Hermann

1985 'The Early and the Imperial Kingdom: A Processural Model of the State in Early Medieval India,' H. Kulke & D. Rothermund eds., *Regionale Tradition in Südasien*, Franz Steiner-Verlag, Wiesbaden, and later reprinted in [Kulke (ed.) 1995].

1993 *Kings and Cults: State Formation and Legitimation in India and Southeast Asia*, Manohar, New Delhi.

Kulke, Hermann (ed.)

1995 *The State in India 1000-1700*, Oxford University Press, Delhi.

Mukhia, Harbans

1981 'Was There Feudalism in Indian History?,' *The Journal of Peasant Studies*, vol. 8, and later reprinted in [Byre & Mukhia (eds.) 1985].

Narayanan, M.G.S. & Veluthat, Kesavan

1978 'Bhakti Movement in South India,' Malick, S.C. ed., *Indian Movements: Some Aspects of Dissent and Reform*, Indian Institute of Advanced Studies, Simla, and later reprinted in [Jha (ed.) 1987].

Ogura, Yasushi

1998 'The Changing Concept of Kingship in the Cola Period: Royal Temple Construction, ca. A.D. 850-1279' in [Karashima 1998b: 39-58].

Ota, Nobuhiro

1998 'Beda Nayakas and Their Historical Narratives in Karnataka during the Post-Vijayanagara Period' in [Karashima 1998b: 100-28].

Quigley, Declan

1993 *The Interpretation of Caste*, Clarendon Press, Oxford.

Raheja, Gloria G.

1988 *The Poison in the Gift*, University of Chicago Press, Chicago and London.

Sastri, K.A. Nilakanta

1955 *The Colas*, second ed. (first ed. in two volumes in 1935 & 1937), University of Madras, Madras.

Shanmugam, P.

1987 *The Revenue System of the Cholas, 850-1279*, New Era Publications, Madras.

Sharma, R.S.

1965 *Indian Feudalism: c. 300-1200*, University of Culcutta, Culcutta.

1985 'How Feudal was Indian Feudalism?,' *The Journal of Peas-*

*ant Studies*, vol. 12, and reprinted in [Byre & Mukhia 1985] and revised print in [Kulke 1995].

1993 'The Segmentary State and the Indian Experience,' *The Indian Historical Review*, vol. XVI, nos. 1-2, 1989-90.

Spencer, George W.

1983 *The Politics of Expansion: The Chola Conquest of Sri Lanka and Sri Vijaya*, New Era Publications, Madras.

Stein, Burton

1977 'The Segmentary State in South Indian History,' in [Fox 1977].

1980 *Peasant State and Society in Medieval South India*, Oxford University Press, New Delhi.

1991 'The Segmentary State: Interim Reflections,' *Purusartha*, vol. 13, 1991, and reprinted in [Kulke 1995].

Subbarayalu, Y.

1982 'The Cola State,' *Studies in History*, vol. IV, no. 2.

Subrahmanyam, Sanjay

1986 'Aspects of State Formation in South India and Southeast Asia, 1500-1650,' *The Indian Economic and Social History Review*, XXIII-4.

Subrahmanyam, Sanjay (ed.)

1990 *Merchants, Markets and the States in Early Modern India*, Oxford University Press, New Delhi.

Takahashi, Takanobu

1998: 'The Treatment of King and State in the *Tirukkuṟaḷ*' in [Karashima 1998b:1-19].

Thapar, Romila

1984 *From Lineage to State*, Oxford University Press, Bombay.

Veluthat, Kesavan

1993 *The Political Structure of Early Medieval South India*, Orient Longman, Hyderabad.

Yamashita, Hiroshi

1998 'God and King in Pre-Devotional Tamil Texts' in [Karashima 1998b: 20-38].

1

# Kingship in Ancient India as Described in Literary Sources and Inscriptions[1]

GEN'ICHI YAMAZAKI

## Introduction

Kings who had shaken off the tribal fetters appeared first in ancient India in the period of the Sixteen Great States, sixth to fifth century B.C. This period gave rise to differing schools of political science focusing on the treatment of the various problems of state policy. Their arguments later developed into the *Arthaśāstra*, originally written by Kauṭilya c. 300 B.C. but was finally compiled as late as c. A.D. 300. Apart from these schools, Brahmans who adhered to the orthodox thought of Brahmanism, and teachers who believed in the heterodox thoughts, i.e., Buddhism or Jainism, also referred to kings and states in their writings.

In my previous articles presented on kingship in ancient India [Yamazaki 1994: 41-130], I took up three literary sources of differing character: the *Dharmaśāstras*, the most important of which is *Manusmṛti* compiled by advocates of orthodox Brahmanism sometime between c. 200 B.C. and A.D. 200; the Buddhist literature, written by believers of heterodox thought c. 500–100 B.C.; and the *Arthaśāstra* compiled by teachers of political science. And through the comparative study of these sources I have elucidated both the common and contradictory views among them on ancient Indian kingship which I will enumerate below.

In the present essay, I would like to compare the conclusions drawn from my previous studies on those literary sources to the kingship described in four inscriptions set down in ancient India: the Edicts of Aśoka (third century B.C.), the Hāthigumphā Inscription of Khāravela (second or first century B.C.), the Junāgaḍh Rock Inscription of Rudradāman (second century A.D.), and the Allahabad Pillar Inscription of Samudragupta (fourth century A.D.). These four constitute the longest inscriptions concerning kingship in ancient India up to the fourth century A.D.

## Kingship in the Three Literary Sources

In my previous studies, I reached the conclusion that the following twelve points summarise the common views held on kingship among the above three literary sources. Accordingly, we may postulate that these points constitute the basic ancient Indian concept of kingship.

1. The king has supreme power over the secular world and serves at the summit of the state; the destiny of the state depends on his abilities and actions.
2. The king is required to govern in accordance with the *dharma*.
3. The most important duty of the king is to protect his subjects and to maintain social and political order; the duty of protecting Brahmans, religious mendicants and religious sects is also stressed.
4. The king is required to have paternal love towards his subjects.
5. The king has been given the *daṇḍa*, the rod symbolising his judicial and military power, to enable him to fulfill his duties.
6. The king has the right to collect taxes and take his share (*bhāga*) as remuneration for fulfilling his duties.
7. Mistaken policies are regarded as neglect in the king's duties, and in this case the execution or banishment of an unjust king is approved.
8. The king is required to possess dignity and ability suitable to his rank, and to act accordingly; *kṣatriya-varṇa* (military caste) origin is desirable, but is not an absolute precondition of the king.
9. The king is believed to be a man of good fortune who is able to bring prosperity to his people through his mystical powers.
10. The king must respect tradition, and he should endeavour not to destroy the indigenous traditional order of another country after conquering it; he should be sufficiently satisfied with the submission of his enemy kings.
11. The king, ruling under the yoke of *karma* and *saṃsāra*, is destined to go either to heaven or hell according to his acts; the king who governs righteously acquires not only his own religious merit but also a part of the merit accumulated by his subjects, but if he governs unrighteously, he receives the same amount of religious demerit.
12. Kingship functions effectively with the help of the bureaucracy and military.

The following six points summarise the views contradictorily held by the three above-mentioned literary sources.

13. Kingship was created by God and was granted to human beings, i.e., God created the original king (*Dharmaśāstras*); kingship was given by the people to the first ruler through some kind of social contract (Buddhist literature). The king's *daṇḍa* and his right of tax collection were originally given by God (*Dharmaśāstras*), or given by the people (Buddhist literature). Accordingly, the king must be charged with the crime of his misrule ultimately to God (*Dharmaśāstras*) or to the people (Buddhist literature). *Arthaśāstra*'s standpoint on this subject is not clear, but is somewhat closer to that of the Buddhist literature.
14. The king is deified (*Dharmaśāstras*); he is not deified (Buddhist literature). Special rituals performed by Brahmans, whose ritual status is higher than the king, are indispensable for his deification. Buddhists' ideal king *cakravartin* is described to have unlimited virtue, not divinity. In the *Arthaśāstra*, the king is required to govern practically and rationally, his deification being utilised only as a temporary expedient.
15. *Dharma* is based on the Vedic or Brahmanical *dharma* (*Dharmaśāstras*); *dharma* is based on the universal law (Buddhist literature). Vedic *dharma* which surpasses the king's authority has been handed down by Brahmans, so that the king must obey their teachings not only religiously but also politically. *Dharma* of the *Arthaśāstra* is closer to that of *Dharmaśāstras*, but in this source the king's order sometimes surpasses the dignity of *dharma*. The order of society is that of the *varṇa-āśrama*, i.e., the four fundamental castes and four stages of life (*Dharmaśāstras*, *Arthaśāstra*), or that of universal law (Buddhist literature).
16. Policy via the skillful use of *daṇḍa* is recommended (*Dharmaśāstras*, *Arthaśāstra*); a non-*daṇḍa* policy is extoled (Buddhist literature).
17. Ritual purity is required of the king (*Dharmaśāstras*); ethical purity is recommended (Buddhist literature). *Dharmaśāstras* explain that the ritual purity of the king who is doing his duty righteously is equal to that of Brahmans who are conducting their religious ceremony.
18. Importance of the king's attachment to sacrificial rites for the prosperity of his kingdom is emphasised (*Dharmaśāstras*); the king is recommended to use the rites as a form of political tactic

(*Arthaśāstra*); sacrificial rites are seen as ineffective and sinful (Buddhist literature).

Concerning the above contradictory views on kingship (items 13-18), we find two extreme views, one is the orthodox standpoint and the other is the heterodox. The standpoint of the *Arthaśāstra*, roughly speaking, holds the ground between these two.

In the following sections, I would like to clarify how the above-mentioned common and contradictory views on kingship are reflected in the inscriptions of our four ancient Indian kings.

## Aśoka

The third Mauryan emperor Aśoka (c. 268-232 B.C.) conquered Kalinga, modern Orissa, eight years after he had ascended the throne. This conquest proved a turning point in his rule. He said himself that seeing the great misery of the Kalinga war, his heart was filled with sorrow and repentance, so that he gave up the policy of military conquest which had been pursued by former kings as well as himself and adopted a new policy of *dharma*. He also became a lay worshipper of Buddhism soon after the war. After that he proclaimed edicts to propagate the new policy, and had them inscribed on rocks and stone pillars.[2]

Here, the kingship described in the edicts will be compared to the above views (items 1-18) derived from the three literary sources.

Items 1 and 2: Aśoka firmly believed that if the king took the initiative to practice the *dharma* and his subjects followed him, prosperity and peace would be achieved. The *dharma* was the basic concept of Indian philosophy and religion signifying universal law and righteousness, though the contents of universal law and righteousness vary from religion to religion. Aśoka specifically selected this word to invest his political ideas with universal character. His *dharma* is closer to the Buddhist *dharma* than the Vedic or Brahmanical *dharma*. With regard to this *dharma* policy, Aśoka's statement is roughly as follows:

> The highest duty of the king is to bring his subjects welfare and happiness both in this world and in the next. Because such welfare and happiness can be achieved through the practice of the *dharma*, the king must take the initiative and teach his subjects the wonderful fruits they will receive from practicing it. Kings of the past did not understand this, but Aśoka is doing his best to practice and teach the *dharma*,

believing this to be the most important duty of the king. Through this policy the debt of the king to his subjects will be paid. Aśoka's ideal will be achieved when the *dharma* is practiced throughout the world for eternity. Conquest through the *dharma* is true conquest, and fame gotten by it is true fame.

Items 3 and 4: Aśoka called all of his subjects 'my sons,' and asked them to love and respect him as their 'father.' His protection extended not only to the slaves and servants but also to the birds and animals. His policy of protection may be summarised as follows:

(1) Injure no living thing; abandon armed conquest; protect and release prisoners; prohibit useless slaughter; restrict castration and branding, and the like.
(2) Provide public welfare services, like medical treatment for all humans and animals; cultivation of medicinal herbs, roots and fruits for humans and animals; digging of wells and planting of trees on the roads for the enjoyment of humans and animals.
(3) Protect and support Brahmans, *śramanas* (religious mendicants), and all religious sects.

Social order based on the *dharma* brings stability to the family, village, district and the state. Eager to attain such order and stability, Aśoka recommended that his subjects practice the following virtues:

(1) Obedience to mother and father; proper courtesy, firm devotion and liberality to friends, acquaintances and relatives.
(2) Obedience, reverence and liberality to Brahmans, *śramanas* and elders.
(3) Proper courtesy to slaves and servants.
(4) Reflection, self-control and respect to others.

The social order thus established might be quite different from that of the *varṇa* system advocated by orthodox Brahmans, which was based on social discrimination.

Item 5: The *danda*, symbolising armed force or punishment, brings pain to living beings if it is used arbitrarily. Aśoka did not discard armed force entirely, but eschewed it until he had reached the end of his endurance.[3] Concerning punishment, he stressed justice, impartiality and penal mitigation. However, he did retain the death penalty, granting only three days postponement to criminals. He gave discretionary power to his judges so that they could perform their duties confidently.

Items 6 and 7: Aśoka explained a policy of providing his subjects happiness as 'acquittance of debt (*ānṛṇya*).' He was definitely aware of a king's duty to protect his subjects, and criticised former kings as having neglected it. But it is not certain whether he used the word '*ānṛṇya*' consciously in relation to his right of taxation or not. From the Rummindei Pillar Inscription of Aśoka, we know that two kinds of taxes, *bali* and *bhāga*, were collected at that time.[4] *Bhāga* means '[king's] share,' but it is not certain if this tax was collected from his subjects by Aśoka consciously in return for his protection policy.

Item 8: The Mauryas likely originated from a powerful clan situated in the middle Ganga valley. They were not recognised as orthodox *kṣatriyas* by conservative Brahmans living in the upper Ganga valley, the homeland of Brahmanism. Possibly because of this, Aśoka did not mention his lineage or his *varṇa* status, but stressed only his ability, deeds and morality. He also expressed his hope that as long as his descendants defended his *dharma* policy, prosperity of the Mauryas would be sure to continue.

Item 9: The titles assumed by Aśoka, such as 'Beloved of the Gods (Devānāṃ priya)' and 'Man of Pleasant Looks (Priyadarśin),' may presumably be understood to show the idea that the king should be a man of good fortune. However, Aśoka himself did not say that his own person was either auspicious or divine, but only stressed that the king should bring happiness to his subjects through his practice and propagation of the *dharma*.

Item 10: Aśoka insisted that his *dharma* was based on ancient tradition. Past kings, he said, ignored tradition and governed unjustly. He called his *dharma* 'ancient custom (*paurāṇī prakṛti*)' and proclaimed the revival of tradition.

When Aśoka embarked on his *dharma* policy, his conquest of the Subcontinent had almost been completed. At that time, Aśoka abandoned his policy of territorial expansion by armed force, and adopted a new policy of world conquest through the *dharma*. This ideal is akin to the reign of *cakravartin*, the Buddhist ideal sovereign. Whether the notion of *cakravartin* was present in Aśoka's *dharma* policy is not certain.

Item 11: Aśoka repeatedly stressed welfare and happiness in this world as well as in the next, and also mentioned that happiness in the next world, i.e., birth in heaven among gods, was more important than the happiness in this world. Aśoka even proclaimed that through the practice of the *dharma* foreign kings and their subjects would become happy and be born in heaven. Lawless persons were described as 'unable to go to heaven,' but 'hell' was not mentioned.

Item 12: Aśoka definitely knew that his *dharma* policy would be realized with the help of his officials. He repeatedly called upon his officials to return 'their debt to him' through the practice and propagation of *dharma*. What is more, he appointed Dharmamahāmātras who exclusively propagated his *dharma* policy.

Let us now compare the contents of the Aśoka inscriptions to the six contradictory views on kingship among the three literary sources.

Items 13 and 14: Aśoka did not comment directly on such problems as the origin or the deification of the king. However, from the fact that he himself was Buddhist, and also from his expression, 'returning the debt,' it is possible to assume that he held to the idea of the origin of kingship as a contract, as did the Buddhist literature. He did not intend to divinise himself, and called himself 'king of Magadha,' avoiding the use of haughty titles like 'emperor (*samrāj*).' 'God' in his moderate title 'Beloved of the Gods' did not mean the Supreme God believed to have created kingship, because Aśoka told in his inscription that gods mingled with men in the peaceful *dharma*-enriching time.[5]

Item 15: Aśoka explained his *dharma* as 'goodness (*sādhu*).' He also explained it more concretely as minimal sin, many virtuous deeds, compassion, liberality, truthfulness, purity of thought, gratitude, firm conviction, and the like. These are aspects of universal morality that are to be honoured by all human beings beyond the boundaries of nation, religion or status. Though his *dharma* holds many aspects in common with Brahmanism, it is incompatible with the *varṇa-dharma* which advocates strict social discrimination. His *dharma* was not the religion of Buddhism itself, but it might constitute a set of political ideas supported by Buddhist social ethics.

Item 16: Though Aśoka abandoned conquest by force and proclaimed non-violence, he neither abandoned his military forces nor abolished the death penalty. However, his *dharma* policy contained no strategy for the skillful use of the *daṇḍa*, as recommended in the *Dharmaśāstras* and the *Arthaśāstra*. It was rather a policy based on non-*daṇḍa* principles.

Item 17: Aśoka did not mention anything about ritual purity or impurity, concepts fundamentally important to the orthodox Brahmanism. Purity (*śauca*), one of the aspects of his *dharma*, should be understood as ethical purity.

Item 18: Aśoka's position was clear on this point. He prohibited Brahmanical sacrificial rites involving the killing of animals because he saw them not only as being absurd but also as being harmful. Prayers which people recite on occasions of disease, travel, marriage or childbirth were also explained as being nearly useless. True happiness and prosperity, said Aśoka, could be achieved by practicing the *dharma*. Festivals held for the propagation of the *dharma* were recommended, but festivals accompanying the sacrifice of animals were not.

In ancient India, the ruler of the secular world could not intervene in the affairs of the religious world theoretically. But actually such intervention often happened as Aśoka's religious policy gave an example.

In conclusion to the above comparison, the descriptions of kingship in the Edicts are more or less in agreement with the twelve common views stated. That is to say, Aśoka proclaimed his *dharma* policy on the basis of kingship as generally defined in ancient India. Concerning the latter six points of controversy, kingship seen in the inscriptions is mostly heterodox, i.e., Buddhist. But Aśoka placed Buddhism side by side with Brahmanism, Jainism and Ājīvikas in his Edicts in an attempt to persuade people that his *dharma* was not the doctrine of one religion but was acceptable universally.

## Samudragupta

Samudragupta (c. A. D. 335-375) was the second emperor of the Gupta dynasty. Kingship mentioned in his Allahabad Pillar Inscription [Fleet 1970: 1-17, Sircar 1965: 262-268], a eulogy written by General Hariṣeṇa and dedicated to his sovereign, stands in opposition to the idea contained in the Edicts of Aśoka. Though the reign of Samudragupta was much later than those of Khāravela and Rudradāman, I would like to take up his inscription here for comparison's sake. The present inscription is much shorter than the Edicts of Aśoka, and its references to kingship are limited. Taking this lack of information into consideration, let us compare kingship in this inscription to the twelve common views listed above.

Items 1 and 2: The view that the king stands at the summit of the state and that the destiny of the state depends on his ability can be seen throughout the inscription. This standpoint is also clear from the title 'supreme king of great kings (*mahārājādhirāja*)' and 'greatest lord (*paramabhaṭṭāraka*),' and from the expression 'he who is the cause of prosperity of the good and the fall of the bad' (*sādhu-asādhu-udaya-pralaya-hetu-puruṣa*). Moreover, Samudragupta was described as having conquered the whole world and as being a man without match in this world. Concerning the policy in accordance with the *dharma*, only the vague expression that 'he binds the hedge of the *dharma* (*dharma-prācīra-bandha*)' is found.

Items 3, 4 and 5: The idea that the protection of his subjects is the highest duty of the king is expressed in the words of Candragupta 'protect the whole earth (*nikhilām pāhy urvīm*),' which were said to have been uttered when he selected and appointed his son Samudragupta to be his successor. Sumudragupta was extoled as having done his best to bestow favours on his subjects, and his protection extended from poets and artists to the poor and the afflicted. Under his rule, orthodox Brahmanical religion prospered, but reference to the *varṇa* order is not found in the inscription. Concerning the *daṇḍa*, Samudragupta's valour and military successes were praised throughout the inscription. About punishment according to the *daṇḍa*, only 'the cause of the fall of the bad' mentioned above is found.

Items 6, 7 and 8: No mention exists concerning tax collection except that conquered kings were ordered to pay tax or tribute (*karadāna*). Though no mention is found of unjust rule, we do see all sorts of implications about the king's dignity, ability and action. For example, he was highly virtuous, handsome, brave and skilled in all kinds of military arts; 'He by his sharp intellect and musical skill puts to shame even gods and demi-gods,' and 'He established his title king-of-poets (*kavirāja*) by various poetical compositions.'

Concerning Samudragupta's origins, his relationship through his mother, Kumāradevī, to the noble lineage of Licchavis (famous *kṣatriya* clan) was stressed. Very likely the Gupta family did not belong to the orthodox *kṣatriya-varṇa*, but belonged to either *brāhmaṇa-*, *vaiśya-* or inferior *kṣatriya-varṇa*. The legitimacy of the Guptas to rule was gained by Candragupta's marriage to the Licchavi Princess. Samudragupta and other Gupta kings after him expressed their pride over and over again in being related to Licchavis in their inscriptions.

Item 9: Concerning the auspicious character of the king, Samudragupta was described as 'of great fortune (*mahābhāgya*),' and the names of his ancestors begin with the epithet *Śrī*, i.e., auspicious, like *Śrī*-Candragupta. Hariṣeṇa, who wrote this eulogy, flattered the king saying that his intellect was expanded by virtue of constantly attending his sovereign's side. This flattery may be related to the popular belief that the king himself was auspicious.

Item 10: The policy of respecting old traditions, including those of the royal families of conquered countries, was adopted by Samudragupta.

The inscription states 'His glory was produced by the favour shown in capturing and liberating [defeated kings],' 'He re-established many royal families that were fallen and deprived of sovereignty,' 'He restored the dignity of the various kings who had been conquered by the strength of his arms.' This policy must be understood in relation to the system of governance widely characterising the Subcontinent at that time. Samudragupta's 'conquest of the whole earth (*sarvapṛthivīvijaya*)' meant conquering and annexing the countries of the Ganga basin, commanding kings ruling beyond the basin or in frontier countries to come to perform obeisance and offer tribute, forcing chiefs or kings in forest territories to surrender, dispatching an army to distant countries in the Deccan and requesting the kings there to submit to him, and requesting kings of even more distant countries, like Sri Lanka and northwest India, to visit him or send maidens and tribute. He was truly 'supreme king of great kings.'

Item 11: The ideas of transmigration, i.e., birth in heaven or falling into hell, are not clearly mentioned in this inscription. But on Samudragupta's gold coins [Allan 1914: cviii-cxii, Sircar 1965: 274-275] we often find the inscription 'wins heaven by good deeds (*sucaritair divaṃ jayati*),' which shows his desire to be born in the world of the gods.

Item 12: It is mentioned that a group of high officials (*sabhya*) were present beside the royal family members when Candragupta appointed Samudragupta to be his successor. Again, Hariṣeṇa, who wrote the eulogy, and Tilabhaṭṭaka, who had it inscribed on the stone pillar, were both great generals (*mahādaṇḍanāyaka*), and the former was also foreign minister (*sāṃdhivigrahika*) as well as minister in charge of royal princes or some important duties (*kumārāmātya*). Needless to say, Samudragupta's 'conquest of the whole earth' was actually achieved by his powerful army.

As to the six contradictory views drawn from the three literary sources, we have the following.

Items 13 and 14: No mention is found on the origins of the king or kingship. Concerning the deification of the king, a standpoint quite close to that of *Manu-smṛti* appears. For example, Samudragupta was described as 'equal to Dhanada (Kubera), Varuṇa, Indra and Antaka (Yama),' [6] and was admired as 'a mortal only in following the customs of the world, but is otherwise a god dwelling on the earth (*lokasamaya-kriyānuvidhānamātramānuṣa-lokadhāmadeva*).' Also, the fame of Samudragupta was described to have reached as far as Indra's palace, [7] and his knowledge and ability was said to have surpassed even those of the gods.

Item 15: Although no direct mention is found on this item, it is certain from various sources including land-grant inscriptions that under Gupta rule the Vedic *dharma* was highly esteemed and Brahmans who advocated it played an important role in religion as well as politics.

Item 16: Samudragupta's valour and military successes were praised throughout the inscription. His countless scars from hundreds of battles were described as beautiful ornaments on his body. Samudragupta's conquest of the world was brought about by the skillful use of the *daṇḍa*, which was recommended to the *kṣatriyas* by orthodox Brahmans. His policy was very far from the non-*daṇḍa* policy in the Buddhist literature.

Items 17 and 18: Concerning the problem of purity, we only find vague mention, such as 'his fame is pure (*śuci*) like moonlight,' and 'the fame of the king purifies the Three Worlds (*punāti bhuvanatrayam*).' No mention is found concerning item 18, but from the inscription on Samudragupta's gold coins, we know he held the great sacrifice Aśvamedha which was recommended in the Vedic literature for the universal king.[8] There is no doubt that he also performed other Vedic sacrifices.

As discussed above, the kingship shown in Samudragupta's inscription is in accord with the fundamental idea or common views on kingship in ancient India. And as to the contradictory views, it is quite close to that of orthodox Brahmanism, especially in relation to the deification of the king and the use of the *daṇḍa*.

## Khāravela and Rudradāman

The inscription of Khāravela of the Ceḍi Dynasty was carved on the wall of Hāthigumphā Cave to publish his achievements as the ruler of the Kalinga kingdom [Jayaswal and Banerji 1930: 71-89, Barua 1938: 459-485, Sircar 1965: 213-221], while the inscription of Rudradāman was carved on a rock to celebrate the completion of the repair work of the banks of Lake Sudarśana in the Kathiawar peninsula [Kielhorn 1905-06: 36-49, Sircar 1965: 175-180]. Turning to their thoughts on kingship, we find the following.

Items 1 and 2: Honorific titles of the two kings show the central part they played in formulating state policy. For example, Khāravela was described as 'the supreme king of Kalinga (*Kaliṅgādhipati*),' '*cakravartin* of Kalinga,'[9] 'noble great king (*ārya-mahārāja*),' while Rudradāman was depicted as lord or sovereign (*rājan, pati, svāmin, pārthiva*) and *mahākṣatrapa*, the traditional title of a ruler of Saka origin. With respect to the *dharma*, the former had the honorific title 'king [who protects] the *dharma* (*dharmarāja*),' and the latter was praised as the king who 'loves the *dharma* (*dharmānurāga*).' The inscription of Rudradāman states that he implemented righteous policies to increase his religious merit (*dharma*) and fame (*kīrti*), and that his subjects were achieving the three objectives of life–the *dharma, artha, kāma*–through his efforts.[10]

Items 3 and 4: Khāravela's royal titles 'king giving peace (*kṣema-rāja*)' and 'king giving prosperity (*vṛddharāja*)' clearly show that a king's first duty was to protect his subjects and to maintain social order. Concerning this duty he mentioned such achievements as the construction and repair of the capital city, tanks, canals, parks and temples; reverance to all religious sects; and liberality to Brahmans, townsfolk and countrymen alike. He was also said to have entertained the citizens of the capital by holding festivals and musical events.

In the inscription of Rudradāman, the duty of king to protect subjects was emphasised. For example, he was 'selected as king (*patitve vṛta*)' by people of all *varṇas* for their protection and he did his best to make his townsfolk and countrymen happy. More concretely, he did not torment his subjects by either taxation, forced labour or arbitrary tribute (*kara-viṣṭi-praṇayakriyā*)[11]; he bestowed gifts every day; he protected cows and Brahmans; and he defended towns and villages from robbers, snakes, wild animals and epidemics. The repair of Lake Sudarśana was also a part of this policy. Rudradāman, it is said, protected the lives of his subjects and vowed to abstain from killing men for the rest of his life, except in battle.

Item 5 will be examined in relation to item 16 below.

Items 6, 7, 8 and 9: In Khāravela's inscription no direct mention is found concerning items 6 or 7 except that his efforts to reduce or exempt all taxes were mentioned as a part of his gifts to his townsfolk and countrymen. However, there are many references to items 8 and 9, such as 'noble,' 'prosperous,' 'brave,' and the like. He possessed an excellent and auspicious mark (*praśastaśubhalakṣaṇa*), and had a beautiful brown-coloured body (*śrīkaḍāraśarīra*). His fame in the virtues resounded throughout the world; he was learned in all kinds of sciences and had a brilliant talent for music. He held a Sprinkling Coronation Ceremony of a Great King (*Mahārājābhiṣecana*), which was a demonstration to remind his subjects of his *kṣatriya* origin.

In the descriptions concerning items 6 and 7, Rudradāman was collecting taxes, tolls and revenues (*bali-śulka-bhāga*) fairly. When his subjects grieved over the seemingly hopeless condition of the banks of Lake Sudarśana, he completed the difficult repair work, using a vast amount of money from his own treasury without casting the burden upon others. The descriptions concerning items 8 and 9 are similar to those of Khāravela. For example, Rudradāman was brave and skilled in all military arts; he was endowed with most auspicious marks (*paramalakṣaṇavyañjana*); he possessed a royal fortune (*rājalakṣmī*), and was talented in poetry and music; he was handsome and well versed in every field of learning. He was proud of winning a king's daughter as his wife through the Svayaṃvara, a ceremony in which a princess chooses her husband among suitors belonging to *kṣatriya* families. This may be understood as his claim of *kṣatriya* origin, but because in reality he belonged to the Sakas of Central Asian origin, he was likely looked down upon by native kings and Brahmans. This is suggested from the words in the inscription that he crushed the Yaudheyas, who boasted of their *kṣatriya* origin and refused to submit.

Items 10, 11 and 12: Not many descriptions pertaining to these three points are found in the Khāravela's inscription. He asked submission from distant enemies; as a Jaina believer he venerated holy men freed from transmigration (*arhats*); and he commanded a strong army consisting of elephants, chariots, cavalry and infantry.

In Rudradāman's inscription, he boasted of his fame in restoring defeated kings. He also hoped for an increase of the *dharma* and fame (*kīrti*). Since this '*dharma*' seems to have meant 'religious merit,' we may suppose that he was seeking not only the prosperity of this world but also happiness in the next. Concerning the role of officials, this inscription was inscribed by Kulaipaputra Suviśākha, a minister of Pahlava origin, who supervised the repair work. He was mentioned as receiving the king's order and accomplishing the difficult work despite the opposition from councillors and other bureaucrats. He proudly stated that by his meritorious act, the king's spiritual merit, fame and glory increased. He also explained that Lake Sudarśana was originally constructed for irrigation by Vaiśya Puṣyagupta, provincial governor under the first Mauryan emperor Candragupta, and its canals were constructed by Tuṣāspha, an official of Greek origin, under the third Mauryan emperor Aśoka. Kulaipaputra deemed to inscribe the names of these two officials, his predecessors who lived more than four centuries before, in order to insist that the king's exploits could be achieved only with the support of competent and faithful officials.

Turning to our six contradictory views, we note the following.

Items 13 and 14: Khāravela's inscription does not touch directly on these two points, but the words '*aira*' and '*rājasivaṃsakulaviniśrita*' have been taken up by some scholars as proof of the king's divinity. According to their interpretation, the former means Aila, descendant of Ilā who was the ancester of the lunar race of *kṣatriya* kings, and the latter means 'originated from the family of the king-saint of legendary Vasu.' [12] However, the former probably means 'noble (*ārya*)' [13] and the latter just 'originated from the king-saint's family.' [14] From these words we can fathom Khāravela's pride concerning his noble family, but we cannot assume that he tried to deify himself.

The idea of kingship in Rudradāman's inscription is fairly close to that of heterodoxy. He was chosen to protect his subjects, and he ordered the repair of lake banks to respond to criticism from them. Throughout the inscription, deification is scarcely found. Some scholars insist that the expression 'his name is repeatedly uttered by teachers (*gurubhir abhyastanāma*)' proves that the people of the day believed that merit was gained by chanting the king's name. But this seems rather farfetched. [15]

Item 15: It is difficult to conclude whether or not *dharma* in these two inscriptions should be classified as orthodox or heterodox. However, the fact that Khāravela was a believer in Jainism may place his *dharma* closer to heterodox thought. On the other hand, Rudradāman's inscription mentioned *varṇa*-status, the three objectives of human life (*trivarga*), and the protection of cows and Brahmans. Accordingly, though heterodox-like views were described concerning kingship, his *dharma* may be closer to that of orthodox thought.

Item 16: Though he himself was an avowed believer of Jainism, Khāravela repeatedly boasted of his military accomplishments, and did not proclaim non-*daṇḍa* ideals. His conquests, he dared to say, reached as far as the Ganga plain to the north and to the Tamil regions to the south. He offered victory gifts to Brahmans and built a new palace to commemorate his conquests. But since it was difficult to annex the more distant countries, he was satisfied with making enemy kings bow down at his feet and taking booty from them. Khāravela was given the title *cakravartin* in the inscription of his queen. *Cakravartin* in the Buddhist literature is an ideal king who conquers the world by the power of the *dharma* without using military power. In this case, *cakra*, the wheel, is the symbol of peaceful *dharma*. But the *cakra* of Khāravela's title might not be such a symbol but rather a representation of the king's military might, as seen in the words 'possessing an irresistible wheel, vehicle and army (*apratihata-cakra-vāhana-bala*),' and 'his wheels of victory run on unimpeded (*supravṛtta-vijayacakra*).'

Rudradāman was also proud of his military conquests, and proclaimed his resolution to repel invading enemies, but he also expressed non-*daṇḍa* ideals in such words as 'he abstains from killing men except in battle.' He defeated the Sātavāhana king Śātakarṇi twice, but destroyed neither him nor his kingdom. He also reinstated many deposed kings.

Items 17 and 18: Both inscriptions do not touch directly upon the ritual purity found in orthodox Brahmanical thought. Regarding religion, Khāravela was a lay worshipper (*upāsaka*) of Jainism, calling himself 'a king [who protects] monks (*bhikṣurāja*)' [16] and financially aiding the Jaina order. However, he also called himself 'a worshipper of all religions (*sarvapāṣaṇḍapūjaka*),' 'embellisher of all temples (*sarva-devāyatana-saṃskārakāraka*),' and offered a lot of gifts to Brahmans. His Sprinkling Coronation Ceremony might have been performed by Brahmans. As mentioned above, Rudradāman supported the orthodox religion through the protection of cows and Brahmans, but we do not know how frequently he sponsored Brahmanical sacrifices.

Our examination of kingship in these two inscriptions brings to light the following points. Concerning the twelve common views among our three literary sources, the inscription of Khāravela lacks descriptions on some items, while that of Rudradāman refers to almost every item through one expression or another. Despite such a disproportionate content, no ideas of kingship opposed to the twelve common views can be found in either inscription. We may thus say that both kings ruled based upon the traditional idea of kingship fostered in ancient India. Concerning the latter six points, both inscriptions seem situated midway between Samudragupta's orthodoxy and Aśoka's heterodoxy.

## Conclusion

The objective of this essay has been to clarify how the kingship mentioned in three literary sources is reflected in the inscriptions of four leading ancient Indian kings. There are two principal conclusions to be drawn from this examination. First, all of the four kings governed, or were praised to be governing, based on the fundamental views of kingship in ancient India found common to these three sources. Secondly, kingship described in the inscriptions of those four kings is located between the two extremes, orthodoxy and heterodoxy. Table 1 presents the relationship between our twelve common views of kingship and the content of the inscriptions, while Table 2 denotes the relationship between the content of the inscriptions and the orthodox/heterodox ideas of kingship. In these tables the four kings appear in chronological order.

During the later Vedic age (c. 1000-600 B.C.), when kingship was in the course of development, orthodox Brahmans living in the upper Ganga valley created and developed rituals to invest tribal kings with divinity and supernatural power, the best known of which were Rājasūya, Aśvamedha, Vājapeya, Aindra-mahābhiṣeka, and Punar-abhiṣeka.

In the post-Vedic age (c. 600-320 B.C.), kingdoms governed by semi-despotic rulers rose up in the middle and lower Ganga valley, where heterodox religions were predominant. The kingdom of Magadha was the strongest among them, and eventually led to the building of the first Indian empire under the Mauryas. In this period of Magadhan expansion, the traditional Brahmanical rituals for the deification of kings decreased in importance. The kings of Magadha supported heterodox religions, and strengthened their power not by ritual but by the establishment of a strong military and bureaucracy. This development of kingship reached its peak during the reign of Aśoka.

After the Mauryas, orthodox Brahmanical thought was gradually revived. A few centuries after the reign of Aśoka, the *Manu-smṛti* preached the deification of kings from the standpoint of orthodox Brahmanism. About the same age, the Kuṣāṇas put forward a similar idea through the introduction of the worship of the reigning and deceased kings. These tendencies culminated in the advent of the Guptas, and under this dynasty the orthodox view of kingship was proclaimed. Table 2 indicates that a gradual shift from heterodox to orthodox kingship took place from the age of the Mauryas to that of the Guptas. The same shift is also symbolised by the change of language used in the inscriptions, i.e., from Prakrit which was usually used by the heterodox sects (Aśoka, Khāravela) to Sanskrit which was the sacred language of orthodox Brahmans (Rudradāman, Samudragupta).

Table 1: Inscription Content and Common Views of Kingship

| Common views | 1 | 2 | 3 | 4 | 5 | 6 | 7 | 8 | 9 | 10 | 11 | 12 |
|---|---|---|---|---|---|---|---|---|---|---|---|---|
| Aśoka | ○ | ○ | ○ | ○ | ○ | ▽ | ○ | ○ | ○ | ○ | ○ | ○ |
| Khāravela | ○ | ○ | ○ | ○ | ○ | △ | | ○ | ○ | △ | △ | ▽ |
| Rudradāman | ○ | ○ | ○ | ○ | ○ | ▽ | ○ | ○ | ○ | ○ | △ | ○ |
| Samudragupta | ○ | ▽ | ○ | ○ | ○ | △ | | ○ | ○ | ○ | ○ | ▽ |

○ Reference
▽ Small reference
△ Vague reference

Table 2: Inscription Content and Contradictory Views of Kingship

| Contradictory views | Orthodox ⟷ Heterodox | | | | | | | | | | | |
|---|---|---|---|---|---|---|---|---|---|---|---|---|
| Aśoka | | | | | | | | ○ | ▽ | △ | ⊗ | × |
| Khāravela | | | △ | | ○ | ▽ | | ⊗ | × | | | |
| Rudradāman | | | ▽ | | △ | × | ⊗ | ○ | | | | |
| Samudragupta | ○ | ▽ | △ | × | ⊗ | | | | | | | |

○ Divinity (items 13, 14)
▽ The *dharma* (item 15)
△ The *daṇḍa* (item 16)
⊗ Purity (item 17)
× Sacrifice (item 18)

## Notes

1 This article is based on my previous study [Yamazaki 1994: 221-43]. I owe much to the following studies.

> P.V. Kane, *History of Dharmaśāstra, Ancient and Mediaeval Religious and Civil Law in India*, 8 books in 5 vols., Poona, 1930-62.
> U.N. Ghoshal, *A History of Indian Political Ideas, The Ancient Period and the Period of Transition to the Middle Ages*, Madras, 1959.
> J.W. Spellman, *Political Theory of Ancient India, A Study of Kingship from the Earliest Times to circa A.D. 300*, Oxford, 1964.
> J. Gonda, *Ancient Indian Kingship from the Religious Point of View*, Leiden, 1969.

2 Hultzsch 1925; Sircar 1965; Sircar 1975; Yamazaki 1979: 11-15, 19-20, 303-30.

3 Forest tribes and unsubmissive people on the border land would be subject to military attack when Aśoka lost his patience with them. See Rock Edict XIII and Separare Rock Edict II.

4 Lummindei (Rummindei) village, where Buddha was born, was exempted from *bali*, and villagers had to pay only one-eighth of their produce as *bhāga*. See Rummindei Pillar Inscription.

5 Filliozat [1949: 225-47; 1957: 1-9] explains that those gods (*devāḥ*) mentioned in the Minor Rock Edict refer to divinized kings, but I do not agree with his interpretation.

6 The same words were written in the two counterfeit copper plates of Samudragupta made in the sixth or seventh century [Fleet 1970: 254-57; Sircar 1965: 270-74]. In the Eran Stone Pillar Inscription, Samudragupta is praised as 'In satisfaction he is equal to Kubera and in wrath he is equal to Yama (*Dhanada-Antaka-tuṣṭi-kopa-tulya*)' [Fleet 1970: 18-21; Sircar 1965: 268-70]. Approximately the same words were written about Samudragupta in the inscriptions of his successors, Candragupta II, Kumāragupta and Skandagupta [Fleet 1970: 26-28, 43-44, 49-51, 53-54].

7 Fleet [1970: 10, note 2] explains that Samudragupta was believed to have gone to Indra's palace (*Tridaśapati-bhavana*) after his death, and this inscription was inscribed posthumously. However this view is problematical.

8 Samudragupta issued gold coins to commemorate his performance of the Aśvamedha. On one side of the coin we read 'Supreme king of kings who has matchless valour having protected the earth, wins heaven (*rājādhirājaḥ pṛthivīm avitvā divaṃ jayaty aprativāryavīryaḥ*),' and on the other '[he became] a hero through Aśvamedha (*aśvamedhaparākramaḥ*)' [Allan 1914: lxxvi-lxxvii, 21-23, Plate V].

9 Manchapuri Cave Inscription of the Chief Queen of Khāravela [Sircar 1965: 221-23].

10 I owe this reading to the following research. Kielhorn 1905-06: 44, note 2. Sircar 1965: 78.
11 '*Praṇayakriyā*' may mean voluntary or semi-compulsory tribute [Kielhorn 1905-06: 49, note 4].
12 Jayaswal and Banerji 1930: 80, note 3, 86, note 51; Sircar 1965: 221.
13 Barua 1938: 470, note 151; Sircar 1965: 219, note 5.
14 Kant [1971: 46] denies any relation of this phrase to the king-saint legend.
15 Kielhorn 1905-06: 45, note 14.
16 I do not agree with the reading 'mendicant king' or 'monk king' because this king calls himself '*upāsaka*' and his political achievements are quite removed from the monkhood.

## References

Allan, J.
1914 *Catalogue of the Coins of the Gupta Dynasties and of Śaśāṅka, King of Gauḍa (in the British Museum)*, London.

Barua, B.M.
1938 'Hāthigumphā Inscription of Khāravela, revised edition,' *Indian Historical Quarterly*, XIV-3.

Filliozat, J.
1949 'Les "deva" d'Asoka, "dieux" ou "divines majestés"?,' *Journal Asiatique*, T. 237.
1957 'Les festivités du dhamma chez Asoka,' *Journal Asiatique*, T. 245.

Fleet, J.F.
1970 *Inscriptions of the Early Gupta Kings and Their Successors, Corpus Inscriptionum Indicarum*, Vol. III, third rev. ed., Varanasi.

Hultzsch, E.
1925 ed. and tr., *Inscriptions of Asoka, Corpus Inscriptionum Indicarum*, Vol. I, Oxford.

Jayaswal, K.P. and Banerji, R.D.
1930 'The Hāthigumphā Inscription of Khālavela', *Epigraphia Indica*, Vol. XX.

Kant, S.
1971 *The Hāthigumphā Inscription of Khāravela and the Bhabru Edict of Aśoka, a Critical Study*, Delhi.

Kielhorn, F.

1905-06 'Junāgaḍh Rock Inscription of Rudradāman, the year 72,' *Epigraphia Indica*, VIII.

Sircar, D.C.

1965 *Select Inscriptions Bearing on Indian History and Civilization*, Vol. I, second ed., Calcutta.

1975 *Inscriptions of Aśoka*, third ed., New Delhi.

Yamazaki, G.

1979 *Asyōka-ou Densetu no Kenkyū (The Legend of Aśoka, a Critical Study)*, in Japanese, Tokyo.

1994 *Kodai Indo no Ouken to Syūkyō, Ou to Baramon (Kingship and Religion in Ancient India, Kings and Brahmans)*, in Japanese, Tokyo.

# 2

# The Treatment of King and State in the *Tirukkuṟaḷ*

TAKANOBU TAKAHASHI

## Introduction

The *Tirukkuṟaḷ* (hereafter *Kural*), also called the Tamil Veda,[1] is the most famous and popular work in the history of Tamil literature. The author, Tiruvaḷḷuvar (hereafter Valluvar), was probably a Jain of the fifth or sixth century A.D., although we have almost no authentic information on his life, religion and dates.[2]

The work consists of 1330 couplets divided into 133 chapters of 10 couplets each: the first 38 chapters deal with 'virtues' (*aṟam*), the next 70 with 'wealth' (*poruḷ*), and the remaining 25 with 'love' (*kāmam*). From a terminological point of view, *aṟam*, *poruḷ* and *kāmam* more or less respectively correspond to the Sanskrit terms *dharma*, *artha*, and *kāma*.

There are innumerable books, articles, and papers dealing with the *Kural*,[3] which may be classified into two groups: those that aim to convey the *Kural*'s excellent messages to a broader circle of readers, and those concerned with its various issues, such as its date, author, and relationship with Sanskrit treatises on *dharma*, *artha* and *kāma*. The last issue concerning the relationship between the *Kural* and Sanskrit texts has especially been debated extensively.[4] Furthermore, although there is considerable variety of opinions regarding the interrelationship between them, ranging from the opinion that the *Kural* is a Tamil version of these Sanskrit treatises to one that the *Kural* conversely influenced them, there is a consensus among moderate scholars that its author Valluvar must have had a very thorough knowledge of these Sanskrit works.

Reference has often been made to the *Kural* as the best work on politics in classical Tamil, probably due to its content-structure as well as to our scant knowledge about polity or political ideas existing before

A.D. 600. (See the second Section of the present essay.) Contrary to our expectation, however, the text does not clearly inform us about them. Thus, in the third Section the relationship between the *Kural* and Sanskrit texts, focusing on the *Kural*'s treatment of politics, especially the king and the state, will be reexamined mainly from the viewpoint of the inner structure of the *Kural*, but not from that of parallel or matching passages between them as has usually been done. Moreover, characteristics of its treatment will be clarified. Subsequently, methods of interpreting the text will be argued in the fourth Section in order to manifest why the *Kural* appears to be a treatise on politics. Finally, in the fifth Section the author's motives for composing the treatise will be mentioned.[5]

## Political and Cultural Situation from the Earliest Times to 600 A.D. and Onwards

Before proceeding to the contents of the *Kural*, it is necessary to survey historically and culturally Tamil up to and after the time when the *Kural* was composed.

*Pre-Sangam Period*[6] (*up to first century A.D.*): Some north Indian sources make mention of the countries in south India. Kātyāyana's *Vārttika* on Pāṇini (fourth century B.C.?), probably the earliest among them, refers to the Pandya, Chola and Kerala countries. Also the edicts of Asoka (third century B.C.) make note of the Chola, Pandya, Satiyaputa and Keralaputa. Kauṭilya's *Arthaśāstra* describes the trade with south Indian countries. All of this information, however, only shows that the Tamil area roughly corresponding to present-day Tamil Nadu and Kerala[7] was politically advanced even before the time of Christ. It is also known from the Tamil-Brahmi cave inscriptions (second century B.C. to second century A.D.) found in various parts of the Tamil area that Jains and Buddhists settled there at that time.

*Sangam Period* (*first–third centuries A.D.*): There is a consensus of opinion among scholars that the major portion of Sangam literature can be assigned to the first to third centuries A.D. Although the Sangam texts portray the social and economic conditions of the time, they do not provide any definite information on the political situation. We know from the texts that there were three kingdoms (Chera, Chola and Pandya) and many petty chiefs, all struggling for supremacy. The territories and capitals of these kingdoms have, to some extent, been identified, but very little is known about their polity and political history, and far less is known concerning the petty chiefs, including their number, territory, relationship with the kingdoms, and other important aspects.[8]

It may be noted that the Tamil area in the Sangam age did not form a political unity but a cultural one, as is clearly shown by the texts and the way they were compiled into anthologies.[9] The culture and society mentioned by the texts are quite indigenous, although people were, to some extent, familiar with Aryan culture and ideas and there were some poets from north India including Brahmins.[10]

*Post-Sangam Period* (*fourth–sixth centuries A.D.*): This is called 'the Dark Period' by some historians, since there is an almost total lack of information regarding events in the Tamil area. But it is to be inferred from a Buddhist text and a later grant that some time about A.D. 300 or a little later the Kalabhras (Kaḷappāḷar), denounced as cruel kings (*kali-aracar*), came and uprooted many *ādhirājas*, indigenous Tamil kings, and upset the political order.[11] This political confusion was ended in the last quarter of the sixth century by the activities of two monarchs, Simhavishnu of the Pallavas who may have established themselves in Kanchipuram around A.D. 250, and Kaḍungōn of the Pandyas with their capital at Madurai.

This dark period was marked by the influx of northern culture, languages, religions and customs. Probably under the patronage of the Pallavas and the Kalabhras, Brahmanism, Buddhism and Jainism began to flourish; especially the latter two were becoming increasingly popular in their territories, which is known from the existence of colleges belonging to these sects, such as the Buddhist college at Kanchi.[12] This age was also characterised by great literary activity in Tamil, and the *Kural* was one of its products.

*After the Sixth Century A.D.*: From the sixth century A.D. onwards, we have rather clear historical and archaeological evidence. The period from the middle of the sixth century to the middle of the ninth century A.D. was the age of mutual conflict among three kingdoms: that is, the Chālukyas of Badami in the Deccan, the Pallavas of Kanchi, and the Pandyas of Madurai in the south. The Chālukyas spread their power over the entire area between the two seas by the middle of the eighth century, and in the south the Pallavas and the Pandyas shared the country, whose frontier was shifting about the line of the river Kaveri.

In the sixth century, the Jains, Buddhists, Saivas and Vaishnavas were struggling to gain popularity, and gradually the Saivas and Vaishnavas became considerably popular, while Jainism and Buddhism were on the wane, although the Jains still survived in south India long after Buddhism had declined.

Although Aryanization of the Tamil country had already begun in the previous period, it was carried on very intensively in this age, and under the Pandya-Pallava rulers, Sanskrit began to hold an honoured place as the language of higher literature and culture.

The period from the sixth to the ninth centuries A.D. was the age of a shift from kingdoms to empire. The Cholas, one of the three prominent kingdoms in the Sangam age, were again to rise in the succeeding epoch as one of the most splendid empires known in Tamil history.

## The *Kural*'s Treatment of the King and the State

As mentioned in the previous section, very little is definitely known concerning the southern kingdoms and their polity before A.D. 600. Such being the case, although some political ideas can be gleaned from Sangam or post-Sangam texts, it seems to some critics that 'no better method can be availed of to understand the nature of Tamil monarchy in the period than to discuss some of the salient statements of Tiruvaḷḷuvar on the subject' [Nilakanta Sastri 1975: 67].

The very first couplet of *Poruṭpāl*, the second part of the *Kural*, dealing with the king, the state, wealth and other matters concerning public life, runs as follows:

> He who possesses all these six things, an army, a people, wealth, ministers, friends (i.e. allies) and forts, is a lion among the kings. (381; Drew, ad.)[13]

The king and the six limbs of the state mentioned here apparently correspond to *prakṛti* referred to in Kauṭilya's *Arthaśāstra* (6.1.1), *Mānavadharmaśāstra* (9.294), *Yājñavarkyasmṛti* (1.353), *Kāmandakīyanītisāra* (4.1), and elsewhere, although the *Kural* divides the seven limbs (*aṅga*) mentioned together in the Sanskrit texts into the king and the other six limbs and makes the latter subject to the king.[14]

These seven limbs of the state are discussed one by one in the succeeding chapters as follows: 'the king' in chapters 39–63; 'ministers' in 64–73; 'people' in 74; 'forts' in 75; 'wealth' in 75; 'armies' in 77–78; and 'friends' in 79–83.[15]

This structure, as well as the 'threefold division' system of the *Kural*, may lead to our expectation that the work will provide us with rich, detailed ideas concerning politics, kingship, and the like, during those times. As is often pointed out, however, the *Kural*'s treatment of these subjects markedly differs from that in the Sanskrit treatises on politics such as Kauṭilya's *Arthaśāstra* (hereafter *KAS*) in that it does not inform us as clearly about them as we may expect. Sketching the general and specific features of the *Kural*, we shall see why this is so.

### *The Kural's Less Concrete and Practical or More Abstract and General Attitude*

Let us take as an example the subject 'fort,' one of the seven limbs of the state. *KAS* deals with the 'fort' in chapter 3 of Book 2. Various kinds of forts and their locations are first mentioned, and then all of the details concerning the construction of each fort follow. *KAS* 2.3.4, for example, reads: 'He should cause three moats to be dug round it [a *sthānīya* 'market town' mentioned in 2.3.3—Takahashi], at a distance of one *daṇḍa* from each other, fourteen, twelve and ten *daṇḍas* broad, three-quarters or a half of the breadth deep, one-third (of the surface-breadth) at the bottom or square with the bottom, paved with stones or with the sides (only) built of stones or bricks, reaching down to (natural springs of) water or filled with water coming from elsewhere, with (arrangements for) draining excess water, and stocked with lotuses and crocodiles' [Kangle: 70].

The author of the *Kural*, on the other hand, allots only one chapter (75. The fort), that is, only 10 couplets, to the subject 'fort,' and so he cannot go into elaborate detail about it, but touches only on the principles, as in *Kural* 743.

> Height, breadth, strength, difficult access:
> Science declares a *fort* must these possess. (G. U. Pope)

Likewise, *KAS* 2.4.27 has a detailed list of necessary items within a fort, mentioning 'he should cause to be made stores, capable of being used over a number of years, of all kinds of fats, grains, sugars, salts, perfumes, medicines, dried vegetables, fodder, dried meat, hay, wood, metals, hides, charcoal, tendons, poisons, horns, bamboos, barks, strong timber, weapons, shields and stones' [Kangle: 81], while the *Kural* refers to it only as 'all things needed':

> A fort contains all things needed and also the good (soldiers) to aid in times of need. (746; Takahashi)

The *Kural*'s similar treatment of a subject is found regarding 'army,' another limb of the seven limbs of the state. The whole of chapters 4 and 5 of Book 10 of *KAS* is allotted to the army, dealing elaborately with 'grounds suitable for fighting,' 'functions of the infantry, the cavalry, the chariots and the elephants,' 'arrangement of battle-arrays in wings, flanks and front in accordance with the strength of troops,' 'distribution of strong and weak troops,' and 'modes of fighting of the infantry, the cavalry, the chariots and the elephants.' All these are packed, on the other hand, in the *Kural* into one verse (761) among 20 concerning the 'army' in chapters 77–78 (77. The excellence of the army; 78. Military spirit).

> The army which is complete in (its) parts and conquers without fear of wounds is the chief wealth of the king. (761; Lazarus)

The same happens concerning the topic 'the group of calamities of the army,' discussed in detail in *KAS* 8.5.1–21, which in *Kural* 769 is mentioned in a simple manner:

> An army can triumph if it is free from diminution, war-weariness, and poverty. (769; Lazarus, ad.)

These examples clearly show that the *Kural*'s treatment of subjects is far less concrete and practical in comparison with *KAS*. On the other hand, the *Kural* incorporates in a limited space didactic texts such as 763 or traditional 'heroic (*puṟam*) poems' (actually, all 10 poems in chapter 78 deal with *puṟam*).

> What if (a host of) hostile rats roar like the sea? They will perish at the mere breath of the cobra. (763; Lazarus)

The tendency of Valluvar to intersperse didactic poems among others pertinent to a subject, even though they are too generalised, is found in various other places too, which we will consider next.

*Poems Relevant to the Subject Interspersed among Didactic Poems*

There are several chapters in the second part of the *Kural* where all 10 couplets are concerned with the topic mentioned in their captions, such as chapters 39 ('Kingly excellency'; See below.), 45 ('Seeking association with the great'), 55 ('The right sceptre'), 56 ('The cruel sceptre'), 57 ('Absence of tyranny'), 64 ('The minister'), and 69 ('The envoy'), but they are rather exceptional. In many chapters, maxim-like verses intermingle with ones relevant to the subject, or rather, pertinent poems are interspersed among maxim-like ones.

The following are examples of the latter case. Chapter 76 ('Way of accumulating wealth') of the *Kural* treats 'wealth,' one of the seven limbs. Here again, the *Kural*'s treatment is, unlike *KAS*'s (6.1.10 and 5.2.1–70), very simplified and generalised, and only one distich (756) refers directly to the subject, while all the others mention it in terms of principles for men in general, including a didactic poem, like 757:

> Unclaimed wealth,[16] wealth acquired by taxes, and wealth (got) by conquest of foes are (all) the wealth of the king. (756; Lazarus)
> The babe which love of mercy bears is reared by the bounteous nurse of wealth. (757; Takahashi)

Book 9 of *KAS* mentions 'the activity of the king about to march,' and its first chapter is concerned with the ascertainment of powers (9.1.1–16), place (9.1.17–21) and time (9.1.22–25), to which Valluvar refers in chapters 48 ('Knowing power'), 49 ('Knowing the fitting time') and 50 ('Knowing the suitable place') respectively. Among the 10 couplets of chapter 48 of the *Kural*, only 471 refers to the topic in a direct way, but others, like 475, mention it maxim-wise:

> Let (one) weigh well the strength of the deed (he purposes to do), his own strength, the strength of his enemy, and the strength of the allies, and let him act. (471; Drew, ad.)
> The axle tree of a bandy, loaded only with peacocks' feathers will break, if it be greatly overloaded. (475; Drew)

Concerning the king's knowing the fitting time (chapter 49 of the *Kural* and *KAS* 9.1.17–21) and the suitable place (chapter 50 of the *Kural* and *KAS* 9.1.22–25), the same is true: that is, the *Kural* treats the topic in a generalised, less practical, or maxim-like way, which gives us the impression that the poems relevant to the subject are interspersed among maxim-like verses, and *not* vice versa:

> A crow will overcome an owl in the day time; so the king who would conquer his enemy must have (a suitable) time. (481; Drew)
> The power of one who has a large army will perish, if he goes into ground where only a small army can act. (498; Drew)

*Nominal Treatment of a Subject*

We have so far seen how the *Kural* deals with political subjects in general terms, and how many didactic poems or moral maxims are intermingled with them. There is still another instance where the author of the *Kural* deals with the subject mentioned in the caption by name only.

As already mentioned, chapters 79–83 (79. Friendship; 80. Investigation in forming friendships; 81. Old friendship; 82. Evil friendship; 83. False friendship) are assumed to deal with 'allies,' one of the seven limbs of the state, but none of the 50 couplets treats of it, and they discuss nothing more than what everyone knows as friendship:

> Like learning, the friendship of the noble, the more it is cultivated, the more delightful does it become. (783; Lazarus)
> It is indeed a gain for one to renounce the friendship of fools. (797; Lazarus)
> Of what avail is long-standing friendship, if friends do not admit as their own actions done through the right of intimacy? (803; Lazarus)
> Better ten million times incur the wise man's hate,
> Than form with foolish men a friendship intimate. (816; G. U. Pope)
> One should fear the deceitful who smile sweetly with their face but never love with their heart. (824; Lazarus)

Some may maintain that the subject is implied in the very first couplet (781) among those 50 ones and is referred to in 827, 828, and 830. Couplet 781 reads:

> What things are there so difficult to acquire as friendship?
> What guards are there so difficult to break through by the efforts (of one's foes)? (781; Lazarus)

Apart from the fact that this interpretation itself is inferred from the caption of the chapter, it is almost impossible for readers to read as such, since all the other succeeding couplets have nothing to do with 'allies.' The same is true in the case of poems 827, 828, and 830:

> A weapon may be hid in the very hands with which (one's) foes adore (him) (and) the tears they shed are of the same nature. (828; Lazarus)

Here, the terms, foes (*o<u>nn</u>ār*) and weapon (*paṭai*), signifying the connection with the topic 'allies' are mentioned, but they appear to show 'unfriendly persons' and 'wicked design or ill will' in a general sense due to a lot of surrounding examples exclusively connected with mere friendship but not with 'allies.'

One may evaluate such an author's way of approach in various ways,[17] but one thing is clear: Valluvar's less concrete and elaborate treatment of subjects than Kauṭilya's is not due to limited space in the *Kural* but rather to his approach to them. That is, Valluvar did not *deliberately* go into elaborate detail about political subjects, since although he allocated 50 couplets to the subject, he still did not refer to it.[18]

In concluding this section, we may sum up the *Kural*'s features as follows: Valluvar's concern was to deal with men's personal or social virtues in general, adopting the framework of Sanskrit treatises on *dharma* and *artha.* (The reason he adopted it will be seen later.) In other words, as has often been said, Valluvar deals mainly with the virtues in terms of good, or even idealised citizenry, and not in terms of caste-based or *āśrama*-based *svadharma*,[19] and hence, when he discusses subjects in politics, it appears that he does not address the king or kshatriya, but simply a man. Along with this, his approach to and treatment of political subjects are extremely universal and general even when he *actually*, not in name only, deals with them. This clearly distinguishes the *Kural* from those Sanskrit treatises, even though he used their framework.[20]

Therefore, in spite of the fact that many parallel ideas or matching passages are to be found in the Sanskrit treatises and the *Kural*, it seems *as if* 'the *Kural* is so remarkably free from Sanskrit words' [Popley: 26], and this is why it does not provide us with so much information on politics as expected from its content structure.

## Do all Couplets have Two Meanings?

If the above conclusion is correct, then why has the *Kural* often been referred to as a book of politics in classical Tamil? One obvious reason is the way of interpreting the text, especially the one offered by commentators.

It goes without saying that when reading a text we should take into consideration its total structure or context, either narrow or broad. The *Kural*'s single authorship is commonly accepted as true, and its division into three parts and 133 chapters, as well as the order of chapters, as original, and undoubtedly the interrelationship among couplets, or between couplets and the chapter relevant to them, or among chapters is closer in the second part on 'wealth' than in the other two parts dealing with 'virtues' and 'love.' However, there is a divergence in views as regards the fundamental question of whether or not the *Kural* is a carefully structured, integrated work under a coherent and consistent plan, or to what degree it is structured. Some critics maintain the *Kural* has a perfect structure without any structural gaps, and others offer an opinion that such a perfect total structure of the text is not self-evident.' [21]

Let us cite Kamil Zvelebil's remark as an example of the former viewpoint. The *Kural* 'is structured very carefully, so that no "structural gaps" occur in the text. Every single couplet is indispensable for the structured whole. Every distich has, so to say, two kinds of meaning: if isolated and thus removed from the content-structure, the couplets lose a very important meaning-component—their "structural meaning." An isolated couplet may be charming and interesting in itself, but it is just a "wise saying," a moral maxim, a "literary proverb" in perfect form, possessing, in varying degrees, the prosodic and rhetoric qualities of gnomic poetry. It acquires a "structural meaning" only in relation to other couplets, forming higher patterns, and, finally, in relation to the entire text, which forms a perfect total structure' [Zvelebil 1973: 163]. In this connection, we may define the commentators' way of interpreting the text as follows: They admit to (or attempt to ascertain) the overall perfect structure of the *Kural*, but do not allow two such meanings of each couplet as mentioned above, but rather allow only a single 'structural meaning.'

We have so far neglected this fundamental question concerning the total structure of the *Kural* in order to manifest the *Kural*'s features in contrast with Sanskrit treatises. In the following case, however, we must confront this question.

Sections 39 to 63 deal with the king and kingship. The first chapter (Chap. 39) among them has the caption 'Kingly excellency,' and all the couplets except the first (381) quoted earlier *explicitly* concern the king or his virtues:

> Never to fail in these four things, fearlessness, liberality, wisdom, and energy, is the kingly character. (382; Drew)
> These three things, viz., vigilance, learning, and bravery, should never be wanting in the ruler of this world. (383; Drew, ad.)
> He is a king who is able to acquire (wealth), to lay it up, to guard, and to distribute it. (385; Drew)
> He is the light of kings who has these four things, beneficence, grace, right sceptre, and care for his people. (390; Takahashi)

The next four chapters (40. Learning; 41. Not learning; 42. Hearing; 43. Possession of wisdom) are supposed to give a detailed explanation of the king's 'learning' referred to in 383, but they seem to describe each topic in terms of men in general rather than in terms of the king:

> Let a man learn thoroughly whatever he may learn, and let his conduct be worthy of his learning. (391; Drew)
> It is said that the lore of letters and of numbers are the two eyes of the living one. (392; Takahashi)
> The desire of the unlearned to speak (in an assembly) is like a woman without breasts desiring (the enjoyment of) womanhood. (402; Drew)
> What does it matter whether those men live or die, who can judge of tastes by the mouth, and not by the ear? (420; Drew)
> Not to fear what ought to be feared, is folly; it is the work of the wise to fear what should be feared. (428; Drew)

Although commentators have tried to interpret the couplets in these chapters connected with a king by saying that a king should study these subjects in order to execute his duties perfectly, these as well as all the remaining distichs of the four chapters do not contain any cues that would restrict their interpretation to the context of kingship.[22] How, then, should we read them? Should we categorise them as a 'nominal treatment of a subject' like the chapters concerning 'allies' and regard them as having nothing to do with a king, or, on the contrary, should we follow the commentators and connect all of them with a king? Or, avoiding these two extreme readings, should we adopt an intermediate reading such as 'If all these are necessary for an ordinary man, how much more are they indispensable to a king' [Meenakshisundaram 1969: 118] ?

In many couplets of the *Kural*, whom the author addresses seems ambiguous. The same is true about the following chapter (44. Correction of faults) in which in a few of distichs, a king is addressed:

> Truly great is the wealth of those who are free from pride, anger and lust. (431; Drew, ad.)
> Avarice, over-confidence, and excessive delight are faults in a king. (432; Takahashi)

A king is not directly referred to in 431, but it must be he who is being addressed, since pride, anger and lust, along with the three faults mentioned in 432, are enumerated as the six faults of a king in *KAS* 1.6.1. A king is explicitly referred to in 436 and is implied in 440. In this context, it appears to be natural to assume that the other couplets in the chapter also concern a king, but, if the others concern themselves exclusively with a king, how indeed do they lose their charm. Take, for example, *Kural* 437:

> Who leaves undone what should be done, with niggard mind,
> His wealth shall perish, leaving not a wrack behind. (G. U. Pope)

This could be read as 'The wealth of *the king* who leaves undone what should be done with niggard mind shall perish, leaving naught,' but then it would become a trite, common saying, lacking any implication and significance. If, on the other hand, such 'double meanings' as mentioned before are perceived in these poems, they acquire their poetical merits and charms. So, it is assumed that this kind of reading might have been the way in which Valluvar wished to have them read.

However, do all couplets contain such 'double meanings'? If so, *Kural* 797 seen before (the third Section, third Clause) can be interpreted as:

> It is indeed a gain for a *king* to renounce the friendship of foolish *kings*.

And other distichs in chapters 79 to 83 could be interpreted in connection with 'allies.' But, many instances, especially, of the third part of the *Kural* dealing with 'love' show that this kind of reading is not necessarily true. Take 1140 as an example:

> The foolish laugh at me before my eyes,
> For they have not suffered [the agony] I suffered. (Takahashi)

Who can read this as a wise saying or a literary proverb isolated from the context? This is the last among ten couplets in chapter 114, titled 'Abandonment of reserve,' which deals with a famous theme of classical love poetry, *maṭal-ēṟutal or maṭal-ūrtal* ('To ride a horse of palmyra stems, as a disappointed lover to win his love,' *Tamil Lexicon*),[23] and only when it is read in its intended context does its meaning become clear. That is to say, this has only a 'structural meaning' but not 'double meanings.' Not only this but many other couplets in the third part have only a 'structural meaning.'[24]

Thus, we may conclude that it is not always correct to define the *Kural* as a carefully structured, integrated work under a coherent and consistent plan. However, as has already been mentioned, commentators admit the total perfect structure of the *Kural* and present a single 'structural meaning' to each couplet, such that eventually, its second part, *Poruṭpāl*, seems as if it were a perfect treatise on politics.

## The Author's Motive for Composing the *Kural* and its Influence in Later Periods

*Valluvar's Adherence to the 'Threefold Division'*

As seen in the third Section, Valluvar discusses politics, including kingship, in the second part of the *Kural*, but his treatment of it is, in most cases, quite generalised, and in a few cases, only nominal. This general attitude is also found in his treatment of 'virtues' (*aṟam*) in the first part. However, his treatment of 'love' in the third part differs very much from that of 'virtues' and 'wealth.' He discusses 'virtues' and 'wealth' following the Sanskrit (or pan-Indian?) tradition although there is great variance between the *Kural*'s treatment and the Sanskrit one. On the other hand, he describes 'love' following exactly the Tamil tradition of love poetry (*akam*) which is indigenous to Tamil and has almost nothing to do with the Sanskrit tradition of *kāma*.[25] Moreover, because Valluvar follows the highly conventionalised tradition of *akam* literature, he fails to depict it in a generalised way as in his treatment of 'virtues' and 'wealth.' This can be readily understood if one tries to quote verses from the *Kural*'s third portion on 'love' as maxims for love in general: the total number of such couplets is very limited compared with the other portions.[26] If his concern was, for example, to deal with personal virtue under 'virtues' and with social virtues in general under 'wealth,' unlike specific treatises such as *Mānavadharmaśāstra* and *KAS*, why did he not deal with 'love' in the same way, or why after all did he include the third part on 'love' in the work?

It is probable that the classical *akam* tradition was still influential, so that he could not but follow it. In that case, however, he could have simply omitted including this part in order to keep his work well-balanced and integrated. Hence it is natural to assume that he would have strongly adhered to the 'threefold division' (*trivarga*), even though it is only nominal.[27] The conception of the 'threefold division' itself was not new to him, since reference had already been made to it in some older texts such as the *Tolkāppiyam* and *Puṟanāṉūṟu*.[28] However, it should be noted that the *Kural* was the first treatise in the history not only of Tamil but also of India to deal with all three goals of life *in a single book*. The *Kural* must have been planned as such with the intention that the structure should become its strong point.[29]

### *Valluvar's Motive in Writing the Kural*

Valluvar might have been influenced by the social and cultural milieu of the Tamil country of his times when it was in the process of change due to the impact of Aryan or northern culture, religions and languages. Buddhism, Jainism, Brahmanism and Hinduism were trying to gain ascendancy over one another. It is known from some early Bhakti texts and the *Periyapurāṇam* of a later age that Buddhism and especially Jainism were flourishing in towns and royal courts before the sixth to seventh centuries A.D. Saivism as well as Vaishnavism were also on the rise.

As a Jain, Valluvar shared a common tendency found among the Jains, which is duly mentioned by a critic: 'The Jains were accommodating to popular wishes, for proselytism on a large scale was also one of their main objects. They studied and mastered the language of the people, wrote important works in that language [30] and through such works sought to gain the allegiance of the people' [Vaiyapuri Pillai 1956: 79]. Thus, in order to satisfy such an appetite for literary or intellectual works as was broadly shared by people in the cities and the courts on the one hand, and to match the contemporary political and social climate in south India on the other, Valluvar wrote his work not as a specialised treatise on virtues and politics, but partly as a literary work and partly as a treatise adopting the said device of the 'threefold division.' It is also probable that he pretended for this purpose that 'he belonged to no particular sect but worked out from his own experience a synthesis of the best he could find' in all of the great religions.[31] Consequently, his work achieved great success in a certain respect, as will be seen below.

### *The Kural's Influence in Later Periods*

The *Kural*'s great success in the literary world of succeeding ages is obvious. Many later poets praised it and its author, and borrowed freely or allude to verses from it.[32] It has attracted the attention of many commentators. Because of its popularity, all the great religions in India have claimed its author as belonging to their own sect. Today, many Tamils, especially the educated, learn a great number of verses of the *Kural* by heart[33] and often quote them in response to various situations in life.

As regards the political field, however, there are no indications of kings and leaders of later periods having been influenced by the *Kural*, although present day political leaders often employ verses from the *Kural* as invocations at public gatherings. According to V. Subrahmaniam, 'No stone inscription, *Prasasti* or copper plate seems to refer to him and no prince called himself a follower of the *Kural* while many boasted of following the *Manu Smriti*,' and the same author explains the reason for this to be that, as the work of a Jain, the *Kural* suffered the same process of slow erosion and absorption in Tamil Nadu as Buddhist philosophy did in the rest of India, neglected by Brahmins and Purohitas in south Indian royal courts and even banned from reading by some Saivaites [Subrahmaniam, V.: 388].

However, such an explanation is not only insufficient but improper. As has often been pointed out, Valluvar's approach to political subjects is so general and 'universal, fettered by the conditions of no particular country or age,' and it seems as if 'he is neither concerned with any historical state of society, with its laws and practices, nor with the scientific and objective description of all aspects' [Meenakshisundaran 1969: 32]. Because of the approach and concerns of Valluvar, his work was considered to be neither thorough, detailed, practical, nor finally important as a book on politics. On the other hand, for these very same reasons, it became an excellent 'literary' or 'didactic' work.

## Postscript

In this essay I have dealt with characteristics of the *Kural*'s treatment of kingship rather than the kingship itself mentioned in it, since it is the most important process for a textual understanding, not only of the *Kural* but also of texts in general, to know characteristics of a text including its chronology and sociocultural milieu. This is especially true when we deal with the polity of ancient Tamil. That is why I have mentioned in the second Section in this paper what are known to us about the political and cultural situation in those days from various sources, showing how little is known definitely concerning it.

Nevertheless, some critics describe polity or kingship of classical Tamil as if it were a historical fact. It may be sufficient for us to take two examples. One is N. Subrahmanian's well-known book [Subrahmanian, N.]. Taking the misleading appellation 'Sangam' in the broadest sense (See note 6.), he gleans political ideas, although some of them seem indefinite and unconvincing, from various sources ranging over several hundreds years, neglecting historical, social and cultural changes occurring during that period.

The other is an interesting and thought-provoking paper by Burton Stein [Stein]. The author holds the view that kings in the Sangam era in its narrowest usage, i.e. the first to third centuries A.D., were 'war-like,' 'violent' and 'amoral,' and they had become 'moral' under the influence of Jainism. His view concerning kingship in the Sangam age, however, seems to be incorrect, sustained by misunderstanding or sometimes even distortion of the contents of such earlier works as [Zvelebil 1973] and [Hart], and is found to be contrary to what 'Sangam texts' describe in some respects.

First of all, Stein mentions that both the love (*akam*) and heroic poems (*puṟam*) of the so-called Sangam literature were the works of illiterate bards [Stein: 3], and these 'earlier, primitive' [Stein: 10], and 'rough' [Stein: 11] works came to be refined by the learned poets, especially metamorphosed by Jains from at least the fifth century A.D. [Stein: 10], and finally came to be redacted and to possess their high literary sophistication between the eighth and fourteenth centuries [Stein: 3-4], citing the works by Zvelebil and Hart. But what Zvelebil mentions is that these works, of a highly sophisticated nature, were 'orally' composed, and were then transmitted orally for a long time up to the eighth century A.D. when they were compiled into anthologies [Zvelebil 1973: 23 ff.]. It should be noted here that Zvelebil does not say that the Sangam works came to possess a highly sophisticated nature by the learned poets of later days, but says that they were so from the very beginning, that is, even at the time of their composition. Although there is a divergence of opinion between Zvelebil and Hart regarding the usage of 'oral composition,'[34] Hart shares the same opinion that Sangam poems were originally highly refined, and says that they were composed by learned poets (*pulavaṉ*) of the Sangam age [Hart: 147 ff.]. Thus, both Zvelebil's and Hart's remarks cited by Stein are quite contrary to what he maintains.

Secondly, it is true that there are heroic poems, as well as some love poems, which describe kings or heroes as war-like and violent, but the number of those poems are rather limited and a far greater part of *puṟam* texts are allotted to depict kings' (or chieftains') generosity, or unstableness or transience of this life, or elegies.[35] Stein maintains that these types of texts depicting tragedy and instability of the world or reflecting moral tone had been influenced by Jainism. Apart from his incorrect impression of ancient Tamil poems, based on a misunderstanding of their composition or nature, namely, as being primitive, rough products by illiterate bards, it is not certain at all whether the moralistic component in Tamil ancient poetry was indigenous or arose from the northern influence. The Tamil-Brahmi cave inscriptions and some poets' names show that Jains and Buddhists, as well as Brahmins, had settled in the Tamil area even in those days, and there is a consensus among scholars that their influence had gradually pervaded Tamil culture and society. However, no poem in the body of classical literature gives the date of its composition, and the date of the poets of the classical period is also unknown to us, and, as mentioned by K. A. Nilakanta Satri, even 'the relative chronology of the poets is not clear' [Nilakanta Satri 1957: 501]. According to S. Vaiyapuri Pillai, the total number of poets in classical literature is 473 (See *Caṅka Ilakkiyam.*), and Zvelebil collects the possible biographical data of the 16 most productive poets among them and makes an attempt to reconstruct their relative chronology [Zvelebil 1975: 265–277]. However, even in the case of Kapilar, the most famous poet during the classical period (Note that certainly he was not an 'illiterate bard' but a *pulavaṉ*-type learned poet.), the authenticity of some works attributed to him is suspect.[36] Such being the case, more information and research on poets in the classical period and their relative chronology are necessary in order to convince us that Stein's arguments concerning the Jains' influence on the ancient period are proven to have a strong foundation.

Thirdly, Stein's impression that ancient kings were war-like, violent, and amoral in an age of fierce warfare [Stein: 10] is quite contrary to the impression among those who are familiar with the love (*akam*) poems, comprising more than three-fourths of the total number of classical texts. Apart from their highly conventionalised nature, love poems imply that the society of those days had already become, to a great deal, cultured and sophisticated, and people do not seem to have suffered from the ravages of war. Obviously, concerning this point, namely, the incompatibility of war-like kings and sophisticated courts, further studies are required.

As has often been insisted by Zvelebil, the thorough preparation of more specialised and detailed monographs on each and every aspect of the history of Tamil literature are expected to ensure further advances in the study of this richly rewarding field.

## Notes

1 The *Tirukkuṟaḷ* has eight other names: *Uttaravētam* 'The ultimate Veda,' *Tiruvaḷḷuvar* 'Saint Vaḷḷuvar' (the author's name), *Poyyāmoḻ* 'The false-

less word,' *Vāyuṟai vāḻttu* 'Truthful praise,' *Teyvanūl* 'The divine book,' *Potumaṟai* 'The common Veda,' *Muppāl* 'The threefold path,' and *Tamiḻmaṟai* 'The Tamil Veda.'

2 They have been discussed in innumerable monographs and books. However, none has so far analysed the *Kural*'s date on the basis of the relative chronology between the love (*akam*) poems of the Sangam age (first–third century A.D.) and those of the *Kural*. The present author intends to discuss this in a separate paper, and so he will touch on it only briefly here.

A wide difference is found between these love poems concerning their styles, contents, tone, and other aspects. However, the most crucial evidence for their relative chronology is the difference in the treatment of some themes, such as *kāṭci* 'the first look at each other between the hero and the heroine,' *aiyam* 'the hero's doubt as to whether the heroine is human or divine,' *tuṇivu* 'the hero's realisation, from various signs, that she is human,' and *kuṟippaṟital* 'the mutual understanding of their love for each other.' These themes are neither referred to in the *Tolkāppiyam* (its pertinent portion belongs to c. second–third century A.D. and refers only to *aiyam*), nor dealt with by Sangam texts including later texts in the *Aiṅkuṟunūṟu* (fourth century A.D.; cf. [Takahashi: 49–51, 229–30]). It is Nakkīrar's commentary (c. eighth century A.D.) on the *Iṟaiyaṉār Akapporuḷ* that mentions them for the first time (cf. [Takahashi: 62 ff.]). The *Kural*, on the other hand, allots chapter 109 to *kāṭci* and *aiyam*, poem 1090 to *tuṇivu*, and chapter 110 to *kuṟippaṟital*, and then the theme 'sexual union' follows in chapter 111, which is again contrary to the early literary tradition. Besides, their description seems exaggerated and high-flown, at least to those who are familiar with the mild, moderate tone of the early texts. This shows that the *Kural* belongs to a later date than the Sangam period, say, after the fifth century A.D.

This conclusion matches one of the most convincing pieces of evidence for the *Kural*'s date presented by S. Vaiyapuri on the basis of new forms of functional words appearing in it [Vaiyapuri Pillai 1956: 84–85].

3 Here is a select bibliography for the present study: K. Appadurai, *The Mind and Thought of Tiruvaḷḷuvar*, Sekar Pathippakam, Madras, 1966; A. Chidambaranatha Chettiar, 'Thiruvalluvar's Message to the World,' *Tamil Culture*, Tuticorin/Madras, Vol. IX, No. 2, 1961, pp. 101–8; [Cutler]; S. Gopalan, *The Social Philosophy of Tirukkural*, Affiliated East-West Press Pvt Ltd, New Delhi/Madras, 1979; D. I. Jesudoss, 'The Political Philosophy of Tiruvalluvar,' *Tamil Culture*, Tuticorin/Madras, Vol. II, No. 2, 1953, pp. 142–52; S. N. Kandaswamy, 'Human Values as Found in Suttapiṭaka and Tirukkuṟaḷ,' *Journal of the Institute of Asian Studies*, Institute of Asian Studies, Madras, Vol. VII, No. 2, 1990, pp. 97–106; [Maharajan]; [Meenakshisundaran 1969]; N. Murugesa Mudaliar, 'Polity in Tirukkural,' *Thirumathi Sornammal Endowment Lectures on Tirukkural, 1959–60 to 1968–69 (In Two Parts), Part I – English*, University of Madras, Madras,

1971, pp. 499–620; A. Palaniswami, 'Diplomacy of the Ancient Tamils,' *Journal of Tamil Studies*, International Institute of Tamil Studies, Madras, No. 10, 1976, pp. 28–39; C. R. Rajagopalachari, *Kural: The Great Book of Tiru-Valluvar*, Bharatiya Vidya Bhavan, Bombay, 1965; M. Shanmugasubramaniam, 'Concepts of Law in *Tirukkural*,' *Proceedings of the First International Conference Seminar of Tamil Studies*, Kuala Lumpur, 1969, Vol. 1, pp. 389–97; [Subrahmaniam, V.]; H. W. Tambiah, 'Pre-Aryan Customary Laws,' *Proceedings of the First International Conference Seminar of Tamil Studies*, Kuala Lumpur, 1969, Vol. 1, pp. 352–75; (Translations:) V. V. S. Aiyer, *The Kural or the Maxims of Tiruvalluvar*, Woraiyur, Trichilapalli, 1952; K. M. Balasubramaniam (Tiruvachakamani), *Tirukkuraḷ of Tiruvaḷḷuvar, Tamil text and English translation with notes and comments*, Manali Lakshmana Mudaliar Specific Endowments, Madras, 1962; [Drew and Lazarus]; V. R. Ramachandra Dikshitar, *Tirukkuṟaḷ, in Roman transliteration with English translation*, The Adyar Library, Madras, 1949; Karl Graul, *Der Kural des Tiruvalluver: Ein gnomisches Gedicht über die drei Strebeziele des Menschen* (*Bibliotheca Tamulica*, Tom. III), Otto Zeller, Osnabrück, 1969 (reprint; first ed., London-Leipzig, 1854–65); [Pope]; [Popley].

4 Ramachandra Dikshitar, for example, endeavours to clarify the relationship between the *Kural*'s *Aṟattuppāl* and *Mānavadharmaśāstra*, *Poruṭppāl* and *Arthaśāstra*, and *Kāmattuppāl* and *Kāmasūtra* [Dikshitar: 140-76].

5 In this essay, words in common use, such as Pandya, Chola, Chera, Sangam, and the like, are used instead of Pāṇṭiya, Cōḻa, Cēra, Caṅkam, and such.

6 Although the expression 'Sangam period' is misleading, the present author uses it for convenience' sake, denoting the period when the main corpus of so-called Sangam literature was composed, that is, the first to third centuries A.D. The appellation 'Sangam literature' is also misleading, since the texts implied by the term differ according to critics: in its narrowest usage it signifies the 'Two Anthologies' (*Eṭṭuttokai* and *Pattuppāṭṭu*), while in its broadest usage texts of different dates and categories such as the *Tolkāppiyam* (the oldest grammar including poetics), 'Two Anthologies,' 'Twin Epics' (*Cilappatikāram* and *Maṇimēkalai*), 'Eighteen Minor Works' (*Patiṉeṇkīḻkaṇakku*) inclusive of the *Kural*, are grouped together. Here I use the term in its narrowest sense.

7 It was after the ninth or tenth century A.D. that Kerala developed as its own linguistic and cultural area.

8 N. Subrahmanian gives the number as 120 [Subrahmanian, N.: 44]. More than 300 appellations of the kings and chiefs are mentioned in the Sangam texts (cf. [Vaiyapuri Pillai 1967: 1461 ff.]), but it is difficult to differentiate personal names from titles, epithets, and the like. J. R. Marr enumerates 47 chiefs who figure in *Puṟanāṉūṟu* [Marr: 182 ff.]. According to M. A.

Drai Rangaswamy, many chiefs had their territories within those of the three kingdoms [Rangaswamy].

9 Cf. [Meenakshisundaran 1961: 68] and [Dikshitar: 11].

10 Colophons to a few heroic poems (*Puṟanāṉūṟu* 16, 125, 367, 377) refer to a Chola king who performed the *rājasūya*, one of the sacrifices prescribed for kings, as Cōḻaṉ Irācacūyam Vēṭṭa Perunaṟkiḷḷi, while we do not know if any king performed the *aśvamedha*. According to K. A. Nilakanta Sastri, the *aśvamedha* occurs only once and that in the inscriptions of the far later period of Rājādhirāja I (reigned 1018–54) [Nilakanta Sastri 1975: 451].

11 Of the Kalabhras we have no definite knowledge. Buddhadatta (c. last quarter of fifth century A.D.), an elder contemporary of Buddhaghoṣa, refers to the reign of the blemishless Accuta Vikkantaṉ of the Kalabbhakula. The Vēḷvikkuḍi grant of probably the third quarter of the eighth century A.D. tells us that a cruel king called Kaḷabhra defeated many *ādhirājas* and established his sway over Madurai, among other Tamil districts. Cf. [Srinivas Iyengar: 528 ff.], and see also [Srinivas Iyengar: 437–8] for the original text and his translation of the Vēḷvikkuḍi grant.

12 As for these colleges and various *saṅghas* at Kanchi, see [Minakshi: 253 ff.]. In Madurai, on the other hand, in A.D. 470 a Dravida Sangha is said to have been established by a Jain named Vajranandi; cf. [Srinivas Iyengar: 247, 528] and [Vaiyapuri Pillai 1956: 58 ff.].

13 I often use translations of W. H. Drew (*Kural* 1–630), J. Lazarus (*Kural* 631–1330), and G. U. Pope. But in some cases, I adapt the text from the original; read 'Drew, ad.' as adaptation by the present author of Drew's translation.

14 This is regarded by Nilakanta Sastri as the *Kural* 'introducing a slight but significant change' [Nilakanta Sastri 1975: 66].

15 This classification was formulated not by the author himself but by the commentators, but this may reflect the original scheme of the author. The 1538th stanza in the *Peruntokai*, a collection of so-called anonymous solitary stanzas (*taṉippāṭal*), tells us there were 10 commentaries on the *Kural*. Only five of them, however, are extant, and among them Parimēlaḻakar's commentary, written in the late thirteenth or early fourteenth century, has by far been famous and has exerted tremendous influence on the interpretation of the *Kural*. Although his commentary excels in many respects, he, as an orthodox Śrīvaiṣṇava Brahmin, often reads later Brahmanical ideology into the original text which, as mentioned in the first Section above, seems to have been composed when Tamil society was still on the way to being Aryanized. As for the role of Parimēlaḻakar's commentary, see [Cutler].

16 According to Pope, 'wealth that falls to him as heir.'

17 For example, Meenakshisundaran says, 'The value of this approach in making the abstruse diplomacy clear to and understandable by the ordi-

nary man in the street cannot be easily exaggerated' [Meenakshisundaran 1969: 132].

18 In this regard M. Mudaliar, for example, says, 'the obvious reasons being that organisational details are subject to change and that elaboration would disrupt the scheme and proportions of Tiruvalluvar's work' [Mudaliar: 510], but, as seen in this Section, this is not wholly true.

19 Such being the case, Valluvar never describes the Brahmin as a prop against the king, nor does he even refer to the Purohita. After all, he does not explicitly refer to the Brahmin except in a few distichs such as *Kural* 134 (as *pārppāṉ*), 543 (*antaṇar*), and 560 (*aṟutoḻilōr* 'the men of six duties').

20 Some specific features of the *Kural* in comparison with the Sanskrit treatises are often pointed out as follows. First, the divine origin or divinity of kingship is not suggested anywhere in the *Kural* (cf. [Mudaliar: 528], [Popley: 26], and [Meenakshisundaran 1969: 123–24]). Secondly, the king must act, just as an ideal man: he must be enthusiastic in the performance of his duties, full of wisdom, munificence, high ideals, and justice. Therefore, in the politics of the *Kural* the means must be as pure and desirable as the end itself, and it is not admissible to resort to unjust or evil means for the sake of the end (See, for example, *Kural* 660: 'To lay by wealth through foul means is like preserving water in a vessel of clay that is not baked.'). This forms a striking contrast to other political treatises, such as *KAS*, which justifies Machiavellian-like crooked politics for the sake of the kingdom.

21 N. Cutler writes, 'neither the precise nature of *Tirukkuṟaḷ*'s total structure of meaning nor the degree to which the text is undergirded by a coherent and consistent plan is self-evident' [Cutler: 553].

22 For example, not a single couplet in these chapters mentions the term 'king.'

23 Concerning *maṭal-ēṟutal*, see Takahashi's detailed analysis [Takahashi: 106–114].

24 One may point to, as a crucial example for a structural gap between chapters, the interrelationship between chapters 106 'Begging' and 107 'Fear of begging.'

25 As seen in Note 2, however, we sometimes come across the *Kural*'s new treatment of themes and its exaggerated and high-flown expressions contrary to the moderation of Sangam texts.

26 One may read or quote as ordinary love or maxim poems the following couplets: 1090, 1091, 1099, 1100, 1101, 1102, 1104, 1108, 1121, 1124, 1134, 1183, 1191, 1192, 1193, 1194, 1196, 1201, 1202, 1210, 1233, 1251, 1252, 1257, 1261, 1281, 1289, 1302, 1323, and 1330. N. Subrahmaniam and R. Rajalakshmi present us with an interesting list, 'Some of the Most Reputed and Oft-quoted Verses of the Kural' [Subrahmaniam, N. and Rajalakshmi, R.: 243 ff.], according to which the ratio of the number of

verses quoted to the total number of poems in each part is as follows: 22 to 380 in the first part on 'virtues,' 24 to 700 in the second part on 'wealth,' and 4 to 250 in the third part on 'love.' Thus the ratio becomes 0.58, 0.34, and 0.016 respectively: that is, quotations from the first and second parts occur 36 and 21 times as often as do quotations from the third part.

27 This may remind us of the term *Muppāl* (literally, 'three parts') which is another name for the *Kural*; see Note 1.

28 *Tolkāppiyam Poruḷatikāram* 89:1 reads, '[interlinked] with pleasure, wealth and virtue (*iṉpamum poruḷum aṟaṉum eṉṟāṅku*),' and *Puṟanāṉūṟu* 31:1–2 says, 'the *kāma* and *artha* of the great tradition follow the path of *dharma* (*ciṟappuṭai marapiṉ poruḷum iṉpamum aṟattu vaḻippaṭūum*).' See also *Puṟanāṉūṟu* 28:15; cf. *Kalittokai* 141:3, a text mostly contemporary with the *Kural*.

29 *Nālaṭiyār* (Four Hundred Quatrains), one of the 'Eighteen Minor Works,' probably of the seventh century A.D., is a Jain work, consisting of 40 chapters of 10 stanzas and dealing with three goals. But its treatment of the goals is far more nominal, since it allots only one among the 40 chapters to *kāma* or 'love' (although there are commentators who maintain that the last three chapters deal with 'love'). This could have happened under the strong influence of the *Kural*.

Some critics, including commentators, assert that the *Kural* deals with a fourfold goal (three goals plus 'liberation') on the basis of chapters 35–37, but the conception of a fourfold goal belongs to later periods. There are still some who insist that this fourfold goal is Aryan, while the Tamilian conception consists of a twofold goal, that is, *akam* and *puṟam*, which are the two aspects of life in classical literature. But, as mentioned by Meenakshisundaram, 'this is a literary theory rather than a philosophical principle' [Meenakshisundaran 1969: 23].

30 See, for example, the *Cīvakacintāmaṇi*, a very popular Jain work written by the austere Tiruttakkatēvar (ninth–twelfth century), which is so sensuous that it has made a critic write, 'If there is one book in Tamil literature that should be banned for the young, it is *Sīvaha-sindāmaṇi*' [Jesudasan: 148]; see also the three great Jain poets called 'Ratnatraya' in Kannada literature, that is, Pampa, Ponna and Ranna (tenth century), who all wrote both secular and religious works following the earlier tradition among the Jains (cf. [Mugali]).

31 I quote this passage from T. N. Vasudeva Rao's work, but in a context contrary to his. The original states: 'All the great religions, such as Hinduism, Jainism, Buddhism, and even Christianity, have claimed Valluvar as belonging to their own sect. The likelihood is that he belonged to no particular sect but worked out from his own experience a synthesis of the best he could find in all of them' [Vasudeva Rao: 51].

32 *Kural* 55 is quoted verbatim in *Maṇimēkalai* 22:59–60, which gives us

evidence for their relative chronology. There are a few studies of such quotations from or allusions to the *Kural*; for example, [Sankaran] and [Maharajan]. However, some of the texts which they find to be such are debatable.

33 The Tamils start learning the *Kural* as early as in the lower grades of primary school.

34 The usage of 'oral composition' by Zvelebil is broader than that by Hart; that is, he means by it 'not literate' or 'not written' composition, since he refers to it as 'not visual "consumption" of literature' [Zvelebil 1973: 25]. On the other hand, Hart uses the expression more narrowly as being synonymous for 'extemporization' [Hart:152–54], and so, he denies that Sangam works were 'orally' composed. But, as he himself mentions, 'this is not to say that the poems were not uttered before being committed to writing. It is quite possible that ... the poets spent some time mentally composing their poems and then recited them for the audience, and that they were committed to writing only afterward' [Hart: 154]. Hence, both Zvelebil and Hart signify almost the same method of composing the Sangam poems but use different terminology.

35 These poems are categorised by *Tolkāppiyam* into genres (*tiṇai*), such as *kāñci* (tragedy and instability of the world), *pāṭāṇ* (elegy and praise), or *vākai* (victory).

36 Poems, such as 37–65 of *Kalittokai*, 201–300 of *Aiṅkuṟunūṟu*, and *Kuṟiñcippāṭṭu*, are supposed to be merely ascribed to him. Concerning the later composition of the poems in *Aiṅkuṟunūṟu* and of *Kuṟiñcippāṭṭu*, see, for example, [Takahashi: 229–30, 221 ftn. 2, etc.].

## References


Cutler, Norman

1992 'Interpreting Tirukkuṟaḷ: The Role of Commentary in the Creation of a Text,' *Journal of the American Oriental Society*, Vol. 112, No. 4, pp. 549–66.

Dikshitar, V. R. Ramachandra

1983 *Studies in Tamil Literature and History*, The South India Saiva Siddhanta Works Publishing Society, Madras (reprint).

Drew, W. H. and Lazarus, John

1991 *Tirukkuṟaḷ*, Asian Educational Services, New Delhi (reprint).

Hart, G. L.

1975 *The Poems of Ancient Tamil: Their Milieu and Their Sanskrit Counterpart*, Berkeley, University of California Press.

Jesudasan, C. and H.
1961 *A History of Tamil Literature*, Y. M. C. A. Publishing House, Calcutta.

Kangle, R. P.
1963 *The Kauṭilīya Arthaśāstra, Part II: An English Translation with Critical and Explanatory Notes*, University of Bombay, Bombay.

Maharajan, S.
1979 *Tiruvalluvar*, Sahitya Akademi, New Delhi.

Marr, J. R.
1985 *The Eight Anthologies: A Study in Early Tamil Literature*, Institute of Asian Studies, Madras.

Meenakshisundaran, T. P.
1961 *Prof. T. P. Meenakshisundaran Sixty-first Birthday Commemoration Volume, Collected Papers of Prof. T. P. Meenakashisundaran*, Annamalai University, Annamalainagar.
1969 *Philosophy of Tiruvaḷḷuvar*, Madurai University, Madurai.

Minakshi, C.
1977 *Administration and Social Life under the Pallavas*, University of Madras, Madras.

Mugali, R. S.
1975 *History of Kannada Literature*, Sahitya Akademi, New Delhi.

Nilakanta Sastri, K. A. (ed.)
1957 *A Comprehensive History of India, Vol. II: The Mauryas and Satavahanas, 325 B.C.–A.D. 300*, Orient Longmans, Bombay/Calcutta/Madras.

Nilakanta Sastri, K. A.
1975 *The Cōḷas*, University of Madras, Madras (revised ed.).

Pope, G. U.
1886 *The 'Sacred' Kurraḷ of Tiruvaḷḷuva-Ṇāyanār*, W.H. Allen & Co., London.

Popley, H. A.
1931 *The Sacred Kural or the Tamil Veda of Tiruvaḷḷuvar*, Association Press, Calcutta.

Rangaswamy, M. A. Drai
1968 *The Surnames of the Caṅkam Age—Literary and Tribal*, University of Madras, Madras.

Sankaran, Srimathi Kamala
1978 *Kamban's Treatment of Tirukkural*, Pooram Publications, Madras.

Srinivas Iyengar, P. T.
1982 *History of the Tamils, from the Earliest Times to 600 A.D.*, Asian Educational Services, New Delhi (reprint).

Stein, Burton
1984 'All the King's Mana: Perspectives on Kingship in Medieval South India,' *Papers on Medieval South Indian History*, ed. by B. Stein, New Era Publications, Madras (reprint ed.: original ed., Richards, J. F. ed., *Kingship and Authority in South Asia*, University of Wisconsin, Madison, 1978, pp. 115–67), pp. 1–67.

Subrahmanian, N.
1980 *Śangam Polity: The Administration and Social Life of the Śangam Tamils*, Ennes Publications, Madurai, 1980 (revised ed.).

Subrahmaniam, N. and Rajalakshmi, R.
1984 *The Concordance of Tirukkural*, Ennes Publications, Madurai.

Subrahmaniam, V.
1969 'The Kural's Contribution to Political Thought: A New Analysis of Porutpaal,' *Proceedings of the First International Conference Seminar of Tamil Studies*, Kuala Lumpur, Vol. 1, pp. 376–88.

Takahashi, Takanobu
1995 *Tamil Love Poetry and Poetics*, E. J. Brill, Leiden/New York/Köln.

Vaiyapuri Pillai, S.
1956 *History of Tamil Language and Literature*, New Century Book House, Madras.

Vaiyapuri Pillai, S. (ed.)
1967 *Caṅka Ilakkiyam: Pāṭṭum Tokaiyum*, Puri Nilaiyam, Madras.

Vasudeva Rao, T. N.
1979 *Buddhism in the Tamil Country*, Annamalai University, Annamalainagar.

Zvelebil, K. V.
1973 *The Smile of Murugan: On Tamil Literature of South India*, E. J. Brill, Leiden.
1975 *Tamil Literature* (*Handbuch der Orientalistik*, Zweite Abteilung, 2. Band, 1. Abschnitt), E. J. Brill, Leiden.

# 3

# God as Warrior King: Images of God in Late Classical Tamil Literature[1]

HIROSHI YAMASHITA

## Introduction

The body of ancient Tamil literature known collectively as the *Caṅkam* Classics, which consist of the *Eṭṭuttokai* ('Eight Anthologies') and the *Pattuppāṭṭu* ('Ten Poems'), is a vast collection of short and long poems on love and war. The *Caṅkam* lyrics and idylls, which date back to the early centuries of the Christian era, reveal the social and cultural milieu of the ancient Tamil Nadu relatively free from the overwhelming Sanskritic-Brahmanical influences from northern India. The *Caṅkam* texts, the earliest extant literary corpus ever composed in a Dravidian language, have recently attracted a great deal of attention because of their rich potentiality in academic inquiries and the insights they are expected to afford in illuminating the convoluted history of the formation and evolution of Indian culture.

Though given but scant attention, the religious aspects of ancient Tamil society as depicted in the *Caṅkam* works have been surveyed by scholars, native as well as foreign. Much of this research, however, is in one way or another biased, being prompted by the deep-rooted theistic and devotional tradition lingering on among the Tamils. Some scholars, for example, venture to speak of the total lack of religious sentiment in *Caṅkam* poetry and therefore of the apparent secularism or even irreligious lineaments of classical literature and society prior to the flourishing of devotional religiosity, whereas others seek to secure in the oldest stratum of the corpus itself convincing proof of the theistic or rather monotheistic development of native beliefs presumably of pre-Aryan antiquity.

Provided with the available materials of the extant *Caṅkam* corpus, which are quite limited in quantity,[2] we are naturally faced with constant difficulties in interpreting and reconstructing the cultural, religious and social conditions of the period. In addition, classical Tamil literature itself was quite stylised and standardised with strict rules and conventions not only in poetics but also in content, so that it is not necessarily a good 'mirror' of culture or society operating during those times. We should always keep in mind the limitations of available documents, the quality of the available information, and the probable gap between the actual state of things and what is described in the literature.[3]

When we consider the nature of devotion in southern Hinduism, it is of foremost importance to understand the process of how the Hindu conceptions of god in Tamil Nadu developed from the preceding indigenous notions of the sacred peculiar to Dravidian India.[4] This issue has indeed been discussed previously by some scholars. The foregoing studies, however, mostly remain less persuasive through a lack of concrete textual evidence or convincing proof, and so they require careful reexamination.[5]

In the present paper, I take up for consideration the concepts of god-king or king-god as found in the late classical and therefore pre-devotional Tamil texts, ideas crucial for understanding the specific nature of southern Hinduism in comparison with its northern counterpart. I will trace the early stages of the evolution of these Tamil concepts, citing original verses from pre-devotional literature, especially late classical works.

## The Notion of the King-God

A brief survey of arguments on this point made in previous studies is necessary before proceeding to the examination of the *Tirumurukāṟṟuppaṭai* (= *TM*) and *Paripāṭal* (= *PP*). One of the more notable arguments in this connection is that the Hindu concepts of god in Tamil India owe a great deal to ancient, indigenous ideas about the human king, as a supreme fighter in particular.[6] As G.L. Hart says, *deva*, the word for god, came to mean 'king' in the north, whereas the process was reversed in Tamil Nadu [Hart 1975a: 14].

In his controversial[7] but no doubt thought-provoking monograph on ancient Tamil literature and its cultural milieu, Hart remarks:

> In ancient Tamil society, the king was the central embodiment of the sacred powers that had to be present and under control for the proper functioning of society. The poems indicate that before the advent

of the Brahmins there was no priestly class of higher status than the king; indeed, those members of society who dealt closely with sacred powers were of low status, as will be seen. The king's position is suggested by the fact that words that meant king in ancient Tamil now denote God [Hart 1975a: 13].[8]

According to this notion, an ancient Tamil king, who was a warrior *par excellence* charged with sacred forces, had religious significance as the embodiment of something divine. In his other study on Tamil devotion, Hart further notes, 'First, the new god was modeled on and assimilated to the king. The temple was called *kōyil*, the house of the king (and earlier the name of the king's palace); many Tamil terms for the north Indian god first meant king or still can mean either king or god; the temple is constructed like a palace; and the deity is treated like a king ...' [Hart 1978: 13]. Here, it is apparent from the context that 'the new god' is the god of the Hindu devotional tradition of south India, such as Śiva and Viṣṇu. He also says elsewhere, 'In other words, while the theory of Tamil religion has kept the northern ideal, the practice has adhered to the indigenous model, which demands that gods be modelled after human kings' [Hart 1978: 19].

This idea on king-god has given stimulus to such scholars as F. Hardy, N. Cutler, Indira V. Peterson and G. Subbiah, and has been referred to by them [Hardy 1983; Cutler 1987; Peterson 1989; Subbiah 1991].[9] For example, Hardy, who made an extensive survey on the emergence and development of south Indian Kṛṣṇaism based upon Tamil and Sanskrit sources, points out the historical change in meaning of the words *kōyil* and *nakar* from 'palace' to 'temple,' the shift in bardic patronage, and phraseological parallels like 'the unending fame,' a typical attribute of the classical king, which in the *Paripāṭal* (= *PP*), a late *Caṅkam* text, is used with reference to the god and his temple [Hardy 1983: 137, 225].[10] He apparently takes it for granted that the semantic transition from the 'palace' to the 'temple' took place.

Quoting a passage form Hart, Indira Peterson, a scholar on Tamil devotional literature, writes:

> The Nāyaṉārs' model for the image of Śiva was the Tamil 'king' or local ruler, who was considered to be 'the embodiment of the sacred powers that had to be present under control for the proper functioning of society.' The cult of temple worship in Tamil country after the *Caṅkam* age shows clear evidence of the transference of the idea of

the king with sacred power to the deity in the temple [Peterson 1989: 33].

It is true that in the Tamil devotional tradition, god, or rather God, is often called *kō*, *kōmāṉ*, *kāvalaṉ*,[11] *iṟaivaṉ*, and the like, all of which originally denoted 'king.' Peterson further adds such appellations as *perumāṉ* (ruler), *nampi* (prince), *īcaṉ*, *pirāṉ* and *empirāṉ* (our lord, master) in the *Tēvāram* hymns [Peterson 1989: 34]. These words ultimately refer to God, namely Śiva, with the original implication of 'king.'

As aforesaid, Hindu temples are called *kōyil* or *kōvil* in Tamil, both of which originally meant 'king's (*kō*) abode (*il*).' In this context, it is quite noteworthy that Appar (alias Tirunāvukkaracar), Cuntarar (Cuntaramūrtti) and Tiruñānacanpantar, the *Tēvāram* Trio at the earliest phases of Tamil devotionalism, moved from one temple to another and composed hymns in praise of Lord Śiva in different names at each temple, just as ancient bards went from one palace to another and sang in praise of each king or chieftain to earn their livelihood.

*Abhiṣeka* and *Tirukkalyāṇam*, two elaborate rituals for Hindu deities, also appear to be borrowed from, or modelled after, the royal rituals or customs of Tamil kings.[12] *Abhiṣeka*, in particular, is likely to have its root in the consecration rites, symbolic of kingship and sovereignty, in which the king was anointed in a similar manner now reserved for the icon (*arcā*) [Clothey 1983: 97].[13] The *Tirukkalyāṇam*, the wedding festival of a divine couple performed in Hindu temples, and the *tiruppaḷḷiyeḻucci*, the ritual done or the poem sung for waking up the deity from a bed chamber in an orthodox Hindu temple in south India irrespective of Śaiva or Vaiṣṇava, may also be considered in the same context.[14]

Subbiah questions, however, the idea that the concepts and attributes of the ancient king were transferred to those of God in devotional Hinduism. He thinks that there is a strong conceptual linking between king and god even in the early poems [Subbiah 1991: 34-40].[15] For this reason too, he rejects the general notion that, in the southern tradition, secular literature preceded religious literature [Subbiah 1991: 6-7].

## Literary Examples[16]

The notion of God's conceptual links with ancient kings or royal customs is worth considering and will undoubtedly provide clues and insights relating to the formation of the religious ideas and institutions of southern Hinduism. This idea, however, has yet to be proven on reliable evidence from Tamil literary sources. So far, the parallelism in vocabulary alone has been pointed out by scholars between ancient king and *bhakti* god. It is, therefore, essential to examine the literary materials of the transitional period to fill the gap between the ancient literature (first to third century A.D.) and the early medieval literature (from seventh century) so that we can trace the progress of these ideas from the classical period to the dawn of Tamil devotion.

Here, bearing the above issues in mind, I will take up for comparison the above-mentioned *TM* (from the *Pattuppāṭṭu* collection) and *PP* (from the *Eṭṭuttokai* collection), two texts of the transitional period considered to be forerunners of Tamil devotional literature.[17]

*Tirumāl Hymns of PP*

To begin with, we will go through some verses from *PP*, a collection of long songs of praise, that is distinguished from the other anthologies not merely by its metaphysical awareness of transcendence and immanence of God but also by its devotional lineaments, particularly in the odes dedicated to Tirumāl/Viṣṇu [Yamashita 1995: 104-14].[18] The Tirumāl hymns of *PP* consist of the integral odes, six in number (I, II, III, IV, XIII, XV) and written by different poets, and one fragmentary ode of unknown authorship which is composed of 82 lines.[19]

For example, one passage of a Tirumāl ode reads:

*poruvēm eṉṟavar matantapak kaṭantu*
*ceru mēmpaṭṭa ceyirtīr aṇṇal*
*iruvar tātai yilaṅkupūṇ māal* (*PP* I. 26-28)

> Māl, father of the two (= Kāmaṉ and Cāmaṉ [20]), adorned with brilliant ornaments,
> Breaking the brunt of the spirited foes (= *asuras*),
> Being a superior king[21](= Māl) of absolute perfection and martial greatness!

Another passage goes:

*cērār iṉṉuyir cekukkum*
*pōraṭu kurucil nī yēntiya paṭaiyē* (*PP* II. 48-49)

> The weapon possessed by you (= Māl), the chief of massacres in battlefields,
> Who destroys the dearest lives of his foes (= *asuras*)!

Yet another example reads:

*... oṉṉārk*
*kaṭantu aṭṭāṉ kēḻ iruṅkuṉṟu* (*PP* XV. 44-45)
Iruṅkuṉṟu,[22] whose colour is that of the One (= Māl) who subdued and destroyed his foes!

Here, wondering whether we regard it exclusively as the image of ancient Tamil kings that provides the backdrop to these passages, let us consider some more verses to clarify this point [Yamashita 1995: 22, 37]:

*eḷḷunark kaṭantaṭṭa vikal nēmiyavai* (*PP* I. 58)
You (= Māl) possess the discus powerful enough to defeat and destroy those who abuse you.

*paruti valava porutiṟal malla* (*PP* III. 89)
One (= Māl) with a discus in your right [hand]! Fighter strong in battle!

*nōṉār uyiroṭu muraṇiya nēmiyai* (*PP* IV. 9)
You (= Māl) possess the discus directed against the lives of [your] foes.

*taṇṇaḷi koṇṭa aṇaṅkuṭai nēmimāl* (*PP* XIII. 6)
Māl possessing the discus with *aṇaṅku* of cool grace!

*cerumiku tikiric celva velpōr* (*PP* XIII. 58)
Chief (= Māl) of victorious battles with the discus raised high in battlefields!

*valampuri vayanēmiyavai* (*PP* XV. 59)
You (= Māl) possess the dextral conch and the victorious discus.

The above citations clearly indicate that Tirumāl/Viṣṇu's fight against *asuras* (*avuṇar*) or antigods and his subsequent victory over them were brought about by virtue of his matchless weapons, including a discus (known as *nēmi* or *tikiri*, terms parallel to Skt. *cakra*). This discus, sometimes known by the name of *sudarśana* or 'the disc of the sun' in Epic-Puranic literature in Sanskrit, is the weapon peculiar to God Viṣṇu-Kṛṣṇa. Verses II. 36-49, IV. 9 and XIII. 58 extol the power of the discus weapon.

Kṛṣṇa. Verses II. 36-49, IV. 9 and XIII. 58 extol the power of the discus weapon. Tirumāl annihilates *asuras* or the antigods using this marvelous weapon.

Verses XIII. 30-33 also describe Lord Tirumāl in his fight with the demons. Here he is found to be armed with a plough (*nāñcil*), as commonly known in the Epic-Puranic literature in Sanskrit traditions. This is his aspect of Balarāma/Baladeva, otherwise called Haladhara, Halabhṛt, Halāyudha and Lāṅgalin in Sanskrit, all of which mean 'bearer of a plough.' Similarly, one verse (III. 87) pays tribute to the conch (*koṭu*, synonymous with Skt. *śaṅkha*) as one of the five weapons (*pañcāyudha*) of God Tirumāl. Apart from the above-mentioned weapons, Tirumāl/Viṣṇu's victory gained by his powerful arrows is also referred to in verse XV. 60.

Most passages cited above on the conquests of Tirumāl over the demoniac beings are in one way or other related to the Epic-Puranic myths in which Viṣṇu, assuming various forms, wins a victory over the antigods. Typical references or allusions to these heroic deeds by Tirumāl in *PP* are illustrated in Table 1.[23]

As may be seen in Table 1, it is expressly described in *PP* I. 22-27 how Tirumāl wins a victory by wielding arrows and 'without touching a plough' (*alantoṭā*). This description is likely to afford negative proof of the participation of Balarāma/Baladeva armed with a plough in this battle, although Tirumāl is clearly mentioned along with his Balarāma aspects in a preceding passage (viz. *PP* I. 3-5) [Gros 1968: 170, nn. 14-25]. Tirumāl's victory won by his mighty arrows is also touched upon in verse XV. 60. The verb *kaṭa* in *PP* I. 26 may imply his grand victory over the *asuras* (*avuṇar*), the antigods who were entirely dependent on tricks [Gros 1968: 170, n. 26].[24]

The word *kūntal* as the name of an *asura* mentioned in *PP* III. 31-32 is the literal translation of the Sanskrit noun *keśin*.[25] Therefore, the *asura* Kūntal parallels Keśin, a horse-shaped demon who is slain by Kṛṣṇa in northern mythology. It is evident that the Kṛṣṇa cycle of Sanskrit myths underlies this Tamil legend about Tirumāl's battle against Kūntal.[26]

The account of Tirumāl's measuring the Earth given in *PP* III. 54-56 is no doubt an allusion to Viṣṇu's 'Three strides' (*trivikrama*), a well-known theme as early as in the Rig-Vedic period.[27]

In addition to the exploits given in Table 1, verses III. 87, 89-90, IV. 47, XIII. 15 and XV. 44-45 of the same anthology also lay stress on Tirumāl's aspect as a brave warrior against the *asuras*, though detailed descriptions of weapons are in absence.

Table 1

| Verse | Sinopsis | Weapon mentioned | |
|---|---|---|---|
| I. 22-27 | Tirumāl wins a victory over *asuras* by the use of arrows which fly swiftly like a whirlwind. | arrow (*kaṇai*) (not plough) | Cf. XV. 60 for the victorious arrows of Viṣṇu (Viṣṇu's aspect as Balarāma?) |
| I. 39-40 | Tirumāl, the source of extraordinary valour, is the source of fear as well for those who are opposed to him. | | |
| II. 36-49 | Cut off by Tirumāl with his discus weapon, the heads of *asuras* fall off like coconuts dropped from palm trees. | discus | 'Discus' is given only by allusion. |
| III. 31-32 | Tirumāl subdues the *asuras* Kūntal (Skt. Keśin) in the form of a maned horse. | | Viṣṇu's aspect as Kṛṣṇa. |
| III. 54-56 | When Tirumāl measures the earth [in three steps], *asuras* tremble with fear and escape into the sea. | | Viṣṇu's aspect as Vāmana. |
| IV. 9 | Tirumāl has a discus weapon with which he brings the lives of his enemies under control. | discus (*nēmi*) | |
| IV. 47 | 'O the One (= Tirumāl) who unnerved the opposing powers!' | | |
| XIII. 15 | 'O King of Battle (= Tirumāl) who massacres!' | | |

| | | | |
|---|---|---|---|
| XIII. 30-33 | Tirumāl has a plough with a curved blade with which he ploughs the chest of his enemies just as one ploughs the soil. | plough (*nāñcil*) | Viṣṇu's aspect as Balarāma. |
| XIII. 58 | Tirumāl is the chief (*celvaṉ*) who triumphs with his discus weapon in battles. | discus (*tikiri*) | |
| XV. 44-45 | Iruṅkuṉṟu has the colour of [Māl] who subdued and killed those who fought against him. | | |

The above discussion suggests that, though Tirumāl is sometimes referred to by the appellations otherwise applied to kings and warriors,[28] the basic identity of Tirumāl as a divine fighter is created in the senario of the antagonism and struggle between gods (*devas/suras*) and antigods (*asuras*), a very old, traditional theme dating back to antiquity as early as Rig-Vedic times, or more recently from Viṣṇu's aspect as Śatrughna, 'Destroyer of Enemies.' Moreover, his other aspects as Kṛṣṇa, Vāmana and Balarāma are also found in the Tirumāl hymns. This fact demonstrates that Tirumāl in *PP*, as the warrior god, is also closely related with the concept of *avatāras* or 'Descents,' which is sporadically mentioned or alluded to in the Tirumāl odes of this anthology (see Table 2[29]).

All of the above considerations show that the image of Tirumāl depends heavily on that of Viṣṇu in northern Hinduism and even reveal multifarious aspects of a composite Viṣṇu-Vāsudeva-Nārāyaṇa-Kṛṣṇa. This image of God in *PP* is thus found to be far removed from the indigenous ideas of a king, a fighter *par excellence* in ancient Tamil Nadu, excepting his association with *aṇaṅku* in *PP* XIII. 6 quoted above which makes mention of Viṣṇu's discus charged with the power of *aṇaṅku*, the ambivalent mystic force originating from the Dravidian notion of the sacred. This can be taken, therefore, at least as a sure indication that this ancient Dravidian concept of kingly or sacred power lingered on in the work of the Late Classical Period, though we do not know whether it developed and transformed itself into the new concept of God in the succeeding period.

Table 2

| Name of *Avatāra* | Verse |
|---|---|
| Kūrma (Tortoise) | Fragment I. 64–66 |
| Varāha (Boar) | II. 16–17, 32–35<br>III. 21–24<br>IV. 22–24<br>XIII. 34–36 |
| Nṛsiṃha or Narasiṃha (Man-lion) | IV. 10–21 |
| Vāmana (Dwarf) | III. 18–20, 54–56 |
| Kṛṣṇa | III. 31–32, 83<br>XV. 10–14, 27–28 |
| Haṃsa (Swan) | III. 25–26 |
| Balarāma or Baladeva | I. 1–5<br>II. 20, 22<br>III. 83<br>IV. 38–40<br>XIII. 30–33<br>XV. 13, 19, 28, 55, 57-58 |

*Cevvēḷ Hymns of PP*

We shall now turn our attention to the odes dedicated to Lord Cevvēḷ (= Murukaṉ) in the same anthology. In the Cevvēḷ hymns (V, VIII, IX, XIV, XVII, XVIII, XIX, XXI), as compared with the Tirumāl odes, there seems to be a fewer number of passages that remind us of a brave king or at least a victorious warriors.[30] The most prominent examples are given below as:

> *viṟal veyyōṉ ūr mayil vēl niḻal nōkki* (*PP* VIII. 67)
> Toward the shadow of the spear and the peacock,
> on which One (= Cevvēḷ/Murukaṉ) desirous of victory mounts, ....

> *vāṇmiku vayamoympiṉ*
> *varaiyakalattavaṉai....* (*PP* IX. 57-58)

Skilled in sword and endowed with the power of victory,
Cevvēḷ(/Murukaṉ) with his mountain-like huge chest, ....

*vittakat tumpai viḷaittalāl veṉvēlāṟ* (*PP* IX. 68)
One (= Cevvēḷ/Murukaṉ) endowed with his victorious spear by cultivating(?) a marvelous war, ....

*aṭumpōrāḷa niṉ kuṉṟiṉmicai* (*PP* IX. 71)

The warrior (= Cevvēḷ/Murukaṉ) in massacring battles!
On your mountain (= Tirupparaṅkuṉṟam)....

*... pōr malintu*
*cūr maruṅku aṟutta cuṭarppaṭaiyōyē* (*PP* XIV. 17-18)
Filled with wars,
One (= Cevvēḷ/Murukaṉ) with the weapon of fire (= spear) with which he killed the party of Cūr!

*aṟumukattu āṟu iru tōḷāl veṉṟi* (*PP* XIV. 21)
Gaining a victory with six faces and twelve arms, ....

*piṇimukam ūrnta velpōr iṟaiva* (*PP* XVII. 49)
Lord (= Cevvēḷ/Murukaṉ) of victorious wars, mounted on Piṇimukam!

*pōr etirntu ēṟṟār matukai matantapak* (*PP* XVIII. 1)
The power and the arrogance of the opponents (= *asuras*) being subdued [by the spear], ....

*ceruvēl tāṉaic celva niṉ aṭiyuṟai* (*PP* XVIII. 54)
Lord (= Cevvēḷ/Murukaṉ) with the weapon of a spear used in battle!

*veṉṟik koṭi yaṇi celva niṉ toḻutu* (*PP* XXI. 17)
Lord (=Cevvēḷ/Murukaṉ) decorated with the victorious banner! We shall adore you.

*māṟu amar aṭṭa vai māra vēl peyarppavai* (*PP* XXI. 66)
Swirling around the sharp and strong spear which kills his foes in battle, ....

*o<u>n</u><u>r</u>ārt tēytta celva ni<u>n</u> to<u>l</u>utē* (*PP* XXI. 70)
Lord (= Cevvēḷ/Muruka<u>n</u>) who killed his foes! We shall adore you.

The keynote or undertone of the descriptions of God Cevvēḷ/Muruka<u>n</u> as a divine warrior in *PP* is not much different from that of Tirumāl in the same work examined in the preceding section, except for some differences in the weapon, the name of the hostile demon, and other lesser aspects. The correspondence of the basic traits is derived from the fact that both gods are called upon for the destruction of a malignant power symbolically represented by a specific chief of demons and his army. Here we can confirm the identity of Cevvēḷ/Muruka<u>n</u> as a righteous god, the antagonist of demoniac forces, as commonly seen in the major deities in the Sanskritic traditions and partaken of importantly by Śiva and Viṣṇu.

Cevvēḷ/Muruka<u>n</u>'s exploits as shown in the above examples are in most cases narrated in the context of his decisive battle against *asuras*. Among the same examples, this god is referred to by the epithet *i<u>r</u>aiva<u>n</u>* ('king') in one place (*PP* XVII. 49), while he is designated more frequently (*PP* XVIII. 54, XXI. 17, XXI. 70) as *celva<u>n</u>* ('he who possesses fortune'), a title of a god of probable northern origin and applied to Tirumāl/Viṣṇu in many cases.[31] The same tendency will be observed in *TM* which is considered below.

*The Idyll TM of the Pattuppāṭṭu*

The above verses in the Cevvēḷ hymns of *PP* are composed of rather formulaic expressions, lacking in vivid accounts and graphic descriptions. On the other hand, in *TM* or 'Guide to Muruku,' one of the 10 idylls which is nearly contemporaneous with, or slightly prior to, *PP*, the heroic exploits of God Muruka<u>n</u> are represented somewhat more vividly and dynamically. Some examples from this idyll are given below as:

*ce<u>r</u>unart tēytta cellu<u>r</u>a<u>l</u> taṭakkai* (*TM* 6)
(Muruka<u>n</u>) with his wide arms which killed the foes like thunderbolts.

*pārmutir pa<u>n</u>ikkaṭal kalaṅkavuḷ pukkuc*
*cūrmutal taṭinta cuṭarilai neṭuvēl* (*TM* 45-46)
The flame-like, leaf-shaped long spear with which (Muruka<u>n</u>) went into (the sea), in order to disturb the cold sea in which rocks rise sheer from the water, and defeated the chief of Cūrs!

*irupēr uruvin̲ orupēr yākkai*
*ar̲uvēr̲u vakaiyin̲ añcuvara maṇṭi*
*avuṇar nalvala maṭaṅkak kavil̲iṇar*
*māmutal taṭinta mar̲uvil kor̲r̲attu* (*TM* 57-60)

(Murukan̲) who attacked an *asura* (= Cūr) with a huge body assuming a twofold form (of human and beast?) to strike terror into his heart for fear of being torn in two, and broke the old mango tree with its bunches hanging down to break the brunt of the *asuras*.

*cer̲unart tēyttuc celcama murukkik* (*TM* 99)

Killing and destroying his foes in battles, ....

*ceruvil oruva poruvir̲al maḻḻa* (*TM* 262)

Matchless One (= Murukan̲) on battlefields! Warrior winning a victory!

*vēḷkel̲u taṭakkaic cālperuñ celva* (*TM* 265)

The large, great and wealthy One (= Murukan̲) with his strong hand holding his spear!

*maṇṭamar kaṭantanin̲ ven̲rāṭu akalattup* (*TM* 272)

In the breast [of Neṭuvēḷ/Murukan̲] which is throbbing violently after securing a grand victory, ....

First of all, *TM* 45-46 and *TM* 57-60 given above clearly indicate that, unlike a human warrior or king, God Murukan̲ fights against not human foes but Cūr, the demon-chief who came to be known as Cūrapan̲man̲ in medieval religious literature, and his demoniac corps.[32] In Murukan̲ as a celestial fighter, we can observe the same role that God Tirumāl has in the Tirumāl odes. However, these passages with this vivid description may also show that God Murukan̲ is reflective of a king with his long spear or lance called *vēl* or *neṭuvēl*, which is the weapon typical of an ancient king or chieftain. In *TM*, therefore, God Murukan̲ appears to be featured as, or modelled after, a warrior or king who destroys his enemies as in the *pur̲am* ('exterior'=war) genre of ancient Tamil literature. However, it is also possible that the divine image of Murukan̲ carrying that weapon in his hand was possibly modelled after that of *talaivan̲* or the hero (i.e. lover/husband) of the *akam* ('interior'= love) category of Tamil literature at the same time. Thus Murukan̲, youthful god of the *kur̲iñci* or mountain tract, possesses the double image as a warrior king and as an amorous hero in the *Caṅkam* tradition.

In *TM*, Murukaṉ, as a god of indigenous provenance, is given a Sanskritic image as a conqueror of antigods. We can accordingly observe here the transitional phase of an indigenous god undergoing so-called Aryanization or Sanskritization.

Cūr, the antagonist of Murukaṉ, was originally an anonymous malignant power not sufficiently personified in the earlier stages of Tamil literature. In *PP* and *TM*, however, this demoniac power underwent personification as the chief of antigods, who was to be more decisively anthropomorphised as the head of demoniac beings named Cūrapaṉmaṉ in the Tamil Puranic literature prominent in later periods [Zvelebil 1979: 157- 192; Zvelebil 1981: 26-39; Yamashita 1993, 151-165].[33]

## Murukaṉ as Skanda-Kārttikeya-Kumāra

Generally speaking, the mode of narration and expression in *TM* as a whole appears more fresh and vigorous than that in the Cevvēḷ odes of *PP*. *TM*, which makes mention of such a wider variety of aspects relating to Cevvēḷ as *vēlaṉ* (priest worshipping Murukaṉ with a spear: *TM* 190, 222), *veṟiyāṭal* (ritual dance in frenzy: *TM* 222), *kuravai* (tribal dance among women in sylvan tracts: *TM* 197), *aṇaṅku* (ambivalent mystic power: *TM* 289), *kaḷavēḷvi* (war sacrifice: *TM* 100), and other bloody sacrifices (*TM* 218,232-33) along with Vedic-Sanskritic elements [Subrahmanian 1966: 105], may possibly retain more indigenous or autochthonous traits in worship than *PP*, which is in many ways more Aryanized.[34] The description of *kaḷavēḷvi* (*TM* 100),[35] a gruesome human sacrifice on the battlefield in which ritual cannibalism was performed by a victorious king, strongly suggests that the image of God Murukaṉ is somehow or other associated with or overlapped by that of the warrior-king in ancient Tamil Nadu.

As already pointed out, the references to Murukaṉ as a war-god in *PP*, lacking in vivid descriptions of battles, are somewhat more formulaic and less dynamic than in *TM*. Independent of context, epithets indicating Cevvēḷ/Murukaṉ in the vocative or nominative with some expression of praise for his heroism and strength are sometimes employed in *PP*, as if they were simply the ordinary titles of this god.[36] At the time of *PP*, the image of God Murukaṉ as an antagonist and conqueror of the *asuras* seems to have already been firmly established after the rigid identification of this god with his northern counterpart, Skanda-Kārttikeya-Kumāra. In this anthology, the presumable twofold image of ancient Murukaṉ as an adolescent god and a brave warrior[37] was overlapped and replaced largely by the sweeping image of the Divine Commander in Chief imported from the north.

The identification of Murukaṉ with the northern Skanda-Kārttikeya-Kumāra is found to have already been established in *TM*, and it became more rigid in the Cevvēḷ hymns of *PP*, as descriptions of his destroying of demons are more exhaustively given in this latter anthology. The elaboration of this identification in *PP* is also supported by other textual evidence concerning his destruction of a mountain after his annihilation of Cūr, the demon-chief. The cosmic myth of his piercing the mountain with his spear is not explicitly known in the early stratum of the *Caṅkam* classics as far as I have been able to ascertain.[38] Only in late classical texts like *TM* and *PP* do we encounter this exploit. Table 3[39] compares the two descriptions of this heroic deed in *TM* and the Cevvēḷ hymns of *PP*.

This table shows that, while the name of the mountain destroyed by Murukaṉ is nowhere given in *TM*, it is clearly named Kuruku, which commonly means 'heron,' in *PP* (V. 5, XIX. 36). This name can be readily understood in light of Sanskrit *krauñca*, a word that has the primary meaning of 'curlew' or 'heron.' Needless to say, Krauñca was the name

Table 3

*Tirumurukāṟṟuppaṭai*

| Verse | | Synopsis |
|---|---|---|
| Tirupparaṅ-kuṉṟam | 45–46 | The long, leaf-shaped spear having a flame with which [Murukaṉ] plunged [into the sea], disturbed the cold sea with rising rocks, and defeated the chief of Cūrs. |
| | 57–61 | Cēy (= Murukaṉ) with blemishless victory, limitless fame and a red spear, who attacked [Cūr] by cutting him into two and conquered *asuras* by breaking the base of a mango tree. |
| Paḻamutir-cōlai | 266–267 | O chief of the *kuṟiñci* region of lofty hills who is strong enough to destroy a mountain! |
| | 275 | O the strong one who ruined the clan of Cūr! |

*Paripāṭal*

| | | |
|---|---|---|
| V | 1–10 | The one who destroyed a huge mountain called Kuruku with a spear, with which he, riding the elephant called Piṇimukam, had smashed the rocks in the sea to pieces and cut the base of a mango tree of Cūr to ruin the clan of cruel *asuras*! |
| VIII | 29 | O the one who has a brilliant spear with which he destroyed a mountain! |
| XI | 70–71 | O the victorious warrior with a spear which cuts the base of the mango tree (i.e. cruel Cūr) asunder! |
| XIV | 17–18 | O the one who has the firing weapon which annihilated the clan of Cūr in battle! |
| XVII | 1–4 | O the spear with which [Murukaṉ] dispirited the arrogance of the enemies and destroyed a mango tree (i.e. Cūr) in the ocean! |
| XIX | 36 | O the one who has the spear which pierced Heron (Kuruku)! |
| XIX | 101–103 | O the one who destroyed the base of the malignant mango tree and ruined the enemy mountain by throwing his faultless spear into it! |
| XXI | 8–9 | What you have in your hand is the spear with which you cut the mango tree regarded by his enemies as their chief asunder and made a hole in the side of a bird. |
| XXI | 28–29 | O the one who destroyed the mango tree! |

of the mountain in which Mahiṣāsura took refuge. It is this mountain that Skanda-Kārttikeya-Kumāra finally destroyed in Sanskrit myths.[40] It is obvious that the Tamil myth-makers gave the name Kuruku to the mountain in Murukaṉ myths, bearing the name of Krauñca in mind.[41]

This indicates that the Tamil myth of Murukaṉ's piercing the mountain is most probably a borrowing from the northern mythology of the adolescent god Skanda-Kārttikeya-Kumāra. It is noteworthy that, in both texts, this episode is introduced quite abruptly, not naturally or organically in context, as a mere addition to the main body of the narrative

Table 4

| Verse | Synopsis |
|---|---|
| V. 26–29 | An embryo was produced as the result of the long sexual union of Śiva and Umā. |
| V. 30–35 | For the sake of Indra who had become the chief of gods by making a vow to kill Śiva's embryo, Śiva, the Consistent One, tore the embryo into pieces. |
| V. 36–41 | The seven Munis gathered the fragments. Their wives swallowed them, kept them in their wombs and nurtured them. But when the wives found themselves unable to bear these fragments any longer, they finally performed sacrifice by throwing them into a fire. |
| V. 42–45 | Excepting Cāliṉi (=Arundhatī), six members of the Seven Mothers shining in the northern sky swallowed the fragments which had been protected by the Three Fires. |
| V. 46–49 | Thus the wives of the Ṛṣis (=Six Kṛttikās) became pregnant without violating their own chastity and gave birth to Murukaṉ on a lotus-bed in a lake [called Caravaṇa] in the Himālayas. |
| V. 50–54 | Being aware of Murukaṉ's birth, Indra armed with flaming *vajra* challenged Murukaṉ to battle. In a few moments, the six pieces took the form of six persons and then became united into one. |
| V. 55–56 | Murukaṉ, though unarmed, defeated Indra in a battle that was no more than sport for this adolescent god. |
| V. 57–70 | The gods, recognizing Murukaṉ as the chief of their army, presented his twelve hands with various things as his weapons; Agni gave a cock, Indra a peacock, Yama a goat, and the other gods other things. |

of Murukaṉ-Cūr antagonism. This may also attest to the derivation of this story from its northern parallel.

The rigid identification of Murukaṉ with the northern god of war in the Cevvēḷ hymns of *PP* is also confirmed in the birth story of Cevvēḷ/ Murukaṉ, the outline of which is given in Table 4 [Yamashita 1989: 164-165].

What is most important regarding the birth myths of God Murukaṉ is that the earlier stratum of Tamil literature does not provide rich information on his birth and parentage. We can expect somewhat detailed accounts only in *TM*. Further details are narrated in *PP*. The comparison of the above account in *PP* with the probable Sanskrit parallels shows that the story of Murukaṉ's birth as given in *PP* is coincident in outline with the accounts in the Epic and Puranic literature of the birth of Skanda. The story in *PP* is, therefore, a Tamil version of the Sanskrit tales of Skanda's birth.

## Concluding Remarks

The foregoing discussion has clarified that in *TM* and *PP*, the overlapped syncretism of Murukaṉ and Skanda is already firmly established by way of the identification of the myths of their birth, their antagonism with demons, and other aspects. Cūr, a personified malignant force in the early *Caṅkam* texts is also anthropomorphised and portrayed as the chief of antigods hostile to Murukaṉ in both texts just like *asuras* in the Vedic-Sanskritic texts. This discussion elucidates, however, that the image of Murukaṉ in *TM* shows comparatively more affinity to the warrior-king depicted in the *puṟam* texts of the earlier centuries since he is described in *TM* as having a long lance in his hand. In *TM* we also find the description of gruesome human sacrifice on the battlefield, which reminds us of the similar depiction made in the *puṟam* texts. Some features of the ancient Tamil king, therefore, seem to have lingered on and been associated with the otherwise Aryanized Murukaṉ in *TM*. The most notable aspect in this relation is the mention of *aṇaṅku* associated with the discus possessed by Tirumāl in *PP*. This clearly shows that the ancient Dravidian concept of the sacred or kingly power still remained effective in the changed realignment concerning the concept of God in the fifth century. It is extremely difficult, however, to argue from these pieces of evidence for the deep indebtedness of the concept of Tamil devotional gods to the concept of ancient Tamil king, as subtly supposed by some scholars.

In conclusion, the remarkable notion on the concept of Tamil gods of a devotional nature greatly indebted to that of ancient kings remains yet to be proved even after this examination of the texts of the later *Caṅkam* works composed at the dawn of the *bhakti* movement. Further studies, including the examination of some other texts of the *Caṅkam* as well as the *bhakti* works, are still required to clarify the relations between the two. The issue on the sacredness/secularity of the king in the early *Caṅkam* period also should be studied in this relation, as the assumed relations of the ancient kings and the devotional God would change according to whether the king was considered to be sacred or not in early times.

## Notes

1 This monograph is 'preliminary' because the literary materials examined here are not exhaustive and the *Kalittokai*, a late *Caṅkam* work, for example, is tentatively ruled out of consideration. Similarly, the *Cilappatikāram, Maṇimēkalai* and some other post-*Caṅkam* texts, as well as important didactic works composed before the dawn of the devotional phases of Tamil literary history, are also disregarded in this article as a matter of convenience. Much still remains to be done.

An earlier version of this paper was presented at a seminar on '*Bhakti*' held at Takushoku University in December 1997 and, after considerable revision, at a symposium on 'Religion and Metaphor' at Tenri University in May 1998. Thanks are due to the participants for their valuable comments and criticisms.

2 *Caṅkam* literature contains in all 2,381 poems attributed to 473 poets in the *Eṭṭuttokai* and the *Pattuppāṭṭu*.

3 For the gap between archaeological findings and descriptions in ancient Tamil texts, see [Maloney 1975: 1-33].

4 For the ideas of the divine as exposed in the vocabulary of 'god,' see [Yamashita 1988].

5 A rare exception is Shulman's remarkable study on Tamil *sthalapurāṇas* (*talapurāṇam*) [Shulman 1980], in which he puts insightful interpretations on local legends of Śaiva shrines based on his vast knowledge and intensive survey on the subject.

6 For the characteristics of ancient kings and their milieu in Tamil country, see [Kailasapathy 1968] and [Marr 1985].

7 For example, Zvelebil [Zvelebil 1981: 13-25] notes, 'I cannot agree with a great many points of Hart's provocative book' and semantically poses a question about the idea of 'sacred power,' the key concept of Hart's interpretation of ancient Tamil society.

8 See also [Hart 1975] and [Yamashita 1991].

9 Cf. [Yamashita 1991: 27-41].

10 For the term *nakar* (*DED* 2943; DEDR 3568), see further [Yamashita 1987: 117, 230; S.K. Chatterji 1958: 83].

11 For the term *kāvalaṉ*, see [Gopalakrishnan 1990].

12 Here also, it should be noted that there is a similar kind of difficulty as pointed out in the Introduction.

13 A. Good stresses the similarities between temple and court ritual and says, 'temple coronations must obviously be compared with the actual coronations of Indian kings; [Good 1987: 50]. Apart from the royal origin of the *abhiṣeka* ritual, Clothey introduces its symbolic roots going back to the Vedic sacrifice. See [Clothey 1983: 98].

14 Cf. [Cutler 1987: 202]. Clothey [Clothey 1983: 50] presents another interpretation of *tirupaḷḷiyeḻucci* as an ancient custom in which damsels arose early in the morning and sang while parading through the streets. This notion, however, is not widely accepted.

15 This linking was, according to Subbiah, sufficiently strong in Tamil culture and, in introducing the theme of 'praise' (*pāṭāṇ* or *pāṭāṇṭiṇai*), the grammarians always explain that the term refers to the praise of both mortal heroes and immortal gods [Subbiah 1991: 39]. In this context, I point out *Puṟanāṉūṟu* 56 by Nakkīrar, in which Pāṇṭiyaṉ Naṉmāraṉ, a king and the hero of the poem, is compared with gods such as Śiva, Balarāma and Murukaṉ. The theme in which a king is likened to a god is called *pūvainilai* and is known in early *Caṅkam* poems.

16 In this chapter when illustrative examples are introduced from *PP* (and not *TM*), internal or external *sandhis* are occasionally untied, with the result that *cīrs* or metrical feet are separated into words or even morphemes for convenience' sake, thus enabling the readers to construe or analyse the citations easily.

17 I use U.Vē. Cāminātaiyar's editions as the original for both texts. Nothing certain can be said concerning the dates of *PP* and *TM*. From several sources of evidence, it may be surmised only tentatively that both texts were composed after the formation of the bulk of the so-called *Caṅkam* works and before the dawn of the devotional literature, namely between the third and sixth centuries A.D.

18 We find a sign of devotional nature in a recurring pronominal term *aṭiyēṉ* ('we as slaves') in *PP* which reminds us of the concept of *aṭiyār* ('devotees as slaves of God') in medieval *bhakti* literature.

19 For a detailed study of the Tirumāl hymns of this anthology, see [Yamashita 1995: 73-157].

20 There are several possibilities concerning the identity of Kāmaṉ and Cāmaṉ. See [Gros 1968: 170, n. 28].

21 Here the word *aṉṉal*, which literally means 'king,' is employed to denote 'god.'

22 *Iruṅkuṉṟu* is supposed to be the name of an earthly mountain sacred to Tirumāl. It literally means 'Black Mountain,' which reminds us of the

colour of Lord Kṛṣṇa devastating the demons.

23 Cf. [Yamashita 1995: 79-80].

24 This usage of *kaṭa* is also found in *PP* XV. 45.

25 Cf. Parimēlaḻakar's commentary (*Paripāṭal Mūlamum Parimēlaḻakar Uraiyum*, notes by U.Vē. Cāminātaiyar, fifth edition, Madras, 1980) on *PP* III 31-32.

26 For Kṛṣṇa's combat myths, including his fight with *asura* Keśin, see [Preciado-Solis 1984: 93-100].

27 As in the *Ṛg-Veda*, however, such names as Vāmana (Dwarf) and Mahābali (alias Bali, a demon chief) never appear in this passage. The dwarfish form of the Lord is nowhere mentioned in this paragraph.

The Rig-Vedic myth of Viṣṇu's 'Three strides' does not make mention of his form as a dwarf. (See, for example, *Ṛg-Veda*, L. 154, VII. 100.) It is in the Brāhmaṇa literature that Viṣṇu in the disguise of a dwarf is clearly mentioned in relation to his *trivikrama* episode. Cf. [Macdonell 1981(1898): 39,41].

28 E.g. *aṇṇal* ('king': *PP* I. 27, XIII. 15), *kurucil* ('king': *PP* II. 49), *mallaṉ* ('boxer', 'wrestler': *PP* III. 89), and *maḷḷaṉ* ('warrior': *PP* III. 90). As for the identification of Tirumāl with a king or vice versa, see [Ēkāmparanātaṉ 1986: 26].

29 Cf. [Yamashita 1995: 84].

30 This may indicate that the image of a fighter or warrior is more intrinsic to Tirumāl/Viṣṇu of northern origin than to the indigenous Murukaṉ, who is predominantly characterised by miscellaneous elements in worship as will be seen below.

31 In his Tamil Index [Subrahmanian 1966: 387], N.Subrahmanian identifies the title of *celvaṉ* exclusively with that of God Tirumāl (=Viṣṇu). Hardy also regards *celvaṉ* merely as one of the titles peculiar to Tirumāl [Hardy 1983: 218]. Hart, on the other hand, considers the same title or epithet to mark gods of foreign origin, more particularly of northern, Sanskritic provenance, who are characterised by benevolence and auspiciousness [Hart 1975a: 63]. We can find this title, as Hart suggests, applied not only to Tirumāl/Viṣṇu (*TM* 151, *Akanāṉūṟu* 175, *PP* IV. 10, VIII. 58) but also to Lord Śiva (*Akanāṉūṟu* 181, *Puṟanāṉūṟu* 6). If Hart is right, *celvaṉ* should be regarded not as an epithet or name of one particular deity, but as a title or designation of a certain category of gods. The problem of the title *celvaṉ* is of importance and may merit a detailed study.

32 The only exception is his exploit of destroying a mountain with his spear given in *TM* 266-67. This will be discussed below.

33 Zvelebil observes that, in the *Kantapurāṇam* of Kacciyappa (fourteenth-fifteenth century A.D.), the struggle between Murukaṉ and Cūr assumed the dimensions of a war on the model of the antagonism between Rāma and Rāvaṇa. Cf. [Zvelebil 1981: 33] and [L'Hernault 1978: 19-20].

34 Brahmanical terms and concepts appear more frequently in *PP* than in *TM*.

See [Hardy 1983: 208] and [Yamashita 1995: 130-33].

35 The details of this sacrifice, see [Hart 1975: 33-36].

36 The examples are as follows: *PP* VIII. 67 (*viṟal veyyōṉ*: 'One desirous of victory'), IX. 68 (*veṉvēlāṟ*: 'One endowed with his victorious spear'), IX. 7 1 (*aṭumpōrāḷa*: 'the warrior massacring in battles'), XIV. 17-18 (*cuṭarpaṭaiyōyē*: 'One with the weapon of fire'), XVII. 49 (*velpōr iṟaiva*: 'lord of victorious wars'), XVIII. 54 (*ceruvēl tāṉaic celva*: 'lord with the weapon of a spear '), XXII. 17 (*veṉṟi koṭi yaṇi celva*: 'lord decorated with the victorious banner'), and XXII. 70 (*oṉṟārt tēytta celva*: 'lord who killed his foes').

In this connection, it is to be noted that Murukaṉ's character as a military hero receded into secondary status when his aspect as a preceptor or philosopher became comparatively dominant in the Chola era. See [Clothey 1983: 23].

37 Zvelebil assumes that the Murukaṉ's heroic myth of antagonism against Cūr was already widely known and well-established in the first century A.D. [Zvelebil 1981: 4-5, 29-30; cf. Yamashita 1993: 155]. Murukaṉ's aspect as a beautiful youth is frequently implied in *akam* contexts [Hardy 1983: 146]. The name Murukaṉ or Muruku itself means 'tender age,' 'youth,' or 'young man' [Burrow & Emeneau 1984: 447].

38 The theme of god's interference with mountains is sporadically found in Indo-Aryan myths around Kṛṣṇa, Viṣṇu, Indra, and the like, as pointed out by [L'Hernault 1978: 18].

39 Cf. [Yamashita 1995: 154].

40 This episode is narrated, for example, in the 'Vanaparvan' of the *Mahābhārata* and in the *Vālmiki-Rāmāyaṇa* (adh. 58). Cf. [Gros 1968: 193, n. 9, 219, n. 29] and [L'Hernault 1978: 16].

41 The derivation of Sanskrit *krauñca* from Tamil (or rather Dravidian *kuṟiñci*) is proposed by a scholar [Shashi Asthana 1976: 144]. Though interesting, this etymology is far-fetched, being not well supported by available linguistic evidence.

## References

Burrow, T. & M.B. Emeneau

1984 *A Dravidian Etymological Dictionary* (second edition), Oxford University Press, Oxford.

Chatterji, S.K.

1958 'Contribution from Different Language-Culture Groups,' *The Cultural Heritage of India*, vol. I, The Ramakrishna Mission Institute of Culture, Calcutta.

Clothey, F.W.
1983 *Rhythm and Intent: Ritual Studies from South India*, Blackie & Son Publishers Pvt. Ltd., Bombay.

Cutler, N.
1987 *Songs of Experience: The Poetics of Tamil Devotion*, Indiana University Press, Bloomington and Indianapolis.

Ekamparanatan, E.
1986 *Kōyilum Iṟaivaḻipāṭum*, Chennai (Madras).

Good, A.
1987 'Divine Coronation in a South Indian Temple,' V. Sudarsen, G. Prakash Reddy and M. Suryanarayana eds., *Religion and Society in South India (A Volume in Honour of Prof. N. Subba Reddy)*, B. R. Publishing Corporation, Delhi.

Gopalakrishnan, R.
1990 *Religion and Mysticism in the Periyapurāṇam*, University of Madras, Madras.

Gros, F.
1968 *Le Paripāṭal: texte tamoule*, Institut Français d'Indologie, Pondichéry.

Hardy, F.
1983 *Viraha-bhakti: The Early History of Kṛṣṇa Devotion in South India*, Oxford University Press, New Delhi.

Hart, G.L.
1975a *Poems of Ancient Tamil: Their Milieu and Their Sanskrit Counterparts*, University of California Press, Berkeley.
1975 'Ancient Tamil Literature,' B. Stein, ed., *Essays on South India*, University of Hawaii Press, Honolulu.
1978 'Nature of Tamil Devotion,' M.M. Deshpande and P.E. Hook eds., *Aryan and Non-Aryan in India*, University of Michigan Press, Michigan.

Kailasapathy, K.
1968 *Tamil Heroic Poetry*, Oxford University Press, London.

L'Hernault, F.
1978 *L'iconographie de Subrahmaṇya au Tamilnad*, Institut Français d'Indologie, Pondichéry.

Macdonell, A.A.
1981 (1898). *Vedic Mythology*, Motilal Banarsidass, Delhi.

Maloney, C.
1975 'Archaeology in South India,' B. Stein ed., *Essays on South India*, University of Hawaii Press, Honolulu.

Marr, J.R.

1985 *The Eight Anthologies: A Study in Early Tamil Literature*, Institute of Asian Studies, Madras.

Peterson, I.V.

1989 *Poems to Śiva: The Hymns of the Tamil Saints*, Princeton University Press, Princeton.

Preciado-Solis, B.

1984 *The Kṛṣṇa Cycle in the Purāṇas: Themes and Motifs in a Heroic Saga*, Motilal Banarsidass, Delhi.

Shashi Asthana

1976 *History and Archaeology of India's Contact with Other Countries*, Delhi.

Shulman, D.D.

1980 *Tamil Temple Myths: Sacrifice and Divine Marriage in the South Indian Śaiva Tradition*, Princeton University Press, Princeton.

Subbiah, G.

1991 *Roots of Tamil Religious Thought*, Pondicherry Institute of Linguistics and Culture, Pondicherry.

Subrahmanian, N.

1966 *Pre-Pallavan Tamil Index*, University of Madras, Madras.

Yamashita, H.

1987 *Religious Aspects of Early South India with Special Reference to Tamil Classical Literature* (Unpublished Ph. D. Thesis submitted to the University of Madras).

1988 'Deivamu to Kadavuru: Kodai Tamiru Sekai no "kami"' (Teyvam and Kaṭavuḷ: Conceptions of 'God' in Early Tamil Nadu), *Indogaku Shūkyōgakkai Ronshū* (*Studies in Religions East and West*), Vol. 15.

1991 'Minami-Indo no Bunka, Shakai ni okeru Josei to Joshin no Mondai (Jo)' (Women and Goddesses in South Indian Culture and Society: An Introduction), Nippon Bukkyō Gakkai (Nippon Buddhist Research Association) ed., *Bukkyō to Josei* (*Buddhism and Women*), Kyoto.

1993 'Myths of the Divine Antagonism: A Note on Murukaṉ and Cur in Early Tamil Literature,' *Chi no Kaikō: Bukkyō to Kagaku* (The Encounter of Wisdom between Buddhism and Science), *Tsukamoto Keishō Kyōju Kanreki Kinen Ronbunshū* (Felicitation Volume presented to Prof. Tsukamoto Keishō on his 60th birthday), Heirakuji Shoten, Tokyo.

1995 'Some Remarks on Tirumāl/Viṣṇu Cult in Early Tamil Religion and Literature with Special Reference to the Tirumāl Odes of Paripāṭal,' *Tōyō Bunka Kenkyūsho Kiyō* (The Memoirs of the Institute of Oriental Cultures), No. 126.

Yamashita, H. and Furusaka, K.

1989 'The Emergence of Murukan: A Study on the Formation of the Tamil Myths of His Divine Birth,' *Ōsaka Kyōiku Daigaku Kiyō* (Daiichi Bumon, Jinbun Kagaku) (Memoirs of Osaka University of Education), Ser. I, Vol. 38, No. 2.

Zvelebil, K.V.

1979 'The Nature of Sacred Power in Old Tamil Texts,' *Acta Orientalia* XL.

1981 *Tiru Murugan*, Institute of Asian Studies, Madras.

4

# Polity and Kingship of Early Medieval Rajasthan: an Analysis of the Nadol Cāhamāna Inscriptions

MASAHIKO MITA

## Introduction

In early medieval Rajput kingdoms, land was often assigned to the persons who belonged to the same clans as those of the kings. Such land distribution has been considered by some scholars like U.N. Ghoshall and A.C. Banerjee as concrete instances of 'the type of monarchies organised on clan lines, afterwards so widely prevalent in Rajputana' [Ghoshal 1929: 236], and the Rajput polity in the early medieval period has thus been understood in the same context as that of the 'clan-monarchy' of the later medieval Rajput states [Banerjee 1962: 48].

This 'clan-monarchy,' often representing a model of 'traditional Rajput polity' is said to be a clan-based state system where land is assigned to the ruling clan members as their own hereditary possession with the political structure and state-locality relations being consequently based on clanship [Tod 1829, vol. 1: 153-245; Banerjee 1962: 127-28; Fox 1971; etc.]. A concrete instance of this in the history of Rajasthan was presented by G.D. Sharma, who analysed a sixteenth-century territorial system of the Marwar kingdom of the Rathors called *bhāī-bandh.*[1]

Contrary to U.N. Ghoshal, N. Ziegler suggests that this clan system of Rajputs is depicted in the historical records and chronicles from the Mughal and later periods [Ziegler 1976]. Furthermore, the existence of such a typical Rajput system as mentioned above in pre-Mughal India has been doubted by several historians [Saran 1952: 4; Kolff 1990: 71-116; Tambs-Lyche 1997: 36-41]. However, this claim would leave us with another question, that is, how we should understand the land distribution among the royal clan members of early medieval Rajputs if their polity was indeed not based on clanship.

This essay will discuss the manner of land assignment of a twelfth-century kingdom of Marwar, that of the Nadol Cāhamānas, [2] focusing on kinship hierarchy, local administration of the kingdom and the nature of assignees' land possession, in order to clarify the nature of its polity and kingship. Through this discussion, we will reach the conclusion that there is a distinct absence of clan structure and the lack of hereditary chieftaincies in the constitution of the Nadol Cāhamāna kingdom, which differs from the clan-based polity and kingship of later medieval Rajput kingdoms.

The Nadol Cāhamāna kingdom is said to have been founded in the last quarter of the tenth century by Lakṣmaṇa who, as a son of Vākpatirāja of the Śākambharī Cāhamānas, had branched off from the main family. From that date onwards, the kingdom lasted more than two hundred years until it declined and fell through a series of battles waged against the Muslim armies of Muhammad Ghorī towards the end of the twelfth century or the beginning of the thirteenth century.

The territory of the kingdom, which occupied the southern parts of modern Pali and Jodhpur districts, can be said to have been of small or medium size in early medieval India. Situated in the northernmost part of an area into which the political influence of the Caulukyas of Gujarat extended, the Nadol Cāhamānas did not always enjoy their independence, and temporarily came under the Caulukya's suzerainty in the twelfth century.

The Nadol Cāhamāna kingdom also constitutes a very valuable example of the subordinate kingdoms or *sāmantas* of the Gujarat empire. For among the *sāmanta* principalities of Rajasthan and Gujarat, the Nadol Cāhamāna kingdom is the only example which provides us with a wealth of information about the structure of polity from the epigraphical records. [3]

However, our analysis here will be confined to the internal political structure of the Nadol kingdom, and will not extend to the overlord-feudatory relations between the Caulukyas and the Nadol Cāhamānas. This latter topic will be a future research focus.

Although the Nadol Cāhamānas have a long history spanning more than 200 years, the available inscriptions range from V.S. 1124 (around A.D. 1067) to V.S. 1251 (around A.D. 1194), with very few inscriptions available for the eleventh century. [4] Therefore, the period of our analysis will be limited to the twelfth century.

## Intermediaries Figuring in the Epigraphical Records

Let me begin by citing a typical stone inscription of the Nadol Cāhamānas, dated V.S. 1233, found amidst the ruins of a Jaina temple at Lalrai:

> On the third of the bright half of Vaiśākha in the [Vikrama] year 1233, under the rule (*rājya*) of two *bhoktṛs* of the village of Saṃnāṇaka (Sonana), *rājaputra* Lākhaṇapāla and *rājaputra* Abhayapāla, four *seī* of barley corn from [the field called] Khāḍisīra were granted by Bhīvaḍā, Āsadhara and all the cultivators living in Paḍideha (the location unidentified), to the god Śāntinātha in connection with the *yātrā* festival of the Gūrjaras for their merit. Whoever violates [the grant] is torn up by the sin. May happiness be with us. Equally, one *harothu*(?) of barley corn out of the *arahaṭṭa* (a water-drawing device) of the village Bhāḍiyāuā (Barwa) was granted by all the cultivators, i.e., Āsadhara, Sīroiya and others, [to the same god] for the merit of Vīlha. [*EI*, 11, pp. 50-51] [5]

It notes that some grants were made by all the cultivators of Paḍideha and Barwa to the god Śāntinātha probably at Lalrai, under the *rājya* of two *bhoktṛs*, or 'possessors of revenue,' of Sonana. The two *bhoktṛs*, Lākhaṇapāla and Abhayapāla, are mentioned also in another Lalrai inscription of the same year [*EI*, 11, pp. 49 ff.], which refers to them as sons of the Nadol king Kelhaṇa, and records that they made a grant of barley corn out of an *arahaṭṭa* at Barwa under the *rājya* of their father, the Nadol king. It is worth noticing the term *rājya*, meaning some kind of political domination, which is used for the *bhoktṛs* as well as for the king. And the fact of the donation by the *bhoktṛs* from the *arahaṭṭa* indicates their claim to the toll of the *arahaṭṭa*. Thus, it is evident from these two inscriptions that the *bhoktṛs* possessed, at least, the revenues from Sonana and from the *arahaṭṭa* at Barwa, and exercised their political or administrative power over Sonana and its surrounding area composed of Barwa, Paḍideha and other villages. Therefore, these records clearly show the existence of intermediaries who, lying between the king and villagers, enjoyed the revenues gained from villages and ruled over some territory including the revenue-deriving villages.

Many instances of such political intermediaries figure in the Nadol Cāhamāna inscriptions, for example:

> For the festival of the goddess Bahughṛṇa belonging to the village

> of Vālahī (modern Bali) which is enjoyed as *grāsā* (a kind of landed possession often seen among Rajputs) by *rājñī* Tihuṇaka, .... [*EI*, 11, p. 33, ll. 2-3] [6]

This passage demonstrates the fact that queen Tihuṇaka possessed (*bhujyamāna*) Bali, but does not tell us whether she had any administrative role there.

> In the village of Jhāṃmara, just one *dramma* [of money] out of the village cess (*grāma-lāga*) was granted to the god Māhagaṇasvāmin by Nāṃnaḍa Rāṣṭauḍa, son of Samagha. [*JPASB*, 12, p. 104, ll. 5-7][7]

Here, Nāṃnaḍa of the Rāṣṭauḍas made a grant from the village cess from which it can be inferred that the cess at Jhamara was under his control.

Thus, the existence of the intermediaries can be seen from the following three patterns of expression in the Nadol Cāhamāna inscriptions: (a) terms derived from the verb √*bhuj* (to enjoy, possess), like *bhoktṛ* (enjoyer, possessor), *bhujyamāna* (being enjoyed, being possessed), *bhukti* (possession or possessed territory), which indicate personal 'possession' of taxes and cesses imposed on villages in the context of the early medieval Rajasthan; (b) records of donations of certain taxes, tolls and cesses by particular persons, who can be taken as intermediary strata possessing these revenues; and (c) mention of some persons ruling (*rājya*) over certain areas. In the above manner, Table 1 represents the intermediaries under the Nadol Cāhamāna rule revealed from the inscriptions.

## Titles and Ranking: Royal Kinsmen and the Others

Most of the intermediaries figuring in the inscriptions had their own titles as shown in Table 1. They can be classified into two broad groups in terms of their meaning. The first is their administrative title or official post like *balādhipa* (leader of the army), *mahāsāhaṇiya* (chief military officer), *bhaṇḍārin* (officer in charge of the treasury), *talāra* (city police), *Māṇḍavyapurādhipati* (ruler of Māṇḍavyapura or modern Mandor) and *Pallādhipa* (ruler of Palla or modern Pal), all of which indicate a specific role in the state administration of the Nadol Cāhamānas. The second is the title of their political status or rank which does not reflect any particular administrative roles but rather royal status, i.e., *kumāra* or *yuvarāja* (heir apparent), *rājaputra*, *rājñī* (queen), *rāuta*, *ṭhakkura*, *rāṇaka*, and the like, most of which are derivatives from '*rājan*.'[8]

This table also interestingly shows that the royal kinsmen did not have an administrative title with the one exception of *Māṇḍavyapurādhipati*. Among them, *yuvarāja* or *kumāra* is, of course, heir apparent to the king, generally the eldest son of the reigning king, as is inferred from the Nadol copper plates of V.S. 1218.[9] Except for this heir apparent and *rājñīs*, all other royal kinsmen have the title of either *rājaputra* or *mahārāja-putra*.

*Rājaputra* literally means 'a son of the king,' but it was not only conferred on the sons of the kings in the Nadol Cāhamāna kingdom. In the Bamnera copper plates, *rājaputra* Ajayasiṃha (No. 15) was mentioned as the son of *mahārājāputra* Kumārasiṃha, and not as the son of the kings Ālhaṇa and Kelhaṇa reigning in V.S. 1220 and 1223 respectively. *Rāja-putra* Lākhaṇapāla and *rājaputra* Abhayapāla (No. 22) were not sons of King Kelhaṇa but of his younger brother *mahārājaputra* Kīrtipāla.[10]

However, these two titles were not bestowed on the members of Rajput families other than the Cāhamānas. Also in Table 1, we find four persons who were evidently the members of non-Cāhamāna Rajputs, i.e., Guhilas, Rāṣṭrakūṭas or Rāṣṭauḍas, and Sauluṃkīs (Solaṅkīs) (Nos. 7, 14, 17 and 19). None of them employed the title *rājaputra*, but they held another title of status like *rāuta* and *ṭhakkura* and an administrative title like *balādhipa* and *talāra*, neither of which were bestowed on the Cāhamānas.

Furthermore, the holders of these two titles do not seem to have been the members of the other Cāhamāna families such as the Śākambharī Cāhamānas, but were confined to the Nadol Cāhamānas. They seem to have been close relatives of the reigning kings. Among the epigraphical instances, the remotest royal kinsmen from a reigning king are *rāja-putra* Ajayasiṃha, *rājaputra* Lākhaṇapāla and *rājaputra* Abhayapāla, who were all nephews of the reigning king Kelhaṇa (Nos. 15 and 22).

From the above discussion, we can conclude that these titles were allowed to be used solely by the royal kinsmen, and through such a title system they were distinguished from other ruling members who did not belong to the Nadol Cāhamānas.

It can be assumed from the meaning of '*mahā*' (great) that there would have been a difference in rank between *mahārājaputras* and *rāja-putras*. According to the inscriptions, this seems to have depended on whether or not one was the son of the reigning king. In the reign of Ālhaṇa, for instance, his eldest son Kelhaṇa [*EI*, 11, pp. 43 ff.], second son Gajasiṃha (No. 13) and third son Kīrtipāla (No. 12) all called themselves *mahārājaputras*. In the reign of the next king Kelhaṇa, his son Soḍhaladeva (No. 27) was the governor of Mandor and designated as *mahārājaputra*. On the other hand, as mentioned above, Ajayasiṃha, who was the son of *mahārājaputra* Kumārasiṃha, was *rājaputra* (No. 15), and so also were Lākhaṇapāla and Abhayapāla (No. 22), the sons of Kīrtipāla who was a younger brother of the reigning king Kelhaṇa. Reflecting these two such tiers of titling among the royal kinsmen, the sons of the reigning kings, *mahārājaputras*, took distinguished parts in the state administration. For instance, when King Ālhaṇa issued the ordinance against slaughter (*amāri-rūḍhi, abhaya-dāna-śāsana*) in V.S. 1209, it was approved by his sons, Kelhaṇa and Gajasiṃha.[11]

In this manner of titling, whenever a new king ascended to the throne, the ranks of the ruling clan members must have been changed according to the degree of their kindred relation to him. Thus, during the reign of Ālhaṇa, the title of his son Kumārasiṃha was *mahārājaputra* [*EI*, 13, pp. 207-8.],[12] but after Kelhaṇa succeeded the throne, his title was changed to *rājaputra*.

From the above analysis of the titles of political intermediaries, it can be said that the Nadol Cāhamānas adopted a title system based on kinship relations which distinguished the royal kinsmen from the other ruling strata of the kingdom, and furthermore, the sons of the reigning king from the other royal kinsmen. Although non-Cāhamāna clan members could also participate in the rule of the Nadol Cāhamāna kingdom, the Nadol Cāhamāna members enjoyed certain priority in land assignment, which is indicated by more frequent reference to the Cāhamāna members than the others in the inscriptions, also as shown in Table 1. The title system adopted by the Nadol Cāhamānas must have functioned to maintain such political superiority of the royal kinsmen among the members of the ruling class of the Nadol kingdom.[13]

## Village Assignment as an Administrative System

The royal kinsmen and the title holders of other clans were stationed at villages as the *bhoktṛs* or 'possessors' of many types of revenue gained from the villages, again as shown in Table 1. In this section, we will mainly focus on the spatial distribution of their political power, which can be traced from the epigraphical records, and which will roughly show the territorial system of the kingdom.

*Bhoktṛs*, or the 'enjoyers or possessors,' of towns and villages were not merely 'possessing' (*bhujyamāna*) a certain portion of the produce of the villages, but also exercised political authority (*rājya*) over particular areas including the villages in their possession. The fact of their political rule can be deduced directly or indirectly from the inscriptions. The case of two *rājaputra bhoktṛs* of the village of Sonāṇa (No. 22) shown in the first section is a typical example; their political rule seems to have extended to other villages, Barwa and Paḍideha.

Also in the case of heirs apparent (*yuvarāja* or *kumāra*), the situation was almost the same. In V.S. 1238, *kumāra* Jayatasiṃha (No. 26) issued a *śāsana* (grant charter) with which he granted to the god Pārśvanātha eight *drammas* every year out of *dāny-udgrānaka* of Sevadi which was in his possession [*EI*, 39, pp. 179 ff.].[14] In this copper-plate charter, there is no mention of the name of the king, as if to imply that Jayatasiṃha had been the reigning king. Also the Sevadi stone inscription of V.S. 1172, while recording that at the town (*pattana*) in his possession, Sevadi, *yuvarāja* Kaṭukarāja granted eight *drammas* to Thallaka, does not mention the reign of the Nadol king (No. 2). From these two records it is evident that heirs apparent could issue grant charters at their own discretion, which means that they did not merely receive the taxes from Sevadi but also exercised political power over it. Moreover, in the same way as the *bhoktṛs* of Sonāṇā their political power was evidently extended to other villages. The Paldi inscription of V.S. 1249, while recording a donation by *mahaṃ* Rājadeva in the village of Paldi, mentions the *pañcakula* (some political organ of the village) headed by *mahāmātya* Vālhaṇa subject to (*tat-pāda-padm-opajīvita*) the heir apparent Jayatasiṃha (No. 26).[15] Although this village was not definitely mentioned as his own possession, Jayatasiṃha ruled over it through his own official. Paldi was situated in the southwest frontier of the kingdom which undoubtedly bordered on the territory of the Candrāvatī kingdom of the Paramāras and, at the latest after V.S. 1239 [*EI*, 11, pp. 52-54], of the Jalor Cāhamānas. The heir apparent might thus have been responsible for control over this frontier from his base of Sevadi.

Another important base was Māṇḍavyapura (modern Mandor), where *Māṇḍavyapurādhipati* or the ruler of Mandor occupied the fort (*durga*).[16] Before discussing this territory though, we must note the unique position of Mandor in the kingdom of that time.

The spatial distribution of the villages mentioned in the inscriptions of the Nadol Cāhamānas (See map.) clearly shows an open space between Nadol and Mandor. Actually there were villages in this space, and among them was the major city of Pali,[17] where many epigraphical records of grants still survive in the temples.[18] Nevertheless, there is no inscription which indicates Nadol Cāhamāna rule. Instead, we have a copper plate of the Guhilas of Mewar dated V.S. 1140, which recorded that the Guhila king Vijayasiṃha granted the fifth part of the produce of Pallī-*grāma* (modern Pali) to an *ācārya* (a priest),[19] as well as a stone inscription dated V.S. 1209 in which the reign of the Caulukya king Kumārapāla was inscribed.[20] All of them seem to indicate that Pali and its surroundings were beyond the political influence of the Nadol Cāhamānas, or if not so, that their political control over Pali was unstable and sometimes fell into the hands of other dynasties as is shown by the records of the Guhilas and Caulukyas. Interestingly, perhaps related to this vacuum of Cāhamāna power, every religious grant recorded in the inscriptions was made within each of these two areas of Nadol and Mandor; in other words, one living in the Nadol area always made grants to temples in the Nadol area while one in the Mandor area did so similarly to those in the Mandor area, with no grant going beyond this vacuum area. Therefore, the Nadol kingdom was undoubtedly, at least, composed of two spatial segments, i.e., the Nadol region and the Mandor region with the city or the fort of Mandor constituting the centre of the latter.

The Mandor rulers made Mandor their political base for controlling the region, but they neither directly ruled over the whole region, nor received the revenue of the whole region as their own *bhujyamāna*. The following inscription dated V.S. 1236 illustrates the political situation prevalent at Osian, located in the northern frontier of the Mandor region:

> In the reign of *mahārāja* Kelhaṇa, and when his son, Kuṃmarasiṃha Siṃhavikrama, is the *Māṇḍavyapurādhipati* and Kīrtipāla is a *rājyavāhaka* (executor of *rājya*) [of this place], in the temple of Sañcikādevī of Upakeśa (modern Osian) which is his *bhukti* (territory in his possession)....[21]

This record clearly shows the existence of the ruler (*rājyavāhaka*) and possessor of Osian, Kīrtipāla, under the Mandor ruler Kuṃmarasiṃha Siṃhavikrama, who indirectly controlled Osian through the Osian ruler.

Such indirect control in the Mandor region can equally be seen in other villages. Jhamara was occupied in V.S. 1219 by Jasadhavala Saulumkī (Solaṅki) who was a *balādhipa* ('leader of the army') subject to the Mandor ruler Gajasiṃha (Nos. 13 and 14), and in V.S. 1227 by Nāṃnaḍa Rāṣṭauḍa (Rāṣṭrakūṭa or Rathor) who received some revenue from the village (*grāma-lāga* : 'village cesses') (No. 19). Jhamara was 'the most important village among the four villages in the land' (*asya tu bhūmyāṃ pādra-caturnāṃ madhye pradhāna-pādra-śrī-Jhāṃmara-sthāne*) [*JPASB*, 12, p. 104, ll. 4-5], which suggests that their political control extended to these three villages of lesser importance. The Mandor rulers would have ruled over the group of four villages through these intermediaries of Jhamara. Between V.S. 1241 and 1250, under the *rājya* of the Mandor ruler Soḍhaladeva, Pal was controlled by *bhaṇḍārin* Yaśovīra, which is evident from his title *Pallādhipa* or 'the lord of Pal' (No. 28).

In the Nadol Cāhamāna kingdom, some non-Cāhamāna people could also acquire the seats of *bhoktṛs*, though examples of this are not many. Among them, however, we have comparatively detailed information about *rāuta ṭhakkura* Rājadeva of the Guhila clan (*anvaya*), who was the *bhoktāri* (*bhoktṛ*) of Nadlai in the mid-twelfth century (No. 7). The duties imposed on the loads of bull carts coming from and going to Nadlai were his own share (*svīy-ādāna*) [*EI*, 11, pp. 36 f.], and a certain portion of oil from an oil mill in Nadlai was also his share [*EI*, 11, pp. 41 f.], though it is not certain that these two kinds of revenue comprised the entire share assigned to the *bhoktṛ* of Nadlai.

Additionally, Rājadeva also seems to have exercised political power over Nadlai. The Nadlai inscription of V.S. 1202 [*EI*, 11, pp. 42 f.] says that Rājadeva who had control over Nadlai made a grant to the Mahāvīra temple. But here all the merchants of Nadlai, Badārī (modern Borli) and Abhinavapurī (unidentified) assembled together into *deśī* (a kind of guild) and determined the grant items according to the standard of the load tax (*pāilā lāga-māne*), which were two *rūās* for each 20 *pāilās* of loads on bullocks and one *rūā* for each cart filled with commodities. Although Rajadeva was mentioned as the grantor, these grant items were not his own share. This is because if they had been his property, then he could freely have made grants and should not have had to make the merchants fix the amount of the load cess, as in the case of his grant in V.S. 1195 [*EI*, 11, pp. 36 f.].[22] This grant, therefore, was not his personal grant from his own share but probably, so to speak, a kind of public grant or common grant made by the residents of Nadlai, which was granted in the name of Rājadeva as the head or chief of Nadlai on the basis of his political power entitled by the king.[23] Possibly, as the grant was public in kind, the merchants needed to assemble and determine their contribution to it.

In V.S. 1200 *rāṇaka* Bhanana (No. 10), who was apparently of a non-Cāhamāna clan as is evident from the fact that his homeland was Karṇāṭa, exempted the dancing girls (*pramadā kula*) of all the gods of Usapa-pattana from the *daśa-bandha*. If the *daśa-bandha* was a tax equal to one-tenth of the income as was interpreted by D.R. Bhandarkar [*PRAS, WC*, 1909, p. 45], it proves that he had the right of exemption in taxation at Usapa-pattana. Further, the Nadlai inscription of V.S. 1228 says that *rāṇā* Lakhamaṇa executed *rājya* in Borlī (No. 20); probably he was also of the non-Cāhamāna clan because of his title *rāṇā*

It is worth noting that the chiefs of Jhamara in the Mandor region appear to have been appointed by the Mandor rulers. A passage of the Jhamara inscription dated V.S. 1219, '*mahārājaputra-śrī-Gajasiṃgha-deva Māṃḍavyapur-āsīt tasya valādhipo Sauluṃkī Jasadhavala*' [*JPASB*, 12, p. 102, ll. 2-6], indicates that the chief Jasadhavala was not a subordinate to the king but to the Mandor ruler Gajasiṃha, as is evident from the expression 'his *balādhipa*' (*tasya valādhipo*). And in V.S. 1227, when the post of the Mandor ruler had already been transferred from Gajasiṃha to Cāmuṇḍarāja, the chief of Jhamara also changed to Nāmnada (Nos. 13, 14, 18 and 19). A similar instance can also be found in the territory of the heirs apparent, as was mentioned earlier: *mahāmātya* Vālhaṇa, head of the *pañcakula* of Paldi, who was dependent (*tat-pāda-padm-opajīvita*) on the heir apparent Jayatasiṃha (No. 26). This 'subinfeudation,' so to speak, can be seen, in our records, only in the case of the heirs apparent and the Mandor rulers, which indicates that both of them had such exceptional power that they ruled over the vast areas through their own retainers.

The above examples of the political power of the intermediaries allow us to draw a rough sketch of the structure of territorial administration of the kingdom. The Nadol Cāhamāna territory was composed of at least two segments, i.e., the Nadol region and the Mandor region, the latter of which was controlled by *Māndavyapurādhipatis*. They occupied the fort of Mandor and controlled the villages through the local rulers, some of whom were appointed by the Mandor rulers. In the Nadol region, the southern border area was under the charge of the heirs apparent who controlled the area from Sevadi in almost the same way as the Mandor rulers. In other areas of the Nadol region, which seem to have formed the heartland of the kingdom, some important towns and villages like Nadlai, Sonana, Borli, Bali, Sanderav and Korta were distributed to other royal kinsmen and non-Cāhamānas to enable them to control their surrounding villages. These local rulers were granted the revenue possession as a source of funds for the expenditure on their political activities. Thus, it is apparent that the 'land distribution' to royal and non-royal people served at the same time as a measure for controlling the territory of the kingdom, and therefore practically constituted the distribution of the local rulership.

Lastly, let us take up a very interesting village assignment which has been considered typical of Rajput land distribution; i.e., the 12 villages attached to Nadlai which were assigned to *mahārājaputra* Kīrtipāla by King Ālhaṇa and *kumāra* Kelhaṇa before V.S. 1218 (No. 12). Groups of 12, 42 and 84 villages in early medieval North India have often been taken as the administrative divisions of Rajput kingdoms [Ghoshal 1929: 259-60]. However, as far as the 12 villages of Nadlai are concerned, it is hard to consider them as an administrative unit. As is evident from the map, these 12 villages were rather widely dispersed. In addition, the assignee Kīrtipāla does not seem to have settled in Nadlai, which is suggested by the fact that he issued the copper-plate charter dated V.S. 1218 not from Nadlai but from the capital Nadol. [24]

It is worth noting that this assignment was made as '*prasāda*.' We also have a valuable copper-plate charter of the Candellas dated V.S. 1311 that records a village grant to *rāuta* Abhi as a *prasāda* or a bounty for his distinguished military service in the battle [*CII*, 7, Pt. 3, pp. 495-98]. Although we do not know whether Kīrtipāla rendered military service before V.S. 1218, it is plausible that this 12-village assignment was a bounty for some service rendered by him and not necessarily made for local administration. [25]

## Nature of Land Possession and Its Distribution System

The above discussion makes it clear that the Nadol Cāhamānas distributed important villages to their kinsmen and a few non-Cāhamānas as well to enable them to control local areas effectively. However, as far as the existing Nadol Cāhamāna inscriptions indicate, their possession of such assignments did not constitute their own hereditary estate. *Ṭhakkura* Rājadeva of the Guhilas was the *bhoktṛ* of Nadlai at least between V.S. 1195 and 1202 (No. 7). During or before 1218, however, Kīrtipāla, the third son of the reigning king Ālhaṇa, received 12 villages including Nadlai as an assignment (No. 12). Sonana, which was assigned to Kīrtipāla as one of these 12 villages, was in turn shifted into the possession of *ṭhakkura* Aṇasīha, probably of a non-Cāhamāna clan, in V.S. 1228 (No. 21). Furthermore, in V.S. 1233, the same village was in the joint possession of two *rājaputra bhoktṛs*, Lākhaṇapāla and Abhayapāla, who were sons of the above-mentioned Kīrtipāla Cāhamāna (No. 22). In the Mandor region, the village of Jhamara was under the control of Jasadhavala of the Saulumkīs in V.S. 1219 (No. 14), but in V.S. 1227 it was controlled by Nāmnaḍa Rāṣṭauḍa (No. 19). Thus, each of these examples clearly indicates its shift in possession from one family to another, which means that their assignments were not hereditary in nature. Again, it is worth noting that in the epigraphical records of the Nadol Cāhamānas there is no example to confirm the inheritence of assignments from father to son.

In the case of the heirs apparent, the situation was somewhat different: every heir apparent possessed Sevadi. From the inscriptions, we can identify five names of heirs apparent: Kaṭukarāja in V.S. 1167-72 (No. 2), Sāhaṇapāla in V.S. 1192 (No. 6), Jayatasiṃha in V.S. 1200 (No. 8), Kelhaṇa in V.S. 1218 [*EI*, 9, pp. 66 ff.; *IA*, 40, pp. 144 ff.] and Jayatasiṃha in V.S. 1238-49 (No. 26). Except for Sāhaṇapāla and Kelhaṇa,[26] either they were entitled to the revenues of Sevadi or they settled there and ruled the neighbouring villages.[27] These facts indicate that the seat of the Sevadi ruler was ordinarily fixed as that of the heirs apparent. This means that the rulership and the revenue entitlement at Sevadi were merely attached to the *status* of *kumāra.* Thus, the heirs apparent did not hold the territory of Sevadi as their own hereditary estate.

The Mandor rulers ruled over the Mandor region which geographically formed a relatively isolated territory. The rulers themselves, however, could not function independently, for they did not control the region as their own hereditary domain. The Nadol Cāhamāna inscriptions mention five *Māṇḍavyapurādhipatis* and inform us of their titles and their kinship positions in the royal family. Table 2 clearly shows that the Mandor rulers were the sons of the reigning kings, excluding *kumāras*, and that they were vested with the title of *mahārājaputra.*[28] This fact negates that the post of *Māṇḍavyapurādhipati* was a hereditary seat. This is because, when a new king ascended to the throne, the Mandor ruler inevitably had to give his seat to the next 'new son' of the 'new king.' Thus, not only the Sevadi rulers but the Mandor rulers were also changed on the occasion of the royal succession.

As for the other royal kinsmen, their assigned revenue entitlement seems to have often been changed on the occasion of the royal succession as well. In the Nadol Cāhamāna inscriptions, with the one exception of *rājaputra* Ajayasiṃha,[29] there is no instance of their revenue entitlement at one village extending over the reigns of two kings. Secondly, all the royal kinsmen who held assignments seem to have been close relatives of the reigning kings as mentioned in the second section. If the assignments distributed among the royal kinsmen had been their own inheritable estate, we would find in the inscriptions Cāhamāna clan members of much remoter degrees of kinship from the reigning kings. Hence, this fact indicates frequent redistribution of their assignments. This redistribution might have been inevitable though because, on the occasion of royal succession, new *kumāra* and a Mandor ruler emerged and their former assignments must have been given to other royal kinsmen for controlling the local areas.

However, it may be improper to say, as some historians do, that the Nadol Cāhamāna polity is a bureaucratic despotism where the absolute king legally decides on a policy and executes his power through many bureaucrats and that the appointment and dismissal of their posts are always at his discretion.[30] In the Nadol Cāhamāna polity, the king often needed his sons' approval to issue ordinances, which is discribed in the Kiradu inscription dated V.S. 1209, as mentioned earlier.[31] And the heirs apparent seem to have had prominent authority equal to 'kingship,' as is inferred from the Nadol copper plates dated V.S. 1218 which mentions that Kelhaṇa became 'the *kumāra* having his own *rājya*' (*kumāro nija-rājya-dhārī*) [*EI*, 9, p. 69, l. 16]. And more importantly, distribution of land and posts to the royal kinsmen does not seem to have depended on the king's favour but rather on their positions in the kinship hierarchy of the royal family. Thus, the Sevadi rulers and the Mandor rulers were bound to be *kumāras* and *mahārājaputras* respectively.

This difference of their entitlement from the assignment by king's favour can be readily illustrated by comparing the land grant documents issued by the Sevadi and the Mandor rulers with that by the assignee *mahārājaputra* Kīrtipāla (No. 12) mentioned at the end of the third section. When grantors themselves issued land grant charters (*śāsanas*), the authority of their possession of the land was usually specified.[32] Thus, when Kīrtipāla issued a *śāsana* of religious grant out of the Nadlai 12 villages, he specified that the villages had been assigned by favour (*prasāda*) of king Ālhaṇa and *kumāra* Kelhaṇa. On the other hand, however, any example of grants made by the Sevadi and the Mandor rulers does not mention *prasāda* of the king but specifies the royal genealogy descending to him (Nos. 2, 10 and 26). Interestingly, none of these three records gives the names of the reigning kings so that the grantors appear as if they were independent kings. This form of recording indicates that *kumāras* and the Mandor rulers did not owe their power base to the kings' will but to the fact that they were the sons of the Nadol Cāhamāna kings.[33]

We may thus conclude from the above discussion that the Nadol Cāhamānas distributed local rulership to the royal kinsmen according to their positions in the kinship ranking of the royal family in which the reigning king held the highest position, and that as the ranking was renewed whenever new kings ascended the throne, the distributed land never formed the basis for an individual estate.

In the case of the non-Cāhamāna clans as well, the assignees inevitably changed on the occasion of redistribution of land among the royal kinsmen. Non-royal intermediaries of the nodal points in the Mandor region seem to have been appointed by the Mandor rulers,[34] such that they were often replaced by others when the Mandor rulers changed. The same thing probably happened with the intermediaries under the king and the Sevadi rulers.[35]

The nature of their entitlement, however, is different from that of the royal kinsmen on one point: it was not based on the authority of their clan. In the inscriptions, they did not assert the dignity of their own clans though some of them were well-known Rajput clans like Rathors, Guhilas and Solaṅkis. In some cases rather, even their relationship to their clan itself cannot be identified from the inscriptions. Besides, they seem to have originally been neither local chiefs nor members of dominant clans of the areas of which they were appointed to rule. In some cases, in fact, it seems that several Rajput clans settled together in one area and none of them could claim exclusive dominance. For example, again as mentioned, the rulership of Jhamara was occupied by a member of the Solaṅkis in V.S. 1219 but in V.S. 1227 by that of the Rathors, which suggests that these two Rajput clans settled together in Jhamara and its surrounding area. If this were not the case, they would have been brought from other areas by the royal family. In either of the two cases they did not owe their rulership to their clan dignity but to the fact that they were appointed to the post by their master: the king, the Sevadi ruler or the Mandor ruler. They could neither acquire nor maintain the rulership without the royal appointment. It is worth noting that the difference in the authority of rulership between the royal kinsmen and non-royal clan members corresponds to the gap in the rank between them indicated by their titles as discussed previously in the second section.[36]

## Concluding Remarks

The Nadol Cāhamāna system thus far discussed leads us to three aspects of polity of the kingdom: (1) no *sāmanta* or hereditary chief, (2) non-despotic, and (3) non-clannish.

(1) The system of the transfer of assignments directly indicates that the local rulers of the Nadol Cāhamānas were not indigenous local chiefs

or local magnates who had permanent bases there. Rather they might be classified into royal officials and thus be similar to *iqṭādārs*. This kingdom did not adopt the territorial system where the posts of local governors were left to the chiefs of the local principalities. Hence, the Nadol Cāhamānas did not form their own *sāmanta* system composed of hereditary *sāmantas* in their own territory, though Nadol kings themselves constituted a *sāmanta* or feudatory of the Caulukyas of Gujarat.

(2) The kingship of this system is rather different from the typical despotism founded on full-fledged bureaucracy. The relatively powerful authority of heirs apparent and *mahārājaputras* and their check over the king, along with the customary selection of the governors of Sevadi and Mandor on the basis of kinship relations, seems to be inconsistent with the typical image of despotism. In addition, that the royal kinsmen composed exclusive ranks of *mahārājaputra* and *rājaputra* and that the greater part of the local rulership were assigned to them do not point to the sort of despotism in which the despot ruled over the whole territory with his own bureaucrats working at his beck and call. I would rather suggest that the royal family members jointly ruled over the entire kingdom with the assistance of the subordinates of other clans and that the king was merely a patriarch of the family.

(3) If 'clan' is conceptualised as a group whose members believe themselves to be descendants from a particular ancestor, the Nadol Cāhamānas did not have a true clan system. In the *bhāī-bandh* system of the late medieval Marwar, one of the typical clan systems of Rajputs, the kingdom was composed of many small principalities whose chiefs were considered to be the same clan members descending from certain illustrious king, and they jointly entered into the conquest of and defense against other kingdoms with a direct descendant serving as their own king and distributed the conquered land among them as part of their own inheritance [G.D. Sharma 1975; 1977: 1-10]. But in the case of the Nadol Cāhamānas, the 'royal kinsmen' composed of *mahārājaputras* and *rājaputras*, etc., were confined to the close relatives of the reigning king, whose extent is that of a family rather than a clan. Here the core of the ruling group and its hierarchy was not a past king but a present reigning king. Thus, on the occasion of a new king's accession to the throne, the composition of their kin ranking was inevitably changed; and consequently, their land distribution never formed their hereditary estate; we can see here a clear contrast between the clan system and the polity of the Nadol Cāhamānas.[37]

As for external relations too, there is no evidence of clan collaboration in the history of the early medieval Cāhamānas. Although the Nadol Cāhamānas branched off from the Śākambharī Cāhamānas and recorded it in their inscriptions as such,[38] they were, at least through the latter half of the twelfth century, an ally or subordinate of the Caulukyas who stood against the Śākambharī Cāhamānas [D. Sharma 1975: 148-60; Majumdar 1956: 23-168]. Thus, the polity and kingship of the Nadol Cāhamānas was by no means based on clanship; they did not have any constant clan relations but only formed the royal family.[39]

The Nadol Cāhamāna polity was thus considerably different from the later medieval Rajput polity; how the early medieval system was transformed into the later medieval one will be discussed in detail in the future.[40]

Table 1 Assignees or Local Rulers under Nadol Cāhamāna Rule

| No. | Date (V.S.) | Assignee or Local Ruler | Title | Clan | Assignment or Political Base | Reigning King |
|---|---|---|---|---|---|---|
| 1 | Last quarter of the 11th century? | Yaśodeva | *balādhipa* | — | Sevadi | — |
| 2 | 1167-72 | Kaṭukarāja | *yuvarāja* | Cāhamāna | Sevadi | Aśvarāja |
| 3 | 1167 | Uppalarāka | *mahāsāhaṇiya* | — | 4 villages near Sevadi (*arahaṭa*) | Aśvarāja |
| 4 | 1187 | Viṃsāraka | — | Cāhamāna | Morkha (oil-mill) | —[1] |
| 5 | 1189 | Timatā | *rāuta* | — | Nadlai (probably) | Rāyapāla |
| 6 | 1192 | Sāhaṇapāla | *mahārājaputra kumāra* | Cāhamāna | Nanana | Rāyapāla[2] |
| 7 | 1195-1202 | Rājadeva | *ṭhakkura rāuta bhoktāri* | Guhila | Nadlai | Rāyapāla |
| 8 | (Siṃha?) 31 (V.S. 1200?) | Jayatasīha | *yuvarāja* | Cāhamāna | Sevadi | Kaṭudeva |
| 9 | 1200 | Tihuṇaka | *rājñī* | (royal kinswoman) | Bali (*grāsā*) | Jayasīha (Jayatasīha?)[3] |
| 10 | 1200 | Bhanana | *rāṇaka* | non-Cāhamāna (from Karṇāṭa) | Usapa-pattana | — |
| 11 | Undated | Sahajapāla | *mahārāja[putra]* | Cāhamāna | Mandor | Rāyapāla[4] |
| 12 | 1218 | Kīrtipāla | *mahārājaputra* | Cāhamāna | Nadlai along with 12 villages | Alhaṇa |
| 13 | 1219 | Gajasiṃha | *mahārājaputra* | Cāhamāna | Mandor | Alhaṇa[5] |
| 14 | 1219 | Jasadhavala | *balādhipa* | Saulumkī | Jhamara (*balādhipābhāvya*) | Alhaṇa |

| No. | Date (V.S.) | Assignee or Local Ruler | Title | Clan | Assignment or Political Base | Reigning King |
|---|---|---|---|---|---|---|
| 15 | 1220-23 | Ajayasiṃha | *rājaputra* | Cāhamāna | Korta (pieces of land) | Alhaṇa to Kelhaṇa |
| 16 | 1221 | Ānaladevī | *rājñī* | (royal kinswoman) | Sanderav (*rājakīya-bhoga*) | Kelhaṇa |
| 17 | 1221 | Pātu and Kelhaṇa | *talāra* | Rāṣṭrakūṭa | Sanderav (*talārābhāvya*) | Kelhaṇa |
| 18 | 1227 | Cāmuṇḍarāja | *mahārājaputra* | Cāhamāna | Mandor | Kelhaṇa |
| 19 | 1227 | Nāṃnaḍa | — | Rāṣṭauḍa | Jhamara (*grāma-lāga*) | Kelhaṇa |
| 20 | 1228 | Lakhamaṇa | *rāṇā* | — | Borli | Kelhaṇa |
| 21 | 1228 | Aṇasīha | *ṭhakkura* | — | Sonana | Kelhaṇa |
| 22. | 1233 | Lākhaṇapāla and Abhayapāla | *rājaputra bhoktṛ* | Cāhamāna | Sonana Barwa (*arahaṭa*) | Kelhaṇa |
| 23 | 1236 | Kuṃmarasiṃha Siṃhavikrama | *Māṇḍavyapurādhipati* | Cāhamāna | Mandor | Kelhaṇa |
| 24 | 1236 | Kīrtipāla | *rājyavāhaka* | Cāhamāna? | Osian | Kelhaṇa |
| 25 | 1236 | Jālhaṇadevī | *rājñī* | (royal kinswoman) | Sanderav | Kelhaṇa |
| 26 | 1238-49 | Jayatasiṃha | *kumāra rāja* | Cāhamāna | Sevadi | Kelhaṇa |
| 27 | 1241-50 | Soḍhaladeva | *mahārājaputra* | Cāhamāna | Mandor Ghaṃghānaka | Kelhaṇa |
| 28 | 1241 | Yaśovīra | *bhaṇḍārin Pallādhipa* | — | Pal | Kelhaṇa |

Notes

1 The Nadlai inscription of V.S. 1187 does not mention the name of the reigning king who was actually Ratnapāla or Rāyapāla.
2 No mention of Rāyapāla, but it is evident from Nos. 5 and 7.
3 D.R. Bhandarkar identifies this Jayasīha with that of the Caulukya dynasty, and his dependants Āśvāka with the Cāhamāna king Aśvarāja (Nos. 2 and 3). But D. Sharma points out from the colophon of the *Supārśvanāthacarita*, a contemporary work, that in Māgha, V.S. 1199, Kumārapāla, the successor of Jayasiṃha, was already on the throne, and identifies him with Jayatasīha, son of Kaṭudeva of No. 8 [D.Sharma 1975: 150].
4 This inscription is so considerably damaged that we cannot read the name of the reigning king, but we can infer the reigning king Rāyapāla from the description of his relation, father of Sahajapāla, and the latter's title *mahārāja[putra]*. See the fourth Section and Note 28.
5 No mention of the reigning king, but it is evident from the Nanana copper plate record of V.S. 1219-20 [*EI*, 39, pp. 17 ff.] that the king was Alhana at that time.

References:

1. *EI*, 11, pp. 30 ff. 2. *EI*, 11, pp. 28 ff.; 30 ff. 3. *EI*, 11, pp. 30 ff. 4. JI, no. 842. 5. *EI*, 11, pp. 34 ff. 6. *EI*, 33, pp. 238 ff. 7. *EI*, 11, pp. 36 f.; pp. 41 f.; pp. 42 ff.; JI, no. 845. 8. *EI*, 11, pp. 33 f. 9. *EI*, 11, pp. 32 f. 10. *PRAS*, *WC*, 1909, p. 45. 11. *ASI*, *AR*, 1909-1910, Pt. 2, pp. 102 f. 12. *EI*, 9, pp. 68 ff.; *IA*, 40, pp. 144 ff. 13. *JPASB*, 12, pp. 102 f. 14. *Ibid.* 15. *EI*, 13, pp. 207 f.; pp. 208 ff.; pp. 210 f. 16. *EI*, 11, pp. 46 f. 17. *Ibid.* 18. *JPASB*, 12, p. 104. 19. *Ibid.* 20. *EI*, 11, pp. 47 f. 21. *Ibid.* 22. *EI*, 11, pp. 49 f.; pp. 50 f. 23. *JI*, no. 804. 24. *Ibid.* 25. *EI*, 11, pp. 51 f. 26. *EI*, 39, pp. 179 ff.; *JI*, no. 955; *Śodh Patrikā* 23, 2, p. 68. 27. *JPASB*, 10, p. 407; p. 409. 28. *JPASB*, 10, p. 407.

Table 2 Relations of *Māṇḍavyapurādhipatis*

| No. | Date (V.S.) | *Māṇḍavyapurādhipatis* | Nadol Kings | Relations |
|---|---|---|---|---|
| 1. | Undated | *mahārāja[putra]* Sahajapāla | Rāyapāla | Son of Rāyapāla and Padmalādevī, and a brother of *kumāra* Sāhaṇapāla. |
| 2. | 1219 | *mahārājaputra* Gajasiṃha | Ālhaṇa | Second son of Ālhaṇa and Annalladevī, and a younger brother of kumāra Kelhaṇa. |
| 3. | 1227 | *mahārājaputra* Cāmuṇḍarāja | Kelhaṇa | Son of Kelhaṇa, and a brother of *kumāra* Jayatasīha. |
| 4. | 1236 | Kuṃmarasiṃha Siṃhavikrama | 〃 | 〃 |
| 5. | 1241-50 | *mahārājaputra* Soḍhaladeva | 〃 | 〃 |

References:
1. *ASI, AR*, 1909-10 Pt. 2, pp. 101-3. 2. *JPASB*, 12, Pt. 2, pp. 101-3. 3. *Ibid*., pp. 103-4. Cf. D. Sharma 1975: 158. 4. *JI*, no. 804.
5. *JPASB*, 10, pp. 406-7; p. 409.

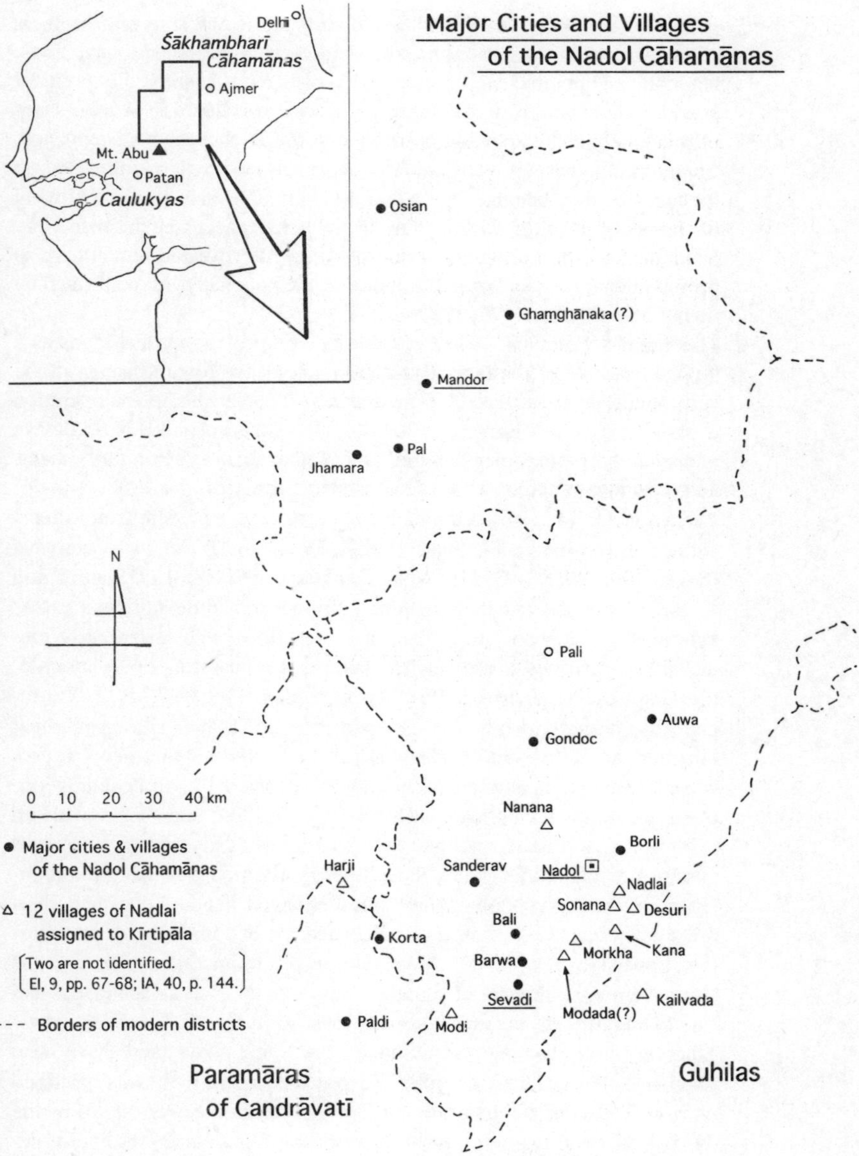


Major Cities and Villages of the Nadol Cāhamānas

## Notes

1 In this system, conquered land was distributed to the sons and brothers of the king, and their hereditary holding of land was sanctioned. Each landholder appointed his officers and could freely exercise his political power within his territory. Their territory was considered to be their share of the collaborative activities in which the ruling clan members engaged. Therefore, the basis of their landholding sanctioned by the king rested on the fact that they belonged to the ruling clan rather than merely enjoying the favour of the king. Although territorial holders accepted the suzerainty of the head of the ruling clan (i.e., the king), they treated him simply as primus-inter-pares, and even the choice of the king had to be confirmed by them [G.D. Sharma 1975; 1977: 1-24].

2 The Nadol Cāhamānas has often been taken up by many historians as a typical example of the land distribution among the royal kinsmen in the early medieval period. A.C. Banerjee sees it to be 'due to the operation of the clan system' [Banerjee 1962: 48]. R.S. Sharma and B.N.S. Yadava understand the assignments of the Nadol Cāhamānas as hereditary estates, and consider the polity as a feudal system [R.S. Sahrma 1980: 143-45; Yadava 1973: 144, 147], but this is not correct, as is evident from careful studies of inscriptions like those of K.K. Gopal and B.D. Chattopadhyaya [Gopal 1963-64: 92-93, 101; Chattopadhyaya 1990: 85]. D. Sharma and A. Sudan term the assignments *jāgīrs* without providing sufficient explanation of the concept, and, therefore, seem to recognise the early medieval land distribution as being the same as that operating in the later medieval system [D. Sharma 1975: 229-30; Sudan 1989: 127]. B.D. Chattopadhyaya properly points out that 'the distribution of land among the royal kinsmen' as in the Nadol Cāhamānas is one of the 'certain new features of land distribution and territorial system' associated with the emergence of early Rajputs [Chattopadhyaya 1976: 71-72], but does not provide an explanation of what constituted the structure of polity in which the land system was operating. Thus, though he rightly indicates that the assignments of the Nadol Cāhamānas 'often changed hands', 'the fact' does not signify much to him beyond 'the existence of some kind of pressure' [Chattopadhyaya 1990: 85]. We should therefore understand 'the fact' as being the normal manner of land distribution of the Nadol Cāhamānas and should enquire into the mechanism of their polity.

3 Thus far, more than 40 inscriptions of the Nadol Cāhamānas have been published. Most of them are religious grant records, which were inscribed on stone slabs and pillars of temples, or inscribed on copper plates by the dynasty as royal charters. In the case of the Cāhamānas, like the kingdoms of Śākambharī, Nadol and Jalor, existing copper plate charters are scarce. In fact, in the case of Nadol Cāhamānas, we can count only 10 such charters.

4 V.S. 1024 and 1039 have been presented as the date of Lakṣmaṇa mentioned in inscriptions [Tod 1829, vol. 1: 292]. However, the former inscription has been lost and the latter date is mentioned in the Nadol inscription of Kelhaṇa, V.S. 1223 (Bhandarkar List, No. 327). Thus no original text of his own inscription is currently available. Recently, Nadol was excavated and an inscription of Lakṣmaṇa dated V.S. 1025 is said to have been discovered [*Times of India*, New Delhi, June 6, 1992, 13]. But the text does not seem to have been published yet. Moreover, the Nadol inscription of Jendrarāja dated V.S. 1124 published by R.V. Somani (*Varadā* Vol. 19, Pt. 1 &2, p. 13) does not provide interesting information for us.

5 *saṃvat 1233 Vaiśākha-sudi 3 Samnāṇaka-bhoktā (bhoktārau) rājaputra-Lākhaṇapāla-rājaputra-Abhayapāla (pālau) tasmin rājye varttamāne cā° Bhīvaḍā Paḍideha-vāsī sū Āsadhara (raiḥ) samasta-sīra-sahitai (taiḥ) Khāḍisīra-ja (ya) va-madhyāt javā (yavāḥ) se 4 Gūjarī-jā (yā) trā-nimittaṃ śrī-Śāntināthadevasya dattā (dattāḥ) pū (pu) ṇyāya / yaḥ ko=pi lupyate (lopayati) sa pāpona (pāpena) chidyate // maṃgala[ṃ] bhavatū (tu) // tathā Bhaḍiyāuā-arahaṭṭe Āsadhara-Sīroiya-samasta-sīraṇa javā (yavāḥ) harothu (hāraka?) 1 Gūjara-tṛ-yātrahi (?) Vīlhasya puṇy-ārthaṃ // 1*

6 *rājñī-śrī-Tihunaka-grāsā bhujyamāna-Vālahī-grāmasya satka-śrī-Bahughṛṇadevī-yātrā nivi(rmi)ttaṃ ....*

7 *śrī-Jhāṃmara-sthāne deva-śrī-Māhagaṇa(?)svāmi Rāṣṭauḍa-virau(?) śrī-Samagha-suta- Nāṃnadena grāma-lāga-madhyāt pradatta-dra 1 mekaṃ (-draṃ° 1 ekaṃ) eva lāgaṃ pradattam //*

8 The Prakrit term *rāuta* is said to derive from the Sanskrit *rājaputra* [*CII*, 3 (ed. by J.F. Fleet), p. 218, fn. 1; Sircar 1966: 279], and *rāṇaka* from the Sanskrit *rājanaka* (lit., royal kinsman) [Sircar 1966: 276]. As for *ṭhakkura*, its etymology is very problematic. While there is a suggestion that it was derived from the Turkish term *tegin* [Sircar 1966: 340], I. Habib considers the Turkish *tarkhān* to be a better candidate for its origin [Habib 1994: 13-14]. In any case, all of them were the titles generally bestowed on petty local rulers subordinate to the kings (*mahārājādhirājas* and *mahārājas*). The ranking is, however, very hard to reconstruct. Some historians have attempted but do not seem to have succeeded in ranking them (e.g., Prasad 1990: xxii-xxiv]. The ranking does not seem to have been fixed on an all-Indian level but is flexible and arranged differently according to the needs of the times and regions.

9 The copper plates [*EI*, 9, pp. 68 ff. and *IA*, 40, pp. 146 f.], ll. 11-17, say, among the three sons of the king Alhaṇa, the eldest, Kelhana, became *kumāra*. See also Table 2. However, the heir apparent does not seem to have always been the eldest son of the king. In the Kiradu inscription of V.S. 1209 [*EI*, 11, pp. 43 ff.], Kelhana, like his younger brothers, only had the title *mahārājaputra*, and was not entitled *kumāra*, which might indicate that the heir apparent was selected from the sons of the king after the candidates had become adults.

10 For their relations, see the inscriptions listed in the 'References' of Table 1.

11 Kiradu inscription dated V.S. 1209 [*EI*, 11, pp. 43-46]. This ordinance was signed by the king and approved by two *mahārājaputras*: *svahastoyaṃ mahārāja-śrī-Ālhaṇadevasya* // *śrī mahārājaputra-śrī-Kelhaṇadeva-matam=etat* // *mahārājaputra-Gajasiṃhasya mataṃ* // (ll. 17-18)

12 The father of Kumārasiṃha is not mentioned in the inscriptions. D. Sharma, without presenting any grounds for his supposition, seems to identify this Kumārasiṃha as Kuṃmarasiṃha Siṃhavikrama who is the son of Kelhaṇa mentioned in the Osian inscription, V.S. 1236 [D. Sharma 1975: 158]. Incidentally, in V.S. 1220 Ajayasiṃha, a son of Kumāra-siṃha, made a land grant in the reign of Ālhaṇa, father of Kelhaṇa. If we assume that one would have been born when his father was 20 years old and that Ajayasiṃha would have been 15 years old in V.S. 1220, then the reigning king Ālhaṇa would have been 75 years old, *kumāra* Kelhaṇa 55, and Kumārasiṃha 35 according to Sharma's supposition. And as the latest record of Kelhaṇa is dated V.S. 1250, we must assume that he would have been an active king until 85. It is therefore much more reasonable to infer that Kumārasiṃha would not be identical with Kuṃmarasiṃha Siṃhavikrama and, consequently, would not have been the son of Kelhaṇa but of Ālhaṇa.

13 That the royal kinsmen enjoyed some privilege in land assignment can also be seen in the Śākambharī Cāhamāna records. The Harsa inscription, V.S. 1030, of the Śākambharī Cāhamānas says that *duḥsādhya* (leader of policemen) Dhandhuka, probably of a non-Cāhamāna clan, granted a village in his own possession (*svabhujyamāna*) with permission of the king (*svāmy-anumataḥ*), but that the sons and the brothers of the king made a land grant without such permission [*IA*, 42, p. 64, ll. 33-40]. The title system in which the titles, *rājaputra* and *mahārājaputra*, were solely held by the royal kinsmen, however, appears to have been unique to the Nadol Cāhamāna kingdom. Generally, the title *rājaputra* is said to have been conferred on petty rulers and not confined to particular lineages, as is evident from *Aparājitapṛcchā* (*sūtras* 78 and 81) and others [Inden 1981; Sircar 1965: 15-16; Yadava 1973: 32-37, 149-150].

14 P.R. Srinivasan says that *dāny-udgrānaka* is *udgrānaka* (a kind of tax) for *dāna* (gift) and thus its meaning is 'share of taxes reserved for gift' [*EI*, 39, p. 180].

15 In this inscription Jayatasiṃha is described as *rāja*, but undoubtedly in the period of the inscription, V.S. 1249, the king Kelhaṇa had not resigned his throne in favour of Jayatasiṃha yet, which is evident from the same inscription which mentions the reign of *mahārājādhirāja* Kelhaṇa. Accordingly, I have no idea why he employed the title *rāja*.

16 See l. 23 of a copper plate of the Nadol Cāhamānas. The text is in D. Sharma 1975: 213 ff.

17 Pali, along with Nadol and Jalor, was attacked by Vigraharāja IV of the Śākambharī Cāhamānas in his expedition to southern Rajasthan in the middle of the twelfth century [*EI*, 26, p. 105, v. 21], which indicates that Pali was one of the major cities in south Rajasthan.

18 P.C. Nahar edited nine eleventh-twelfth century inscriptions of the Jaina temples of Naulkhā Śāṃtināth and Somnāth in Pali [*JI*, pp. 199-206].

19 *EI*, 31, pp. 237 ff. Interestingly, the inscription records in the last line Cāhamāna *rājaputra* Raṇadhavala as the *dūtaka* (executor or messenger) of this grant.

20 *PO*, 1, No. 2, pp. 41 ff.

21 '*śrī-Kelhaṇadeva-mahārāja-rājye tat-putra-śrī-Kuṃmarasiṃha-Siṃhabi-krame śrī-Māḍavyapurādhipatī ... dabhikānvīya-Kīrtipāla-rājyavāhake tad-bhuktau śrī-Upakeśīya-śrī-Sañcikādevi-devagṛhe...*' [*JI*, No. 804].

22 In this case, he granted a part of his own share of the load cess to the god Nemināttha without enquiring of merchants.

23 It is hardly plausible to think that this grant was simply an illegal activity or an excess of his authority because it was inscribed plainly and openly. Thus, if it was not illegal, it cannot but be considered as a grant coming from his administrative authority.

24 Nadol copper plates of Kīrtipāla, V.S. 1218 (No. 12 of Table 1), l. 19.

25 *Rājakula-pala* (oil share of the royal family) in Nadlai enjoyed by Rudra-pāla, Amṛtapāla and *rājñī* Mānaladevī in V.S. 1189 [*EI*, 11, pp. 34 ff.] might possibly have been a collective possession of the royal family which was enjoyed by the royal kinsmen who did not have administrative duties. For, in the same inscription, Timaṭā having the title *rāuta* is listed as the witness of the donation made by them; he seems to have been a local chief of Nadlai (No. 5 of Table 1).

26 We cannot unfortunately ascertain from the existing inscriptions that *kumāra* Sāhaṇapāla and *kumāra* Kelhaṇa were the rulers of Sevadi.

27 See the third section.

28 A few letters after '*mahārāja*' are damaged in the title of Sahajapāla of No. 1, but considering that he was the son of the king Rāyapāla and that the titles of other Mandor rulers were *mahārājaputra*, it seems quite natural to fill in the blank with '*putra*'. In the case of Kuṃmarasiṃha Siṃhavikrama of No. 4 too, we can properly infer from his relationship, son of the king Kelhaṇa, that his title *mahārājaputra* would have been merely omitted.

29 See, No. 15 of Table 1. *Rājaputra* Ajayasiṃha or Ajayarāja donated irrigated land to a brahmana called Nārāyaṇa three times, all of which are recorded on the copper plates of V.S. 1220, 1223 and an undated one. The record of V.S. 1220 falls during the reign of Ālhaṇa, and the other two during the reign of Kelhaṇa. But the grant items were not the revenue from Korta but were parcels of land. Probably Ajayasiṃha was not the governor of Korta but simply owned the cultivated fields in Korta as his own property.

30 As far as the present studies on Indian history are concerned, most Marxist historians like D.D. Kosambi and R.S. Sharma do not support Marx's theory of Oriental despotism linked with the Asiatic mode of production. Rather the historiography on individual dynasties in early medieval India tend to describe kingship and polity as bureaucratic despotism or absolute monarchy. For the cases of the Cāhamāna dynasties, see D. Sharma 1975: 219-20; Singh 1964: 273-74.

31 See Note 11.

32 Reference to the authority of possession is often seen in the cases where grantors' land possession originated in the *prasāda* assignment by their overlords. For instance, in the Bombay Secretariat copper plate document dated in V.S. 1231, *mahāmandaleśvara* Vaijalladeva proclaimed the granting of Ālaviḍagāṃva village after mentioning the fact that he had been assigned Narmadātaṭā *maṇḍala* through the favour (*prasāda*) of his overlord Ajayapāla Caulukya [*IA*, 18, pp. 80 ff.].

33 In addition, the revenue possession assigned to the royal kinsmen was not necessarily a remuneration for their administrative service as in a bureaucracy. As mentioned in Note 25, some of them seem to have benefitted from villages without having provided administrative service.

34 See the third section.

35 What has been discussed here does not necessarily refute the succession of the titles themselves of non-Cāhamāna clan members but rather their successive political bases. For instance, the *bhoktṛ* of Nadlai was *ṭhakkura rāuta* Rājadeva of Guhila family (No. 6 of Table 1), whose father Ūdharaṇa also held the title *rāuta*. But the former delegated chief in charge of Nadlai was not Ūdharana but probably *rāuta* Timaṭā (See Note 34). Probably Ūdharaṇa had a rulership elsewhere in the kingdom.

36 Such shifting and unstable holding of political assignments discussed thus far can be seen in the religious grants as well, as pointed out by B.D. Chattopadhyaya. According to him, in the Nadol kingdom, there were different nodes with which individual villages were connected as a mechanism for channelling village resources, and the link between the nodes and their respective villages were temporary and often changed [Chattopadhyaya 1990: 70-92]. If this is true, not only secular and religious grants but all the revenue channels of the Nadol kingdom would have been changeable. Such a type of revenue system would correspond to the Nadol Cāhamāna polity as presented in this paper.

37 For the details about the comparison between the Nadol Cāhamāna system and the *bhāī-bandh*, see the conclusion of my paper [Mita 1996: 47-50].

38 Nadol copper plates of Kīrtipāla, V.S. 1218 [*EI*, 9, pp. 68 ff.; *IA*, 40, pp. 144 ff.], and undated Mandor inscription of Sahajapāla [*ASI, AR*, 1909-1910, Pt. 2, pp. 102 f.].

39 The question arises as to whether or not this polity of the Nadol kingdom can be the norm of the *sāmanta* principalities of Rajasthan, i.e., the Jalor

Cāhamānas, the Candrāvatī Paramāras, the Bhinmal Paramāras and the Guhilas. This is a very difficult question to answer because these *sāmanta* polities do not offer very rich information about the intermediary strata as in the Nadol Cāhamānas. The inscriptions of these kingdoms do not seem to show the dominance of the royal kinsmen in the administration. Therefore, the distinct domination of the royal kinsmen over the state administration might be unique to the Nadol Cāhamānas. But the non-existence of hereditary chiefs in these kingdoms might similarly be suggested from the epigraphical records, which mention very little about the intermediaries in spite of the abundant records of religious grants. For if hereditary local chiefs or landed nobles had existed, these grant records should have referred to their names as local rulers or grantors. Therefore, it is not unreasonable to judge that even in other *sāmanta* principalities, hereditary chieftainship had not yet formed in early medieval Rajasthan.

40 As for the transformation into the later medieval clan system, I have presented a supposition in my paper [Mita 1996: 50].

## Abbreviations

*ASI, AR*: *Archaeological Survey of India*, Annual Report.

*CII*: *Corpus Inscriptionum Indicarum*, Archaeological Survey of India, New Delhi.

*EI*: *Epigraphia Indica*.

*IA*: *The Indian Antiquary*.

*JI*: *Jaina Inscriptions*, Vol. 1, edited by P.C. Nahar, second ed., Delhi, 1983 (first ed., 1918).

*JPASB*: *Journal and Proceedings of the Asiatic Society, Bengal*.

*PRAS, WC*: *Progress Report of the Archaeological Survey*, Western Circle.

## References

Banerjee, A.C.

1962 *Lectures on Rajput History*, Calcutta.

Chattopadhyaya, B.D.

1976 'Origin of the Rajputs: The Political, Economic and Social Processes in Early Medieval Rajasthan,' *Indian Historical Review*, 3 (1), pp. 59-82.

1990 'Villages, Wells and Rulers in South-eastern Marwar: Aspects of Rural Settlements and Rural Society in the Kingdom of the Nadol Cāhamānas,' *Aspects of Rural Settlements and Rural Society in Early Medieval India*, K.P. Bagchi & Company, Calcutta, pp. 70-92.

Fox, R.G.

1971 *Kin, Clan, Raja, and Rule: State-Hinterland Relations in Preindustrial India*, Oxford University Press, Bombay.

Ghoshal, U.N.

1929 *Contributions to the History of the Hindu Revenue System*, Calcutta.

Gopal, K.K.

1963-64 'Assignment to Officers and Royal Kinsmen in Early Medieval India,' *University of Allahabad Studies: Ancient History Section*, pp. 75-103.

Habib, I.

1994 'Linguistic Materials from Eighth-Century Sind: An Exploration of the Chachnāma,' *Symposium Paper of Indian History Congress*, 55th Session.

Inden, R.

1981 'Hierarchies of Kings in Early Medieval India,' *Contributions to Indian Sociology* (N.S.), 15 (1-2), pp. 99-125.

Kolff, D.H.A.

1990 *Naukar, Rajput and Sepoy: The Ethnohistory of the Military Labour Market in Hindustan, 1450-1850*, Cambridge University Press, Cambridge.

Kulke, H.

1995 'Introduction: The Study of the State in Pre-modern India,' H. Kulke ed., *The State in India: 1000-1700*, Oxford University Press, New Delhi.

Majumdar, A.K.

1956 *Chaulukyas of Gujarat*, Bharatiya Vidya Bhavan, Bombay.

Mita M.

1996 'Land Distribution and Kinship of the Nadol Cāhamānas: Structure of Rajput Polity in 12th-Century Rajasthan,' *Journal of the Japanese Association for South Asian Studies*, 8, pp. 27-57.

Prasad, P.

1990 *Sanskrit Inscriptions of Delhi Sultanate: 1191-1526*, Oxford University Press, New Delhi.

Saran, P.

1952 'The Feudal System of Rajputana,' P. Saran, *Studies in Medieval Indian History*, Delhi, pp. 1-23.

Sharma, D.

1975 *Early Chauhan Dynasties*, second ed., Motilal Banarasidas, Delhi (first ed. 1959).

Sharma, G.D.

1975 'Concept of Kingship and the Marwar Nobility during the 16th Century,' *Proceedings of Indian History Congress*, 36th Session (Aligarh), pp. 157-65.

1977 *Rajput Polity: A Study of Politics and Administration of the State of Marwar, 1638-1749*, Manohar Publishers & Distributors, New Delhi.

Sharma, R.S.

1980 *Indian Feudalism: c. A.D. 300-1200*, second ed., Macmillan, Madras (first ed., 1965).

Singh, R.G.

1964 *History of the Chahamanas*, Varanasi.

Sircar, D.C.

1965 *The Guhilas of Kiśkindhā*, Sanskrit College, Calcutta.

1966 *Indian Epigraphical Glossary*, Motilal Banarasidas, Delhi.

Sudan, A.

1989 *A Study of Cahamana Inscriptions of Rajasthan*, Research Publishers, Jodhpur.

Tambs-Liche, H.

1997 *Power, Profit and Poetry: Traditional Society in Kathiawar, Western India*, Manohar Publishers & Distributors, New Delhi.

Tod, J.

1829-32 *Annals and Antiquities of Rajasthan*, edited with an introduction and notes by W. Crooke, 3 vols.; reprinted, Low Price Publications, Delhi, 1990.

Yadava, B.N.S.

1973 *Society and Culture of Northern India in the Twelfth Century*, Central Book Depot, Allahabad.

Ziegler, N.P.

1976 'The Seventeenth Century Chronicles of Mārvāṛa: A Study in Evolution and Use of Oral Tradition in Western India,' *History in Africa: A Journal of Method*, 3, pp. 127-53.

# 5

# The Changing Concept of Kingship in the Cōḷa Period: Royal Temple Constructions, c. A.D. 850-1279

YASUSHI OGURA

## Introduction

It is well known that the regional kingdoms of the medieval period that appeared in east, central and south India, were intensively involved in temple construction. As a result, a number of enormous royal Hindu temples emerged in these regions from about the eleventh to the thirteenth century. Some of the notable examples are the Lakṣmaṇa temple (c. A.D. 954) and the Khaṇḍāriya Mahādeva temple (first quarter, eleventh century) at Khajuraho, the Udayeśvara temple at Udaipur (1059-80), the Liṅgarāja temple at Bhuvanesvar (mid-eleventh century), the Jagannātha temple at Puri (1135), and the Sun temple at Konarak (1238-58). The Rājarājeśvara temple at Thanjavur (1003-10) and the Rājendreśvara temple at Gangaikondacholapuram (third decade, eleventh century), built by thė Cōḷa kings Rājarāja I and Rājendra I respectively, stand out among these impressive royal temples.

These royal temples ostensibly displayed the power and strength of the builder to his subjects as well as competing rivals. But it should be also noted that these temples played an important role in the royal *dāna* strategy to establish king's legitimacy over his subordinates. There is no doubt that the religious authority of the king provided by his imperial temple would have minimized the cost of government. At the same time the legitimacy thus acquired must have served as a complement to his administrative systems which were comparably vulnerable except in a few cases. Therefore, the kings of the regional kingdoms of the medieval period made their greatest efforts in various forms to make the most of the traditional religious institution of the Hindu temple in order to establish their legitimacy. But the actual process might have differed in details according to the cultural region. This essay focuses on the temple building activities by the Cōḷa kings flourished in south India from the late ninth to thirteenth century A.D. By arranging their royal temples chronologically, we will deduce, through the nature of each construction, the political intentions of the kings who built them.

## Early Phase (850-1000): Image of Goddess, Local Śiva Shrines and Paḷḷippaḍais

In the middle of the ninth century A.D., Vijayālaya (c. 850?-71),[1] captured Thanjavur, the capital of his neighbouring clan of Muttaraiyars and founded the Cōḷa dynasty. According to the Tiruvalangadu plate of Rājendra I (1012-44), Vijayālaya dedicated an image of the goddess Niśumbhasūdanī in the city of Thanjavur to commemorate his victory.[2] Although he left no temples of his own,[3] not less than a hundred small temples were constructed during the late ninth and tenth centuries with granite stone in the Kaveri delta, many of which were converted to stone from the original wooden or brick structure. These changes went side by side with the expansion of the early Cōḷa dynasty.

These temples, so far generally called 'early Cōḷa temples', have been studied by several scholars such as Nilakanta Sastri [1955: 693-709], Balasubrahmaniyam [1966, 1971], Barrett [1974], Hoekveld-meijer [1981], Dhaky [1983a], and Dehejia [1990]. These scholars speculate by and large that by the time of Āditya I (871-98/907), a Cōḷa stone tradition must have been well established in the Kaveri delta region. The basis for this assumption is the description in the Anbil plates of Sundara Cōḷa (957-73/975?). It is mentioned there that Āditya I was the one 'by whom the row of large temples of Śiva, as it were banners of his own victories, lofty and unacquainted with defeat or collapse, was built of stone on the two banks of Kaveri River from the Sahya mountain ... even to the ocean.'[4] Seemingly solely based on this information, Balasubrahmaniyam ascribed even more than forty temples to the reign of Āditya I [Balasubrahmaniyam 1966: 82-85]. But it seems natural to suppose that other patrons like the Muttaraiyars, the Irukkuvēḷs and the Paḻuvēṭṭaraiyars would have been responsible for some of these constructions. Recent studies tend to use more detailed classification, paying more attention to patrons other than the Cōḷa dynasty [Rajan 1975: 240-300, Rajan 1983, Dhaky 1983b].

Scrutinising a royal involvement in these temples, however, presents a very difficult problem, since very few temples bear royal foundation inscriptions. The scholars mentioned above, generally seem to have assumed that almost all of these temples were built by the Cōḷa royal patrons be they kings, a queen, or some of king's officers. But a question may arise whether temples classified by these authors by using dynastic labels were indeed built by the royal family itself or by others, whether independent chieftains or rich landholders. It is true that these temples show similar stylistic peculiarities, but a common style does not always mean the same patronage. It may mean at most a common tradition on the part of the artisans who built them. Therefore it might be difficult to deny cases in which some influential chieftains or landholders in a particular area hired the same group of artisans who were working for the Cōḷa royal family to have built temples of their own. This would be a limitation that seems to be inherent in the classification of architectural styles using dynastic labels.

Recently Kaimal has boldly argued that Āditya I did not build any temples at all, basing herself on the very fact that temples built in his reign lack his foundation inscriptions [Kaimal 1996: 33-66]. She goes on to say that even the succeeding king Parāntaka I (907-954) did not built any temples except for a very few cases. Thus, according to her, the early Cōḷa kings were basically indifferent to temple building, because of their scanty resources for such costly projects, at least before the time of Uttama Cōḷa (971-988), when his mother Sembiyan Mahādevī showed her strong munificence by patronaging temple construction. Kaimal starts her argument by giving stress to the importance of inscriptional data. She points out that the date of the Anbil plates is half a century later than the reign of Āditya I. She concludes that since there is no foundation inscription found to indicate his involvement in temple construction, it simply means that the account in the Anbil plates merely represents an interpolation of the idea of kingship in the later period.

As for the lack of Āditya I's foundation inscription, former writers have also noticed this. Dhaky, for example, wrote that 'there are no inscriptions of Āditya I which concern the building of temples; and the few inscriptions known of royal queens are donative in nature' [Dhaky 1983a: 148].[5] But he still believes that Āditya I, or some members of the royal family (and some officers on his behalf), were substantially involved in temple construction. He gives the example of the famous Nāgeśvara temple at Kumbhakonam, concluding that this temple, although it is of a moderate size, could be regarded as a royal structure from the richness of its embellishment and the excellence of its workmanship. His explanation for the lack of a foundation inscription itself is, however, ambiguous. He says simply that it is possible that Āditya I did not think it proper to record his name as builder of such ancient shrines [*ibid.*]. By the same criteria of style, Dhaky ascribes the Brahmapurīśvara temple and the Koraṅganātha temple, both of which are masterpieces of tenth-century temples, to the construction activities of Parāntaka I, although they also lack foundation inscriptions of this king. In this way, basing himself on style as well as inscriptional data, Dhaky classified a large number of temples into a group called 'Cōḷas of Tañjāvūr: Phase I' under the heading of the 'Early Cōḷanāḍu style.' Though his primary concern is not with the clarification of the patronage of each temple but with a general trends in the architectural style of each period, it is true, as Kaimal states, that such a classification might still cause the misunderstanding that so many temples were related to the early Cōḷa kings themselves.

On the other hand, Kaimal's argument is also not without difficulties. First of all, as Kaimal herself admits, her arguments are based on the negative evidence that there have been found no foundation inscriptions. But it is not so unusual for a temple not to have such an inscription, even if it is a royal building. For example, no foundation inscriptions have been found in the monumental Rājendreśvara temple at Gangaikondacholapuram, though there is no doubt from other evidence that Rājendra I (1012-44) built it [Srinivasam 1983a: 241].[6]

Secondly, if temples such as the Nāgeśvara, the Brahmapurīśvara, and the Koraṅganātha, were not built by Cōḷa kings, then there arises the question of who built them. These temples are no inferior in the perfection of their entire construction as well as the detail of their embellishment, than, for example, the Mūvar Kōvil built by the Irukkuvēḷ king Bhūti Vikramakesarī, who was a close relative and loyal ally of Āditya I [Dhaky 1983b: 200]. Therefore if such buildings are to be ascribed to independent local forces other than the Cōḷas, the Irukkuvēḷs, the Paḻuvēṭṭaraiyars, or the defeated Muttaraiyars, they must have been so rich and influential that they appeared more visibly on the political stage of this period than Cōḷas. If there did not exist such forces strong enough to build such excellent temples, should we then consider that these temples were built by temporary foreign invaders like the Rāṣṭrakūṭas or the Pāṇḍyas, who hired architects working in the invaded region?

Third question concerns Kaimal's interpretation of the Anbil plates. Elsewhere in her article, Kaimal tries to see the development of the idea of kingship in three cases of temple construction by Parāntaka I, all of which can be attested by inscriptions. One is the construction of the entire structure of the Kōdaṇḍarāmeśvara temple at Tondaimanadu, while the other two works are only on parts of temples. Among these latter two, the first is the finishing work on the upper portion of the *vimāna* (beyond the *kuḍapaḍai* [7]) in the Gomukteśvara temple at Tiruvaduturai and the second is the dedication of a golden roof for the *cit-sabhā* at Chidambaram Naṭarāja temple. She insists that Parāntaka I's intention can be assumed in both cases to have been to spend his limited resources on deliberately selected works so as to have a maximum visual advertisement effect as royal protector of Śaivism [Kaimal 1996: 57, 59]. Thus she concludes that such an awakening consciousness of a new form of kingship is reflected in the wording of the Anbil plates that boasts Āditya I's great undertaking, which is, according to her, baseless. But if the possibility that Āditya I built temples is to be excluded, and only a very limited involvement can be ascribed even to his son Parāntaka I, this would mean that, when Sundara Cōḷa had this inscription executed, there would have been virtually no precedents of temple builders among his ancestors since, as both Dhaky and Kaimal agree, Gaṇḍarāditya (949-957), Parāntaka I's successor, did not construct any royal temple. Even during the reign of Sundara Cōḷa himself very few temples were built, and none from royal patronage [Dhaky 1983a: 176-78]. In such circumstances, who could gain the idea that temple construction was a great royal undertaking? [8] Was it a sudden revival of the Pallavas' idea of kingship as the protector of Śaivism at its zenith in the eighth century? If not, he should have had at least some precedents of active builders in his lineage. Since Gaṇḍarāditya, and of course Vijayālaya, can be excluded with certainty, we might expect that the involvement in temple construction by either Parāntaka I or Āditya I must have been somewhat more intensive than Kaimal supposes. Thus we may still be inclined to consider that such excellent monuments like the Nāgeśvara, the Brahmapurīśvara and the Koraṅganātha, with such refined decoration, are Cōḷa royal monuments. The earlier kings did not feel it necessary to leave their names inscribed there, probably owing to their lack of understanding that temples were important political devices. Some other temples sharing common style with them might also be assigned to the patronage of these kings. But as for this latter conjecture, it should be admitted that we have no supporting evidences at all.

These difficulties, however, should not diminish the importance of Kaimal's argument in which she clearly points out problems arising from the dynastic classification of architectural styles. In the follwing discussion, her table [Kaimal 1996: 39 Fig. 3] is to be consulted with our additions of the above-mentioned temples most probably constructed during the reigns of Āditya I and of Parāntaka I.

The royal temples of this period are to be classified into two groups. One is a group of temples having a sepulchral nature that were built over the remains of kings who died in war. The other is a group of temples that were converted to stone from those originally situated (or sometimes newly built) in the sacred places of the Tamil religious tradition.

In the first category, we should notice the Kodaṇḍarāmeśvara temple in Tondaimanadu built in 941 by Parāntaka I. This is the first royal Cōḷa temple in the sense that it is datable on the clear basis of its foundation inscription. This temple was built on the border of Toṇḍaināḍu and Āndhradeśa on the spot where Parāntaka I's father Āditya I died in the battle. Kodandarāma is another name of Āditya I, and as may be inferred from the name of temple, it enshrines a *liṅga* named after him. Such funerary temples, called *paḷḷippaḍai*, appeared first in the late ninth century [9] and not only had they become very common in the Cōḷa royal family in this period, but they also continued to be built until about the twelfth century.

Kaimal relates such funerary temples directly to traditional Tamil warrior culture but attention should be given to the fact that these temples were presided over by pontiffs belonging to the Pāśupata sect.[10] When a Pāśupata *guru* (teacher) died, his body was not burned but buried, and his disciples built over his remains a *liṅga* named after him, and sometimes a temple was built to enshrine the *liṅga*.[11] The spread of the Pāśupata sect in the Kaveri delta area in this period is attested by many inscriptions indicating the existence of their *maṭhas* all over this region [Sastri 1955: 647-52]. Since the extensive influence of the Śaiva Siddhānta sect was felt only after the time of Rājendra I, the Pāśupata sect must have represented the Śaivism of this period. Therefore there is no wonder that a Cōḷa king, having presumably received his *dīkṣā* ceremony from his Pāśupata *guru* as a devout Śaiva, was buried in the manner of the Pāśupata.

It might be, however, still possible to regard the *paḷḷippaḍai* as a syncretistic fusion of such a Śaivaite tradition and Tamil warrior culture, which latter is supposed to be related to the so-called hero-stone tradition. In hero-stones or memorial tablets made between about the fifth to sixth and the twelfth century in Tamil Nadu, often a pedestal or a shrine is depicted, and this is said to be 'the precursor of the later day *paḷḷippaḍai* shrines erected over the remains or the place of the dead heroes.'[12]

A close affiliation between megalithic tombs and memorial stones can also be inferred from records copied from Megalithic tomb structures, showing also that the practice of erecting dolmens for those who had met a heroic death continued until a very late period.[13]

In this regard, Kaimal is right to infer from these *paḷḷippaḍais* a heroic kingship that would have given foremost legitimacy to the kings who built them. Indeed the *paḷḷippaḍais* they constructed were solely for their relatives who had died a heroic death in battle.[14] In the days of continuous warfare, to memorise such warrior-kings who were considered to have become god-like heroes when enshrined in a temple and to insist on a living king's heroic lineage directly connected to the deified dead, must have had the effect of giving him a strong legitimacy over his subordinates, even if it was limited to the small circle of the court.

At the same time, however, a fusion of Śaivism with such an earlier idea of kingship in this temple of Parāntaka I suggests that Śaivism was already deeply rooted in the Cōḷa court of his reign. It seems to indicate indirectly that Kaimal's assertion that both Āditya I and Parāntaka I, except for a few cases, did not build any temples, is difficult to accept completely.

The royal temples of the second category are invariably as moderate in size as other temples throughout this early period. This also applies to the royal *paḷḷippadai*s. These are not comparable in size to either the royal temples of the Pallavas in their heyday or those of the Cōḷa kings from Rājarāja I onward, and this suggests a scarcity of resources on the part of patrons for spending in large-scale temple construction. These temples, however, show an obvious shift of royal patronage from the goddess Niśumbhasūdanī, worshipped as a tutelary deity within the circle of the Cōḷa family on a clan level,[15] to the god Śiva. Now they have become the protector of Śiva, who possessed a far more universal nature. Throughout this early period, the location of royal temples of this category was limited to the traditional sacred places that showed each local manifestation of Śiva. Therefore the royal enterprise could not go beyond the acknowledgment of each local tradition. But there should be no doubt that, following the expansion of the Cōḷa territory, the more they acknowledged each local tradition, the more universal their legitimacy as protector of Śaivism became in much larger areas beyond the nuclear region of the Cōḷas.

In the later stage of this earlier period, their political sensitivity to royal temple construction seemed to have been intensified by Sembiyan Mahādevī, mother of Uttama Cōḷa. Her apparently strategic involvement in temple building and generous donations seems to have gone beyond simple munificence. She constructed a number of temples inscribed with her foundation inscription. She seems to have also strengthened the royal relationship with the Naṭarāja temple at Chidambaram. The royal approach to Naṭarāja who had come to assume the character of a universal Sanskritized god in this period,[16] was most probably begun by Parāntaka I, as was mentioned above, in the form of the donation of a golden roof for the *cit-sabhā*. This might have been followed by the frequent inclusion of an image of Naṭarāja into the iconographic scheme of temple walls, which was otherwise very conservative. This inclusion is particularly to be seen in the temples built by Sembiyan Mahādevī. Moreover, she projected her own identity upon her Umā-Maheśvara temple in Konerirajapuram where her natal star was regularly celebrated [Balasubrahmaniyam 1966: 168, Kaimal 1996: 62]. She even named one of her temples in Kuttalam Cōḷīśvara, in a manner that had not been seen before her, thus clearly imprinting the royal presence there. Furthermore, the temple in the village called Sembiyan Mahādevī contained a portrait image of herself that was regularly worshipped [Sastri 1955: 453]. All of these aspects foreshadows the well devised political strategy in a large-scale temple building by the next king, Rājarāja I.

## Middle Phase (1000-1078): Imperial Temples and the Cult of the Royal Liṅga

Rājarāja I (985-1012), who succeeded the throne of Uttama Cōḷa in 985, built the enormous Rājarājeśvara temple (later called Bṛhadīśvara) in Thanjavur in the beginning of the eleventh century.[17] When he ascended to the throne, the Cōḷa territory, once extended considerably owing to Parāntaka I's success over the Pāṇḍyas, has shrunk in spite of a recovery by Sundara Cōḷa. The Rāṣṭrakūṭas from the north, as well as an alliance of the Pāṇḍyas, Keralas, and the Sri Lankans from the south, were always threatening the Cōḷas. Rājarāja I first made inroads into the south and defeated the Pāṇḍyas and the Keralas, and then subjugated the northern part of Sri Lanka with his navy. As for the north, he sent a large army led by his son Rājendra and defeated Satyāśraya of the later Cālukya dynasty that succeeded the Rāṣṭrakūṭas. As a result of these victories, the Cōḷa army carried back enormous booty, most of which was bestowed on the Rājarājeśvara temple. Thus the temple was a monumental work primarily for showing off the wealth and power of the Cōḷa kingdom that was beginning to take the shape of huge empire. While temples built by kings of the earlier period were located in the traditional sacred places of the Tamil country and were in that sense strongly bound to old ties, this temple was built in the newly founded capital of Thanjavur which was selected by the will of Rājarāja I himself. It is said that his royal palace was located next to this temple. Following him, Rājendra I (1012-44), his son, also founded the Rājendreśvara temple (later also called Bṛhadīśvara), almost the same in size and style, in his new capital of Gangaikondacholapuram. These temples formed a completely new category of the imperial temple which was completely different in scale as well as style from temples built before, and the temples of this category would continue to be built until the end of the dynasty.

Besides location, size, and style, there is another aspect that characterises these imperial temples. It is the incorporation of the king's name in the names of temples, that is, the *liṅga* enshrined in them was called after the king who dedicated it. Names like 'Rājarājeśvara' or 'Rājendreśvara' can be understood primarily as 'Lord (Śiva) of the king Rājarāja' or 'Lord of the king Rājendra.' But at the same time they leave at least the grammatical possibility of interpreting them as 'Rājarāja as Lord' and 'Rājendra as Lord' and so on. Such naming of the *liṅga* is not unique to these Cōḷa kings, and we have a number of examples all over India [18] and more remarkably in the Khmer kingdom of Cambodia, which latter case has been discussed by a number of scholars in the context of the so-called *devarāja* cult. [19] Nonetheless it has a particular importance here in that it appeared in the royal temples of the Cōḷas for the first time, that is, it indicates the first emergence of the cult of the royal *liṅga* among them. This might have meant a significant change in their idea of kingship. Here we should make a distinction between this type of *liṅga* and the *liṅga* also called after a king that was enshrined in a *paḷḷippaḍai* as mentioned above, since in this latter case, worship was meant for a deseased king who was considered to have been united with the god Śiva after his death. This is somehow in accordance with the Pāśupata tradition. But in the case of imperial temples, the *liṅga* was called not after a dead but after a living king. We do not have any textual evidence to explain such a custom properly. Accordingly we could speculate whether it was meant as the apotheosis of a living king.

There are many instances to show that the worship conducted in the Rājarājeśvara temple was centred on the king Rājarāja I himself. It is widely known that in the circumambulatory passage surrounding the *garbhagṛha* a number of portraits of royal family members used to be displayed, among which the portrait sculpture of Rājarāja I bearing a close resemblance to the god Śiva is found.[20] Moreover, temple walls bear thirty representations of Śiva in his Tripurāntaka ('Destroyer of the Three Citadels of Demons') form and it has been suggested that the popularity of this theme at this temple may have served as a symbol of Rājarāja I's military strength and imperial authority.[21] The same motif is also found in a mural painting on the wall of circumambulatory passage [Venkataraman 1985: 124-29]. Moreover, the biggest festival was held every twelve years according to the king's natal star. Some of these characteristics had already appeared in the temples built by Sembiyan Mahādevī as described above. But it is important to notice that each of these elements appeared here in its fully developed form. It seems as if all efforts were made to direct the whole course of worship towards the king himself.

In spite of all these appearances, however, we should not overlook another aspect in the scheme of iconography at this temple. There is a wall painting in which Rājarāja I and his three queens are worshipping the Naṭarāja Śiva as pious devotees. Here there is no trace of apotheosis of the king. The painting is found on the wall of the same circumambulatory passage in which the portrait statue of Rājarāja I and the painting of the Tripurāntaka, both of which were mentioned above, are located. They would seem to be completely contradictory. Moreover there is no inscriptional evidence to suggest that Rājarāja I did proclaim himself to be a god in public. The larger Leiden grant suggests to the contrary when it says 'when the king became a god' [*Epigraphia Indica* xxii]. Referring to his death, it tells us simply that while living, he was just a man, although it indicates at the same time that he was regarded as a god after his death.

Rājarāja I donated to this temple not only a number of images in bronze, but also a huge amount of jewels, precious stones, silver, gold and so on that had been taken as booty from his enemies.[22] His family starting with his elder sister Kundavai as well as high officials followed him to make donations on a large scale. Moreover not only from the villages in his nuclear area of the Kaveri delta but also from those of more distant regions including Karnataka, Andhra Pradesh, and northern part of Sri Lanka, lands were donated to this temple, taxes were levied for its sole use, and workers were collected for temple service. Thus the Rājarājeśvara temple became the richest social unit of that time. From its property the temple loaned cash to the villages in its neighbourhood with interest of more than 12 per cent. With such interest the property of the temple became ever larger, while at the same time the economical development of the nuclear area surrounding the capital Thanjavur was promoted. In many cases the labour for temple service was provided by the Brāhmin villages established according to the king's policy of *agrahāra*. The cultural influences of such Brāhmin villages over surrounding areas were not of minor significance. Therefore Rājarāja I's policy must have created economical and cultural network on a large scale radiating from the Rājarājeśvara temple [Spencer 1969: 42-56]. In this way, the Rājarājeśvara temple succeeded in combining the worship of Śiva in traditional local shrines scattered all over his territory and created a unique religious identity there. In this social context, it is clear that this temple was intended to be nothing other than the main political device in Rājarāja I's centralised royal *dāna* strategy. It was there that the king, redistributing his property accumulated as booty to his subjects, played the role of a pious devotee of Śiva and thus assured his legitimacy. It looks like he was at most a high priest who represented for Śiva for the common devotees.

But how should we harmonise the two apparently contradictory images of the king Rājarāja I at this temple? Here it is necessary to remember that the *paḷḷippaḍais* continued to be built in this period. It seems that both Rājarāja I and Rājendra I were less active than earlier kings in constructing them for their relatives. Rājarāja I is known to have built two sepulchral temples. One was the Ariñjigai-Īśvara temple at Melpadi for his grandfather Ariñjigai who died at Arrur in battle, and the other was the Kandalīśvara temple at Tenneri for Uttama Cōḷa. Rājendra I also built the Pañcamahādevīśvara temple in Ramnathan Koil for Pañcavaṉmahādevī, his stepmother. Except for the last case, these temples retain the nature of the royal *paḷḷippaḍais* of the early period in that they were meant to memorialise heroic kings. This means that the idea of heroic kingship remained in this period. As concluded above, the erection of *paḷḷippaḍais* in the earlier period, gave kings the legitimacy that connected them to the deified hero. If this was the case, it should next be asked if such a god-like nature was shared by living kings as well. Although mixed with Śaivism, the worship at *paḷḷippaḍais* must have been a kind of ancestor worship that had, most probably, its root in the tradition of megalithic culture. Whether living kings had a sacred nature of their own before south India had been strongly influenced by Sanskrit culture, is not certain. But it might not be so unnatural to assume the existence of a king's sacred and spiritual nature, as is inferred from much evidence in other cultures in the world.[23] If we are allowed to take such external evidence into consideration, we would be inclined to think that the Cōḷa kings still might have retained such a somewhat sacred and god-like nature, which was materialised at their imperial temples in the form of the naming of the *liṅga* after the king, the iconographic scheme, and royal ritual and so on. It should be added that such a large scale materialisation would have been possible when Rājarāja I had ensured his supreme position as an emperor with huge resources at his disposal.

Why, then, did this aspect of the king's god-like nature not fully develop? In this regard, we have to take into consideration the presence of Brāhmins who played a significant role in the court as *rājapurohitas* as well as in the management of these imperial temples. Their name suggests that they had migrated from north India and that most of them belonged to the Śaivasiddhānta sect [Takashima 1994: 41-53, Takashima 1989: 41-57]. Although the existence of *maṭhas* of this sect in the Kaveri delta region has been ascertained from at least the tenth century onward, the names of their *ācāryas* appeared in the Cōḷa court only from the time of Rājarāja I. Their strong influence over kings was attested in various occasions [Sastri 1955: 452]. We may wonder whether it was they who placed restrictions on the development of the sacred aspect of the king. In other words, it could be considered that a compromise might have been reached between the king who had the god-like self-image, and the *rājapurohitas* whose framework of orthodox northern Brāhmanism required the king to be subordinate to the Brāhmins in the sacred matters. Was it because of this compromise, that the images of Rājarāja I represented in the art, ritual, and political economy of the Rājarājeśvara temple are so complicated and contradictory? At any rate, he was neither a god nor a common devotee. If there is a definition for him, it would be that of a god-like devotee.

The custom of creating an image of the king resembling a god which was particularly evident among the Pallavas as well as Southeast Asian art, the genealogical portions of *praśasti* that trace the origins of the dynasty to gods, also common to the Pallavas as well as the Cōḷas, and even the *aṃśa* theory persistently described in the Brāhmanic literature such as the *Manu-smṛti*, could be regarded as the results of a similar compromise. Scholars like Derett [1957: 67], Filliozat [1966: 95-106], and Scharfe [1989: 96] refuse to see the deification of the king in the name of the *liṅga* called after a living king. But it seems that they have been caught in the trap of a dichotomy in that they have made a clear-cut distinction between god and man.

To sum up, in the worship of royal *liṅga* at imperial temples, we can detect some resonances of early ideas of kingship entertained before Sanskritization in which the king was concidered to be in charge of both the sacred and the secular realms. But this could not be fully developed owing to the increasing influences of the Śaivasiddhānta Brāhmins who migrated to this region in this period and eventually acted as advisers to the kings. As a result of a compromise between the kings and these Brāhmins, imperial temples had a double nature. One aim was to exalt the king as the god-like king by various iconographic and ritualistic devices and as such legitimised him. The other was to characterise the king as a supreme representative of the god Śiva. In the latter instance, the aspect of the king as a pious devotee of Śiva was emphasised and played an important role in his *dāna* strategy that also provided him with legitimacy.

In the kingdoms in Southeast Asia, notably in Cambodia, a row of imperial temples of similar characteristics was built where the cult of the royal *liṅga* was also very common. But there the imperial temples were not only monuments to display royal power but also royal tombs where the remains of the king were buried. As a result, the king's god-like aspect seemed to have fully developed there. In south India, however, royal sepulchral temples were never combined with the imperial temples. It might be said that faced with the already deeply rooted Brāhmanism, the kings in south India, even Rājarāja I, could not push their sacred aspect to the fore. But as for the *rājapurohitas*, they seemed to have been unable to establish the king completly within the framework of Brāhmanism. Thus, they had to allow the king to play the role of supreme priest. Although this period can be characterised as the time when incorporate kingship in Kulke's model was established,[24] it seems that the earlier mode of kingship, whether it can be characterised as 'heroic' or 'divine,' coexisted with the new idea of incorporate kingship.

## Late Phase (1070-1279): Patronage of the Chidambaram Naṭarāja and Emergence of Ammaṉ Shrines

When Adhirājendra (1068-1070) was assassinated and the line of Vijayālaya became extinct, the Eastern Cālukya prince Rājendra took the throne with the title of Kulōttuṅga I (1072-1122) and inaugurated the Cōḷa-Cālukya line. This line lasted for two hundred years, and the nature of royal temple policy changed drastically in this period.

Although Kulōttuṅga I did not have any temple built for himself, the succeeding kings generally followed the custom of building imperial temples that was established in the middle phase. Also the custom of naming the imperial temple after the builder king and the cult of the royal *liṅga* seemed to have continued throughout the period. Vikrama Cōḷa (1118-1135) who succeeded Kulōttuṅga I, built his Vikramacōḷīśvara temple at Vikramacholanallur [Venkataraman 1985: 74, Barasubrahmaniyam 1979: 167-71]. This is now a rather neglected monument, but two others, that is, Rājarājeśvara temple (Airavateśvara temple) at Dharasuram built by Rājarāja II (1146-1172) and Tribhuvanavīleśvara temple (Kampahareśvara temple) at Tribhuvanam (Tribhuvanavīlapuram) built by Kulōttuṅga III (1178-1218), stand out among the many temples of this late phase. In minor details these imperial temples show some advances, but in size as well as style they follow rather faithfully the model of the Rājarājeśvara temple built by Rājarāja I.

But the naming of the Tribhuvanavīleśvara temple merits attention. This temple was so called after one of the titles of Kulōttuṅga III, meaning 'the hero who conquered three worlds.' This is the common name of Śiva and has something more abstract than a name like Rājarājeśvara in which the king's most familiar personal name is directly connected to the name of the temple. This is felt also in another name of the temple, that is, 'Kampahareśvara,' meaning the god who relieved the gods, or the Cōḷa king of shivering out of fear (*kampa*) [Srinivasan 1983b: 312]. This implies directly the god Śiva himself. Particularly in the latter case, but also in the former, we notice that the king's personality has faded from the naming of the temple. Two Tamil inscriptions state that 'the temple was dedicated to the Iṟaivar (Śiva), adored by Ari (Viṣṇu) and Piramar (Brahmā), so that the whole world may worship and praise Him' [*ibid.*]. It seems as if all the worship was meant only for the god Śiva and not for the king at all. In this regard, we should also notice that in the thirteenth century, Rājarājeśvara temple as well as Rājendreśvara temple came to be called by rather abstract names as Bṛhadīśvara rather than their original names after their respective builders.

The Tribhuvanavīleśvara temple was consecrated by the king's *rājapurohita*, Īśvara Śiva, the spiritual son of Śrīkaṇṭha Śambhu and the author of a theological treatise, the *Siddhāntaratanākara* [*ibid.*, Sastri 1955: 399]. It is confirmed that the Śaivasiddhānta sect had firm roots in the whole of the Tamil country by the twelfth century and took the place of the Pāśupata and other older sects [Swamy 1975: 167-209]. The Śaivasiddhānta sect is said to have had an advantage that it placed a stress on the *parārthapūjā*, that is, the worship for the benefit of others, as opposed to the Pāśupata sect, which emphasised *ātmārthapūjā*, or worship for oneself [Takashima 1989: 48]. The former, having systematised the *bhakti* movement, succeeded in establishing a theory and a practice for the salvation of common people and held an established position in the Śaivism of the Tamil country. Its presence at the court is ascertained from the time of Rājarāja I by the names of *rājapurohitas*, that is, Īśāna Śiva Paṇḍita[25] and Śarva Śiva in the reign of Rājarāja I and Rājendra I, Śrīkaṇṭha Śiva in the reign of Vikrama Cōḷa and so on.

Therefore it would be wondered if their increasing influence over the court as well as the common people prevented the kings from giving their imperial temples a personal flavour. In other words, the lack of the king's personality in the cult of temple indicates that the Brāhmins at the court had come to exercise a clear advantage over the kings. Notably in the Tribhuvanavīleśvara temple, there was no place for the king to project his god-like image on his own temple, since it appears, in this monument marking the culmination of great Cōḷa temples, that the king was now deprived not only of his god-like character but also of the role of the supreme priest or of the representative for the god and degraded to a lay protector of Śaivism.

This situation might have been reflected in the condition of *paḷḷippaḍai* of this period. There is an indication that the *paḷḷippaḍai* was regarded as improper, as may be inferred from the case of Pañcavaṇmahādevīśvara temple in Ramnathan Koyil built by Rājendra I, where an attempt can be seen to have been made to erase the word '*paḷḷippaḍai*' from the inscription [Sastri 1955: 453]. We have also a record showing that an attack on a *guhai* (monastery) occurred in A.D. 1200 in the reign of Kulōttuṅga III [Sastri 1955: 652, Sethuraman 1992]. *Paḷḷippaḍai* and *guhai* are closely related institutions, and *paḷḷippaḍai*s were especially under the control of the Pāśupata sect. Therefore it could be surmised that these incidents may have indicated increasing disapproval of the sect or at least of the custom of *paḷḷippaḍai*. At any rate there is no possibility for the kings to emphasise their heroic or sometimes divine legitimacy as they did in the preceding periods.

The shift of the source of legitimacy from the king's own person, whether he be regarded as hero or divine, to the universal Śaivism is also suggested by the remarkable emphasis on the patronage of Naṭarāja at Chidambaram by these later Cōḷa kings. As was mentioned above, Kulōttuṅga I did not build any temple for himself, but he and his successor Vikrama Cōḷa, through their minister Navalokavīla, spent their entire energy on enlarging and embellishing the Naṭarāja temple at

Chidambaram. Such intense involvement in the Naṭarāja temple was continued to Kulōttuṅga III, who dedicated the famous Nṛtta Sabhā (a dancing hall for Śiva as the king of dance). It was in their time that the temple took its present-day shape, converted from a small temple to a large complex. The patronage of the Naṭarāja temple by Cōḷa kings has a long history going back to Parāntaka I, as was described above. Naṭarāja first appeared as a sculpture on the wall of royal temples of the early period. Countless bronze images of him were made side by side and came to be worshipped inside of the imperial temples along with the *liṅga* as an anthropomorphic manifestation of Śiva. In this regards, the shift of the capital by Rājendra I from Thanjavur to Gangaikondacholapuram might be explained, at least partly, in relation to Chidambaram, since Gangaikondacholapuram is located midway between Chidambaram and Thanjavur.[26] At any rate, now Naṭarāja became virtually the tutelary deity of the dynasty. It should be also noted that it was in this same period that royal patronage of the Raṅganātha at Srirangam was also strengthened. The increasing importance given to these Sanskritized universal deities might have meant the degradation of imperial temples as centres of the worship in the empire. In these circumstances it seems that the legitimacy based on the king's own person would not have made sense at all. Instead the shift of their patronage to a pan-Indian Sanskritized god, even though kings had to give up their divine self-image, must have offered them a much more universal legitimacy that they could advocate against other competing dynasties.

If this is regarded as a legitimisation in a horizontal direction then, that in a vertical direction is probably reflected in the emergence of Ammaṉ shrines at imperial temples. Ammaṉ shrines where a goddess is enshrined had appeared already at the time of Rājendra I. But it is important here that all the imperial temples of this late phase came to attach an Ammaṉ shrine to form a pair with the *vimāna* where a royal *liṅga* was enshrined. This is considered to have been primarily an architectural expression of Sanskritization in which aboriginal goddesses were more and more assimilated to Hinduism as consorts of Śiva. But it would also have meant the absorption of independent clans in the broad region, who were worshipping aboriginal goddesses as their tutelary deities, into the Cōḷa empire.

Therefore a current of Sansktitization in this period eventually provided kings with a more consistent and stable basis for their legitimisation, in exchange of their divine self-image.

## Conclusion

The royal involvement in temple building by the Cōḷa kings described above rather clearly shows the nature of their legitimacy, which changed over the time. In the early phase (850-1000), their project started from the construction of sepulchral temples and the patronage of local Śiva shrines by converting them to stone structures. The former were solely meant for their relatives who had died heroic death in war, and they thus assured the kings of the legitimacy of their lineage by being connected to heroic warriors. While such a form of legitimacy might have been accepted only in a small circle of the Cōḷas on a clan level, the latter represented the germination of a political consciousness of the effect of royal temple building. At the same time, the enlargement of patronage from their tutelary goddess Niśumbhasūdanī to Śiva at local shrines scattered over a larger area beyond their nuclear region would have provided them with a more universal legitimacy as protectors of Śaivism. Therefore, in the later stage of this early phase Sembiyan Mahādevī extensively put her energy in converting old structures to stone and build stone temples and inscribed her name, thereby imprinting the existence of the dynasty. Thus royal temples came to play a significant role as political devices in her *dāna* strategy.

In the middle phase (1000-1078), the latter form of legitimacy seemed to have been fully developed, as was inferred from the case of the Rājarājeśvara temple built by Rājarāja I. The king Rājarāja I donated extensively to the Rājarājeśvara temple, and through the economical and cultural network radiating from the temple he redistributed to his subjects his property accumulated as booty from his enemies.[27] At the same time, however, the earlier form of legitimacy remained in this period in the form of the cult of the royal *liṅga* at imperial temples of a new category as well as royal sepulchral temples that had continued to be built since the early phase. It went side by side with the newer form of legitimacy. The coexistence of both forms of legitimacy seems to suggest a compromise between kings and the Brāhmins who had come to have a great influence over king's temple policy as his advisers. As a result, kings retaining their divine and heroic aspects, had to play a role of the highest devotee or, at best, the supreme priest.

In the last phase (1070-1279), although imperial temples continued to be built where a *liṅga* named after a king was installed, king's own personality gradually faded away, as is to be inferred from the naming of temples. Instead the kings of this period all made great efforts in the enlargement and embellishment of the Naṭarāja temple at Chidambaram. At the same time they began their patronage of the Raṅganātha temple at Srirangam. These facts indicate the older form of legitimacy completely lost its validity and the king's legitimacy came to depend on his nature as a pious devotee of a pan-Indian Sanskritized god. This was the result in a part of the victory of the Brāhmins over kings, but mainly of the king's need to rule a wider region with a minimum cost. Such a strategy can be seen also in the case of Ammaṉ shrine that came to be attached to imperial temples.

Thus the form of legitimacy was drastically changed during four hundred years of the Cōḷa period. Roughly speaking, it developed from a simple heroic and divine form in the early period to a more sophisticated Saskritized form in the later period, while in the middle transitional period, both forms were mixed together. These changes seem to approximately correspond with the development of kingship in Orissa,[28] but their details significantly differ from those of the Eastern Indian example. Regional differences should be considered also in relation to Khmer kingdom in Cambodia. A systematic comparison of these kingdoms would provide a clearer picture of the nature of regional kingdoms in the middle ages.

## Notes

1 Throughout this essay, I have adopted the dating of Michael Meister, ed., *Encyclopaedia of Indian Temple Architecture, South India, Lower Drāviḍadeśa 200 B.C. –A.D. 1324.*

2 The Tirvalangadu plates of Rajendra Cola, *South Indian Inscriptions*, 1920, 3, no. 3, #205.

3 The well known Vijayāla Cōḷīśvara temple at Narttamalai carrying his name, often classified as an 'early Cōḷa temple,' originally belonged to the Muttaraiyars whom he defeated. This temple came to be so called in a later period.

4 The Anbil plates of Sundara Cōḷa; *Epigraphia Indica*, Calcutta, 1919-1920, vol. 15, no. 5. 68, translated by T.A. Gopinatha Rao.

5 See also Barrett [1974: 49]; 'not a single one of these temples carries an inscription with a foundation date or with a direct reference to Āditya I as founder.'

6 In Orissa it is also common for no foundation inscription to have been found. Donaldson [1990: 95-120].

7 There is disagreement sorrounding the understanding of this architectural term. Dhaky interprets it as the *jagatī* below the *kumuda*. In this case

almost all of construction from the base to the finial would have been built by Parāntaka I [Dhaky 1983a: 175].

8 The genealogical *praśasti* of Uttama Cōḷa ascribes active temple construction to his mythical ancestor, the king Kaccahapan. Spencer [1984: 415-32]. It is confirmed from inscriptions that by the time of Uttama Cōḷa royal involvement in temple building was fairly established. In that sense it would be natural for him to ascribe active temple building even to his mythological ancestor in order to legitimise his own activity.

9 The earliest *paḷḷippaḍai* in inscriptions was of Rājāditya Mahādeva of Western Gaṅga, who built it for his father Pṛthivīgaṅgaraiyar at Solapuram where he died; this was in the eighth year of Vijayakampa [Balasubrahmaniyam 1971: 89-90].

10 N. Sethuraman [1987: 9-37]. In many cases their *maṭhas* were attached to a *paḷḷippaḍai*.

11 The earliest example can be seen in the Mathura pillar inscription of Candragupta II. It is said that the Pāśupata *guru* Udītācārya constructed two shrines in memory of his two teachers and installed the Śiva *liṅgas* in the shrine. Tirumūlar of the seventh century A.D. clearly describes such a procedure. [Sethuraman 1991: 29-37].

12 K. G. Krishnan, 'Hero-stone Inscriptions of the Pallava Times,' R. Nagaswamy, ed., *Seminar on Hero-stones*, Madras, 1974, quoted in Settar [1982: 187].

13 Settar [1982: 186], quoting N. Krishnan.

14 Some of the later *paḷḷippaḍais* have a different character. They were built sometimes for the mother or sister of a king and just for their memory.

15 Kaimal regards this goddess as the clan deity of the Cōḷa and insisted on her aboriginal origin, based on the analysis of Nagaswamy; see Kaimal [1996: 36, 53] and Nagaswamy [1977: 39].

16 For a brief account of the development of the Chidambaram Naṭarāja temple, see Kulke and Rothermund [1990: 142-44].

17 As for the following historical account of the Rājarāja I, see Sastri [1955], Srinivasan [1983: 223-24], Balasubrahmaniyam [1977], and Venkataraman [1985].

18 For example, Avantisvāmin temple built by an Utpala king Avantivarman in the ninth century in Kashimir; the Udayeśvara temple by Udayāditya Parāmāra in the eleventh century in Malwa; Rājasiṃheśvara temple by Pallava king Rājasiṃha in Kanchi in the eighth century; closer to the Cōḷas, the example of Uttamadānīśvara temple in the ninth century, built by a Muttaraiyar chieftain, Uttamadāni.

19 There are a number of works treating this subject; for a bibliography, see Kulke [1978].

20 J. Sundaram [1958: Plate 8]. Such royal portrait statues are found more commonly in Southeast Asia.

21 Gary J. Schwindler, 'Speculations on the Theme of Siva as Tripurāntaka

as it appears during the Reign of Rājarāja I in the Tanjore Area, c. A.D. 1000,' at the annual meeting of the Association for Indian Studies, 1981, quoted in Huntington [1985: 528].

22 Venkataraman listed items of these donation; see Venkataraman [1985: Appendices].

23 See the classical work by Frazer; *The Golden Bough. Study in Magic and Religion*, London, 1913 (third edition). Dumont considered that in India kings surrendered their original function as priests to the Brāhmins in as early as the Vedic period; see Dumont [1970: 62-88].

24 For a brief account, see Kulke and Rothermund [1990: 130-31] and Kulke [1978: 125-37].

25 His affiliation is not certain. The name Īśāna Śiva seems to suggest his affiliation to the Śaivasiddhānta sect. But Sethuraman insists that the name ending with the word '*paṇḍita*' means an affiliation to the Pāśupata sect; see Sethuraman[1991].

26 A similar example of a shift of the imperial capital in relation to the state god is reported in Orissa; see Kulke [1980: 30-40].

27 Such an attitude appears to correspond with his various efforts intended to build up a centralised administrative network. See Karashima [1984: Introduction xxvi].

28 See articles in Eschmann, Kulke and Tripathi [1978].

## References

Balasubrahmanyam, S.R.

1966 *Early Chola Art, Part One*, New York.

1971 *Early Chola Temples, Parantaka I to Rajaraja I (A.D. 907-985)*, Bombay, Calcutta, New Delhi, Madras.

1977 *Middle Chola Temples, Rajaraja I to Kulottunga I (A.D. 985-1079)*, Amsterdam.

1979 *Later Chola Temples, Kulottunga I to Rājendra III (A.D. 1070 -1280)*, Faridabad.

Barret, Douglas E.

1974 *Early Cola Architecture and Sculpture; 866-1014 A.D.*, London.

Dehejia, Vidya

1990 *Art of the Imperial Cholas*, New York.

Derrett, J.D.M.

1957 *The Hoysaḷas*, Madras.

Dhaky, M.A.

1983a 'Cōḷas of Tañjāvūr: Phase I,' Michael Meister ed., *Ency-*

*clopaedia of Indian Temple Architecture, South India, Lower Drāviḍadeśa 200 B.C.- A.D. 1324*, Delhi.

1983b 'Irukkuvēḷs of Koḍumbāḷūr,' Michael Meister ed., *Encyclopaedia of Indian Temple Architecture, South India, Lower Drāviḍadeśa 200 B.C.- A.D. 1324*, Delhi.

1983c 'Paḷuvēṭṭaraiyars of Paḷuvūr,' Michael Meister ed., *Encyclopaedia of Indian Temple Architecture, South India, Lower Drāviḍadeśa 200 B.C.- A.D. 1324*, Delhi.

Donaldson, Thomas Eugene

1990 'Rsis, Gurus and Kings in Orissa Temple Art,' Claudine Bautze-Picron ed., *Markandeya: Essays in honour of Dr. James C. Harle*, Delhi.

Dumont, Louis

1970 'The Conception of Kingship in Ancient India,' *Religion, Politics and History in India: Collected Papers in Indian Sociology*, Paris/The Hague.

Eschmann, A., Kulke, H. and Tripathi, B. C.

1978 *The Cult of Jagannath and the Regional Tradition of Orissa*, New Delhi.

Filliozat, J

1966 'New Researches on the Relations between India and Cambodia,' *Indica* 3, pp. 95-106.

Frazer, J.G.

1913 *The Golden Bough, A Study in Magic and Religion*, London (third edition).

Hoekveld-meijer, Gerda

1981 *Koyils in the Cōḷamaṇḍalam: Typology and Development of Early Cōḷa Temples*, Amsterdam.

Huntington, Susan

1985 *The Art of Ancient India – Bhuddist, Hindu, Jain*, New York and Tokyo.

Kaimal, Padma

1996 'Early Cōḷa Kings and "Early Cōḷa Temples": Art and the Evolution of Kingship,' *Artibus Asiae* 56(1/2), pp. 33-66.

Karashima, Noboru

1984 *South Indian History and Society: Studies from Inscriptions A.D. 850-1800*, Delhi.

Kulke, Herman

1978a 'Royal Temple Policy and the Structure of Medieval Hindu Kingdom,' Anncharlott Eschmann, Herman Kulke and Baya

Charan Tripathi eds., *The Cult of Jagannath and the Regional Tradition of Orissa*, New Delhi.

1978b *The Devaraja Cult*, New York.

1980 'Legitimation and Town-Planning in the Feudatory States of Central Orissa,' Jan Peiper ed., *Ritual Space in India: Studies in Architectural Anthropology (Artand Archaeology Research Paper XVII*), London.

Kulke, Herman and Rothermund, Dietmar

1990 *History of India*, London (paperback edition).

Nagaswamy, R.

1977 'A Note on Niśumbhasūdanī installed by Vijayālaya Chola in Tanjore,' *Lalit Kalā* 18, p. 39.

Rajan, K.V. Soundara

1975 'Early Pāṇḍya, Muttaraiyar and Irukkuvēl Architecture,' Prammod Chandra ed., *Studies in Indian Temple Architecture*, New Delhi.

1983 'Muttaraiyars of Nēmam and Sēndalai,' Michael Meister ed., *Encyclopaedia of Indian Temple Architecture, South India, Lower Drāviḍadeśa 200 B.C.- A.D. 1324*, Delhi.

Sastri, K.A. Nilakanta

1955 *The Cōḷas*, Madras (second edition).

Sethuraman, N.

1987 'Presidential Address,' *Studies in Indian Place Names* 8, pp. 9-37.

1991 'Crusade against Guhai(Monastery),' *Journal of Epigraphical Society of India* 17, pp. 29-37.

Settar, S.

1982 'Memorial Stones in South India,' S. Settar and Gunther D. Sontheimer eds., *Memorial Stones: a study of their origin, significance and variety,* Darwad and Heidelberg.

Sharfe, Hartmut

1989 *The State in Indian Tradition*, Leiden.

Spencer, George W.

1969 'Religious Networks and Royal Influence in Eleventh Century South India,' *Journal of the Economic and Social History of the Orient* 12 (part 1), pp. 42-56.

1984 'Heirs apparent: Fiction and Function in Chola Mythical Genealogies,' *The Indian Econimic and Social History Review* 21(4), pp. 415-32.

Srinivasan, K.R.

1983a 'Cōḷas of Tañjāvūr: Phase II,' Michael Meister ed., *Encyclopaedia of Indian Temple Architecture, South India, Lower Drāviḍadeśa 200 B.C.- A.D. 1324*, Delhi.

1983b 'Cōḷas of Tañjāvūr: Phase III,' Michael Meister ed., *Encyclopaedia of Indian Temple Architecture, South India, Lower Drāviḍadeśa 200 B.C.- A.D. 1324*, Delhi.

Sundaram, J.

1958 *The Great Temple at Tanjore*, Tanjore (second edition).

Swamy, B.G.L.

1975 'The Golaki School of Saivism in the Tamil Country,' *Journal of Indian History* 53, pp. 167-209.

Takashima, Jun

1989 'Early History of the Saiva Matha: 8th to 13th century (in Japanese),' *Journal of the Japanese Association for South Asian Studies* 1, pp. 41-57.

1994 'Establishment of Siva Cult,' Noboru Karashima ed., *The Dravidian World* (in Japanese), Tokyo.

Venkataraman, B.

1985 *Rājarājeśvaram – The Pinnacle of Chola Art*, Madras.

# 6

# Vijayanagar Nāyakas in Tamil Nadu and the King

NOBORU KARASHIMA

I previously published two studies on the rule of Vijayanagar *nāyakas* in the northern part of Tamil Nadu by compiling the lists of *nāyakas* appearing in the Vijayanagar inscriptions of Chingleput and North Arcot Districts respectively [1990, 1998]. For the same purpose, I have since then also examined the Vijayanagar inscriptions of South Arcot, Tiruchirapalli and Thanjavur Districts. I shall therefore discuss in this essay the characteristics of the *nāyaka* rule in the northern and central parts of Tamil Nadu comprising the five districts, which constituted the core area of the Vijayanagar rule in Tamil Nadu, in relation to the issues of Indian kingship.[1] The discussion will focus on the relations that the *nāyakas* of the above area (five districts) had with the king.[2]

I define a *nāyaka* in all of these studies as one who posseses any one or more of the following four qualifications: (1) a *nāyaka* title, including its Tamilised or Telugu form such as *nāyinār*, *nāyaniṅgāru*, etc.; (2) his own territory referred to as his *nāyakattanam* or *sīrmai* (*sīma*); (3) status as an agent (*kāraiyattukku-kartarāna* or *kāriyattu-kaḍava*) of the king; and (4) membership of a regiment of *nāyakas* (*nāyakappāḍi*). This definition was formulated primarily for the purpose of ascertaining the actual number of *nāyakas* whose appearance is recorded in the inscriptions of each district. Nevertheless, there seems to be no reason to alter this definition in the argument for the functioning of a *nāyaka* system during a certain period of Vijayanagar rule in Tamil Nadu. Most of the individuals who have one or two of the last three qualifications (Nos. 2-4) are also qualified by having a *nāyaka* title (No. 1), though not *vice versa*, and the activities of *nāyakas* described in those inscriptions present a considerable similarity indicating the cohesion of this group. Therefore, most of those who are selected for inclusion in these lists can be regarded as belonging to the same sociopolitical group of people called '*nāyaka*.'

Table 1

| | Cg | NA | SA | TT |
|---|---|---|---|---|
| Total | 124 | 144 | 142 | 85 |
| 1351-1375 | 1 | 0 | 1 | 0 |
| 1376-1400 | 1 | 1 | 0 | 0 |
| 1401-1425 | 1 | 3 | 0 | 0 |
| 1426-1450 | 1 | 3 | 4 | 6 |
| 1451-1475 | 2 | 6 | 4 | 3 |
| 1476-1500 | 12 | 15 | 13 | 7 |
| 1501-1525 | 23 | 34 | 25 | 13 |
| 1526-1550 | 36 | 29 | 34 | 14 |
| 1551-1575 | 14 | 21 | 39 | 10 |
| 1576-1600 | 13 | 12 | 15 | 15 |
| 1601-1625 | 13 | 11 | 6 | 13 |
| 1626-1650 | 7 | 9 | 1 | 4 |

However, it is also obvious from the study of them that a certain hierarchy existed in the group, for example, between those who had close relations with the king and those who worked for some superior *nāyaka* or exercised their power in a small locality. This point remains to be studied further.

## Number of Nāyakas in the Five Districts

The names of 162 *nāyakas* as defined above were collected from the Vijayanagar inscriptions in Chingleput District (Cg) by counting the same name only once for each inscription. Of these 162, if we exclude the duplicate names appearing in more than one inscription by identifying them, there remain 124 individual *nāyakas*. Likewise, in North Arcot District (NA), out of the 222 occurrences of *nāyaka* names in the inscriptions, 144 individual *nāyakas* are counted; in South Arcot District (SA), out of 275 occurrences, 142 *nāyakas*, and Tiruchirapalli and Thanjavur Districts combined (TT, the same arrangement afterwards), out of 131 occurrences, we find 85 *nāyakas*. The chronological distributions of those individual *nāyakas* in each district are as above (Table 1).[3]

This pattern of the chronological distribution of *nāyakas* in the five districts further supports the inference I repeatedly suggested in my previous works [1992: 107; 1998: 65] that the *nāyaka* rule in Tamil Nadu was established towards the end of the fifteenth century. In studies undertaken in the past, however, some scholars have simply presumed that *nāyakas* engaged in their activities throughout the Vijayanagar period from the beginning, whereas some others have insisted that such a system was only imagined in the mind of Portuguese merchants who recorded the activities of *nāyakas* in their travels.[4] My argument that the *nāyaka* rule was established as a system towards the end of the fifteenth century is further reinforced by the emergence in the inscriptions of *nāyakattanam*, the territory bestowed by the king on *nāyakas* for their management, only from the end of the fifteenth century. The *nāyaka* system seems to have functioned in Tamil Nadu for more than one hundred years from the last quarter of the fifteenth century, even though its smooth operation seems to have been considerably disturbed towards the end of the Vijayanagar rule by the aggressive behaviour of some *nāyakas* seeking their independence.

The district-wise distribution of *nāyakas* shows us that their activities were concentrated to a considerable extent in North and South Arcot Districts, and also to a fair extent in Chingleput District. In contrast, in Tiruchirapalli and Thanjavur Districts, which were the core area of the Chola rule, we find a much lesser number of *nāyakas* reflecting the inactivity of *nāyakas* in the area except in the later period when the Thanjavur *nāyakas* increased their power. Important to note here is that one of the reasons for the concentration of *nāyakas* in North and South Arcot Districts was the evident economic development of that area during the thirteenth and fourteenth centuries as marked by the increase in the number and occurrence of the revenue terms relating to industries and commerce in inscriptions, such as *paṭṭaḍai-nūlāyam* and *taṟi-kaḍamai* [Karashima 1992: 31-32, Shanmugam 1989]. This development must have allured the Vijayanagar kings to send a larger number of *nāyakas* to the area.

In Dharmapuri, Salem, Coimbatore, Pudukkottai, Madurai, Ramanathapuram and Tirunelveli Districts, to the west and south of the above five districts, many inscriptions also yield names of *nāyakas*. However, as these districts comprised the peripheral area of the Vijayanagar rule in Tamil Nadu, I shall reserve the study of *nāyakas* in that area for some other occasion.

If we examine the taluk-wise distributions of *nāyakas* in each district, they are as follows with all occurrences of each *nāyaka* name being counted, if the inscription differs (Table 2).

The above patterns also denote some concentrations in the appearence of *nāyakas* in particular taluks, which seem to correspond to the differences in ecological and sociopolitical conditions seen among the taluks.

Table 2

| Cg | (162) | NA | (222) | SA | (275) |
|---|---|---|---|---|---|
| Chingleput | 59 | Arakkonam | 3 | Chidambaram | 60 |
| Kanchipuram | 50 | Arni | 73 | Cuddalore | 11 |
| Madhurantakam | 4 | Chengam | 15 | Gingee | 28 |
| Ponneri | 2 | Cheyyar | 14 | Kallakurichchi | 26 |
| Saidapet | 5 | Gudiyattam | 6 | Tindivanam | 31 |
| Sriperumbudur | 14 | Polur | 73 | Tirukkoyilur | 80 |
| Tiruttani | 4 | Tiruppattur | 5 | Villupuram | 30 |
| Tiruvallur | 18 | Tiruvannamalai | 8 | | |
| Madras City | 6 | Vellore | 2 | | |
| | | Walajapet | 1 | | |
| | | Wandavasi | 22 | | |

| Tp | (95) | Tj | (36) |
|---|---|---|---|
| Kulittalai | 12 | Kumbakonam | 8 |
| Lalgudi | 1 | Mannargudi | 1 |
| Musiri | 3 | Mayuram | 5 |
| Perambalur | 6 | Nagapattinam | 2 |
| Tiruchirapalli | 73 | Nannilam | 6 |
| | | Papanasam | 4 |
| | | Pattukkottai | 1 |
| | | Sirkali | 2 |
| | | Thanjavur | 7 |

Actually, those concentrations seem to derive from the existence of some important temples (for example, Kanchipuram, Chidambaram, Srirangam, etc.), *nāyaka* regiments (for example, Padaividu) or prosperous *nāyaka* families (for example, Gingee) in particular taluks.

*Nāyaka* regiments (*nāyakappāḍi*), as cited above, to which no proper attention has been paid in the past studies, may require some explanation. As I have pointed out in a previous study, [5] the *nāyakappāḍis* seem to have been organised on the basis of communities. We find in the inscriptions in our study area of this essay, Kuṟumba, Kamma and Kannaḍiya *nāyakappāḍis*, and in Pudukkottai District, a peripheral area, Kolla *nāyakappāḍi*.[6] Though Kannaḍiya cannot be said to be a community in a strict sense meaning the speakers of Kannaḍa language, Kuṟumba, Kamma and Kolla can certainly be taken as meaning particular communities, which reminds us of the community-wise organisation of the Chola army in and after the eleventh century.[7] Though the percentage of *nāyakas* belonging to these regiments remains less than five per cent, further studies will be required on this organisation. Some *nāyaka* families should also be taken up for studies through examining all of the extant inscriptions. One of the focal points in such a study of *nāyaka* families should be an examination of when and how deeply these *nāyakas* established their power locally to enable them to develop into feudal lords.

## Nāyakas' Concern with Temples and Taxation

One of the activities of the *nāyakas* conspicuously described in inscriptions is their tax remission. Sometimes they appear as executors of the king's order for remission of taxes on temples such as *jōḍi* and *sūlavari*, but more often they appear themselves to remit taxes on artisans and merchants, such as *paṭṭaḍai-nūlāyam* (consolidated tax on the people of workshops). *Kāṇikkai* (meaning 'presents'), which had weighed as the heaviest burden on the people during the early period of the Vijayanagar rule, is another kind of tax often remitted by *nāyakas* during the later period. In the Vijayanagar taxation, [8] however, we may discern three different levels of the tax-levying authority, namely those of the king, *nāyakas* and *nāṭṭavars*. Though it is no easy task to categorise individual taxes into groups according to these authority levels, *jōḍi* and *sūlavari* can be categorised as the taxes of the king's level, as they were mostly remitted by the king, as stated earlier. Likewise, *paṭṭaḍai-nūlāyam* which was mostly remitted by *nāyakas* without any reference to the king can be categorised as the tax belonging to the *nāyaka*'s level, though there are some cases in which *nāyakas* asked the king for remission or gave merit to the king in their remission. *Nāṭṭu-viniyōgam*, *nāṭṭu-kāṇikkai*, etc., the taxes relating to the *nāḍu* organisations, can be categorised as belonging to the *nāṭṭavar*'s level.

Despite the existence of those different levels of tax-levying authority, *nāyakas* seem to have handled or been involved in all the levels of taxation. As we have already seen, the king often instructed *nāyakas* to remit *jōḍi* and *sūlavari* imposed on temples. There are several sixteenth-century inscriptions in South Arcot District in which *nāṭṭavars* swore to the *nāyaka* and his agent in the locality and also to the king the remission of the taxes which the former *nāṭṭavars* had imposed on the Kaṇmāḷa community [Karashima 1992: 159]. Concerning the rights enjoyed by *nāyakas*, however, one important point remains unclear, that is, the extent to which the king controlled the taxation in *nāyakas*' territories. This point takes into consideration also the question of whether or not the so-called 'crown land' existed in the kingdom under direct management by the king's officers.

Scholars had long believed that *paṇḍāravāḍai* (*bhaṇḍāravāḍa*) was the crown land managed directly by the king's officers and that the rest of the land in the kingdom was parcelled out to *nāyakas* as their territories (*nāyakattanam*).[9] This view implied that *nāyakas* were free to manage their territory including overseeing tax collection. I have clarified elsewhere, however, that *paṇḍāravāḍai* was not the 'crown' land, but the 'taxable' land as opposed to the 'tax free' land granted to temples (*dēvadāna*) or Brāhmaṇas (*agrahāra*), and that as such it did exist in *nāyakas*' territories too [Karashima 1992: 205-8]. In support of this there are many inscriptions in which a *nāyaka* sought the king's permission for converting *paṇḍāravāḍai* in his territory into *dēvadāna* or *agrahāra*.

We may presume from the above that the king had detailed knowledge of the revenue of each *nāyaka*'s territory. In actuality we have some direct evidence supporting this point. An inscription [*AR* 1942/43-98] dated 1548 records that King Sadāsivadēvarāya sent an accountant to Sūrappa Nāyaka's territory in NA District to remit the king's portion of the taxes paid by the people to Sūrappa Nāyaka's palace. The text can also be interpreted as meaning that the king remitted the tax to be paid to the king's palace by Sūrappa Nāyaka. Either interpretation, however, affords us the opportunity to say that the king had detailed knowledge about the taxation in *nāyakas*' territories. According to another inscription [*SII*, xxiv, 363] from Srirangam dated 1513, King Krishṇadēvarāya seems to have ordered Vīrayyar Daṇṇāyaka to increase the amount of tax exemption of Srirangam temple's estate (*tiruviḍaiyāṭṭa sīmai*) instead of allowing him to take for himself (?) all the taxes in his own estate (*sīmai*) between a certain two rivers. Though the meaning of this text leaves some ambiguity concerning the tax collection in the *nāyaka*'s own *sīrmai*, this also underscores the king's detailed knowledge of the revenues of the locality and his control of the taxation 'through' *nāyakas*.

Another thing we can readily notice from the inscriptions in relation to *nāyakas* is the great interest they had in temples. All of the *nāyakas* seem to have been eager to associate themselves with the temples of his locality. There is a good number of inscriptions recording tax remission by *nāyakas* in favour of temples or the donations of land/village along with its revenue to temples. Moreover, there are some inscriptions which record the appointment of a *nāyaka* as a temple functionary such as an administrator (*sthāna-nirvāham*), guardian of the sacred precincts (*tirumēni-kāval*), watchman (*talārikkam*) of temple villages, and the like

[Karashima 1992: 25]. As many of the temples of this period developed into huge economic institutions, each possessing a great many villages and conducting daily public services on a grand scale, their association with a temple must have considerably benefitted *nāyakas* in innumerable ways. As a prime example, Tirumalai Nāyaka of Padaividu appears in one inscription as one of the temple authorities in the assignment of a temple land to a certain individual, and in some other inscriptions he himself appears as the lessee of a temple village [Karashima 1992: 21].

As is evident from the past studies, artisans such as weavers, smiths and oil-pressers were given accommodation in temple streets together with certain merchants, and temples seem to have even controlled their production activities [Mahalingam 1955: 378-79]. As *nāyakas* were quite eager to develop industries in their territory, they naturally encouraged artisans and merchants by remitting the taxes such as *paṭṭaḍai-nūlāyam* and endeavoured to control those who were living in temple streets. For *nāyakas*, temples must have been important in that sense also. Additional significance that temples had for *nāyakas* concerns their function as an important communications means in the state ruling network. As will be discussed later, the stone walls of temples functioned as the message board, through which *nāyakas* publicised their charity as well as their relations with the king and locality. All such clearly advantageous aspects must have been a source of prompting for the *nāyakas* to maintain their association with temples in a variety of ways.

## Nāyakas' Relations with the King

Here we shall examine the specific relation these *nāyakas* had with the king. As stated earlier, many *nāyakas* held *nāyakattanams* as their own territory (*sīrmai*), and there are some cases in which their *nāyakattanams* are specifically stated as having been bestowed by a certain king. For example, Chiṉṉa Chevvappa Nāyaka (TT) was bestowed his *nāyakattana-sīrmai* by Srīraṅgadēvarāya [*AR* 1968/69-275], Muttuveṅkaṭappa Nāyaka (SA) also by the same king [*AR* 1936/37-254], and Sūrappa Nāyaka (SA) by Sadāsivadēvarāya [*AR* 1937/38-465]. Though subinfeudation cases are also seen in inscriptions, in which a superior *nāyaka* bestowed a part of his *nāyakattanam* on his subordinate *nāyaka*,[10] it is presumed that all the *nāyakattanams* were initially bestowed by one king or another.

Some *nāyakas* were designated as *aḍaippam* (page as a betel bearer) showing their close relation to the king, for example, or as *mahā-pradhā-*

Table 3

| Designations | Cg | NA | SA | TT | Total |
|---|---|---|---|---|---|
| *Mahāmaṇḍalēśvara* (provincial governor) | 3 | 1 | | | 4 |
| *Mahāsāmantadhipati* (provincial governor?) | | | | 1 | 1 |
| *Mahāpradhāni* (chief minister/governor) | | 1 | | 1 | 2 |
| *Pradhāni* (minister) | | | 1 | | 1 |
| *Rājyam-kartar* (*pārapattiyam*) (governor) | 1 | | 2 | | 3 |
| *Daḷavāy* (commander) | 5 | 2 | 1 | | 8 |
| *Vāsal* (chief palace guard) | 5 | 2 | 5 | 2 | *8[11] |
| *Aḍaippam* (page bearing betelnuts) | 4 | 4 | 3 | 1 | *11 |
| *Kāriyattu-kaḍava* (agent of the king) | 7 | 2 | 5 | | 14 |
| *Avasaram* (writer) | | | 1 | | 1 |
| *Sēvagam* (servant) | 5 | | | | 5 |
| *Pāda-sērvai* (royal servant) | | | | 1 | 1 |
| *Mugappāvāḍai* (page bearing a towel) | 1 | 2 | | | 3 |
| *Bokkisham* (state accountant) | | 1 | | 1 | 2 |
| *Vāsal-karaṇikkam* (court accountant) | | 1 | | | 1 |
| *Ūḻiyam* (servant) | 1 | | | | 1 |
| *Pallakku-sērvai* (palanquin guard) | | 1 | | | 1 |
| *Taṇḍu* (palanquin officer) | 1 | | | | 1 |
| *Kaṭṭiyam* (herald) | | 1 | 1 | | 2 |
| Total | 30[12] | 19 | 19 | 7 | |
| Number of *nāyakas* | 124 | 144 | 142 | 85 | |

*ni* (chief minister/governor) indicating their ranking position in the government. If we select such cases for analysis, they appear district-wise as above (Table 3).

Though the study of these designations remains insufficient to reveal the actual function of their offices in some cases, there is no doubt that they represent important offices in the Vijayanagar court and government. Table 3 shows us therefore that 10 - 20 per cent (16 per cent on average) of *nāyakas* of the regions served the king in his court or in the government as important officials and attendants, This immediately brings to memory the statement made by Nunes, the Portuguese merchant who stayed at Vijayanagar during Achyutadēvarāya's reign, that '200 captains (*nāyakas*) were always with the king at the capital' and that 'only sometimes they visited their territory, where they had their agent for its management' [Sewell 1970: 355]. Though we are not certain at present how many *nāyakas* existed in the Vijayanagar kingdom during each of the king's reigns, there is no doubt that a certain number of *nāyakas* were required to stay at the capital to serve the king directly or to work in the government as important functionaries. This is further proof that *nāyakas* were neither local magnates who exercised their political power in their own right nor merely a group of intruding military leaders as both presumed by Stein [1980: 423; 1982: 105]. Indeed, their political power was legitimised and delegated only by the king.

Another noticeable fact concerning the relations *nāyakas* had with the king is the practice of a great many *nāyakas* giving religious merit (*puṇṇiyam* or *danmam*) to the king in their charity deeds such as donation of land/village to a temple or tax remission in favour of a temple. This act of merit-giving to the king can be interpreted as a way of showing *nāyakas*' fidelity to the king with the purpose of strengthening their position in the state ruling system or securing the king's favour by pleasing him. Surely there must have been many things for which they wished to seek the favour of the king. Notably some inscriptions record a *nāyaka*'s request to the king for the remission of taxes on a certain temple in his territory. In one of them [*AR* 1934/35-60] we are told that Timmappa Nāyaka, who succeeded in having the temple exempted from certain taxes through his request to the king, received in turn some villages for his own management from the temple.

An interesting aspect of the relations between the king and *nāyakas* is revealed by two sets of records on the rebellious *nāyakas* in both inscriptions and literature. First, two Kanchipuram inscriptions [*AR* 1919-584, *SII*, xvi, 102] tell us that when the improper execution of Achyutadēvarāya's order by Sāḷuva Nāyaka (Chellappa) came to be known, the king went himself to Kanchipuram to implement his desire that an equal number of villages be granted to Varadarāja and Ēkāmbaranātha temples in Kanchipuram. Moreover, Rājanātha Ḍiṇḍima's *Achyutarāyābhyudayam* records the story that the rebellious Chellappa was chased down for punishment by a general sent by Achyutadēvarāya [Ayyangar 1919: 158]. This is confirmed to a certain extent by another inscription [*SII*, xxii-1, 253] denoting that Vīranarasiṅgarāya Nāyaka (Chellappa), who had not executed Krishṇadēvarāya's order of tax remission for a temple, was chased and caught in Travancore by Tirumalai Nāyaka. In the second set, according to the *Kōyil Oḻugu* (Temple History) of Srirangam temple [Sastri and Venkataramanyya 1946: 76-77] and also to *Achyutarāyābhyudayam* [Ayyangar 1919: 108-9], Kōnēridēva, a *mahāmaṇḍalēśvara* ruling the Tiruchirapalli area who oppressed Srirangam temple by imposing maliciously heavier tax on it, was finally subdued by the army led by Narasā Nāyaka (a *de facto* king). Contemporary inscriptions in the Tiruchirapalli area reveal his rebellious disposition towards the king [Karashima 1992: 74-78] which must have been the reason for his being subdued and summarily punished.

The above examinations demonstrate that all the Vijayanagar *nāyakas* in the study area participated in the state administration in one way or other and were placed under the control and vigilance of the king. Their relations with the king revealed by inscriptions was nothing other than 'political.'

## South Indian Kingship

We shall explore here the issues of kingship more generally by also examining the incidents of other south Indian states. To do so, we must first consider the character of our source material, that is the inscriptions. The majority of the inscriptions are, as is well known, engraved on stone walls of temples, though we have some number of inscriptions engraved on copper plates preserved in a house or on rocks in a hill or stone slabs planted in a field. The inscriptions on temple walls record mostly the donation of certain objects including land/village to the temple by people including a royal family, or the remission of taxes by tax-levying authorities such as the king, local chiefs or *nāyakas*, *nāṭṭavars* (*nāṭṭars*), etc. in favour of the temples. However, inscriptions recording tax remission in favour of the locality or certain communities do appear having nothing to do with the temples on the walls of which they are engraved. Still others record the political compact between local chiefs or the resolution of the villagers on some matter or of the people who rose up in open revolt against the oppression laid upon them by some authority. This variety in the contents of temple inscriptions suggests that these inscriptions had in essence a proclamatory character, which was closely related to the function of temples as the nexus of local as well as state communication networks. Of course, temple walls were also used as a sort of storage for preserving the records of important matters, but even more significantly, they were primarily used as the message board for and by the contemporaries of the locality.[13]

Another important feature of these inscriptions, particularly from the perspective of kingship studies, is their mentioning of the king's name usually in the initial part. Though the actual ways of mentioning differ to a certain extent from dynasty to dynasty, most of the temple inscriptions have a passage referring to the ruling king with his regnal year, being accompanied further, in the case of certain later dynasties, by the year in the Śaka/Kali era and/or a cyclic year. In those regions (or times) where (or when) the Śaka era was unfamiliar to the local people, the king's regnal years served as dates. However, reference continued to be made to the king's name in the Vijayanagar inscriptions in Tamil Nadu together with the year in the Śaka era or in some other dating system. This reference to the ruling king is thus inferred to have had some meaning other than dating. If we consider the message-board function of the temple walls and inscriptions, it is quite understandable that the king's name was a prominent part of the inscription, through which he wished to convey his message to the local people.

By way of example, during the Chola period, Rājarāja I introduced a new practice of putting a standardised eulogy (*praśasti/ meykkīrti*) of the king into most of the temple inscriptions [Krishnan 1981: 157]. His victory in a battle or his conquest of an enemy's territory was added to the eulogy within a year or so, showing a remarkable uniformity of his eulogy in the inscriptions. This type of eulogy-making that he had established was followed by the kings succeeding him including those of other dynasties, showing clearly the effort by those subsequent kings to make the people of their kingdom aware of their glorious achievements and even feel their presence in the locality. This was certainly a stratagem for ensuring that the kingship penetrated into every locality of the kingdom.

At the same time, however, if we look at the matter from the viewpoint of local people, the reference to the king's reign must also have meant their recognition of, or support given to, the king. In the Islamic world there was a practice of referring to the ruling king in the *khuṭba* conducted every Friday in the main mosque of the locality, which embodied the local people's recognition of the king. Thus, the king's name to which reference was made in temple inscriptions must have incorporated both such double meanings of penetration and recognition of the kingship as well as occasionally revealing the tension existing between the ruler and the ruled. It thus goes without saying that the area in which the inscriptions are found bearing a king's name constituted the kingdom. It is interesting to notice that the *nāyakas* who established practically independent power in some area towards the end of the Vijayanagar rule often omitted the names of the Vijayanagar kings in their inscriptions. The same was the case of the two *nāyakas* who became rebellious in the lower valley of Kaveri River during the fifteenth century [Karashima 1992: 72-81].

Another point we have to consider is the problem of revenue collection by the king in the form of various taxes levied on the people and products. A large number of tax terms appear in temple inscriptions, with 422 different terms having been collected from the published Chola inscriptions [Karashima 1984: 74-84] and 635 terms from both the published and unpublished Vijayanagar inscriptions in Tamil Nadu [Karashima 1992: 186]. At first glance, these large figures may cast some doubt on the existence of any clear taxation policy in those kingdoms. If we examine the frequency of their appearing in the inscriptions, however, it will become apparent that in the Chola kingdom seven particular terms commonly appear in all four periods of the Chola rule and in both the two main areas of the kingdom (Chōḻamaṇḍalam and Jayaṅkoṇḍachōḻamaṇḍalam) more than twenty times.[14] This is also true in the Vijayanagar kingdom where five terms appear in all seven periods of its rule and in all the four divisions of the present study area for more than twenty times.[15] The distinct frequency in the appearance of these select terms confirms the existence of certain revenue policies in force in these kingdoms. However, the composition of these basically important terms differs from one kingdom to another reflecting the independent revenue policy of each kingdom.[16]

If we compare the percentage of the inscriptions recording tax remission as their main purpose among the whole inscriptional corpus of each state between the Chola and Vijayanagar states, the percentage of the Vijayanagar inscriptions seems to be greater with a large number of them actually noting that kings or *nāyakas* remitted certain taxes in favour of a temple or a certain locality. The Chola inscriptions on the other hand record as their main purpose the land/village donations to temples or Brāhmaṇas, but always specify whether the tax is to be paid by the donor or by some corporate bodies in the locality or is to be relinquished and exempted by the higher authority. Thus, in both cases these inscriptions reveal that the tax was a great concern for both the king and the locality. Concerning the exaction of tax, tension or conflict is seen to have often arisen between the ruler and the ruled. During the early Vijayanagar period, many instances of peasants' or artisans' desertion of their village or workshop occurred because of the heavy burden of taxes levied on them.[17] The severity of this oppression can be understood by the open revolt in the fifteenth century of the peasants and artisans against the Vijayanagar administrators as well as their landlords [Karashima 1992: 141-58].

The revenue collection made by the king from his subjects in the form of tax was one form of the warranted and legitimised conduct of the king as set out in the *Dharmaśāstras*. The king had the right to collect from his subjects usually one-sixth of their produce. At the same time, though, it was the king's duty to protect his subjects from invasions by outsiders and to maintain the social order to ensure that they could live peacefully [Mahalingam 1955: 22, 162]. The idea that social disorder would prevail if there was no (righteous) king has repeatedly been expressed in literary sources, and it is interesting to find confirmation of this idea in the inscriptions. The phrases given to the traitors to an established social order, such as *rāja-durōhi* (traitor to the ruler), *nāṭṭu-durōhi* (traitor to the locality), *iṉa-durōhi* (traitor to the community) and *śiva-durōhi* (traitor to the god), appear mostly in the inscriptions of the thirteenth and fourteenth centuries in the northern part of Tamil Nadu[18] after the decline of the Cholas but before the establishment of the Vijyanagar power, namely the place and time for which no 'proper' king ruled.

The thirteenth and fourteenth centuries also mark the period when the people of the lower stratum of society organised themselves into large territorial assemblies such as *periya-nāḍu* for their own protection or into certain community-based assemblies such as *valaṅgai* (right hand) and *iḍaṅgai* (left hand) challenging the hierarchical social order which had been created and maintained by the people of the upper stratum, namely the Veḷḷāḷas and Brāhmaṇas [Karashima 1992: 141-58; Aiyer 1955]. In contrast, during the heydays of the Cholas and the Vijayanagar kings, no such symptom of social disorder or protest appeared, though we do not know whether or not the people were indeed content with the state rule of the time. The most important means for maintaining the order in society was without any doubt the military power (*daṇḍa*) exercised by the king. Protection and punishment are the two sides of the authority coin. Regarding the use of military power for punishment, we have already seen the case of Chellappa Nāyaka who, for betraying the king's order, was chased down and caught by another *nāyaka* during Achyutadēvarāya's reign. Some other similar cases are also citable. Concerning protection, however, inscriptions provide us with only a few examples. Rare among them is the assurance of protection given by Muttukrishṇappa Nāyaka to those people (*kuḍis*) who desired to come and settle in the newly established street in Chidambaram that 'they need not be afraid of anything other than the fury of the wind and the heat of the sun' [Karashima 1992: 27].

Lastly we shall consider the sociopolitical relations between the king and the ruling elite who worked for the state as intermediaries between the king and common people in their locality. During the Chola period, particularly in its earlier half, the ruling elite comprised basically the local leaders (*nāṭṭars*) of the landholding Veḷḷāḷa community, on which was based the king's power. They must therefore have claimed their special relations with the king simply on the basis of their being local leaders of the Veḷḷāḷa community. However, Rājarāja I attempted to reform their relations with him for the purpose of building a systematic administration system under the Brahmanical (or Iranian) idea brought from the north [Karashima 1984: xxvi]. In doing so, he assigned them and some members of other communities also to certain offices such as *srīkāriyam* (officials in charge of temples), *tiṇaikkaḷam* (revenue officials) and *karaṇam* (accountants), and conferred on them such titles as *mūvēndavēḷān*, *pallavarayan*, *viḻupparayan*. In recruiting them, the king probably also considered their personal quality in addition to their communal identity.

At the same time, the Chola kings attempted to depend on the sociocultural strength of the Brāhmaṇa community to facilitate their state administration, for which they granted villages to a large number of Brāhmaṇas who were invited from the Deccan and recruited them as officials in their government under the title of *brahmarāyan*.[19] Thus, these Veḷḷāḷa and Brāhmaṇa officials constituted the ruling elite in the Chola state, and the ideology which provided a strong basis for the Chola ruling system was communal as well as Brahmanical [Veluthat 1993: 17-19]. However, we need not take this concept of the Chola kings of incorporating Brāhmaṇas into the state ruling system in its narrow 'religious' sense. Even though Rājarāja I is thought to have tried to deify himself in the form of a *liṅga* enshrined in the Brihadīśvara temple in Thanjavur, this should also be understood in the broader context of his effort to centralise the state under his powerful hegemony [Ogura 1998].

In the Vijayanagar state, the intermediaries serving between the king and local people were certainly *nāyakas*. As already stated, *nāyakas* were granted their territory (*nāyakattanam)* by the king and ruled it on his as well as on their own behalf, though there were some *nāyakas* who served other *nāyakas* instead of serving the king directly. Such subordinate *nāyakas* were granted their territory by the *nāyakas* who were considered superior in their serving the king and for whom they worked in turn. However, all *nāyakas* were in effect responsible to the king, whether directly or indirectly, for the management of their respective territories and for fielding soldiers for participation in military campaigns. According to Nunes, they had to remit to the king a certain proportion of the revenues of their territory as well as to maintain the prescribed military forces for the king's command [Sewell 1970: 370]. In their own territories, however, they behaved as the lords having under them their own agents, or some intermediary class of people such as *nāṭṭavar*, who controlled the production and trade in their locality.

Judging from their names, most of the *nāyakas* who worked in the study area must have been either Kannaḍigas or Telugus, though it is not so easy to ascertain their community. In *Rāyavācakamu*, we come across at least two different communities of *nāyakas*,[20] and *nāyakappāḍis* in the inscriptions suggest the existence of more than three other communities among *nāyakas*. Certainly, there must have been some *nāyakas* who were related to the royal family. However, the communal identity or relations similar to those existing between the early Chola kings and their ruling elite cannot be surmised to have existed between the Vijayanagar kings and the *nāyakas*. The Vijayanagar territory was vast indeed, incorporating into it quite a variety of communities belonging to different language groups. Communal relations could therefore not have been the main ideological base that tied the king with the *nāyakas*.

Rather the substantial tie that bonded the king and the *nāyakas* to ensure state rule cannot be anything other than the bestowal of a *nāyaka*-ship (*nāyakattanam* in the real sense of the word) on them. Being obligated by the granting of territory to them for their management, the *nāyakas* swore their fidelity to the king, remitting to him a certain proportion of the revenue generated in their territory and maintaining for him a certain military force. Importantly, this granting of a *nāyaka*-ship seems to have been made based mostly on the personal quality or merit of each *nāyaka* and not on the consideration of any special relations such as particular inter-community relations [Ota 1998].

Though we are not sure at present from where this idea of granting *nāyakattanam* derived, if not from the Kakatiyas or the Hoysalas, its apparent resemblance to the granting of *iqṭā'*, *soyūrghāl* or *jāgīr* in some Islamic countries cannot be denied. Though many scholars including Nicholas B. Dirks [1987] regard this relation seen between the king and a *nāyaka* as that of gift-giving and -receiving practised in the Brahmanical social order, we would be better to regard it as a political tool common to many different cultures.[21]

In conclusion, we may say that the relation the king had with local peoples through intermediaries changed in accordance with the development of the social formation, and accordingly also changed the ideology which supported the kingship. The study of Indian kingship from the perspective of Brahmanical rituals basing on examination of ancient religious texts or on analysis of the present-day caste relations and rituals has contributed greatly to our understanding of Indian society. To gain an even better understanding of Indian society, however, further study should also be encouraged from the aspect of historical development or inevitable changes in society by examining such contemporary source materials as inscriptions.

## Notes

1 I am extremely thankful to Prof. Y. Subbarayalu of Tamil University and Prof. P. Shanmugam of Madras University, who greatly helped me in collecting inscriptional materials and in reading them for this study. Permission for access to the unpublished inscriptions was granted by Drs. K.V. Ramesh, M.N. Katti and M.D. Sampath, Directors of Epigraphy, Archaeological Survey of India, to all of whom I am very grateful.

2 One of the key points of the 'segmentary state' theory put forward by Burton Stein, to which I am not in agreement, is the idea of 'ritual sovereignty'. He denied the king's exercise of 'political sovereignty' over the kingdom, and according to him, both the Chola *nāṭṭars* and the Vijayanagar *nāyakas* were politically independent from the authority of the king who exercised only his ritual sovereignty over them. The main purpose of my previous study [1998] was to dispute this idea. In the final stage of his study, however, Stein abandoned his previous idea on sovereignty, suggesting rather the combination of its 'ritual' and 'political' aspects [1991]. Other scholars have also argued for the combination of these two aspects in their interpretation of the Indian kingship [Dirks 1987; Kulke 1982; Chattopadhyaya 1983] even prior to Stein, which is more reasonable and acceptable to me. However, this idea of combining ritual and political, or religious and secular, depends heavily, in some cases, on the anthropological analyses of the Brahmanical texts as well as on the present-day caste relations and seems to pose the danger of blurring the significance of historical development or change of the state and society. The purpose of this essay is therefore to review the political aspect of kingship from the perspective of the historical development of the state and society, specifically to swing purposefully the pendulum to the opposite end in an endeavour to reinfuse the historicity into the study of Indian kingship.

3 In order to equate as closely as possible the chronology of *nāyakas* to the actual events as they presumably occurred, I have deducted 25 years from the year of the inscription, if the *nāyaka* is stated as the father of the *nāyaka* who had the inscription recorded. In a like measure, I deducted 50 years for a grandfather, 20 years for an uncle, and 10 years for an elder brother.

4 Strangely enough, neither the scholars who argued for the working of the *nāyaka* system nor the opponents of such an interpretation have ever done

empirical studies on *nāyakas* by examining the inscriptional texts. For this, see [Karashima 1992: 83].

5 N. Karashima, 'Nāyakappadis Appearing in Vijayayanagar Tamil Inscriptions,' M.D. Sampath ed., *Shri K.G. Krishnan Felicitation Volume*, Mysore, forthcoming.

6 This Kolla-*nāyakappāḍi* seems to have been located in Togamalai in Tiruchirapalli District, for which see *IPS*, 710.

7 We have evidence on the working of the Paḷḷi and Churutimān communities as soldiers. For Paḷḷis, see [Subbarayalu 1981] and for Churutimāns, see [Karashima 1984: 30].

8 For the Vijayanagar taxation, see [Karashima 1992: 183-204; Karashima *et al.* 1993: 37-51].

9 The view expressed by N. Venkataramanyya [1935: 170] has been simply followed by Burton Stein [1980: 412, 420] and others.

10 Achchutappa Nāyaka seems to have obtained his *nāyakattanam* from his lord Koṇḍama Nāyaka [*SII*, xvi, 294, 295]. Another Koṇḍama Nāyaka received Vīrapāṇḍyanallur-sīrmai from Nalankishṭṭaṇappa Nāyaka [*AR* 1934/35-240].

11 In the case of the numbers with an asterisk in this 'Total' column, some deduction is made for the same *nāyaka(s)* appearing across the districts.

12 The figure 30 is obtained by deducting three *nāyakas* of *kāriyattu-kaḍava*, who are also *daḷavāy*, from the total number (33) for Cg.

13 This aspect of temple inscriptions has been discussed in [Karashima 1996].

14 The seven terms are *antarāyam, ech-chōṟu, kaḍamai, kuḍimai, muṭṭaiy-āḷ, taṭṭār-pāṭṭam* and *veṭṭi*. See [Karashima 1984: 72].

15 The five terms are *āḷ-amañji, kāṇikkai, maravaḍai, māvaḍai* and *taṟik-kaḍamai*. See [Karashima 1992: 229].

16 If we compare the seven basic taxes of the Chola period with the five of the Vijayanagar period, the difference in their taxation is clear. The Pandyan taxes also attest to this. See [Karashima 1984: 112-13].

17 N. Karashima, 'Weavers' Desertion of Their Places in Fifteenth-Century Tamil Nadu,' *Dr. K.V. Ramesh Felicitation Volume*, Mysore, forthcoming.

18 *SITI*, 525 (*śiva*, *nāṭṭu*, *iṉa*, A.D. 1342); *SII*, vii, 118 (*rāja*, *nāṭṭu*, A.D. 1258?); *IPS*, 340, 341 (*rāja*, *matru*, *nāṭṭu*, Sundara-Pāṇḍya-7); *IPS*-285 (*nāṭṭu*, *śiva*, Sundara-Pāṇḍya-13?); *SII*, vi-58 (*nāṭṭu*, *guru*, Rājarāja III-23); *SII*, vi-456 (*śiva*, Rājādhirāja?); *AR* 1943/44-268 (*śiva*, *nāṭṭu*, Rājarāja III-17).

19 For the title of *brahmarāyan*, see [Karashima 1984: 58-60], and for the migration of Brāhmaṇas, see the introduction of [Krishnan 1984].

20 Reḍḍis and Kammas are referred to therein, for which see [Wagoner 1993: 121].

21 Wagoner discusses the problem of Islamic culture adopted in the Vijayanagar court [1996].

## References

Aiyer, K.V. Subrahmanya

1955 'Largest Provincial Organizations in Ancient India,' *Quarterly Journal of the Mythic Society*, NS. vol. 45 (1954-55), no. 1, pp. 29-47, no. 2, pp. 70-98, no. 4, pp. 270-86 and vol. 46 (1955), no. 1, pp. 8-22.

Ayyangar, S. Krishnaswami

1919 *Sources of Vijayanagar History*, University of Madras, Madras.

Chattopadhyaya, Brajadulal

1983 'Political Process and the Structure of Polity in Early Medieval India: Ploblems of Perspective,' Presidential Address. Ancient India Section, *Proceedings of the Indian History Congress*, 44th Sesion, Burdwan, later reprinted in Chattopadhyaya, *The Making of Early Medieval India*, Oxford University Press, Delhi, 1994 and [Kulke 1995].

Dirks, Nicholas B.

1987 *The Hollow Crown: Ethnohistory of an Indian Kingdom*, Cambridge University Press, Cambridge.

Karashima, Noboru

1984 *South Indian History and Society: Studies from Inscriptions A.D. 850-1800*, Oxford University Press, New Delhi.

1990 'Vijayanagar Nayakas in Chingleput District Inscriptions,' *The Memoirs of the Institute of Oriental Culture*, The University of Tokyo, No. 112, pp. 93-135, later in [Karashima 1992: 83-113].

1992 *Towards a New Formation: South Indian Society Under Vijayanagar Rule*, Oxford University Press, New Delhi.

1996 'South Indian Temple Inscriptions: A New Approach to Their Study,' *South Asia*, NS. XIX-1, pp. 1-12.

1998 'Vijayanagar Nāyaka and King: An Examination of Nāyakas in North Arcot District Inscriptions,' *Acta Asiatica* 74 (*Kingship in South Indian History*, ed. N. Karashima), pp. 59-99.

Forthcoming (a) 'Weavers' Desertion of Their Places in Fifteenth-Century Tamil Nadu,' *Dr. K.V. Ramesh Felicitation Volume*, Mysore.

Forthcoming (b) 'Nāyakappadis Appearing in Vijayayanagar Tamil Inscriptions,' M.D. Sampath ed., *Shri K.G. Krishnan Felicitation Volume*, Mysore.

Karashima, Noboru *et al.*

1993 (Y. Subbarayalu, P. Shanmugam, M.N. Katti and Cynthia Talbot) 'A Statistical Study of Revenue Terms in Vijayanagar Inscriptions,' *Journal of the Epigraphical Society of India*, No. 19, pp. 37-51.

Krishnan, K.G.

1981 *Studies in South Indian History and Epigraphy*, New Era Publications, Madras.

1984 *Karandai Tamil Sangam Plates of Rajendrachola I*, Archaeological Survey of India, New Delhi.

Kulke, Hermann

1982 'Fragmentation and Segmentation Versus Integration? Reflections on the Concept of Indian Feudalism and the Segmentary State in Indian History,' *Studies in History* 4, pp. 237-63.

1995 (ed.) *The State in India 1000-1700*, Oxford University Press, New Delhi.

Mahalingam, T. V.

1955 *South Indian Polity*, University of Madras, Madras.

Ogura, Yasushi

1998 'The Changing Concept of Kingship in the Cōḷa Period: Royal Temple Construction, ca. A.D. 850-1279,' *Acta Asiatica* 74 (*Kingship in South Indian History*, ed. N. Karashima), pp. 39-58.

Ota, Nobuhiro

1998 'Beda Nayakas and Their Historical Narratives in Karnataka during the Post-Vijayanagara Period,' *Acta Asiatica* 74 (*Kingship in South Indian History*, ed. N. Karashima), pp. 100-128.

Sastri, K.A. Nilakanta and Venkataramanyya, N.

1946 *Further Sources of Vijayanagara History*, Vol. III, University of Madras, Madras.

Sewell, Robert

1970 *A Forgotten Empire*, second Indian edition, India Book House, New Delhi.

Shanmugam, P.

1989 'Pattadai and Industries in the Tamil Country under the

Vijayanagar Rule,' *Journal of Asian and African Studies* 37, (Tokyo), pp. 31-49.

Stein, Burton

1980 *Peasant State and Society in Medieval South India*, Oxford University Press, New Delhi.

1982 'Vijayanagar c. 1350-1564,' Tapan Raychaudhuri and Irfan Habib eds., *The Cambridge Economic History of India*, vol. I, Cambridge University Press, Cambridge (Indian edition, Orient Longman, Hyderabad, 1984).

1991 'The Segmentary State: Interim Reflections,' *Purusartha*, vol. 13, later reprinted in [Kulke 1995].

Subbarayalu, Y.

1981 'Social Change in Tamil Nadu in Twelfth and Thirteenth Centuries,' paper read at the Second Annual Conference of South Indian History Congress, Trivandrum.

Veluthat, Kesavan

1993 *The Political Structure of Early Medieval South India*, Orient Longman, Hyderabad.

Venkataramanyya, N.

1935 *Studies of the History of the Third Dynasty of Vijayanagara*, University of Madras, Madras.

Wagoner, Phillip B.

1993 *Tidings of the King: A Translation and Ethnological Analysis of the Rayavacakamu*, University of Hawaii Press, Honolulu.

1996 '"Sultan among Hindu Kings": Dress, Titles, and the Islamicization of Hindu Culture at Vijayanagara,' *The Journal of Asian Studies* 55-4, pp. 851-80.

7

# Bēḍa Nāyakas and their Historical Narratives in Karnataka during the Post-Vijayanagara Period

NOBUHIRO OTA

## Introduction

In the southern Deccan plateau after the decline of the Vijayanagara kingship caused by its defeat in the battle of Raksasi Tamgadi in A.D. 1565, many politico-military leaders descended from the semi-tribal Bēḍa caste and, bearing the title of *nāyaka* (hereafter called Bēḍa Nāyakas), ruled their own estates semi-autonomously for almost two centuries. They did so until the Mysore kingdom under the *de facto* kings Hyder Ali and Tippu Sultan established its centralised dominance over the region in the late eighteenth century.

The focus of this essay is on the 'histories' of two families of Bēḍa Nāyakas, one residing in the eastern part of present-day Chitradurga district and the other in the northern part of present-day Tumkur district. 'Histories' here refer to the narratives as made up and believed by these families rather than to chronological accounts of what actually happened to them. The sources are two family histories,[1] namely the *Niḍugallu Arasugaḷa Vaṃśāvaḷi* (Family history of the Nidugallu kings)[2] and *Nāyakanahaṭṭi Bakhairu* (Memoir of Nayakanahatti),[3] which are respectively the genealogical accounts of the two Nāyakas of Nidugallu[4] and Nayakanahatti that were written down in the late eighteenth century. In these texts I will mainly deal not with the chronologically later parts, which are, comparatively speaking, of more historical value, but with the more 'fictional' and legendary parts covering their distant ancestors from the mythic founders to the estate-building direct progenitors.

Needless to say, the vanities and hopes of little kings who believed or wanted others to believe that they had great ancestors, long histories as rulers, and great power are woven into these ancestor legends. Therefore, any attempt to reconstruct their history by uncritically utilising them will invariably fail. The study by Citraliṃgayya [1987], though it is almost the one and only work entirely devoted to the histories of the Bēḍa Nāyakas in eastern Chitradurga, must be said to be one example of such a failure. But my main concern here is not to expose the fictitiousness of these narrative histories but rather to discover the logic and terminology on the basis of which these 'fictional' histories were invented and narrated, the self-perceptions represented therein, and the historical context that needed or made possible such self-perceptions.

As for studies of family histories in south India, the work of Dirks [1987b] must not be left unmentioned. He applied the method of structural analysis to the family history of a little king in the Tamil region and tried to clarify the narrative structure inherent in the text. By way of contrast, I would like to locate the text in its historical context and consider the meaning of the self-perceptions of the Bēḍa Nāyakas appearing in the texts in relation to the historical and political circumstances in which they were situated when the texts were composed. Therefore, besides an analysis of the texts themselves, I shall try to reconstruct their history as far as possible on the basis of contemporary inscriptions[5] and other source materials.[6] With regard to the inscriptions, I will also pay considerable attention to their eulogistic and panegyric parts (*biruḍāvaḷi*), which praise the accomplishments and characters of the kings and their ancestors, as representations of their self-perceptions.

Here I would like to state my premise in dealing with the self-perceptions of the Bēḍa Nāyakas. The identity of the Bēḍa Nāyakas is, as their name suggests, a compound of two essentially contradictory identities, 'Bēḍa' and '*nāyaka*.' As is shown later, this duality is reflected in their ancestor legends. My interpretation of *nāyaka* identity is as follows. It is well known that many military leaders with the title of *nāyaka* played active and important roles in the history of the Vijayanagara kingdom. Their social backgrounds and origins were diverse and their identity as *nāyakas* was primarily defined in relation to the Vijayanagara kings to whom they offered military services and whose sovereignty they shared through gifts of symbolic resources such as titles, emblems and lands. In this sense, *nāyaka* is a generic term for military leaders, and they can be understood to form a non-descent and non-caste 'open status group.'[7] Therefore, the *nāyaka* identity is fundamentally contradictory to Bēḍa identity based on descent and caste. My concern is to trace the process whereby these seemingly incompatible identities came to coalesce in the personalities of the Bēḍa Nāyakas and their historical circumstances.

## The History of the Bēḍa Nāyakas in Eastern Chitradurga

First let us briefly consider the internal structure of the Bēḍa caste.[8] The Bēḍa caste was broadly divided into the two endogamous groups of Myāsa Bēḍas and Ūra Bēḍas with the majority of Bēḍa Nāyakas belonging to the former. The Myāsa Bēḍas are subdivided into several exogamous groups called *beḍagu* in Kannada. The Nidugallus and Nayakanahattis, along with the Nāyakas of Ratnagiri[9] and Hosakote[10] in eastern Chitradurga, belonged to one of these *beḍagus* called Enumalōru. In addition, the Nāyakas of Chitradurga and Samtebennuru, for instance, belonged respectively to the Kāmagēti and Pūvala *beḍagu*.

That the above-mentioned four Bēḍa Nāyakas in eastern Chitradurga belonged to the same exogamous clan is reflected in their historical narratives. The genealogy of Raṃgappa Nāyaka of Ratnagiri recorded in an inscription [*EC*, xi, Hr-6] dated Śālivāhana Śakha year of 1514 (hereafter abbreviated as S; the roughly corresponding Christian era is gained by adding 78 years) starts with a founder whose name is indecipherable because of physical damage, and he was followed by Kāmi (i.e., Kāma), Abbi (i.e., Abbe) and Kāma in genealogical order. The genealogy of the Nidugallus given in their inscriptions and the *NAV* begins with the founder named Tippa, and he was succeeded by Kāma, Abbe and Bomma. One finds that, though the founder is not ascertainable, these two genealogies are identical with regard to the names of their ancestors in the second and third generations, and the brothers of the fourth generation, Bomma and Kāma, are assumed to have been the direct progenitors of the Nidugallus and Ratnagiris respectively. The genealogical table of the Hosakotes attached to the *NAV* also made Īśvara, a brother of Bomma, the progenitor of the Hosakotes. Their history as estate rulers in the region started in the mid-sixteenth century, in the case of the Nidugallus with Hoṭṭeṇṇa of the third generation after the aforesaid Bomma, and in the case of the Ratnagiris with Lakṣmīpati of the ninth generation after Kāma, Bomma's brother. As is suggested by this difference in the number of generations covering the same period, these genealogies must be considered spurious.

We find another representation of the common genealogical identification shared by the four Bēḍa Nāyakas in the legend of brothers who divided and inherited the ancestral estate. The 'Account of Indrandroog' says that Yallappa Nāyaka of Hosakote, Timmaṇṇa Nāyaka of Nidugallu, Saraja Raṃgappa Nāyaka of Ratnagiri, and Mallappa Nāyaka of Nayakanahatti were brothers and divided the ancestral estate among themselves and ruled their own parts respectively [*MNM*, 422]. According to the 'Historical Account of Doodairee,' Tippa, the mythic founder of the Nidugallus, was given by 'Narasinxloo Kistna Rayaloo' (i.e., Kṛṣṇa Rāya?) of Vijayanagara the country 'as far as Pavagud (i.e., Pavagada) in the east, Bollore (i.e., Bellara?) & Beedeeree (?) on the southeast, Chitteldroog (i.e., Chitradurga) on the west, Moolcalmooroo (i.e., Molakalmuru) on the north and Aradkeira (i.e., Eradikere) to the northeast,' and his seven sons divided and inherited it [*MNM*, 271]. The number of brothers is here given as seven instead of four. The motif of the divided inheritance of seven brothers was a widespread motif in the semi-historical accounts of little kingdoms in contemporary south India,[11] and 'seven' is a symbolic and conventional number in this motif. The *NAV* and *NB* also contain both the common genealogical identification and the legend of the brothers' divided inheritance in slightly different forms. Needless to say, these legends and genealogies are fictional. But one point that should be emphasised is that they tried to legitimise their rule of the estates by appealing to the ideology of genealogy and kinship.

Next let us consider the process of the estate building of the Bēḍa Nāyakas.

The Bēḍas were mobile groups who lived by hunting and cattle farming in hilly tracts and were marginal to the local agrarian societies. In the area of present-day Chitradurga district, the Bēḍas accounted for 17 per cent of the entire population in the early twentieth century and were the second largest caste after the Vīra Śaiva caste of some 21 per cent of the population.[12] But from the point of view of land control, they could not be reckoned as being dominant. According to statistics gathered from the late eighteenth century in the then Dodderi district located in the middle of eastern Chitradurga, Bēḍas accounted for 19 per cent of the number of households. But their holding of ploughs, which roughly corresponded to the extent of their land-holdings, was only 13 per cent of the total such number. On the other hand, the four agricultural castes together, including the Kuṃcaṭiga and Pakka Nāḍu Reḍḍi accounted for 25 per cent and 52 per cent respectively of the number of households and ploughs [*MNM*, 264]. In the then Talaku district neighbouring Dodderi district 'there are great numbers of *Boya* (i.e., Bēḍa) people. They are generally employed as *Sibendy* Peons (footsoldiers) and some of them cultivate lands' [*MNM*, 257]. Even this degree of control of agricultural production, though by no means dominant, was achieved only after the two-century rule of the Bēḍa Nāyakas, and their control of land and agriculture in the sixteenth century must have been less. As is described below, the founders of the Bēḍa Nāyakas are assumed from the legends of their distant ancestors to have migrated from outside the region. This also reflects their character as being outsiders to local agrarian society. Their rule of the estates was not the direct result of the autonomous development of a local agrarian community with a long history but rather originated from land gifts by the Vijayanagara kingship.

Among the four Bēḍa Nāyakas, the Nidugallus appear first in contemporary inscriptions. According to an inscription dated S. 1481 [*EC*, xi, Cl-54], Hoṭṭeṇṇa Nāyaka was given Dodderi *sīme* as a military fief (*amara māgaṇi*) by Tirumala Rāja, a brother of Aḷiya Rāma Rāya, the *de facto* king of that time. Though no inscription of his descendants has been found predating the mid-seventeenth century besides one dated S. 1537 [*EC*, xi, Cl-25],[13] it is to be surmised that they gradually extended their dominance from the basin of Vedavati River around Dodderi to the eastern hilly tract. In the early seventeenth century they displaced the family of Timmaṇṇa Nāyaka, who had ruled the Nidugallu region until then, and moved from the plain fort of Dodderi to the hill fort of Nidugallu and ruled both Dodderi and Nidugallu *sīmes*, comprising the western half of Pavagada Taluk and the greater part of Callakere Taluk [*MNM*, 368; NAV, 107]. From the late seventeenth century their estate was gradually invaded by powerful neighbouring Nāyakas, namely, Rayadurga from the north and Chitradurga from the west. When the estate was finally absorbed by the dominion of the Mysore kingdom in the late eighteenth century, it comprised merely the western half of Pavagada Taluk and the region around Parasuramapura.[14]

The first appearance of the Ratnagiris in contemporary inscriptions is that of Lakṣmīpati Nāyaka in an inscription dated S. 1492 [*EC*, xii, Mi-10]. According to this inscription, he was given Dodderi *sīme* (located in present-day Tumkur district and not its namesake held by Hoṭṭeṇṇa Nāyaka as a military fief) as a fief (*māgaṇi*) by one Caivappa Nāyaka, who himself was given that *sīme* as a fief (*māgaṇi*) by Tirumala Rāya, the first king of the Āravīḍu dynasty. His son Raṃgappa Nāyaka held Agali *sīme* as a military fief (*amara nāyakatana*) [*SII*, ix-2, 690]. They seem to have first ruled from Sira. But when Sira was made the strategic centre of the Adil Shahs after their first Karnataka expedition in A.D. 1637, they moved to Ratnagiri, about 23 km northeast of Sira. From this time they were obliged to pay tribute to the Muslim superintendents dispatched to

Sira by the Adil Shahs and, after their downfall, by the Mughals. Finally, in the late eighteenth century, Tippu Sultan of Mysore put an end to their local rule.[15]

It is difficult to trace the history of the Nayakanahattis because of a lack of contemporary inscriptions of historical reliability. But based on fragmentary descriptions scattered throughout the accounts of other Nāyakas, it is to be inferred that in the mid-seventeenth century they had established local rule over the region around Nayakanahatti. Afterward they became subject to Madakari Nāyaka IV (A.D. 1721-48) of Chitradurga, and except for only one village named Gajjaganahalli near Nayakanahatti, all their estate was taken away in the early eighteenth century [*MNM*, 34, 37-8; *NB*, 33f].

Tracing the history of the Hosakotes is also difficult. Their one and only inscription of historical reliability is that of Baḍa Timmaṇṇa Nāyaka, dated S. 1601 and found at Hosakote [*EC*, xii, Pg-70]. The 'Account of Indrandroog' says that in the mid-seventeenth century they were deprived of Kumdurpi by the Nāyakas of Rayadurga and moved to Hosakote [*MNM*, 422]. In the late eighteenth century, along with the Nidugallus and the Ratnagiris, they were deprived of their estate by the Mysore kingdom.

Among the four Bēḍa Nāyakas in eastern Chitradurga, the local rule of the Nidugallus and Ratnagiris began with the assignment of fiefs by the Vijayanagara kingship. But all eastern Chitradurga was not assigned to one common ancestor as the legendary accounts claim, and parts of the region were assigned separately to these Nāyakas as well as to other Nāyakas. In Nidugallu, Timmaṇṇa Nāyaka and his son Immaḍi Timmaṇṇa Nāyaka ruled Nidugallu *rājya* (or *nāḍu*) under Vijayanagara sovereignty from the late Tuḷuva period. Their inscriptions are chronologically distributed from S. 1476 to the year of Pārthiva (i.e., S. 1507) [*EC*, xii, Pg-39; *SII*, ix-2, 665; *EC*, xii, Si-31; *EC*, xii, Pg-40; *EC*, xii, Pg-38; *EC*, xii, Pg-63; *EC*, xii, Pg-37; *SII*, ix-2, 687; *AR* 1917-6]. In Hiriyuru, Keṃcappa Nāyaka and his descendants held Hiriyuru *sīme* as a military fief (*amara māgaṇi*), and the chronological distribution of their inscriptions is from S. 1489 to S. 1531 [*EC*, xi, Hr-47; *EC*, xi, Hr-79; *EC*, xi, Hr-85; *EC*, xii, Si-3; *EC*, xi, Hr-88; *EC*, xii, Si-1; *EC*, xi, Hr-56].

In the political disturbances and uncertainty following the late sixteenth century, when the Vijanagara kingship was waning and Muslim power had penetrated from the north but was not yet strong enough to establish practical dominance, local rule was established and consolidated by one's own power, especially militarily. In the almost incessant struggles and wars with powers from both within and without eastern Chitradurga, the Nidugallus and Ratnagiris fought through to maintain their estates for about two centuries, even though they were compelled to move their seats of power and experienced changes in their estates. On the other hand, Timmaṇṇa of Nidugallu and Keṃcappa of Hiriyuru failed to maintain their fiefs assigned by the Vijayanagara kingship and disappeared as a result of the assaults of the Nidugallu Nāyakas and Chitradurga Nāyakas respectively in the early seventeenth century. In these politically disturbed times, both the Hosakotes and the Nayakanahattis presumably built up and consolidated their estates.

Given the vicissitudes of the Nāyakas in the region, how then should the legend that all eastern Chitradurga was bestowed on the founder and afterwards divided among brothers be understood? The premise of the legend is a political map of the four Nāyakas ruling independently in the region in the seventeenth century and its object is to explain and legitimise that political reality. It hid the political disturbances ruled by the law of the jungle and the dynamic process of estate-building by means of the veil of the static ideology of genealogy and kinship. The historical fact of separate fief assignments to the Nidugallus and Ratnagiris under the Vijayanagara kingship was modified to the endowment of the whole region to a mythic common founder and a subsequent divided inheritance. That is, their rule of estates was legitimised not only in relation to the Vijayanagara kingship but also by the ideology of descent and inheritance. We shall thus consider in the following sections the coexistence of these two essentially different modes of logic through which the status of the Bēḍa Nāyakas was constructed in the ancestor legends.

## An Analysis of the Legend of Distant Ancestors in the *Niḍugallu Arasugala Vaṃśāvaḷi*

The *NAV* begins with the legendary biography of the mythic founder named Tippa Rāja. Then follows the genealogy of the Nāyakas until the late eighteenth century. In between are inserted brief descriptions of the most important political events. In the last part it is recorded that Vīra Hoṭṭeṇṇa Nāyaka served Hyder Ali of Mysore with his own followers. I shall try to analyse the early and legendary part of the text from the mythic birth of the founder to the establishment of the estate by the direct progenitor. Passages quoted below, among which the first follows, are my own summarised translations:

> A seven-year-old girl living in Harati Sarvada near Bijapur in the north conceived the son of the Sun god while she was praying to him. Being afraid that its honour would be damaged by the unmarried girl's conception and delivery of a child, her family secretly abandoned the newborn baby in a dunghill (*tippe*) at a hamlet where Dharani Kāma Nāyaka lived with a large herd (*kaṃpaḷa*). One day Kāma Nāyaka found the abandoned baby whom a she-buffalo had been suckling of its own accord and named him Tippa Rāja after the dunghill (*tippe*) where he was found.

Sarvada, where the mother of the founder is assumed to have lived, is a village located about 15 km southwest of Bijapur on the banks of Doni River. The legendary motif of migration from Sarvada in the north is shared with the Ratnagiris.[16] Because of a lack of reliable sources, it is impossible to ascertain the original place of the Nāyakas. But in an account of the Nayakanahattis who belonged to the same exogamous clan, the founder is presumed to have migrated from the hilly tract around the famous Srisailam in present-day Kurnool district. One must therefore be cautious about accepting the legendary migration from Sarvada as a historical fact. Why, then, did such a legend exist? And why from Sarvada and not from some other place?

Sarvada is the original site of Sarvada Maṭha (monastery) of the Vīra Śaiva sect, which had close connections with the Nidugallus.[17] It would thus seem appropriate for the migration from Sarvada to be interpreted as a semi-historical story so as to express the close ties between the *maṭha* and the Bēḍa Nāyakas. The 'Historical Account of Doodairee' goes one step further to claim that the girl conceived the son of the god Śiva at Sarvada (Sārvāḍēśvara) [*MNM*, 269].

The impregnation of a virgin girl by the Sun god and the subsequent abandonment of the newborn baby remind us of the birth of Karṇa, a half-brother and enemy of the Pāṇḍava brothers. But the birth legend of the primogenitor should not be interpreted simply as a motif copied from the famous *Mahābhārata*. A close tie between the founder and the Sun god appears in a different form in the distant ancestor legend of the Nayakanahattis too. The motif of a founder closely related to the Sun god may originally have been a traditional legend about the origins of that particular exogamous group. The meaning of the motif that a she-buffalo suckled the infant founder is quite clear. The name of the exogamous group to which the Nidugallus belonged was Enumalōru, and it derives from *enumu*, meaning a 'she-buffalo' in Telugu. This motif tries to explain the special or 'totemic' importance of a she-buffalo to them. That a sacred cow voluntarily suckles a *liṃga* hidden underground or in an ant-hill, which is then discovered by men surprised at the scene, has become a topos in the mythic accounts of Hindu temples. By replacing a sacred cow with a she-buffalo and a *liṃga* with the infant founder, the relationship between the founder and she-buffaloes was homologised to the indivisibility between Śiva and sacred cows and the sacredness and superhuman character of the founder at which were hinted.

The founder's stepfather is said to have tended a herd (*kaṃpaḷa*). There is a custom among the Myāsa Bēḍas to sanctify a herd of cattle as the property of gods and to leave it with holy attendants [Kṛṣṇamūrti Hanūru 1993: 126-9; Kariśeṭṭi Rudrappa 1995: 68-70]. Through his stepfather and his herd, the founder also obtained the holiness entailed in attendance on a sacred herd.

According to folk religion, if a baby is put on a dunghill (*tippe*) and its ear is pierced, it will grow into a healthy child. Such a baby is often named Tippēsvāmi or Tippaṇṇa if a male or Tippamma if a female [Caṃdraśēkhara Kaṃbāra 1985: 948]. The naming of the founder as Tippa is clearly in accordance with this folk belief. But it is not sufficient for fully understanding why he was so named. As is noted below, the legend of distant ancestors, especially the founder, in the *NAV* corresponds with the *biruḍāvaḷi* in inscriptions of the seventeenth century. Moreover, this *biruḍāvaḷi* was itself not completely original to the Nidugallus, but was composed by appropriation and redefinition of that of Cikka Tippa Bhūpāla, who ruled from Nidugallu in the late fifteenth century. He is of course totally different from Tippa in the legend. But it seems unnatural to consider this coincidence a mere accident. The name Tippa itself may also have been appropriated along with his *biruḍāvaḷi* and associated with a familiar folk belief to give birth to the motif of an infant abandoned in a dunghill (*tippe*) in the ancestor legend.

Through this mythic birth of the founder, the Nidugallus tried to depict a self-image closely connected with terminology and legends suitable for establishing their status as champions of the caste or exogamous clan:

> Muddamma and Bīramma, two daughters of Cikkaṇṇa Gouḍa, went daily to Bijapur to sell milk and yogurt. One day the Padshah of Bijapur saw the beauty of the two girls and proposed marriage. Kāma Nāyaka migrated with the family of Cikkaṇṇa Gouḍa southward to protect the girls from the Padshah. They reached Paṃpā and set-

tled there. After some time, one day when Kṛṣṇa Rāya was out hunting tigers, Tippa, who had grown into a boy and was playing with friends at the time, killed the hunted tiger with an arrow. Impressed by this feat, the Rāya asked Kāma about him, and after hearing that he had been found in a dunghill, he said to Kāma 'The earth is mine and the dunghill is my property; there is thus no relation between the boy and you (*bhūmi nammadu tippe namma adhīna śiśu ninage saṃbaṃdhavilla*).' The Rāya made Tippa an attendant, had him marry a daughter named Vīramma of Keṃcappa Nāyaka, who had already been in his attendance (*tamma baḷi idda*), and gave him the land where Kāma Nāyaka had a cowshed after naming it Kāmaḷāpura.

After some time, a wrestler named Bahadara Malaka, an attendant of a Padshah of Delhi, came to Vijayanagara and proposed to fight a duel. Tippa, representing all the wrestlers in the city, stood on the field and fought him with a sword (*kaṭṭāri*) in his right hand. He moved his sword so quickly that his enemy did not notice the musk paste put on his forehead by the point of the sword. Tippa won and cut the enemy's body into pieces. The Rāya gave him a reward of a white conch, a discus and magnificent anklets and the title of 'the champion of the beautiful swordsmen, the defeater of Bahadara Maluka (*Bahadara Malaka saptāṃga haraṇa*), the wearer of the lion-shaped forehead ornament (*siṃha lalāṭa*), *Gaṃdabhēruṃda* (mythic bird with two heads), and the chief jewel of heroes (*kali bhāṣiṃga*).' The Rāya also gave Tippa the country of 'Harati Sarvada 66,000 *sīme*' and ordered him to rule permanently and enjoy it for generations (*śāśvatavāgi rājyavāḷikoṃḍu anubhavisikoṃḍu iru*).

Emigration to protect females who are forced to marry by kings of 'low' caste or Muslims is a topos in the legendary accounts of little kingdoms in south India. Here this widespread motif is not only adopted, but details are added to the effect that the girls in question were selling milk and yogurt. This detail is consistent with the fact that Kāma Nāyaka tended a herd and makes the narrative seem more probable and natural.

In the royal city of Paṃpā (Vijayanagara) where the founder emigrated with his stepfather, the transactions with the Vijayanagara kingship occurred. In these two episodes of the killing of a wild tiger and a Muslim wrestler, the Nidugallus represent their identity as a *nāyaka* who offered martial services to and received gifts of honours, emblems and lands from the Vijayanagara kingship. In the text the title postfixed to Tippa is generally *rāja*, but from his son onward, *nāyaka* is postfixed to personal names. This means that through martial services offered to the universal king at the royal city, the Nidugallus acquired the identity of *nāyakas*. In the first episode, Tippa is declared by Kṛṣṇa Rāya to have 'no relationship' with his stepfather and enters into a matrimonial relationship with a *nāyaka* in attendance on Kṛṣṇa Rāya. These symbolise the supra-descent character and openness of the group of attendants named *nāyakas* that formed around the Vijayanagara kingship.

On the other hand, it should not be overlooked that even in this episode, which seems to overcome the ascribed identity, details of Bēḍa background are interwoven. The bow and arrow which Tippa used are familiar to the Bēḍas, whose traditional occupation is hunting. That he killed a tiger reminds us of the famous legendary Bēḍa hero Gādri Pāla Nāyaka who died in a fight with a wild tiger to protect a divine herd [Kṛṣṇamūrti Hanūru 1993: 42-3]. What is further significant here is the reference to Kamalāpura, which is a hamlet located in the southern suburb of the former city of Vijayanagara and means literally the 'town (*pura*) of lotuses (*kamala*).' This name was modified to Kāmaḷāpura, that is, the 'town of Kāma' so as to be naturally interwoven into the story of the migration of Kāma and Tippa. One copper plate of dubious authenticity[18] records that one of the Nayakanahatti Nāyakas received tax-free land in Kamalāpura from a Vijayanagara king. These deliberate modifications and persistent references imply the special importance attached to Kamalāpura by the Bēḍa Nāyakas or Bēḍas as a whole. A recent sociological study also attests to the close relationship that exists and might have existed between the Myāsa Bēḍas and this same locality.[19] Unfortunately, what the actual relationship was remains to be clarified by further research.

In the second episode, Tippa acquired the hereditary estate as his reward for another martial service. It should firstly be pointed out that this episode represents the explanation or narrative version of part of the *biruḍāvaḷi* in the inscriptions. The process of composing the *biruḍāvaḷi* by appropriation and redefinition will be considered in the next section. Here it is to be noted that the correspondence between one of the main episodes of the entire ancestor legend and the *biruḍāvaḷi* gives an important clue for inferring the period when the ancestor legend was composed.

What matters here is the name of the country that was given to Tippa, namely, Harati Sarvada. Needless to say, this is also the name of the birthplace of the founder. Judging from the following parts of the *NAV* and the aforementioned description in the 'Historical Account of Doodairee,' the country given to Tippa must have been eastern Chitradurga. Although its history is not known, Harati, located in modern Hiriyuru Taluk, must have once been a regional centre of eastern Chitradurga, as the ruins of a relatively large fort there suggest [Girija 1991: 384-390]. Apart from the Nidugallus and Ratnagiris, many Bēḍa Nāyakas, including Keṃcappa of Hiriyuru, appear in inscriptions found in this region with the place name of Harati prefixed to their personal names. Though unfortunately its origins and circumstances remain to be clarified, Harati was a symbolic centre of eastern Chitradurga. But a village named Sarvada cannot be found in this region. Conversely, a village with the name of Harati cannot be found in the region around Bijapur. By combining the names of the site of his departure and destination into the fictitious place name Harati Sarvada, Tippa's spatial movement became a round trip between Harati Sarvada and Vijayanagara.[20] Tippa's symbolic return to his ancestral places seems to signify the restoration of the ascribed identity that had once been negated through service to the universal king in his royal city. His contact with the Sun god, she-buffalo and *kaṃpaḷa*, which gave him the identity of a Bēḍa or Enumalōru, occurred in Harati Sarvada, and by his return to another Harati Sarvada he recovered that identity: [21]

> The three generations of Tippa Rāja, Kāma Nāyaka and Abbe Nāyaka ruled and enjoyed Harati Sarvada. The two sons of Abbe were Īśvara Nāyaka and Bomma Nāyaka. The former ruled the Harati Sarvada *sīme*. The latter reclaimed land from the forest in the basin of Vedavati River after securing the permission of a Vijayanagara king. He founded the three villages of Gōtaṭāka, Callakere and Dodderi one after another. In the last one, he constructed a fort from where he ruled the country from the hill pass of Gonuru in the west to Nidugallu in the east, where he constructed a fort and a market town .

The name of Tippa's son is identical with that of his stepfather. Although the *NAV* does not give a special explanation of this coincidence, it seems to symbolise the recovery of his tie with the stepfather once denied by Kṛṣṇa Rāya.[22]

Bomma is said to have surrendered the ancestral estate to a brother and obtained a new one in the Vedavati basin. This is another version of the legend of the brothers' divided inheritance and makes it clear that

Bomma was the direct progenitor of the Nidugallus. Īśvara, who inherited the ancestral estate, is supposed to have been the progenitor of the Hosakotes. The country Bomma is supposed to have ruled roughly corresponds to the largest extent of the estate of the Nidugallus in the mid-seventeenth century. The statement that Bomma constructed a fort and a market town in Nidugallu is erroneous because even before the Vijayanagara period, Nidugallu had been a regional centre and gave its name to the surrounding country. That Bomma was made the fictional builder of the estate and seat of power in the seventeenth century indicates the important position he is supposed to have occupied as the direct progenitor in the *NAV*.

In other accounts, Gosikere is said to have been founded by Bomma [*MNM*, 367], and so Gōsaṭāka in the above account must be Gosikere. Although Gosikere might not have actually been a seat of the Nidugallus, it must be pointed out that Gosikere was one of the centres of activity of the aforesaid Sarvada Maṭha, six head monks of which had their tombs there [Girija 1991: 152]. Given the close relationship between the *maṭha* and the Bēḍa Nāyakas noted above, it is safe to assume that the special emphasis given to Gosikere in the ancestor legend was another means of symbolically expressing that relationship. The 'Historical Account of Doodairee' says that Tippa reclaimed the forest around Gosikere and built a temple for the god Sārvdāḍēśvara [*MNM*, 271]. Although this account associates its foundation with Tippa and not Bomma, it reflects the importance of Gosikere as the site of the Vīra Śaiva *maṭha*. It can also be said that by making use of two centres of the *maṭha*, the symbolic round trip to the royal city is expressed again.[23]

In the following part of the *NAV*, Hoṭṭeṇṇa Nāyaka appears as a great-grandson of Bomma. He is probably identical to his namesake who held Dodderi *sīme* as a fief in the aforementioned inscription dated S.1481. That he is specifically said to have ruled Dodderi *sīme* in the *NAV* may indirectly reflect the historical fact that Hoṭṭeṇṇa was the first family member to rule in eastern Chitradurga. His grandson was Timmaṇṇa Nāyaka, who moved from Dodderi to Nidugallu in the early seventeenth century, and this accords chronologically with the period of Hoṭṭeṇṇa. After the shift to Nidugallu, all the following Nāyakas were named Timmaṇṇa or Hoṭṭeṇṇa. This contrasts with the fact that before the aforesaid Hoṭṭeṇṇa all Nāyakas had different names, and it suggests that the periods of Hoṭṭeṇṇa and his grandson Timmaṇṇa were important milestones in the history of the Nidugallus.

The ancestor legend in the *NAV* reflects the dual identity of the Bēḍa Nāyakas. In one respect they were champions of the caste or clan, and in another respect they were *nāyakas* of non-descent and open character who offered martial services to the universal king. These two identities are attached respectively to the birthplace, Harati Sarvada and to the royal city of Vijayanagara. The founder Tippa made a symbolic round trip to Vijayanagara and eventually returned to the birthplace closely connected with the ascribed identity.

## An Analysis of *Biruḍāvaḷi* in Inscriptions

As was noted earlier, the ancestor legend, especially the founder legend in the *NAV*, corresponds with the *biruḍāvaḷi* of inscriptions from the seventeenth century. The *biruḍāvaḷi* was not completely original to the Nidugallus, but was composed by the appropriation and redefinition of an existing model. The following are the *biruḍāvaḷi* of Timmaṇṇa Nāyaka of Nidugallu in an inscription dated S.1592 [*EC*, xii, Pg-46] and the original one of Cikka Tippa Bhūpāla in an inscription dated S.1409 and found at Nidugallu [*EC*, xii, Pg-54]. The translations are mine, and the upper- and lowercase letters in parenthesis indicate corresponding passages, e.g., (A)-(a).

Timmaṇṇa Nāyaka

The auspicious and prestigious *nāyaka*, (A) the champion who defeated Nāyakas who broke their word, (B) the hero who protected those who sought refuge and defeated those who opposed him, (C) the champion of the beautiful swordsmen, the musk fighter (*kastūri kōlāhala*), (D) the terrifying form of Śiva for the hostile army, (E) the champion of all who do and do not praise him, (F) the decapitator of Mesa, (G) the *liṃga* worshipped by both friend and foe, (H) the subduer of the kings' army, (I) the defeater of Bahadara Malaka, the wrestler who protected the herd of she-buffaloes (*yanumala maṃda pārthika malla*), the paramour of courtesans who are enemy kings, he who is honoured with a conch (*saṃkha*) and a discus (*cakra*), and is the wearer of magnificent anklets.

Cikka Tippa Bhūpāla

(c-1) The champion of beautiful men, (c-2) the king with a sword (*kaṭhāri rāya*), (d) the terrifying form of Śiva for the hostile army,

(e) the champion of all who do or do not praise him, (f-1) the champion who took the head of Mesa, (a) the champion who defeated kings and Nāyakas who broke their word, (b) the hero who protected those who sought refuge, (g) the *liṃga* worshipped by both friend and foe, (i) the defeater of Bahadara Malaka's kingdom, (h) the subduer of the Hoysala army, (f-2) the decapitator of Holekallu Bomma, the companion of Nārāyaṇa, the man wholly devoted to Hari *bhakti*, the worshipper of the lotus feet of the god Tiruveṃgaḷanātha.

Among the fifteen elements that make up the *biruḍāvaḷi* of Timmaṇṇa Nāyaka, nine elements have been appropriated from that of Cikka Tippa Bhūpāla. As for the reason for this appropriation, it can only be guessed from the historical circumstances. One possibility is that after the Vijayanagara kingship had disappeared in all but name, they tried to legitimise their rule of the estate in relation to and in continuation with the past rulers of the locality.[24] In south India, the acquisition of honours (*biruḍu*) means the acquisition of (part of) the substance and character of those who gave them or had had them until then. But the Nāyakas of Nidugallu did not simply imitate nor borrow the *biruḍāvaḷi* of Cikka Tippa, and partly changed its form, reinterpreted it, and added new and original elements.

The *biruḍāvaḷi* of Cikka Tippa includes elements that are based on political events in early fourteenth century south India. This implies, though as yet uncertified, that his ancestor fought on the side of the Saṃgamas who struggled against both Muslim and Hindu politico-military powers to establish the Vijayangara empire. 'Hoysala' (h) is, needless to say, the dynasty that held sway over south Karnataka before the Saṃgamas. Once appropriated, the proper noun Hoysala was displaced by the common noun *rāya*. 'Holekallu Bomma' (f-2) can be identified with a namesake who had the title of *mahāsāmaṃta* and ruled Nidugallu Rājya in the early fourteenth century [*EC*, xii, Si-8; Venkata Ramanayya 1990: 46].

The Kannada original of (I)-(i) is *Bahadara Malaka saptāṃga haraṇa*. Generally speaking, *saptāṃga haraṇa* in *biruḍāvaḷis* means 'those who defeat (the army of ) a hostile kingdom,' and *saptāṃga* refers to the seven elements of a kingdom, usually the king, ministers, territory, fort, treasury, army, and allies [Chitnis 1990: 34]. Given that the *biruḍāvaḷi* of Cikka Tippa was based on the history of the early fourteenth century, Bahadara Malaka can be identified with the famous Muslim general Malik Kafur, who led the huge army of the Khiljis into south India. The

Nidugallus literally borrowed this element and then reinterpreted it. As the episode of Tippa's fight in Vijayanagara shows, 'Bahadara Malaka,' who was originally a symbol of the Delhi Sultanates, was transformed into a wrestler from Delhi. Accordingly, the seven parts (*saptāṃga*) were reinterpreted as the constituent elements of a human body, usually the head, eyes, ears, mouth, legs, arms, and heart.

Among the original elements added by the Nidugallus, the most important is 'the auspicious and prestigious *nāyaka* (*śrīmanmahānāyakācārya*).' This title, combining *nāyaka* and *ācārya*, which means 'spiritual guide,' is peculiar to the Bēḍa Nāyakas, and it quite often appears in the *biruḍāvaḷis* of other Bēḍa Nāyakas besides the Nidugallus.[25] Unfortunately, its real connotation and genesis are still not clear, but it was of special importance to the Nidugallus as Bēḍas. The original term for 'she-buffaloes' in 'the wrestler who protected the herd of she-buffaloes' is *yanumala*. This is another form of *enumu* in Telugu. In Kannada, in which the *biruḍāvaḷi* is written, the form *emme* is much more widely used. The term *yanumala* has been purposefully selected and used here. Thus it is not incorrect to interpret it simply as 'she-buffalo' like the editor and translator of the *EC*, but the author of the *biruḍāvaḷi* who chose the Telugu form must have had in mind Enumalōru, the name of the exogamous group to which the Nidugallus belonged. This is important for demonstrating the self-perception of the Nidugallus as clan champions.

Next let us confirm the correspondence between the episode of Tippa's fight in the *NAV* and the *biruḍāvaḷi*. The whole setting of the episode in which he defeats Bahadara Malaka is nothing other than element (I). Element (C) tallies with the fact that his weapon was a sword. That he is said to have put musk paste on the forehead of the enemy is in accordance with 'musk fighter,' a seemingly strange element in the *biruḍāvaḷi*. 'He who is honoured with a conch and a discus, the wearer of magnificent anklets,' being the parts of titles given as a reward, also appears in the *biruḍāvaḷi*. The episode of Tippa's fight in the *NAV* can be said to represent the narrative version of parts of the *biruḍāvaḷi*. Especially the appropriated elements (I) and (C) structure the general setting of the episode. It can be safely said that only after the *biruḍāvaḷi* had been composed by appropriation and redefinition was the episode created.

Given the importance of the episode in the whole sequence of the ancestor legend, it seems highly probable that the entire ancestor legend was created after or in conjunction with the composition of the *biruḍāvaḷi*.[26] Because of the nature of the problem, it is very difficult to verify this hypothesis. But I can give the following circumstantial evidence to support it. Firstly, the name of the founder in the legend is identical with the holder of the original *biruḍāvaḷi*. The name of Tippa does not appear in the genealogy of the Nidugallus given in the aforementioned inscription of Hoṭṭeṇṇa Nāyaka of the sixteenth century. The mythic founder with the name of Tippa appears neither in the ancestor legend of the Nayakanahattis who belonged to the same endogamous group nor in the legends transmitted among the Bēḍa community. These facts show that the founder named Tippa and his legendary biography did not exist before the appropriation of the *biruḍāvaḷi* of Cikka Tippa Bhūpāla started.

The relatively long *biruḍāvaḷi* of Hoṭṭeṇṇa Nāyaka in the aforementioned inscription dated S. 1481 is, apart from the very common elements such as 'the champion who defeated Nāyakas who broke their word' and 'the hero who protected those who sought refuge,' different from the model provided by Cikka Tippa Bhūpāla. Moreover, in this inscription, like those of the Ratnagiris of the sixteenth century, the place name Koteyakere[27] was prefixed to the name of the ancestors. But in the seventeenth century this was replaced with Harati. Correspondingly, the ancestor legend in the *NAV* totally omits Koteyakere and mentions Harati in the form Harati Sarvada as the original place of the founder. The place names prefixed to personal names are, generally speaking, their ancestral places and are important in giving a certain identity to the persons. I think the change of place name also shows a change in the self-perception and recognised descent of the Nidugallus between the sixteenth and seventeenth centuries.

The composition of the ancestor legend forming the main part of the *NAV* along with the imitation *biruḍāvaḷi* in the inscriptions represented a series of operations whereby the Nidugallus reconfirmed and redefined their own status and identity in the new historical and political circumstances of the mid-seventeenth century when the Vijayanagara kingship became totally nominal and the Nidugallus became substantially independent lords. They had a history of *nāyakas* who had served the Vijayanagara kingship at its zenith in the sixteenth century as military leaders. Their memory along with the title of *nāyaka* was maintained in the seventeenth century in the form of the legend of the martial services the founder Tippa offered to the universal king in the royal city. But just as the founder Tippa finally accomplished the symbolic return to his birthplace and recovered his ascribed identity as a Bēḍa, so would the Nidugallus of the seventeenth century, who had transformed themselves into lords in their symbolic birthplace in eastern Chitradurga, seem to have rediscovered and redefined their identity as Bēḍas. One can find this new trend in the deliberate addition of the name of the exogamous clan to the imitation *biruḍāvaḷi*. What matters here is the historicity of the emphasis of Bēḍa caste identity. It was obscure in the early days of the Nidugallus, who were then primarily *nāyakas* as military leaders serving the Vijayanagara kingship in its heyday, and became clearer and more articulate in the ancestor legend and the *biruḍāvaḷi* composed in the seventeenth century.

## An Analysis of the Ancestor Legend in the *Nāyakanahaṭṭi Bakhairu*

The *NB* begins with a legendary account of the founder Mallayya and gives the genealogy of his descendants until the late eighteenth century interspersed with descriptions of some important events. Though there is one specified date in the fourteenth century recorded at the beginning, the meaning or explanation of this date is not given. The *NB* ends with Baṃgāra Mallappa Nāyaka, who followed Hyder Ali in his expedition into Malabar in 1766 and died in the siege of Calicut. In the following, I would like to analyse the early semi-legendary part of the text from the mythic founder Mallayya to Bōdi Mallappa Nāyaka, who seems to have compiled the original version of the text. The passages quoted below are my own abridged translations:

> In the sacred forests called Karimale and Bilimale east of Srisailam hill lived Kāṭa Nāyakana Mallayya and his six brothers with a herd (*kaṃpaḷa*) of one hundred thousand cattle and five hundred *mesa*. Once when a drought had continued for twelve years, they migrated with twelve gods kept in boxes (*peṭṭige dēvaru*) to the west searching for grass and water and finally settled and established a fold (*haṭṭi*) for the *kaṃpaḷa* to the east of Guru Guhēśvara hill.

In relation to Srisailam, supposed to have been the original place of Mallayya, it must be noted that the god of Srisailam Mallēśvara is invoked at the start of the text. Mallēśvara, more familiar as Mallikārjuna, is enshrined in a large ancient temple at Srisailam. That there are many Nāyakas named Malla besides the founder in the genealogy of the Nayakanahattis also suggests a close relationship between them and Mallikārjuna (or Mallēśvara) at Srisailam. Though it is impossible to determine their actual original place, we can recognise the same method as that found in the case of the Nidugallus of appropriating the site of a closely affiliated religious authority as their own original place.

'Kāṭa Nāyaka' in the name of the founder means a leader (*nāyaka*) of forest people (*kāṭa*). Just as in the case of Tippa in the *NAV*, the founder tended a *kampaḷa*, which is a herd of cows sanctified for the gods of the Myāsa Bēḍas. *Peṭṭige dēvaru* means literally 'gods (*dēvaru*) in boxes (*peṭṭige*),' and they are the most important gods among the Myāsa Bēḍas. They number twelve in all.[28] The status of Mallayya as a leader of forest people at the head of five hundred *mesa*, or Myāsa Bēḍas, is defined in relation to the two most sacred objects of the Myāsa Bēḍas.

Mallayya first emigrated to a place near the hill of Guru Guhēśvara. Later Mallayya prayed to him when he was besieged by a Vijayanagara army. Guru Guhēśvara (literally, a preceptor presiding in a cave) must therefore have been a saint intimately affiliated with the Nayakanahattis, but the *NB* does not give any further clues for identifying him as a historical person. In Nayakanahatti there are two tombs of Tippērudra Svāmi, a famous Vīra Śaiva saint, in one of which Myāsa Bēḍas act as priests. According to a legendary account, he once meditated in a cave (*guhe*) near Callakere [Girija 1991: 167- 70]. Guru Guhēśvara in the text might be another name of Tippērudra Svāmi on the ground that he once meditated in a *guhe*.

> A saint filled with light (*bhavya mūrti*) from Vijayanagara made a tour of the country. One day he came to see Mallayya and recognised that he was a *sāraṇa* born as a boon from the Sun god. After receiving abundant gifts from him, the saint went back to Vijayanagara and told the king about Mallayya. The king became angry because Mallayya had migrated to his kingdom without asking his permission (*hukum*) and sent an army to defeat him. When Mallayya was besieged by the army, he prayed to the Sun god, Parvata Mallēśvara (i.e., Srisailam Mallikārjuna) and Guru Guhēśvara. He then moved the herd as he wished and defeated the besieging army. Next, the Vijayanagara king sent 33 concubines to arrest Mallayya. Their dances and music won his favour and they succeeded in seducing him into making a wager with his own life as the stake. But with only a single cry Mallayya made the herd ascend the hill and won the bet. Surprised at the miracle, the concubines fled back to Vijayanagara and reported to the king that he was not human but a *śaraṇa* (*mānavanallā śaraṇa saṃtatti*).

The first stage of the transaction between a Vijayanagara king and the Nayakanahattis described here is not friendly but hostile. It is of special importance that Mallayya frustrated the king's attempt to arrest him twice by his superhuman prowess in controlling the herd at will. Notably, the power of the king was not effective before the superhuman power of the attendant of the sacred herd.

The founder Tippa in the *NAV* was, as already noted, a son of the Sun god. That Mallayya is said to have been born as a boon from the Sun god is another variation of the motif of a Sun-affiliated founder. Because of this close affiliation, Mallayya prayed to the Sun god at the crucial moment for victory.

It is interesting that Mallayya is called *śaraṇa* by the saint and the concubines. *Śaraṇa*, of Sanskrit origin, means generally 'protector, protection, refuge,' but especially in the Kannada-speaking region it denotes a follower of Vīra Śaivism. However, its usage in the *NB* differs from both of these. The saint praised Mallayya as a *śaraṇa* born as a boon from the Sun god and reported him to the Vijayanagara king as 'a *śaraṇa* manifested as a human being (*sākṣāt śaraṇa puruṣa*).' The concubines commented that he was 'not human but a *śaraṇa*.' From these usages, *śaraṇa* in the text can be interpreted as a man with superhuman power and sacredness. That is, the terminology of Vīra Śaivism, which is foreign to the Bēḍas, has been appropriated to express the holiness of Mallayya tending a sanctified herd.

> Being interested in Mallayya, the king invited him to Vijayanagara through the saint filled with light. The king, highly pleased, called him 'the eldest son of the kingdom (*saṃsthānakke mukhya maga*)' and gave him many gifts. The king bestowed many gifts on the *kampaḷa* too and worshipped it with his queen. The king and Mallayya together milked the *kampaḷa* into an offering box (*ḍabbi*) of the god Hampe Virūpākṣa and made a twelve-point agreement concerning Mallayya's rights. These included the right to collect a certain tribute from those marrying and cultivating land. It was also ordered that when he moved with the *kampaḷa* and twelve *peṭṭige dēvaru*, villagers en route would be obliged to offer food and send a message to neighbouring villages. When the king finally sent Mallayya off, he gave a royal order (*hukum*) that he and his descendants should maintain customs and good practices, including those pertaining to marriage among people of the Vālmīka clan in 54 countries (*coupamnāru dēśagaḷalli yirru vālmīka vaṃśastha jana*), and pun-

ish those who violated them and that they should enjoy the status of chief of the clan as long as the sun and moon existed. Mallayya established a settlement with folds (*haṭṭi*) at the foot of a hill near Kumdurpi and traveled around personally to see that the customs of his caste (*yī janarugaḷu*) were observed and to punish those who violated them.

The second stage of the transaction between the Vijayanagara king and Mallayya turned out to be friendly. Mallayya was invited to the royal city by the king who appreciated his braveness shown in defeating the royal army. Just as the founder Tippa temporarily lost his descent identity as a Bēḍa at Vijayanagara in the *NAV*, Mallayya transcended his biological descent and became a son of the Vijayanagara kingship. The pseudo-son (*kumāra*) relationship with a Vijayanagara king as pseudo-father was one of the ultimate expressions of *nāyaka* identity, which was defined primarily in relation to the Vijayanagara kingship.[29]

But the case of Mallayya is different from that of Tippa in one crucial point. The descent-based status of Mallayya as the champion of the caste or clan was confirmed by the universal king at his royal city. The Vijayanagara king permitted him to move freely with his *kampaḷa* and twelve *peṭṭige dēvaru*, the two most sacred objects of the Bēḍas, and officially endorsed his status as a hereditary chief of 'people of the Vālmīka clan in 54 countries.' '54 countries' are, according to the traditional Hindu perception of the world, all the countries comprising this world. 'Vālmīka clan' denotes the Bēḍas, who claimed to be descendants of the famous saint-poet Vālmīki, author of the *Rāmāyaṇa*.[30] It is further significant that the *kampaḷa* attested to the endorsement and affirmation of his status. There are some defects in the part of the text which I have translated as 'Mallayya milked the *kampaḷa* into an offering box of the god Hampe Virūpākṣa,' and its meaning is not clear. But my interpretation that the transaction is witnessed by both the *kampaḷa* and Hampe Virūpākṣa, the most sacred symbols respectively for Mallayya and the Vijayanagara kings, the latter of whom used the epithet Virūpākṣa in their inscriptions claiming to rule the kingdom on behalf of the sovereign god Virūpākṣa, cannot be far off the mark. That the king with his queen bestowed gifts on and worshipped the *kampaḷa* also implies that the king recognised the Bēḍa tradition symbolised by the sacredness of the *kampaḷa* in relation to which Mallayya's status was defined.

Afterwards Mallayya moved his settlement to Gosikere and his six brothers shifted respectively to Ratnagiri, Midigesi, Horkoṭṭi (i.e., Hosakote), Nidugallu, Samkaragallu, and Kumdurpi.

That seven brothers dispersed to different places is another version of the motif of the brothers' divided inheritance indicating the psuedo-consanguineal ties among the four Bēḍa Nāyakas in eastern Chitradurga. It should be noted that in this version Mallayya is clearly ranked as the eldest among the seven brothers. This would seem to be an attempt to affirm the supremacy of the Nayakanahattis over the other Bēḍa Nāyakas in the region on the principle of kinship.

Mallayya had three sons, Sūradevina Pāpa Nāyaka, Torrela Malla Nāyaka, and Gādri Pāla Nāyaka. The son of Torrela Malla was Jagaḷūru Pāpa Nāyaka. Sūradevina Pāpa fought with Hoṭṭeḷa (i.e., Hoṭṭeṇṇa) Nāyaka over the right to tend the *kaṃpaḷa* and twelve *peṭṭige dēvaru* on the occasion of a festival and won. His son Kākaḷa Nāyaka moved with the *kaṃpaḷa* and twelve *peṭṭige dēvaru* to Nayakanahatti, then covered with forest, and reclaimed and settled a *haṭṭi.* His grandson Giḍḍēra Nāyaka offered anklets embellished with pearls to the *kaṃpaḷa.*

Sūradevina Pāpa Nāyaka, the eldest son of Mallayya, succeeded the father. Among the sons and grandsons of Mallayya, Jagaḷūru Pāpa Nāyaka and Gādri Pāla Nāyaka are of special interest. These two persons are legendary heroes of the Bēḍas who were deified after their death and are even today tutelary gods of the Bēḍas and are worshipped at their respective tombs located in the modern Chitradurga district [Kṛṣṇamūrti Hanūru 1993: 42-50, 252-72]. These two heroes are of course mythic and legendary rather than historical, and so their inclusion in the genealogy of the Nayakanahattis is almost certainly erroneous. But by this manipulation the legitimacy of the Nayakanahattis as the champions of the Bēḍas is again asserted.

'Hoṭṭeḷa Nāyaka' in the text must be one of the Nidugallus. Though the historical authenticity of this quarrel is dubious and cannot be confirmed, the point of the episode is fairly clear. It asserts the importance of the two most sacred objects, *kaṃpaḷa* and *peṭṭige dēvaru*, for the Bēḍa Nāyakas, whose status and legitimacy must be constructed in relation to them, and the supremacy of the Nayakanahattis who actually tend them. This episode can also be understood as a legendary expression of the political rivalry among the Bēḍa Nāyakas belonging to the same exogamous group. The migration with the sacred objects to Nayakanahatti and Giḍḍēra Nāyaka's offering to the *kampaḷa* also underscore the politics of the Nayakanahattis who tried to construct and define their own status in relation to the sacred symbols of the Myāsa Bēḍas.

After the period of Bōdi Mallappa Nāyaka, a son of Giḍḍēra, the descriptions of the *NB* become of relatively more historical value. He is said to have married Girijamma Nāgati, a sister of Cikkaṇṇa Nāyaka (A.D. 1675-1686) of Chitradurga, and this makes it possible to determine the period of his life. He was the first 'Malla' since the mythic founder, and many of his descendants came to call themselves Malla. This indirectly suggests that the ancestor legend beginning with the founder Mallayya in the *NB* was composed during the time of Bōdi Mallappa Nāyaka.

The leitmotif of the ancestor legend in the *NB* is that the Nayakanahattis are the legitimate chiefs of the Bēḍas and superior to all the other Bēḍa Nāyakas. Many symbols and idioms of the Bēḍas, such as *kaṃpaḷa*, the twelve *peṭṭige dēvaru*, the deified Bēḍa heroes, and the Sun god legend, were appropriated and integrated into a genealogy that tried to establish their status as champions of the caste or clan. In the transactions with the Vijayanagara king, though the acquisition of *nāyaka* identity through martial service is implied, it is pushed into the background by the endorsement by the universal kingship of the indigenous traditions and idioms of the Bēḍas in relation to which the status of the Nayakanahattis as the champions of the Bēḍas was constructed. Compared with the *NAV*, the *NB* obviously stresses their descent-based identity as Bēḍas or Enumalōrus and pushes their non-descent, open identity as *nāyakas* into the rear. This may be partly attributed to the historical fact that the Nayakanahattis did not have direct experience nor memories of service as *nāyakas* in the capacity of military leaders at the zenith of the Vijayanagara kingship.

## Conclusion

In the ancestor legends of the Bēḍa Nāyakas composed in the seventeenth century, the ascribed Bēḍa identity based on descent and caste was no less emphasised than was non-descent and acquired *nāyaka* identity, though both are fundamentally contradictory. When we consider the historical significance of this, it must not be overlooked that the articulation of identity based on descent and caste was not such an uncommon phenomenon in the historical narratives of other little kings in contemporary south India. For example, the famous Keṃpē Gouḍa of Bangalore and his descendants belonged to the Morasu Okkaliga agriculturist caste and called themselves 'of the fourth clan (*caturtha gōtrada*),' namely, *śūdras* ranked fourth in the *varṇa* system [*EC*, xii, Kg-12]. In a family history of the Nāyakas of Pavagada, who were Ere Gollas, a sub-group of a cowherd caste, the issue of caste plays a pivotal role [*MNM*, 395-407]. Furthermore, during this period the legend came to circulate widely in south India that the Saṃgamas who established the first dynasty of the Vijayanagara Empire were of the Kuruba shepherd caste, although there are no descriptions in contemporary sources implying that they were actually so. The earliest records of this legend in Kannada appear in two works by Tirumalārya, a minister-cum-poet in the court of Cikka Dēva Rāja Oḍeya (A.D. 1672-1704) of Mysore. In his *Cika Dēva Rāya Vijayam* [Narasiṃhācār and Rāmānujaiyaṃgār 1896: 22] and *Cikka Dēva Rāya Vaṃśāvaḷi* [Krishnaswami Ayyangar 1986: 303], he called the Saṃgamas 'the Kuruba kings (*kuruṃba rāyaru*).' [31] Of course the legend cannot be determined as being true or false because of a lack of reliable sources. What matters is that caste identity among the politico-military elite grew so strong that it reached back in time to involve the Saṃgamas. After the late sixteenth century, when the Vijayanagara kingship rapidly declined, descent-based caste identity tended to grow and be articulated, and this was fundamentally contrary to the open status of the *nāyaka* among the politico-military elite. The heavily Bēḍa-coloured self-images in the ancestor legends of the Bēḍa Nāyakas were examples (probably extreme) of the representation of this general trend rather than exceptional cases resulting from their actual peculiar 'tribal' background.[32]

Though the causes of this historical transformation must have been complex, one cause was the change in the political roles and functions of *nāyakas*. In the early sixteenth century at the zenith of the Vijayanagara kingship, they were literally leaders (*nāyaka*) of the army. Even though they were granted fiefs (*nāyakatana* or *amara māgaṇi*), their endowments seem to have been changed within a short period, and long and stable relationships between *nāyakas* and particular regions did not develop. But from the late sixteenth century, when the central kingship started to decline quickly, *nāyakas* came to be lords (*saṃsthānika*) ruling particular regions for longer periods, and their right to rule was inherited by their descendants.[33] The new reality of the hereditary and semi-permanent rule of estates and the need to legitimise it must have impelled them to develop a genealogical awareness. The fact that many family histories such as the *NAV* and *NB* were composed in and around the courts of little and big kings testifies most eloquently to their keen sense of genealogy. The development of this genealogical and descent consciousness might have given new life or new spirit to the caste-based identity that had been, at least partly, negated or hidden by the *nāyakas*' open status, which was primarily defined in relation to the Vijayanagara kingship.

For warlords such as the Bēḍa Nāyakas, who did not have consanguineal ties with the dominant elite in local agrarian society, the maintenance and consolidation of ties with martial Bēḍa followers might have been a top priority on their agendas for political survival at a time of political disturbances and uncertainty. But they could never take the loyalty of their Bēḍa followers for granted. The relationship between them was not always as stable as their 'tribal' appearance would suggest, but was sometimes full of tension. For example, Sūrakāṃta Raṃgappa Nāyaka of Chitradurga was assassinated by his own soldiers mainly consisting of Bēḍas on the ground that they had not received regular pay [*MNM*, 9]. Given these political circumstances, the self-images of the Bēḍa Nāyakas as champions of the Bēḍas were not unrelated to the needs of their realpolitik to maintain and strengthen the loyalty of their martial Bēḍa followers.

The self-images closely connected with idioms and legends that tried to establish their status as champions of the Bēḍa caste or clan in the ancestor legends of the Bēḍa Nāyakas are inseparable from the historical and political circumstances of the seventeenth century when the prototype of the legends may have been composed. They are not mere mythic and obscure recollections of distant ancestors before they participated in the political Great Tradition composed of the universal Vijayanagara kingship and the open status group known as *nāyaka*. Rather they are representations of a descent identity rediscovered and redefined in the new political circumstances after the collapse of the Great Tradition.

In this essay I have, at the risk of simplification, contrasted the post-Vijayanagara politics based on genealogy, descent and caste with the open and dynamic political system of the Vijayanagara kingship at its zenith, which depended on services offered by military leaders. My presupposition that the military leaders who shared the sovereignty of the Vijayanagara kingship through gifts of honours, titles and lands constituted an open status group and developed a group identity under the name of *nāyaka* remains a hypothesis to be verified by further research.

My tentative conclusion is that the formation of the family histories composed of idioms and logic particular to the Bēḍa caste was closely connected with and the consequence of the consolidation of their local rules. As already explained, the Bēḍas were numerically dominant in eastern Chitradurga, but the agricultural production there was under the control of a few agricultural castes. Concerning this point, the rule of the Bēḍa Nāyakas was different from the case of the Pudukottai kingdom studied by Dirks, where the caste organisation headed by the king reached down to villages and supported the political rule both administratively and ritually [Dirks 1987a: Parts 3 & 4]. Given this, the local agricultural groups' support must have been indispensable for the stability of the Bēḍa Nāyakas' rule. But the family histories analysed here do not seem even once to have tried to target them in their attempt to legitimise the local rule. Though this is beyond the scope of this essay, to understand historically this seemingly curious silence and the almost exclusive obsession with Bēḍaness, a great deal more must be made known about the administrative and ritual setup of their local rule.

**WESTERN CITRADURGA**

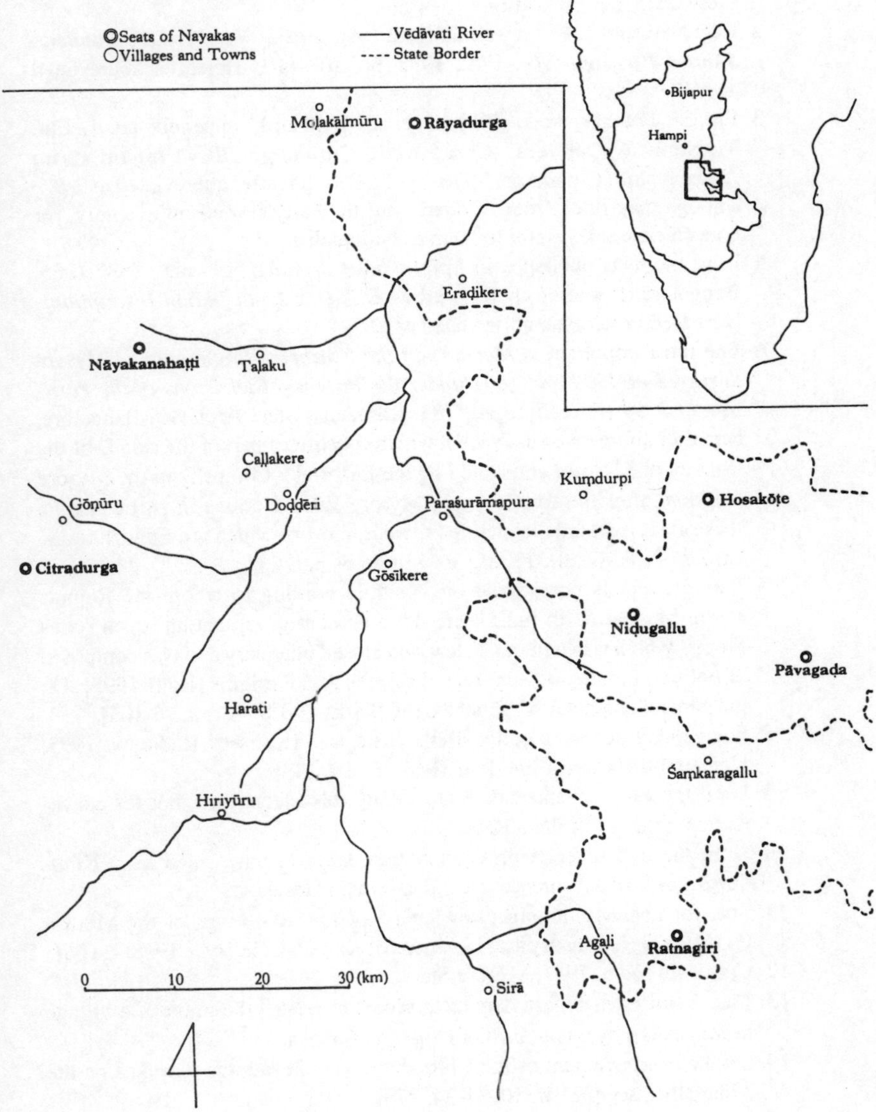

## Notes

1 Though the texts mainly recording the histories of the families of little kings during this period bear various titles such as *vaṃśāvali*, *bakhairu*, and *kaiphiyattu*, they are similar in content and style such that I call all of these texts 'family histories.'

2 Rā. Narasiṃhācār ed., 'Niḍugallu Arasugaḷa Vaṃśāvaḷi,' *Kannaḍa Sāhitya Pariṣatpatrike*, 17-2, 1932, pp. 103-110. Hereafter abbreviated as *NAV*.

3 Eṃ.En. Prabhākar ed., 'Nāyakanahaṭṭi Bakhairu,' appendix no. 1, Eṃ. Vi. Śrīnivās et. al. eds., *Caṃdravaḷḷi, Citradurga Jilleya Itihāsa kurita Lēkhanagaḷu*, Citradurga, 1976, pp. 26-35. Hereafter abbreviated as *NB*.

4 Though they ruled from Dodderi until the early seventeenth century, for convenience sake I refer to them as Nidugallus.

5 I use the texts published in *Epigraphia Carnatica*, 19 vols., 1886-1965, Bangalore (hereafter abbreviated as *EC*) and *South Indian Inscriptions*, New Delhi (hereafter abbreviated as *SII*).

6 The most important is *Memoirs of the Northern Purgunnahs of Mysore Surveyed in 1800 and 1801 under the Provincial Divisions of the Partition of 1799* (microfilm, no. 785, Karnataka State Archives, Bangalore, hereafter abbreviated as *MNM*), which constitutes part of the results of the 'Survey of Mysore' conducted by the East India Company in the Mysore kingdom after the fourth Anglo-Mysore War. I utilise in particular the 'Historical Accounts' contained therein, most of which are English translations of the so-called Kaifiyats written by natives.

7 This concept is borrowed from Kolff, according to whom the Rajputs of pre-Mughal north India were not a descent group but an 'open status group,' which was without a clear and closed boundary and was composed of politico-military adventurers of diverse social origins [Kolff 1995]. On the general character of Nāyakas, see [Dirks 1987a: 43-52, 96-106].

8 For general accounts of the Bēḍa caste, see [Kariśeṭṭi Rudrappa 1995; Kṛṣṇamūrti Hanūru 1993; Iyer 1988: ii, 197-238].

9 Until the early seventeenth century they ruled from Sira, but for convenience' sake, I call them Ratnagiris.

10 Until the mid-seventeenth century they seem to have ruled from Kumdurpi, but for convenience' sake, I call them Hosakotes.

11 See, for instance, the ancestor legend of the little kings of the Morasu Okkaliga agriculturist caste in southeast Karnataka in [Iyer 1988: i, 105].

12 *Census of India*, 1931, Mysore State.

13 This inscription, highly damaged, seems to record the grant of a village headmanship by a grandson of Hoṭṭeṇṇa Nāyaka.

14 On the encroachment of the Chitradurga and Rayadurga Nāyakas on the Nidugallus, see [*MNM*, 10, 33-34, 278].

15 For the history of the Ratnagiri Nāyakas, see 'History of Midigesi Chiefs,'

*Mysore Archaeological Report*, 1946, pp. 24-31; 'Kaifiyat of Ratnagiri,' in [Mahalingam 1972: 318-20].

16 According to 'Memorandums of Poligars of the Ceded Districts,' Heery Huddeyer (i.e., Hiriya Oḍeya), an ancestor of the Ratnagiris, was a Desai (hereditary local officer) of Sarvada near Bijapur. Later he came to serve a Vijayanagara king with a thousand infantry and was given twelve villages as 'jageer' to maintain the infantry [Firminger 1917: 381].

17 On this *maṭha*, see [Maṃjunāthan 1987]. The head monks of the *maṭha* were also spiritual guides (*pūrvācārya*) of the Ratnagiris, who called themselves disciples and sons (*śiṣyaru makkaḷu*) of the monks [*EC*, xi, Hr-6; *SII*, ix-2, 689].

18 Prabhākar ed., 'Nāyakanahaṭṭif Bakhairu,' appendix no. 2, pp. 35-36.

19 Even nowadays in years when the harvest is good, a group of Myāsa Bēḍas goes to Anegondi to made a ritual gift to descendants of the Āravīḍu family and afterwards goes to Kampli and Kamalapura to meet old relatives living there [Kṛṣṇamūrti Hanūru 1993: 133].

20 The 'Historical Account of Doodairee' gives another version of the symbolic round trip between the birthplace and the royal city [*MNM*, 271]. According to this version, Bommaṇṇa Nāyaka, the great-grandson of Tippa, constructed three villages and named them Harati, Dodderi and Sarvada after the ancestor's place. The construction of villages with the names of ancestral sites can be interpreted as a symbolic return to them.

21 The 'Historical Account of Doodairee' says more clearly, though slightly differently, that the symbolic return to the ancestral place signifies the recovery of Bēḍa descent. According to this account, Tippa was sent to eastern Chitradurga after 'Narasinxloo Kistna Rayalo' included him in the 'Boya (i.e., Bēḍa) Caste' because he was brought up by a Muslim 'Padshah' though his mother was a *kṣatriya* [*MNM*, 270f].

22 The 'Historical Account of Nidigull' clearly states that Tippa named his son after his stepfather [*MNM*, 367].

23 As in this case, the relationship with this Vīra Śaiva *maṭha* is, though indirectly, incorporated into the ancestor legend of the *NAV* at important moments. S. Bayly states that in little kingdoms in the Tamil region of the same period, deified *gurus* were revered as the supernatural patrons of kingdoms [Bayly 1989: 65-69]. The relationship between the Bēḍa Nāyakas and Sarvada Maṭha may be understood in a similar way.

24 The history of Cikka Tippa Bhūpāla and his family is not known because of a lack of sources. In the political disturbances before and after the dynastic change in the Vijayanagara empire from the Saṃgamas to the Sāḷuvas in the late fifteenth century, many independent rulers apppeared in south India. He may have been one of them. In the reign of Kṛṣṇa Rāya, Jaka Nāyaka held Nidugallu *sīme* as a fief [*EC*, xii, Pg-62], and so he must have been displaced in the early years of the Tuḷuvas.

25 See, for example, the inscriptions of the Chitradurga Nāyakas [*EC*, xi, Hr-53; *EC*, xi, Hk-54; *EC*, xi, Jl-46].

26 The earliest example of an imitation *biruḍāvaḷi* of the Nidugallus appears in an inscription dated S. 1578 [*EC*, xii, Pg-42]. But it ends at 'the wrestler who protected the herd of she-buffaloes' in the above translation.

27 Though Girija states it is located in modern Parasuramapura Hobli of Callakere Taluk [Girija 1991: 165], I have been unable to identify it.

28 On the *peṭṭige dēvaru*, see [Kṛṣṇamūrti Hanūru 1993: 118-23; Kariśeṭṭi Rudrappa 1995: 62-3].

29 On the *kumāra* relationship in Vijayanagara politics, see [Dirks 1987a: 101-2].

30 According to legendary accounts, though born to Brahman parents, he grew up among tribal hill people because his parents died soon after he was born. Afterwards he married a tribal girl and became a highway robber. The Bēḍa Nāyakas appropriated the legend on account of the self-image, or that imposed by others, of the Bēḍas, whose lifestyle is 'tribal' and claimed to be *Vālmīka gōtra*, that is, descendants of the children born to Vālmīki and his tribal wife.

31 Many references are found in the Kannada Kaifiyats collected by Colonel Colin Mackenzie around 1800. For example, see [Kalaburgi 1994: 73, 118].

32 To understand the historical process of the reducing of the Nāyakas as an open status group into a mere shell of what they had formerly been and the growth of respective caste identities, the Telugu Balija caste and its history may give an important clue. Many Nāyakas, including the three major Nāyakas in the Tamil area and the Nāyakas of Cannapattana, Beluru, and Rayadurga in the Kannada area, are said to have been Telugu Balijas. The mixed nature of the Telugu Balija caste, comprising originally people of various descents, corresponds with the openness and fluidity of the Nāyakas as an open status group. When and how people of diverse origins came to be a closed descent group and the relationship between that process and the Nāyakas are questions that remain to be resolved.

33 According to Karashima [1992: Chapters 1, 3 , 5], *nāyakas* in Tamil displayed a tendency towards localisation even in the early sixteenth century.

## References

Bayly, S.

1989 *Saints, Goddesses and Kings: Muslims and Christians in South Indian Society 1700-1900*, Cambridge, Cambridge University Press.

Caṃdraśēkhara Kaṃbāra (ed.)
1985 *Kannaḍa Jānapada Viśvakōśa*, vol. 2, Beṃgaḷūru, Kannaḍa Sāhitya Pariṣattu.

Chitnis, K.N.
1990 *Medieval Indian History*, New Delhi, Atlantic Publishers & Distributors.

Citraliṃgayya, Eṃ.Vi.
1987 'Harati Pāḷeyagārana Mūla Vaṃśāvaḷi. Oṃdu Vyāsaṃga,' Lakṣmaṇ Telagāvi ed., *Haratisiri*, Hartikōṭi, Vālmīki Sāhitya Saṃpada, pp. 282-316.

Dirks, N.
1987a *The Hollow Crown: Ethnohistory of an Indian Kingdom*, Cambridge, Cambridge University Press.
1987b 'The Pasts of a Pāḷaiyakārar: The Ethnohistory of a South Indian Little King,' George W. Spencer ed., *Temples, Kings and Peasants: Perceptions of South India's Past*, Madras, New Era, pp. 85-132.

Firminger, W.K. (ed.)
1917 *Fifth Report from the Select Committee on the Affairs of the East India Compay, 28 July, 1812*, repr., Calcutta, R. Cambray & Co.

Girija, Ṭi.
1991 *Citradurga Jillā Darśini*, Dāvaṇagere, Rēkhā Prakāśana.

Iyer L.K.A. (ed.)
1988 *The Mysore Tribes and Castes*, 5 vols, repr., Delhi, Mittal.

Kalaburgi, Eṃ.Eṃ. (ed.)
1994 *Karnāṭakada Kaiphiyattugaḷu*, Hampi, Prasārāṃga, Kannaḍa Viśvavidyālaya.

Karashima, Noboru
1992 *Towards a New Formation: South Indian Society under Vijayanagar Rule*, New Delhi, Oxford University Press.

Kariśeṭṭi Rudrappa
1995 *Myāsa Nāyakaru: Oṃdu Janāṃgika Adhyayana*, Beṃgaḷūru, Kannaḍa Sāhitya Pariṣattu.

Kolff, D.H.A.
1995 'The Rajput of Ancient and Medieval North India: A Warrior-Ascetic,' N.K. Singhi and Rajendra Joshi eds., *Folk, Faith & Feudalism: Rajasthan Studies*, Jaipur, Rawat Publications, pp. 257-94.

Krishnaswami Ayyangar, S. (ed.)
1986 *Sources of Vijayanagar History*, repr., Delhi, Gian Publishing House.

Kṛṣṇamūrti Hanūru
1993 *Myāsa Bēḍara Saṃskṛti*, Beṃgaḷūru, Karnāṭaka Sāhitya Akāḍemi.

Mahalingam, T.V. (ed.)
1972 *Mackenzie Manuscripts: Summaries of the Historical Manuscripts in the Mackenzie Collection*, vol. 2, Madras, University of Madras.

Maṃjunāthan, Ji.Ji.
1987 'Sujñāna Ciṃtāmaṇi hāgu Harati Nāyakara Guruparaṃpare,' *Haratisiri*, pp. 1139-46.

Narasiṃhācār, Es.Ji. and Rāmānujaiyaṃgār (eds.)
1896 *Cika Dēva Rāya Vijayam*, Maisūru.

Venkata Ramanayya, N.
1990 *Vijayanagara: Origin of the City and the Empire*, repr., New Delhi, Asian Educational Services.

# 8

# Kingship, Community and Commerce in Late Pre-colonial Khurdȧ

AKIO TANABE

## Introduction

This essay aims to elucidate aspects of kingship in late pre-colonial Orissa in terms of its interrelationships with the local communities and market. The material for discussion will be based on data from the Khurda kingdom (A.D. 1572-1804) and local communities existing in the region called *gaṛa* or 'fort,' which consisted of several villages centring around a fortress. I will refer to this unit of local inter-village community as a 'fort area' in this essay. I will draw my examples particularly from the state's interaction with Garh Manitri (Fort Manitri) where I conducted intensive anthropological fieldwork as well as historical research.

The interrelationships between the state and local communities that developed from the late sixteenth to eighteenth centuries in Khurda will be formulated in this essay as 'sacrificer state and sacrificial community.' The main concern here is to elucidate the nature of development of state formation, by which local communities were assimilated into the redistributive structure of kingship while maintaining its system of entitlements at the local level. Local communities were to transform themselves into 'sacrificial organisations without sacrificer,' where communities remained as the basic unit of social reproduction but were incomplete without the presence of kingship. The King commanded, when the need arose, control over local resources – both economic and military – with his authority as sacrificer.

These transformations of local communities in interaction with the level of the state seem to be related to the particular historical development of the importance of the 'little kingdom'[1] in late sixteenth to eighteenth century Orissa and in other parts of India. It appears that it was during this period that the interaction and interdependence between the little kingdoms and the local communities were intensified. In discussing the state formation here, it is necessary to consider not 'the State' (with a capital 'S') in terms of 'regimes, kingship, administration and government,' but the 'state' (with a small 's') in terms of 'the various systematic aspects which together and interdependently fostered the growth and development of complex social orders' [Perlin 1985: 451]. This point is particularly important in looking at the characteristics of the interrelationships between the state and society in India during this period.

The investigation of the development of such relationships between the state and local communities in the wider historical context of the late sixteenth to eighteenth centuries, moreover, leads us to consider another important aspect. The introduction of more advanced and universal administrative technology in the local communities in the process of state formation, such as accounting, measuring and use of money, meant not only that these communities in the jungles of the hilly tracts of Khurda were more closely incorporated into the royal redistributive system, but also that they came to be connected to the wider network of the flow of money and goods, specifically the trade and commerce articulated with the growth of the world economy. Such development, in turn, gave distinct character to the fiscal set-ups and politico-military dynamics of the state in the late pre-colonial Khurda.

### *Principles of Kingship and Community*

The principles of pre-colonial Indian society and state will be called here 'community principle' and 'kingship principle.' [2] Here, the community principle refers to the ways in which horizontal cohabitation of people in a locality was aspired to be managed autonomously through a system of entitlements. The kingship principle relates to the aspiration of the state to extend its redistributive power cohesively throughout the vertical relations existing within the kingdom.[3] It is my contention that it is in the dialectics of these principles of community and kingship that seem to lie one of the sources of historical dynamism of sixteenth-eighteenth century Khurda, if not of the whole of India.[4]

In the community principle, what is important is the diversity in the forms of the lifestyles of the various peoples – castes and tribes – and their interdependence as a community, each playing a part of the whole. Forming a community did not necessarily mean a shared lifestyle or viewpoints, but rather, in the case of India, it is precisely the diversity of viewpoints and hierarchisation of different members that characterise its structure. In the hilly tract areas of Orissa, the 'fort areas' formed the primary unit for such horizontal division and integral coordination through the system of entitlements.[5]

In considering the kingship principle, it is necessary to look at it not as an independent outside force working above the community but see how its attempt to extend its redistributive structure interacted with the autonomy-seeking communities, and how it resulted in the particular relationship between the state and community becoming a more dependent one. The attempt of the state to extend its redistributive dominance did not lead to centralisation in the modern sense. Neither did it take a purely ritual character. It is thus necessary to try and delineate the cultural paradigm in which the balance and interrelationship between the state and community were managed in the context of the particular technological and economic stage of history.

### *Sacrificial Idiom in Indian Society and Kingship*

In the formulation of the 'sacrificer state and sacrificial community,' I have tried to avoid both the model of putting the ritual state and pragmatic society in dichotomy as in Geertz [1980] and Stein [1980] and the model which supposed the uniformity of emulating polities as in Tambiah [1985a, 1985b] and Peabody [1991a]. Geertz and Stein are correct in assuming that there were functional divisions between the state and the local levels, despite the assertions of Tambiah and Peabody in their emulative resemblance. But in proposing a kind of disjunction between the ritual and the pragmatic, they fail to treat the relationship between the state and the local levels as a total social phenomenon, which in turn is captured by Tambiah and Peabody's totalising perspective.

If we are to combine the insights provided by both these approaches, we must delineate the functional divisions of the state and community, and at the same time give adequate attention to the intricate systems of exchange and interactions between the two. In other words, we must attempt to describe the relationship between the state principle and community principle in terms that elucidate the cultural paradigm in which the exercise of the redistributive authority of kingship and the social reproduction of autonomy-seeking communities interacted to constitute the state-society complex. The formulation of 'sacrificer state and sacrificial community' is such an attempt.

The idiom of sacrifice has recently attracted considerable attention with the re-evaluation of Hocart's scheme on kingship and caste, in which sacrifice plays the central part [Hocart 1950, 1970]. Recognition of the cosmological significance of the institution of kingship and dominance pace Dumont led a number of scholars to return to and adopt the Hocartian scheme for enhancing the understanding of Indian society, in which the centrality of the king and/or the dominant caste is given importance as the pivotal point of Hindu social organisation. It seems as if now there is a large consensus that caste is a sacrificial organisation among a number of influential scholars [Dirks 1987; Raheja 1988; Quigley 1993, 1994].

When we look at what each of them mean by 'sacrificial organisation,' however, we find that there is actually more diversity than consensus. There seems to be variance over who assumes the central role as sacrificer and where the institution of sacrificial organisation is based. This seems to stem from the scholars' insensitivity, when discussing caste, to the complex relationship existing between the state and community, and the position of sacrificer and sacrificial organisation thereof.

Dirks [1987] takes a king-centred point of view where all of the castes are seen to have been positioned in relation to the king. There does not seem to be enough attention given to the local community which might operate on a different principle than kingship. Raheja [1988] takes the dominant caste to be the main sacrificer, assuming in a rather facile manner that there is a structural equivalence between the king and the dominant caste. She does not seem to be sensitive enough to the difference between the sovereignty of the king and local dominance of the dominant caste, as well as to the possible historical transformation of the nature of the dominance of the dominant caste. Quigley [1993], also adopting the sacrificial model, goes as far as arguing that each caste attempts to emulate the structure of the king's court. He thus in effect ignores the differences between not only the king and the dominant caste but among any of the castes, merely emphasising the emulative aspiration to be sacrificer among all of the castes.

I am also inspired by Hocart's use of the idiom of sacrifice to describe the Indian state and community. However, I would like to employ the idiom with sensitivity to the difference in function between kingship and local community, and to the way the sacrificial organisation was managed in the peculiarly Indian context. It is insufficient to argue that the sacrificial organisation was centred around the king as sacrificer. Rather the sacrificial organisation in the Indian community took its particular form in the system of entitlements.

We should note here that the sacrificial structure of community did not mean that it was an exclusively 'Hindu' system. What I am arguing here is not only that sacrificial organisations are found in other parts of the world, but also that sacrificial communities in India involved a diverse population including the tribals and also Muslims. Moreover, there was so much diversity in religio-social practices even among non-tribal and non-Muslim members that there is no point in talking of a 'Hindu' system as such. The diverse population followed their own religious practices, and sacrificial structure did not mean sharing of beliefs or practices, except that the members were supposed to play their part in support of the whole including participation in community ritual. In the case of Khurda, for example, there were many Muslim warriors including even a Muslim chief in Manika Garh. The Muslim members in Manika Garh also participated in community rituals which included worship of the local tutelary goddesses. This community practice coexisted along with the Islamic belief and practice within the Muslim group. Thus, sacrifice was not a religious institution in the sense of bringing about a shared system of a particular belief, as it allowed diversity to exist in the religious practice. [6] The pre-colonial Indian sacrificial community was both 'secular' in the sense of allowing the co-existence of diverse religious groups and 'religious' as it was related to the value of the whole and the transcendent. The means of approach to the transcendent, that is, the source of power of life, was diverse according to the different role and position of each member, the aggregate sacrificial practice of whom brought about the reproduction of the community as a whole.

The local community was the site of the basic reproductive activities. Each entitlement-holder played a part in the reproduction of the whole in the community as sacrificial organisation. Sacrifice here refers to the actions which were performed as a duty of a part dedicated for the whole. Such sacrificial activities should be thought to have included not only rituals but also politico-economic activities in the cultural paradigm. The duties and shares of each part were defined in the system of assignments and entitlements in the community.

The local sacrificial communities in late pre-colonial Orissa, however, were ideologically incomplete in themselves. They needed the king who functioned as the sacrificer. This did not mean, though, that the sacrificial organisation was directly centred around kingship. The king remained outside sacrificial communities but not disjoined from them, granting authority for the assignments and power of each entitlement-holder through various prestations, and acted as the central organiser of sacrificial activities.

In the following sections, I will trace the development of community and state in their dialectic relationships in Khurda from the late sixteenth to eighteenth centuries. Through its description, I will try to explain and examine the growth and workings of 'sacrificer state and sacrificial community.' Subsequently, I will postulate the meaning of this development of state formation for the wider economy.

## The State and Community in Khurda in History

### *Establishment of the Khurda Kingdom and its Interaction with Local Leadership*

After the collapse of the medieval Orissan empire in 1568 brought about by the Afghan invasion, Ramachandra Deva, the first king of the Khurda Bhoi dynasty, managed to build up a small-scale kingdom with Khurda as its fort capital. He re-established the idol of Lord Jagannath in the temple in Puri which had been plundered, and was able to present himself as the successor of the tradition of the great Orissan empire.[7] His position was further strengthened when the Mughal emperor, Akbar, acknowledged Ramachandra as Gajapati (*gajapati*: the lord of the Elephants) or the paramount ruler of Orissa in 1592. He was also given the rank of 'commander of 3500' and was granted authority over the Khurda kingdom and 31 small kingdoms (*zamindārī*) under his command in the surrounding area.

Before the establishment of Khurda, the hilly tract of Khurda was ruled mainly by Saora 'tribal' chiefs. The establishment of the kingdom here did not mean that the pre-existing petty rulers in the area were totally driven away by him. Rather, the 'conquest' of the region involved the state acknowledging the existing power structure of the locality and putting the petty rulers under his supra-authority.

The indigenous sources say that the Khurda king gained his territory from the king of '*śuddha* Saori' (Purified Saora) who had originally ruled the region. The Khurda king is said to have sacrificed the latter and buried his head under a tree [Pattanaik 1959: 6].[8] At the time of the establishment of the Khurda kingdom, apart from the king who had been sacrificed, there are said to have been four '*śuddha khaṇḍāyat*' and thirteen 'Saori *khaṇḍāyat*' who were autonomous chiefs [Srichandan 1989]. It should be noted here that *khaṇḍāyat* refers not to the caste name but to autonomous chiefs.[9] '*Śuddha*' means 'purified' and the name suggests that the Saōras were purified and became *khaṇḍāyat*. 'Saori' is the adjective form of Saora and this *khaṇḍāyat* was clearly of Saora origin.

The Khurda king had initially probably allowed these indigenous *khaṇḍāyats* of tribal origin considerable autonomy, himself ruling above as the encompassing power of these chiefs. However, in the course of the seventeenth to eighteenth centuries, these chiefs were gradually driven away and replaced by the chiefs of the fort areas called *bisoi* and/or *daḷabeherā* [10] who operated more directly under the king's command and who constituted the military and administrative head of the region as well as the servants of the king. At the time of colonialism, there were only one *khaṇḍāyat* among the four original *śuddha khaṇḍāyats* and four among the original thirteen Saori *khaṇḍāyats* that had remained there.

The history of the relationship between the Khurda kingdom and the region may be seen as a process by which the small-scale polities, such as existing chiefdoms and small kingdoms, were encompassed inside the kingdom, being allowed some degree of autonomy at first. Then gradually there was increasing interference in the regional polities, taking away their autonomy. There were no doubt wars and violent conquests involved in the process whereby the kingship took away the autonomy of the regional small-scale polities and put them under its control. In this process, the existing autonomous chiefs (*khaṇḍāyats*) and small kings (*rājās*) were replaced by fort chiefs (*dalābeherā, bisoi*) who were directly under the king.

Spreading the kingship's control over the regional polity-society, however, did not mean centralisation in the sense of the modern state where bureaucrats and army are dispatched from the central government and the structure of command is unified. As far as the warriors and scribes residing in the regional polity-society were concerned, they were guaranteed not only economic bases but also administrative and military power as well as a ritual capacity from the king, as their office was closely articulated with the administration of polity. In this sense, it can be said that the process by which the state took control over a region paradoxically involved decentralisation and sharing of sovereignty to the localities [cf. Perlin 1985: 475].

On the other hand, at the same time, it is incorrect to view the situation in terms of the 'segmentary state' [Stein 1980] in which the king had ritual suzerainty whereas the region had practical power. It must be noted that the administration and military at the local level contributed greatly to the reproduction of the state. The local society, on the one hand, was dependent on the king for the legitimacy of its authority and power, while on the other, it sent soldiers for the state when necessary, provided administrative services such as revenue collection and accounting for the king, and supported the royalty and ministers financially by providing land and taxes. In this way, the local society had not only a ritual relationship with the kingdom but also a deep-rooted relation of mutual coexistence at the military, administrative and economic levels.[11]

This peculiar kind of development of mutual dependence of the state and community may be understood in terms of 'sacrificial community and sacrificer state.' Its peculiar characteristics may be appreciated if we compare it with the situation of semi-autonomous communities under *khaṇḍāyat* chiefs. In semi-autonomous communities, chiefs were taken to be the distributor of the land to different entitlement-holders.[12] The chiefs did not have to depend on the state for his authority, except that he sent an annual prestation (*nazarānā*) to the greater king as a token of submission.

When the communities were transformed to sacrificial community under the sacrificer state, however, the chief no longer had independent authority. Not only the chief but also each and every entitlement-holder derived legitimacy directly from the king, as presented through oral family histories informing us of how they were called and given entitlements from the king. The entitlement-holders in communities, by accepting the king's sovereignty, were thus granted royal authority to their power and rights. As a token of their hierarchical relationships, each entitlement-holder was to pay *taṅki* (a quit rent) to the king.[13] The community entitlement-holders played their role in the name of the king around whom the sacrificial activities were supposed to be centred. The sacrificial communities were to remain incomplete without the presence of the king as sacrificer.

The king, on the other hand, had to give shares of sovereignty to the entitlement-holders in communities. It was through this giving that the king established his relationship with the local communities and thus gained control over them [Dirks: 1987; Berkemer 1993: 319].[14] The sacrificial communities were the actual sites where activities regarding production took place according to the system of entitlements. The king, while remaining outside communities, acted as the centre and source of authority of the sacrificial organisations in communities as sacrificer through various exchanges, and was thus able to extend his control over the military, administrative and economic resources in the localities.

## Establishment of Garh Manitri

### *The Conquest and Annexation of Garh Manitri*

Let us now look at the process of formation of Garh Manitri (Fort Manitri) as a sacrificial community in its relationship with the state. I have given a brief ethnohistory of the establishment of Garh Manitri elsewhere [Tanabe 1995], so let it suffice here to point out the nature of the transformative process of the area that led to the establishment of the system of assignments and entitlements, which was the substantial basis for the sacrificial organisation.

According to the village oral tradition, the tribal Khonds and then Saoras were the original settlers in the region. The ancestors of the present Caste Hindus are said to have immigrated into the area after annexation of the area into the Khurda kingdom which probably took place around the beginning of the seventeenth century. It is said that after the ancestor of the present chief of the fort (*daḷabeherā*) succeeded in conquering the area which had been under the Ranpur kingdom, Brāhmaṇas and other service castes were invited to the region. Additionally, more Khaṇḍāyats were invited from other forts to support the chief in the military as *pāikas* or foot soldiers. These new immigrant families are said in oral family histories to have received *khañjā* land from the king to support themselves. *Khañjā*, in the ordinary sense, means 'arrangement' and, historically, refers to the 'hereditary assignments of entitlements and duties' granted to the community members. The land attached to such office, that is, *khañjā* land or sometimes called *hetā*, constituted a major part of such allotted shares of resources, and this kind of land given through 'arrangement' of the office seems to have functioned as the basic idiom of the community membership.

It is important to note that these developments did not mean eradication or replacement of the local autochthonous population and culture, which were incorporated into the overall system. The case in point here, as regards Garh Manitri, is the place of the goddess Ramachandi and the tribal population of Khond and Saora who were given places in the newly emerging complex state-social organisation in the area.

One important move by the royalty regarding the autochthonous goddess Ramachandi and the tribal population was the fact that the king constructed a temple for Ramachandi next to the Jagannath temple in the fort, both of which were placed in front of the royal palace. So there came to be established a royal-divine complex of the king's palace and temples of the state deity Jagannath and the local tutelary deity Ramachandi in the village of Garh Manitri. For Ramachandi to be established as a major tutelary goddess of the region, it was considered appropriate for the goddess to have a temple inside the village, although the goddess's original abode on the hill outside the village remained to constitute the centre of her divine power.

In this way, there were close interactions between the state level and the local level in which not only the state god, Jagannath, was brought to the region and worshipped but also the local goddess of tribal origin, Ramachandi, was gradually transformed in its form of worship. The goddess was to be worshipped in a way suitable for the king to be the main patron or the sacrificer (*yājamaṇa*), introducing *pūjā* to be performed by the Brāhmaṇas. At the same time, indigenous features in the style of worship such as possession by the Saora shaman (*kāḷisī*), offerings of animal sacrifice and *puñji* (heaps of a mixture of rice, egg and liquor) by the Khond priest, were maintained and incorporated in the system. The king also donated land for the goddess which was occupied by the Saora shaman and Khond priest as their *khañjā* land for fulfilling their duty towards the goddess. The granting of *khañjā* by the king and its acceptance by the Khond priest and Saora shaman tells us of the main method of the incorporation and acquisition of membership of the tribal population in the community.

The king was not only the *ādya sebaka* (first servant) of Jagannath but also became the patron-sacrificer of the tutelary goddess of Garh Manitri, Ramachandi. By thus being related to both deities, the king could project himself, at least in Garh Manitri, as the patron-sacrificer of the local indigenous goddess while maintaining his position as the king of Orissa, winning both local support and state-level authority.[15]

## *System of Entitlements as the Basis of Incorporating Dynamism*

Thus in the process of establishment of Garh Manitri, castes were brought into the area, and both the people of so-called Caste Hindus and indigenous tribals became embedded in the system of entitlements with its allotted duties and shares (*khañjā*). This system of entitlements was the basis through which different cultural elements and diverse population can be given a place in the community as a united whole through interaction and exchange. It can be said to have been the main system through which the state and society maintained the dynamism absorbing and incorporating new elements into the community structure of the state-society complex. This process of incorporation must have taken place over a long period of time, but I would like to emphasise the fact that this was still an on-going process when the states, especially at the level of the little kingdoms, were developing closer interaction with the local, often tribal, communities in the hilly tract of Orissa in the late sixteenth to eighteenth centuries.

It is important to note here that, although *khañjā* was the fundamental mechanism for the sacrificial community and thus formed the core of the community principle in pre-colonial Khurda, *khañjā* is always stated as being given by the king in family histories. The royal authority represented by the king, which ultimately leads to the divine authority of the Lord Jagannath as the real ruler of Orissa, is indispensable in guaranteeing the legitimacy of holding *khañjā* in the community as the basis of one's social and existential identity. So, although *khañjā* formed the basis of the community structure, it was inseparable from the workings of authority and power of the king from the time of its very allotment. This suggests that in understanding *khañjā*, we must take into account not only the community principle but also the principle of kingship and dominance, which worked together in an overlappingly manner in the formation of the system of entitlements.

In the next section, we will look at the interactions between the state and community more closely, taking as our example Garh Manitri and using the primary resources found in the locality.

## Exchange Relation between the State and Community in Late Pre-colonial Khurda

### *About the Historical Sources*

Sources employed here are administrative documents written or rather etched on palm leaves (*tāḷa patra*) using iron pens (*lekhoṇi*). Such palm leaves were the most popular medium for administrative and religious documents in Orissa until the beginning of the nineteenth century. The documents were written in Oriya scribe letters (*karaṇi*). The palm leaf scripts used as the source here are administrative documents of A.D. 1776 to 1805 which have been preserved by the family of an 'accountant' (*bhuī muḷa*) of Barabati village. These documents were kept in bundles and had become objects of worship during *daśaharā* as the tool of family profession signifying their traditional ruling status. The owner was not aware of the contents of the documents. To the best of my knowledge, there has been no previous research of this kind on administrative documents at the village or fort level in pre-colonial Orissa.

### *System of Entitlements and Assignments*

I will only briefly describe the system of assignments at the community level since I have presented details of it elsewhere [Tanabe forthcoming]. The document first records how the resources for redistribution for entitlement-holders were collected from the 13 villages (12 surrounding villages and the central 'fort itself') that constitute the fort area of Garh Manitri. All the accounting is done in cowry units. There is 13,115 *kāhāṇa* 8 *paṇa* 10 *gaṇḍā* worth of resources in total, which consists of the 'land part' (*bhumi bhāga*) worth 11,103 *kāhāṇa* 5 *paṇa* (84.66 per cent), and 'cowry part' (*kauḍi bhāga*) which are further divided into the 'cash cowry' (*nagada kauḍi*) worth 176 *kāhāṇa* 6 *paṇa* (1.34 per cent) and the rest of the cowry part worth 1,835 *kāhāṇa* 13 *paṇa* 10 *gaṇḍā* (14.00 per cent) that consisted of slash-and-burn fields, mango trees, meals, various goods given at ritual occasions and other items.

The state's direct share from these resources remarkably consisted of only 294 *kāhāṇa* 2 *paṇa* 15 *gaṇḍā*, that is, a mere 2.24 per cent share of the total. It consisted of all of the cash cowry part (176 *kāhāṇa* 6 *paṇa*) and land part (117 *kāhāṇa* 12 *paṇa* 15 *gaṇḍā*).

The remainder of the resources were then distributed among the communal entitlement-holders. They were granted to, according to the classification in the document, 'gods' (*debaha*) including the state-deity Jagannath, family tutelary god of the chief and regional tutelary goddess, 'donation to Brāhmaṇas' (*brāhmaṇa dāna*), 'village level allotted land' (*desa hetā*) given to village administrative officers such as village heads (*desa pradhāna*) and village accountant (*desa bhoi*) as well as village servants such as carpenter, barber and washerman, 'fort-level servants' (*gaṛa sebaka*) such as carpenter, barber, potter, watchman and bedmaker, and the 'payment for foot soldiers' (*pāika bartana*) which included, besides foot soldiers and guards, administrators such as 'chief' (*daḷabeherā*), 'scribe' (*koṭha karaṇa*) and 'collector of fines' (*taṇḍakāra*), as well as 'labourer' (*kāṇḍi*) and 'military musician' (*bājantari*).

### *State's Revenue from the Community*

The state's revenue from the fort area of Garh Manitri totalled 1,942 *kāhāṇa* 15 *paṇa* 6 *gaṇḍā* 3 *kaḍā*, which was 14.81 per cent of the total resources of the area. This comprised: (A) the revenue from the royal government's direct shares, (B) taxes collected from the shares of the communal entitlement-holders and (C) taxes collected from the community. (See Table 1.) The details of each of these are examined below.

Table 1 : State's revenue from the community of Garh Manitri

| From the state's direct share (A) | From tax on communal shares (B) | From miscellaneous community tax (C) | State revenue from Garh Manitri (Total) | Total resources recorded in Garh Manitri |
|---|---|---|---|---|
| 264.11.11.0 | 1,302.14.0.0 | 375.4.12.2.0 | 1,942.15.6.3 | 13,117.12.0.0 |
| 13.62% | 65.53% | 19.32% | 100% | |
| | | | (14.81%) | (100%) |

(A) Revenue from the royal government's direct shares

As regards the direct share of the royal government from the resources available from Garh Manitri, it was a mere 294 *kāhāṇa* 2 *paṇa* 15 *gaṇḍā* as was previously mentioned. The land part, namely the state-owned land, was 1 *bāti* 10 *māṇa* 14 *guṇṭha* 2 *biśwā* which was worth 117 *kāhāṇa* 12 *paṇa* 15 *gaṇḍā*, and from this state tax of 75 per cent namely 88 *kāhāṇa* 5 *paṇa* 11 *biśwā* 4 *paḍā* was collected. The remaining 25 per cent was probably the cultivators' share .

There was also the cash part (*nagada kauḍi*) of 176 *kāhāṇa* 6 *paṇa* that was collected by the state. (See Table 2.) As regards 'tax for slash-and-burn fields,' we know from another part of the documents that 12 *paṇa* was taken per 'plough' (*haḷa*). Thus about 133 spades worth of tax went to the state. Unfortunately, it is very difficult to ascertain the nature of other taxes. However, we can safely assume at least that the 'fish-giving' and 'oil-presser piece tax' probably refer to taxes that were taken in relation to the fish-catching and oil-pressing businesses. These were business activities undertaken outside the primary community structure and thus there was a need for the state to assess taxes directly in these cases. Whatever the contents of these taxes were, it is important to note that the state collected these taxes in cowry cash directly from the villages. This suggests the wide extent of the usage of cowry cash for the payment of state tax as well as for businesses.

(B) Taxes collected from the shares of communal entitlement-holders

These were taxes collected from the shares distributed to the communal *khañjā* holders and consisted of approximately two thirds of the entire state tax (65.54 per cent). Two types of taxes were paid by the *khañjā* holders, namely *taṅkī* and *utnī*. According to the British Report [*Selections I & II*] *taṅkī* meant 'quit rent' that had a specially privileged rate. *Taṅkī* was given to the king as the 'token' [Pfeffer 1978: 428] of their accepting and subjugating themselves to the royal authority by

Table 2 : Contents of the state's direct shares from villages

| Category | Content | Cowry (*kāhāṇa*) amount |
|---|---|---|
| Land part | 75% of *bāti* 1.10.14.2 worth *kāhāṇa* 117.12.15 | 88. 5.11.4 |
| Cash part | 'tax for slash-and-burn fields' (*toilā kara*) | 100 |
| | 'levy for seedlings' (*taḷī kuḷa*) | 47 |
| | 'fish giving' (*māccha diā*) | 18.12 |
| | 'pole tax' (*khuṇṭa kara*) | 2.14 |
| | 'oil-presser piece tax' (*teli khandi kara*) | 2 |
| Total | | 264.11.11.0 |

Note: The total figure does not match, the inconsistency of which is common in this document.

which they received their shares and assignments. As regards *utnī*, it is not certain precisely what kind of tax it was, but it was certainly one levied on *khañjā* holders collected along with the *taṅkī*.

The tax rate varied in accordance with the particular relationship between the state and a *khañjā* holder. Obviously, in cases where there were tax exemptions and tax reductions, the *khañjā* holders were entitled to that much more privilege from the state. The relationships between the royal government and the *khañjā* holders depended on what kind of exchanges existed between the two, that is to say, what kind of function (military, administration, or other) or value (for instance, ritual or religious legitimacy for power) the *khañjā* holder offered and what kind of economic/symbolic resources the kingship gave in return. Taxes were a part of the different exchange relations that existed between the state and the community members in each locality which gave rise to the positioning of the different *khañjā* holders in relation to the king.

Let us then look at how much tax each *khañjā* holder actually paid.

Firstly, out of the resources of 1,018 *kāhāṇa* 13 *paṇa* 10 *gaṇḍā* distributed as the share to the deities, there is no tax levied on the land known as the 'auspicious nectar-like royal banquet' (*śri amṛta maṇoī*), worth 200 *kāhāṇa* 12 *paṇa* 10 *gaṇḍā*, which is the land donated to Lord Jagannath of Puri, the source of legitimacy of the Orissan kingship. This tax exemption is understandable due to the politico-ritual importance of Lord Jagannath to the royal government. Regarding the taxes for the other deities, 818 *kāhāṇa* 9 *paṇa*, there was only a low tax of 6.90 per cent levied on them, the *taṅkī* rate being 6.25 per cent and the *utnī* rate 2.34 per cent. Although the deities other than Jagannath held importance only at the regional or local level, their patronage by the royal government was of considerable significance since the king's legitimacy at the local level depended on how the king presented himself as the sacrificer for the local communities. In contrast, there was a high tax levied on the payment for servants of deities (42.97 per cent).

Out of the 106 *kāhāṇa* land donated to Brāhmaṇas, 50 *kāhāṇa* part was originally the *jagīr* of the state general and this part was exempted from tax. As for the remaining 56 *kāhāṇa*, there was a *taṅkī* of 25 per cent and exempted from *utnī*. The tax for the Brāhmaṇas was relatively low and was obviously a part of the privileges given to the Brāhmaṇas who taught the locals the ideal of the sacrificial community and the significance of the king as the *dharma*-keeping sacrificer.[16]

As regards the tax rates for the officials in the surrounding villages, that of the principal of village heads and tax collector was 34.38 per cent, the village head 44.60 per cent and the village scribe 25.78 per cent. The tax rate for the village servants such as washerman, barber and carpenter in the surrounding villages was 31.25 per cent. Although these tax rates were much lower than that of the state-owned land (75 per cent), they, especially that of village heads, were still relatively high among *khañjā* holders. They received certain privileges as administrative office holders, but seemed to have been considered more as village officers than state administrators. Their position as village officers can be ascertained from the fact that the village heads also received some direct payment from the villages.

The share of the village watchman, who was one of the seven fort servants, 11 *kāhāṇa*, was not taxed. The village watchman was an important profession for the state as it watched over the security of the fort which played a central military function. For the share of the other four fort servants, namely carpenter, barber, potter and bedmaker, 205 *kāhāṇa*, each person was taxed 2 *kāhāṇa* 2 *paṇa* 10 *gaṇḍā* per head which meant a tax rate of 7.38 per cent. The fort servants were more privileged from the tax point of view than village servants despite the fact that the contents of the job hardly differed. This was probably because the fort servants served directly in the fort which was unarguably important for maintaining the functioning of the state.

Military personnel were further privileged as far as tax rates were concerned. First of all, the chief, *koṭha karaṇa* (scribe), tax collector, labourer, and military musicians were exempt from *taṅkī*. Other soldiers paid reduced taxes such as 1 *kāhāṇa* 4 *paṇa* for the fort guard, 1 *kāhāṇa* 8 *paṇa* for the boundary guard and fort watchman, 2 *kāhāṇa* 14 *paṇa* for the rest of the foot soldiers that came to only a 2.47 per cent tax rate on average. With regards the *utnī*, the chief had 100 *kāhāṇa* of the 458 *kāhāṇa* 2 *paṇa* exempted from tax, the labourer was entirely exempted, Maguni Maharata who was a state level soldier had 210 *kāhāṇa* out of 300 *kāhāṇa* exempted. Out of the taxed amounts, there is a specially low rate of 3.91 per cent for the chief, military musicians, the state level soldiers Maguni Maharata and Jagananda, the soldier of the chief's regiment Parakshit Rautray and Sukhadeba Srichandan and 7.81 per cent for other soldiers and guards. It is not clear why the soldiers Parakshit Rautray and Sukhadeba Srichandan in the chief's regiment were given these tax privileges but it might have been as some kind of a special privilege given by the king to these individuals for some particular reason. It was quite common, apart from tax reduction and tax exemption, for the king to endow certain individuals with some privileges such as the use of specific titles or symbols. Thus, the tax rates of the military personnel combining *taṅkī* and *utnī* were very low, ranging from 2.13 to 10.51 per cent. This is not surprising, since the recruitment of military personnel at the community level constituted one of the utmost concerns of the state who depended largely on local forts for their supply of military resources.

(C) Taxes collected from the community

Miscellaneous taxes from the community level were collected under various names such as 'fort deities' (*gaṛa bhagabāt*)[17] 20 *kāhāṇa*, '*kārajī* meals [?]' 28 *kāhāṇa* 14 *paṇa*, 'examination meals' (*parikshā bhāt*) 5 *kāhāṇa*, '*khandhiāṇa* [?]' 3 *kāhāṇa*, 'transport fee' (*bāja kharcha*) 100 *kāhāṇa*, 'prostitute subject tax [?] (*dāri prajā māguṇi*) 100 *kāhāṇa* plus 'land tax' (*māṇa paṇi*) 146 *kāhāṇa* 12 *paṇa* 12 *gaṇḍā* 2 *kaḍā*.

Regarding 'land tax,' out of the usable land of the whole of the Manitri fort area, 80 *bāti* 4 *māṇa* 20 *biśwā* 14 *guṇṭha*, the *jagīr* of the state general (*baksi*), 1 *bāti* 19 *māṇa*[18]– which consisted of the land donated to a Brāhmaṇa, 7 *māṇa* and the land part of Maguni Maharata's soldier salary, 1 *bāti* 12 *māṇa* – was untaxed. On the rest of the taxable land, 78 *bāti* 5 *māṇa* 20 *biśwā* was levied a tax of 1 *kāhāṇa* 14 *paṇa* per 1 *bāti* which makes the *māṇa* land tax 146 *kāhāṇa* 12 *paṇa* 12 *gaṇḍā* 2 *kaḍā*. It has often been presupposed without foundation in previous studies that the land tax comprised the major state revenue in the pre-colonial state, but this clearly was not the case at least in the Khurda kingdom, where land tax constituted only a small part of the state's revenue.

From the structure of the state's tax, one can observe that the state enjoyed a relationship with the locality at three different levels. Category 'A' represents the state's direct relationship with the villages that formed the foundation of production. This constituted a mere 13.62 per cent of the state's revenue. The state rather allowed the resources from the villages to be distributed to the communal *khañjā* holders. This positioning of the state is reflected in the word 'remainder for the state' (*koṭha rahaṇi*) which is the name for the land part of the state's direct share. This suggests that the state only took hold of the remaining land as the direct share after distributing land to the communal *khañjā* holders. The state also took 'cash cowry' tax from the users of the 'slash-and-burn fields,' and from the fishing and oil-pressing businesses, that did not fit the communal entitlement structures. Category 'B' denotes the state's relationship with communal *khañjā* holders. It consisted of 65.53 per cent of the state's tax from the locality and was the most important source of revenue as far as taxes levied from localities were concerned. The state's revenue presupposed the existence of a system of entitlements, which the state not only protected but also was dependent upon for generating the state's income. Category 'C' indicates the state's relationship with the fort area community as a whole. It included land tax as well as meals and transportation fee provided probably for various messengers of the state to the localities. The existence of such taxes also suggests the state's acceptance of and the importance of local communities as politico-social units.

### *The Use of State Revenue in the Region*

There is a surprising factor regarding the use of state taxes which is revealed in the following documents. Let us look first at the document which describes the settlement of state revenue. Unfortunately, the year of the document cannot be ascertained except that it is from the tenth regnal year of a certain Khurda king. We can safely assume from the contents, however, that it is from the end of the eighteenth century to the early nineteenth century. We find the following description there:

> On the ninth day of *Bṛṣaba* month [late May], in the presence of chief (*bisoi*) Paramananda Samantray and state tax collector (*behoraṇa gumāstā*) Raghunath Patnaik, settlement was made for 3,101 *kāhāṇa*.... The expense in the region etc. is (*thānā*[19] *bae ogeraku*) 1,100 *kāhāṇa*, state expense for the palace (*koṭha bae naaraku*) is 2,001 *kāhāṇa*.

What I mean by 'a surprising factor' in the document is that out of the 3,101 *kāhāṇa* collected as state revenue, only 2,001 *kāhāṇa* was taken towards the royal expenditure and 1,100 *kāhāṇa* which was more than one third was used as expenditures for the region in which it was collected.

Table 3 : Expenditure of state tax for gods and rituals in the fort area of Manitri

| Item | Expenditure |
|---|---|
| Sri Satyabādi Deba (deity at Sakhigopal near Puri) | 22.8 |
| 5 sheep for the state (*khaṭhaku bodā 5 goṭā*) | 25 |
| payment along with these sheep [?] (*e bodā salā samiṅga*) | 11 |
| ...[illegible]..., payment for entertaining visitors [?] (*melāṇi karcha*) | 29.4 |
| clarified butter for fire sacrifice (*homa ghia*) | 16.14 |
| ... [illegible]... | 6.12 |
| ... [illegible]... | 20.4 |
| For the sword hut of Ramachandi of this fort, for *Āświna* month festival.[20] | |
| 2 sheep [for sacrifice] | 10 |
| buffaloes [for sacrifice] | 9 |
| Palace offerings [in Garh Manitri] | 22.8 |
| Total of above | 176.10 |
| Present of silver coin at the New Regnal Year (*aṅka bheṭi ṭaṅkā*), 16 rupee[21] | 64 |
| For things, yoghurt, clarified butter, pumpkin etc. | 25 |
| Total [for New Regnal Year] | 89 |
| For the Swing Festival (*doḷa parbaku*) | |
| coloured powder etc. (*abira ogara*) 10 units | 15 |
| sweets (*sāe sākara*) 10 units | 10 |
| chick peas (*chaṇā*), 15 nauti | 5.14 |
| Total [of Swing Festival] | 30.14 |
| For Mesa saṃkrānti [paṇā saṃkrānti festival] | |
| God Mahavir's *paṇā* drink ... | 2 |
| chick peas (*chaṇā*), 12 nauti | 3.8 |
| Shoes, etc. | 10.8 |
| sugar, black sugar, yoghurt, cheese etc. | 5 |
| Total | 21 |
| For mother cow festival (*gasmā* [*gomā*] *parba*) | 25 |
| Feast after fasting (*chhāṛa khai*) | 25 |
| Total [of festivals] | 190.14 |

How it was used in the region is also very interesting. See Table 3 for the details of the expenditures given in this document.

Within the state tax, the expenditure consisted of that for Sri Satyabādi Deba in Sakhigopal near Puri which is important at the state level (22 *kāhāṇa* 8 *paṇa*), 5 sheep which were probably offered to a goddess in the king's name, and the Autumn Festival of the goddess Ramachandi which was important for legitimisation of the king's authority in the region of the Manitri fort.[22] Ramachandi is the tutelary goddess of Manitri fort and the king had a deep-rooted relationship, donating land and building a temple in front of his palace in the village. The Festival of

Table 4 : Salary and allowances from the state to regional officers

| Receiver | Amount |
|---|---|
| Salary holders (*mahinādāra*) | |
| assistant of chief (*śaradāra jānīsī*) | 27 |
| *baiṭhi karaṇa* [scribe] | 45 |
| *hājira karaṇa* [scribe] | 16.14 |
| *koṭha karaṇa* [scribe] | 65.8 |
| *bhumimuḷa* [accountant] | 65.10 |
| Total [of payments] | 220.2 |
| Allowance [?] (*samiṅga*) etc. | |
| allowance for chief | 100 |
| palace (*behoraṇa*) allowance | 100 |
| west door guard (*paśchhima dwara*) allowance | 40 |
| inner guard [?] (*bhītara*) allowance | 15 |
| *paḍihāri* [?] allowance, 3 persons | 45 |
| state tax collector (*behoraṇa gumāstā*) | [79.1]* |
| Total [of allowances] | [379.1]* |

* Illegible but calculated by subtraction from the total of 1,100 *kāhāṇa*.

Ramachandi includes representations of dominance and kingship in the rituals and by carrying out this festival, the legitimacy of the dominance of the king and those who held power and authority in the king's name in the region was confirmed.

Next, it can be seen that state taxes were used to carry out rituals in the Manitri fort area such as the New Regnal Year (held on *suniā* day), Swing Festival (*doḷa parba*), *paṇā saṃkrānti*, Mother Cow Festival (*gomā parba*) and feast after fasting of Kartika month (*chhāṛa khai*). There is another interesting document regarding expenditure for these rituals, which we will leave until later.

Then, there are notes made on salary (*mahinā*) that was paid from the regional expenditure of state tax to the main administrative officers in the region as shown in Table 4.

The 'salary holders' (*mahinādāra*), as they were called, consisted of the 'assistant to the chief'/ *baiṭhi karaṇa* (scribe) (this was the same person as can be seen from another document), *hājira karaṇa* (scribe), *koṭha karaṇa* (scribe), *bhumimuḷa* (accountant). They received their salary from the state taxes for playing important roles in state administration. These officials except for *koṭha karaṇa* did not receive any share of *khañjā* from the fort area and depended solely on the state salary for their existence.

Moreover, the officials like 'chief,' 'west door guard' (*paśchhima dwara*), 'inner guard' (*bhītara*), *paḍihāri* and 'state tax collector' (*behoraṇa gumāstā*), and the king's palace in Manitri village received their allowance (*samiṅga*) from the state taxes. It is not certain how the nature of this allowance (*samiṅga*) differed from the salary (*mahinā*) of the above administrative officers, but this payment was also no doubt given to officers essential for the running of the state. There was no *khañjā* at the fort area level for offices of the west gate guard, the inner guard, and the *paḍihāri* all of who depended for their existence on payment from the state.

The officers of 'assistant of chief'/*baiṭhi karaṇa* (scribe), *hājira karaṇa* (scribe), *bhumimuḷa* (accountant), west gate guard, the inner guard and the *paḍihāri* had no share of *khañjā* from the fort area but only received salary or allowance as state officials. Nonetheless, these officers received a tax-free residential area in the region and seem to have been given other rights as full members of the regional community. Also their positions were hereditary. The important difference between them and *khañjā* holders, however, was the fact that their status was dependent not on the *khañjā* of the local community but on their position as employee officials of the state. This also meant that they did not have *khañjā* land which was a strong basis of identity in the region but were paid salary or allowance in cash cowry or equivalent rice from the royal government. They had more proximity to royalty and perhaps enjoyed some privileges in this relation, but their position in the fort area can be said to have been less deep-rooted than full-fledged *khañjā* holders.

Lastly, there were miscellaneous expenditures such as for oxen for pulling carts (133 *kāhāṇa* 5 *paṇa*). These carts might have been used as a means of communication between the locality and the capital and for other transportation. The transportation and communication between the capital and forts was vital for the state and the fee was duly paid from the tax.

There is another interesting document which deals with the expenditure of state tax in the locality on ritual occasions. (See Table 5.) It shows that apart from the amount spent for the gifts for gods of various levels on ritual occasions, and for Ganesh Puja and Ramachandi Festival that were performed in the fort area as a whole, expenditures of state tax in the region included gifts on each ritual occasions, such as the Swing Festival, *Mesa saṃkrānti*, Mother Cow Festival and New Regnal Year, to important officials working in the state machinery. It is important to note that these gifts were not just payments, but were gifts that were given

Table 5 : Regional expenditures of state tax on ritual occasions

| Item | Expenditure |
|---|---|
| For Lord Jagannath's Rath Jatra (*Śri Jagannāṭh māhā prabhuṅka guṇḍichā jātra*) | 14.4 |
| For offering *tuḷasi* leaf and money gift (*dakṣiṇa*) at the feet of Sri Satyabadi Deba | 22.8 |
| For Śri Gopinath Deba's *rāsa jatra* festival at Barabati | 2.0 |
| For Mahavir's Mesa *saṃkrānti* day *paṇā* drink, at Naranipada | 2.4 |
| For silk on the same occasion [as above] | 0.9 |
| Mugamunda Mahavir *beubathi* [?] | 0.8 |
| Expenditures at the palace [in Garh Manitri] (*behoraṇare bae*): total | 84.6 |
| Swing Festival | 14.12 |
| Mesa Saṃkrānti | 13.12 |
| Mother Cow Festival | 14.4 |
| New Regnal Year | 37.6 |
| Feast after Fasting | 14.4 |
| For *pratihāri* | 7.11 |
| Swing Festival | 1.12 |
| Mother Cow Festival | 3.0 |
| New Regnal Year | 1.2 |
| Feast after Fasting | 1.13 |
| For chief (*bisoi, śaradāra*) Paramananda Samantray | 51. 5.5 |
| Swing Festival | 6.12 |
| Mesa Saṃkrānti | 4.12 |
| Mother Cow Festival | 11.4 |
| New Regnal Year | 21.8 |
| Feast after Fasting | 7. 1.5 |
| State minister's (*diwān sāhebaṅka*) *dasurāt* [?], New Regnal Year present | 4.6 |
| State general's (*baksi sāhebaṅka*) New Regnal Year present | 4.6 |
| Councilor, Mahapatra's (*rājaguru Māhāpatraṅka*) New Regnal Year Present | 4.6 |
| King's New Regnal Year present | 7.8 |
| For *koṭha karaṇa* [scribe] | 5.0 |
| Mother Cow Festival | 2.8 |
| Feast after Fasting | 2.8 |
| For *bhumi muḷa* [scribe] | 5.0 |
| Mother Cow Festival | 2.8 |
| Feast after Fasting | 2.8 |
| For *beherā pradhān* | 2.4 |
| Mother Cow Festival | 1.2 |
| Feast after Fasting | 1.2 |
| For Ganesh Puja (*haritāḷikā*) | 4.8 |
| New Regnal Year (*suniā*) gold coin (*mohara*) | 20.4 |

| | |
|---|---|
| *Āświna parba* [Ramachandi goddess 'great seventh' festival] | |
| Clarified butter for fire sacrifice [homa ghia] | 20.4 |
| Collective (*koṭha*) buffalo | 30.4 |
| Sheep 6 | 30.0 |
| Expenditure for these sheep | 18.0 |
| Fort's Ramachandi's Sword Hut Festival ['great eighth' festival] | 37.10 |
| Athranga Ramachandi's Festival | 2.8 |
| Barabati Ramachandi's Festival | 4.0 |

on each occasion of annual rituals. Many scholars have pointed out that one of the most important ritual functions is the construction of socio-political relations through ritual actions and exchanges. Gifts to the king and the three main ministers on the occasion of the New Regnal Year, for example, were acts that represented the acceptance of the authority of the king and ministers and that reproduce the hierarchical relationship of authority between the state and region. Moreover, the performance of annual rituals by the royal palace inside Garh Manitri village funded by the gifts taken from taxes collected in this region represented and confirmed the authority of kingship in the locality. Also, the fact that officers of this region received gifts from state tax for the performance of rituals symbolically marked their privileged positions in relation to the state. It was also a sign that they could only continue to claim their authority in the region through the state, that is to say, that they were subject to the king's authority. These had the power of symbolic representation particularly since they were ritual actions which took place in marked space and time.

In this way, the collection and expenditure of state taxes demonstrate that the process of collection and redistribution of products in the region were intimately connected to the reproduction of socio-political relations in both the state and the regional levels. Here the image of the state in medieval India hitherto prominent in existing literature as a body outside the local society, extracting the surplus in the form of tax, does not apply. As a matter of fact, the king and ministers who represented the state constituted specific relationships with members of the regional community through various exchanges. In this way, the specific status of each office and the system of dominance and authority were constituted through this act of exchanges.

The state handed out to some entitlement-holders in the region specific privileges in the form of tax exemption and reduction, and made various gifts on ritual occasions, apart from providing salary and payment, and these constituted a part of various exchanges that reproduced socio-political relationships in the locality. Moreover, the king and ministers were provided with gifts of goods on ritual occasions collected from the region and these were also one kind of exchange linking them to the region in a hierarchical relationship. The state accepted products from the region in the form of taxes, but immediately redistributed one third of this to the expenditure in the region, which was devoted to reproducing the redistributive structure of royal authority connecting the state and various entitlement-holders in the regional community. The redistributed products which regional officers received were no longer mere goods but acted as emblems imbued with royal privileges, honour and dominance, once they came as gifts from the king. The regional officers were thus important members of the region and, at the same time, by accepting these gifts they were imparted with the king's authority and power.

### *Communal Entitlements and the State*

The local community realised a horizontal coexistence by the system of entitlements, but at the same time, the various *khañjā* holders and state officials came to be imbued with parts of royal sovereignty and assumed a role as a king's representative in terms of a certain level and quality. In this way, the kingship principle came to have its place within the regional community. The kingship principle was, in fact, as much inseparable as the community principle was from the regional community, since, as we have seen in the ethnohistory of the establishment of fort areas in Khurda, it was in the combination of the workings of both the kingship principle and community principle that the local communities initially came to be formed. The acts of the granting and receiving of entitlements with land, gifts at ritual occasions, salary and allowance, tax exemption or reduction, titles, insignia of royal authority and other privileges between the state and the local entitlement-holders reproduced the aspects of vertical hierarchy of authority based on the kingship principle in the region. The exchange and gifting of resources that was based on the system of entitlements made possible the cohabitation of multiple groups in the region, and at the same time, also constituted the hierarchical relationships of authority centred around kingship.

The basic human, economic and military resources were reproduced at the community level where the system of entitlements functioned as a sacrificial organisation in which each performed its assigned duty for the benefit of the whole. It was the king outside the community but not detached from it, however, that acted as sacrificer who was the source of legitimacy for each entitlement and who assumed the central position in the redistributive network of royal honour and authority through which the king could command political control over economic, administrative and military resources in the localities. The lived world can thus be said to have been formed by the workings and interactions of the two principles of community and kingship, that together constituted the overall structure of 'sacrificer state and sacrificial community.'

## State Revenue, Warfare and Trade

### *State Revenue and Warfare*

Let us now clarify the implication of development of such state-community relationships for the revenue of the kingdom.

We have seen that the actual income the king obtained from communities of fort areas was rather limited. Instead of the state collecting a large amount of tax from each locality and providing them with administrative and military services, the everyday running of the kingdom was dependent rather upon the workings of the system of entitlements in the local communities. The fort areas comprised multiple centres of communities where not only the basis of social reproduction but also various functions of the state were placed.

As regards the income of the kingdom, there was only a meagre amount of *koṭha* lands belonging directly to the king which provided for the immediate wants of the palace, and most of the cultivated land in the kingdom was allotted to communal entitlement-holders as *hetā* (allotted land with a quit rent) and to state officials as *jagīr*. Also other resources, such as fruit trees, dairy products, and cotton products, available for shares were distributed mostly to entitlement-holders.

In the case of Garh Manitri, as we have seen above, the amount of the share, including land, goods and money, which belonged to the state directly was a minimal 2.24 per cent. (Although the rate could probably have been higher in the plain area of Orissa.) The state tax collected from the entitlement-holders and the community, which can be said to presuppose the existence of the system of entitlements in the community, was 12.57 per cent making the total 14.81 per cent. However, more than one third of the state's revenue was spent in the locality itself and only 9.55 per cent of local resources went to the state's treasury.[23]

Besides the small revenue derived from communities, the king obtained *peshkash* or prestation from his subordinate *zamindārs* or *rājās* of the surrounding little kingdoms.[24] Also, his *zamindārs*, chiefs and other principal subjects sent him *nazarānā* or presents of valuables 'upon the occurrence of a new accession, a birth, or marriage, in the family of the chief, or upon some of the principal Hindu festivals.'[25]

However, these gifts from subordinate *zamindārs* together with taxes from communities can not be thought of as having been sufficient for the running of the state. We have to remind ourselves that the state's need for money rose especially in times of war. And since in actual fact, the Khurda kingdom constantly waged wars against the Mughals and surrounding little kings, there was a need for a steady source of money.

Pre-colonial polities continually attempted to enlarge their shares in acquiring resources – economic and symbolic – and this led to competition through which the more adept managed to enlarge their sphere and share [Peabody 1991a: 38]. It is necessary to note here that the system of gifting of *peshkash* and *nazarānā* among hierarchical polities and between rulers and subjects did not mean that stable relationships existed. The Khurda king's authority in relation to Jagannath also never went uncontested. The king's control over the Jagannath cult and thus his divine authority was rather something to be fought over and won in the context of continuing rival claims from neighbouring kingdoms.

Since the constant waging of war meant that the king needed money, from where may we ask did the king get such money?

### *Money, Trade and State Revenue*

We do not have any historical material that can tell us from where the sources for military expenditures came in the Khurda kingdom, and we can only begin to offer new questions here. We may, however, conjecture one possibility that the funding may have been derived from the state tax on trade through which the king earned additional money to enable him to wage warfare. Stein says that in 'patrimonial' regimes of the seventeenth and eighteenth centuries, 'the quantitatively larger resources devoted to military expenditures ... were drawn from increasingly effective taxation on trade wealth, not landed wealth' [Stein 1985: 76]. We have circumstantial evidence supporting the view that the situation was similar in Khurda.

Stein argues that the above-mentioned fact is related to two features of the regime. One is 'a major reliance for state income upon commerce and upon leaders of mercantile groups' and the other is 'the disjunction between state-level authority and an underpolity of local lordships, or chiefs, with considerable and legitimate autonomy from state-level administration, but subordinate to it' [Stein 1985: 76]. These two features fit Khurda rather well. Concerning the first feature, Ewer records that there was 'a very considerable trade between Cuttack and the regions west of Orissa ... formerly conducted through Khoordah.' The king's treasury was enriched 'from *sayer*[26] duties levied on the transit of grain, salt, and every species of merchandise through the territory of Khurda.'[27] With insufficient revenue from local communities and a meagre amount of royal land (*koṭha*: '*khalsa*' in other regions), it would not be unreasonable to assume that state income relied largely, though it is very difficult to know precisely how much, upon this trade tax. About the second feature, the 'underpolity' corresponds, in the case of the Khurda kingdom, to the fort area communities with semi-autonomous reproductive capacity but subordinate to, and ideologically incomplete without, the state. We do not have direct evidence, but with these corresponding features, it would not be unreasonable to assume that the state of Khurda, too, met the military expenditure with the tax on trade, while largely leaving agricultural production at the hands of local communities.

Cotton textile and rice seem to have been the two major items that went into trade from the hinterland of Khurda, besides salt from Chilika Lake. Cotton textile is still today considered to be a speciality of Khurda. There are ecological reasons behind this. Raw cotton was grown in slash-and-burn fields mainly in the jungle, and the hilly tract of Khurda was abundant in such locations. In the case of Garh Manitri in 1828-1830, out of 645.91 acres of cultivated or inhabited land, as much as 128.83 acres (19.95 per cent ) consisted of slash-and-burn fields.[28] They would make millet, usually *māṇḍiā* (*Eleusine corocana*), which was one of the staple foods for subsistence, in the first year and then cotton in the second year in the slash-and-burn fields. In the third year, they would move on to a next patch allowing the used land to regain fertility. The raw cotton must have been given to the cotton-carders (Tuḷabhīṇā) who carded and teased it into cotton wool, then to others (probably women of different castes) who spun it into threads and then to the weavers (Tanti) who turned them into hand-loomed cloth.[29]

The circulation of cowry was clearly vital for such a transaction. The English kept buying a large amount of cowry from Maldives in the seventeenth-eighteenth centuries in order to meet the expenses in eastern India for textile trade and in West Africa for slave trade [Heimann 1980; Perlin 1987]. It is known that, in seventeenth and eighteenth-century Bengal, humble weavers were paid in advance in cowry [Perlin 1986: 1045; 1987: 300, 320].[30] There is no reason to doubt that this was also the case with Orissa of the same period where cowries were widely utilised [De 1952]. This means that cowry went from traders and moneylenders to weavers, cotton-carders, various teasers and spinners, and to various peasants who cultivated slash-and-burn fields, including not only Khaṇḍāyats (warrior-cultivators) but also, more importantly, Bāuris ('untouchable' rock-cutter) and Saoras (tribe) whose dependency on slash-and-burn fields was greater. The level of monetisation in the wider population of the hinterland and the importance of the humble currency of the cowry in late pre-colonial Orissa should thus be recognised more than it is usually assumed.

Some of the cotton textile, thus collected, found its way, through traders, to English and Dutch traders who bought them at the coastal ports of Orissa, though the amount was considerably lower compared to Bengal and Coromandel. As early as in the mid-late seventeenth century, we find mention of Orissa by an English trader, Bowrey, that 'Rare and considerable quantities of callicoes made and sold to the English and Dutch, cut and finish brought over land to them to their territories in Ballaasore in the Bay of Bengala' [Temple ed. 1905]. This means that textiles produced in the hinterland found their way abroad through trade, connecting rural villages surrounded by jungle to the wider world economy.

Rice was another important item for trade. The agricultural surplus of rice was procured through the system of entitlements by which large shareholders received more than could be consumed by the family and dependants. The surplus rice found its way to traders, the payment in return made again in cowry. Additionally, the record of the entitlements suggests that mangoes, oil and fish also probably went into the local market for exchange there. The non-entitlement-holders such as fishermen,[31] oil-pressers, sweet-makers, goldsmith, cotton-carders and weavers, who were producers of market commodities, depended on market exchange for their reproduction.

The inflow of cowry into the peripheral hinterland was thus connected to the procurement of cotton textiles, surplus rice and other commodities by traders. The outflow of cowry back into the coastal centre was partly realised through payment of tax. Bayly emphasises the two ways in which 'revenue demand "prime[d] the pump" for trade' and 'trade "prime[d] the pump" for the revenue demand' [Bayly 1992: 63]. His argument is that the need for procurement of textiles and other goods from the hinterland brought cash into the periphery, and the payment of revenue to the state capital brought cash back into the centre. This view is an insightful extension of the classical view[32] that it was mainly the demand for payment of state revenue that pushed peasants into selling their crops into the market. Bayly shows that this was supported by the flow of cash in the other direction with the payment for commodities into the hinterland.

In Khurda at least, however, we cannot stress the role of the demand of the state revenue for commercialisation of local products. As we have seen before, the flow of local resources into the state's treasury was a mere 9.55 per cent of the total products in the region that came under administrative control. This demand, of course, must have played some part in bringing rice into the market, but it would not have been enough of a 'pump' for all the lively trade that was taking place. Accordingly, we must here assume that there were more commodities that went into the market irrespective of the demand for state revenue.

Subrahmanyam [1990a] takes up the case of the coastal and long-distance rice trade from the port of Basrur in the eastern coast of south India, despite the low rate of land tax in the hinterland, and questions the validity of the 'commercialization through state coercion' hypothesis. In explaining this phenomena, he says, 'there is ... considerable evidence which points to *production for the market*, quite independently of the exigencies of "forced commercialization"' [Subrahmanyam 1990: 46, emphasis by Tanabe]. While I can immediately accept his argument for the flow of rice into the market independently of state revenue and adopt it to my case, I cannot categorically state that there was 'production for the market' at least in Khurda.

As we have seen, the rice was produced and distributed according to the system of entitlements and assignments of the community members. There was no immediate 'production for the market.' [33] The production of rice was rather controlled by the intricate system of allotment of land and cultivators [34] to entitlement-holders. Instead of there being production of rice for the market, the surplus of rice for the market was guaranteed by the unequal allotment of shares supported by the system of entitlements. Here we see that there was no contradiction but rather compatibility and even interdependence between the community-based system of social reproduction and the monetised market economy.[35]

The redefinition of the community-based system of entitlements in terms of cowry currency in the Orissan hinterland is connected to the introduction of higher administrative methods in the locality in the process of development of 'sacrificer state and sacrificial community' from the late sixteenth century. This had the effect of translating the value of products into monetary terms and thus prepared the way for the different kinds of products in the locality to be connected to the wider market economy. Also, we may conjecture that, as the sphere of the local community was clearly demarcated and the entitlements within were defined, there was concomitant development of definition of the sphere of market exchanges outside local communities. The local community and market, rather than being incompatible with each other,[36] may be seen to have developed in a complementary manner.

Here, we may begin to appreciate the wide usage of money and the importance of the market and trade for the extensive population in the hinterland that went hand in hand with the existence of the community-based system of entitlements. Perlin says that 'in the late seventeenth century, and especially in the eighteenth, ... a new type of monetary economy came into being ... characterised by the extension of money-use to large sections of the "humble" population, to peasants, townsmen and textile manufacturers...' [1983: 69]. This applies to Orissa where the expansion of the usage of cowry was connected with developing market exchanges of foods and goods for everyday living by the regional population in local markets (*hāṭa*) as well as to the need of the periphery region to cater to the demand for supplying textiles by the coastal centre.[37]

I have suggested one possibility that it was from this expanding trade both regionally and trans-regionally that the state was able to collect taxes to pay for sustaining its increasingly expensive warfare operations. However, we must wait for the discovery of new materials in order to confirm this point.

## Concluding Remarks

### *State Formation and Transformation of Locality*

The development of the structure of the 'sacrificer state and sacrificial community' in late sixteenth to eighteenth century Khurda can be seen as an irreversible process of change in the locality. It involved introduction of the king's authority as sacrificer without whom the reproduction of the community as sacrificial organisation was not considered possible. The king was the central authority from whom the legitimisation of duties and shares of each entitlement-holder in the community derived. The actual productive activity was done largely by local communities which not only reproduced themselves but also supplied the king with necessities through different assignments, including, importantly, soldiers when the need arose.

The establishment of the system of entitlements in the community was a part of the state formation in which the nature of the fort areas was irreversibly transformed. In the process, all of the resources produced in the locality came to be calculated and recorded in cowry units, thus establishing the basis for more efficient administration. The amount of shares of each entitlement-holder was defined in cowry units and taxes were taken from them by a proportion also defined by cowry units. Moreover, scribes recorded these entitlements and taxes on palm leaf scripts. Introduction of such advanced methods of administration and monetary institutions exerted a strong influence on the locality which subsequently prompted the significant transformation.

It goes without saying here that, after this transformation, even intra-community exchanges in late pre-colonial society in Khurda were quite unlike the non-monetary, custom-based barter system, hitherto called the '*jajmānī* system.' The duties and shares of entitlement-holders were well defined in the administrative records, in monetary terms, and in the system of entitlements which held the local community as the primary unit of reference, rather than individual *jajmān* households as supposed in the *jajmānī* system. They also derived legitimacy from kingship with which the community enjoyed a very close exchange relationship. The development of 'sacrificer state and sacrificial community' in the late sixteenth to eighteenth century can be seen, from one perspective, as a process where the state and its administration entered and commanded more control over community resources, without, however, breaking up the integrity of the community and remaining outside of it. The maintenance of the state of little kingdoms came to be dependent upon the military, administrative and economic resources offered by the local communities of the fort areas which were the basic constitutive units of the little kingdoms as well as the units of social reproduction in the hilly tracts of Orissa. The development of such an intimate and interdependent relationship between the little kingdom and the fort areas represented a new stage in the history of relationships between the state and community, whose dialectics played one of the major roles in the dynamism of Indian history [Stein 1998].

The particular development of state formation in the late sixteenth to eighteenth century, however, not only meant that the localities came to be more closely incorporated into the redistributive network of the state. It also meant that these regions were, in a word, integrated into the wider market economy. Perlin speaks of 'the "library" of categories and techniques' [1985:435] introduced by the state through which regions came to be incorporated into the universalist, money-based economy. Once values, however localised and embedded in different contexts and systems they may be, were transformed into monetary figures, money was left to generate its magical power of making the valued entities exchangeable without causing them to lose their original specific and heterogeneous values [1987: 309].

Such characteristics of money operating against but at the same time preserving society's diversity and heterogeneity found their parallel in the relationship between the state and community. The state put into operation in the locality the advanced administrative method of classification, assessment and recording and also served to make the community ideologically incomplete without the presence of the king as the sacrificer. However, it is important to note that this did not imply the imposition of a universal system. Each community retained its idiosyncratic character in terms of its population and culture according to its specific history, reflected in a different sacrificial organisation and system of entitlements. The king, as the sacrificer, remained outside the community but was not disjoined from it. He was the central common point of reference among the heterogeneous communities.

## *State, Community and Commerce*

The monetisation – though largely ideological– of the system of entitlements and sacrificial organisation was concomitant with the expanding demand of textiles and surplus rice from the coastal centre to the hinterland periphery in the late pre-colonial period. As the local communities were incorporated into the state redistributive structure and the universal monetary figure was introduced, they were, at the same time, integrated to the wider network of market exchange. Those resources that were allotted by the system of entitlements but that were not consumed by the family which included most importantly raw cotton produced in slash-and-burn fields and surplus rice but mangoes, too, as well as the resources only partially redistributed in the system of entitlement (most significantly cotton textiles but also fish and oil), found their way into the market exchange. This would not have been possible without the opening up of communities and the introducing of monetary institutions through the state formation of the late pre-colonial period that significantly transformed the locality. The development of trade and market exchange also nurtured and supported the reproduction of non-entitlement-holder caste people who engaged in the production of market commodities, such as weavers, cotton-carders, fishermen, oil-pressers, sweet-makers and goldsmiths. From one point of view, it was in fact the re-establishment of the system of entitlements that prepared the way for the integration of local communities into the wider commercial and economic sphere.

Though we have seen that the state could rely on the sacrificial organisations of local communities for everyday reproduction, it remains puzzling from where the state procured its extra resources essential for running the state especially for waging its warfare. We know that the state levied taxes on the flourishing trade that was taking place at the regional and inter-regional levels, and we have suggested the possibility that it was this trade tax that provided the state with these financial resources for waging warfare. However, as the nature and amount of the trade tax as well as the structure of the expenditure for warfare remains unknown to us, these points demand further clarification.

With all the limitations in our present stage of knowledge, it is obvious that the management of the state in seventeenth-and-eighteenth century Orissa had to contend both with the aspect of the structural reproduction of the local communities based on the distribution of shares of the products from the land on the one hand, and also with the aspect of the dynamic movement related to the trade and warfare connected to the sea on the other. It could thus be said that the king's two faces – that of the sacrificer and that of the warrior – had to draw upon the two different wheels – one of the sacrificial community based on the land and the other of seaborne trade. It was the king's capacity to connect the two wheels, which kept the chariot of the state running in late pre-colonial Khurda. This chariot, however, was soon to be taken over by the British who gradually and completely altered its design to suit their imperial style of dominance over the land and sea.

## Acknowledgement

I would like to thank Mr. Sabyasatchi Mohanty of Khurda for helping me with the translations and Mr. Laxmidhar Sundaray of Garh Manitri for assisting me with deciphering and copying the palm leaf manuscript and also for providing me with clues for interpreting the data through his knowledge of local history. I am also grateful to Prof. Noboru Karashima, Prof. Hiroyuki Kotani, Dr. Dilip Menon and Mr. Nobuhiro Ota for reading the manuscript and giving me their constructive criticisms and comments. An earlier and longer paper of the same title appeared in *Rituals as Popular Culture: Towards Historico-Anthropological Understanding of Modern Indian Society* edited by H. Kotani in the name of

Steering Committee of the Research Project: Institutions, Networks and Forces of Changes in Contemporary South Asia, Tokyo, 1999.

## NOTES

1 The term 'little kingdom' was first applied to the study of the Indian state by Cohn [1959, 1987] and further developed by Stein [1980], Dirks [1979, 1987], Peabody [1991a, 1991b], Berkemer [1993] and Schnepel [1995]. Paying attention to the level of the 'little kingdom' has offered a new perspective on the politico-ritual process of interactions and exchanges that existed between different levels of polities. In this connection, I should also mention the names of R. Fox [1971] for north India, and L.K. Mahapatra [1977] and Kulke [1978d, 1993a] for Orissa whose works were instrumental in inspiring research toward this direction although they did not use the term 'little kingdom.'

2 For the terminology of principles, I am inspired by Mizushima [1990] who used the terms of 'individual principle,' 'community principle' and 'state principle.' For Mizushima, these principles denote the share-maximising principle of different subjects such as the state, community and individuals. However, when I use the term 'community principle' and 'kingship principle,' I am more interested in the qualitative difference in the structuring principle of the state and community.

3 My employment of the terms 'horizontal' and 'vertical' differs from Srinivas's terminology regarding the 'horizontal solidarity' (solidarity within one caste) and 'vertical solidarity' (solidarity among different castes in the community) [Srinivas 1952].

4 See an attempt by Stein [1998] to describe the evolution of political forms in India in terms of the relationship between states and communities. This perspective seems to provide promising insight into the development of polity and society in India. As to Stein's 'segmentary state,' however, I have some doubts as I discuss below.

5 The details of the system of allotment of various works and of resource distribution and exchange are dealt with in a separate paper [Tanabe forthcoming].

6 Menon also says, 'Religious practices in the region (Malabar) were characterised by their diversity' [1996: 8]. He relates this to the 'secular' character of community denying its 'religious' framework. However, I attempt to go beyond the dichotomy of secular/religious with the cultural idiom of 'sacrifice.'

7 The date of the reestablishment of the cult of Jagannath at Puri is placed by K. N. Mahapatra [1958, 1969] to be in 1575 followed by other historians such as K. C. Mishra [1971] and P. K. Patnaik, whereas Kulke [1978] places it in 1590.

8 There are several instances where an indigenous tribe is said to have been sacrificed at the threshold of the 'Hinduisation of a region.' They often became, though not in Khurda's case, the tutelary deity (*iṣṭadebatā*) of the fort or the chiefdom. Kulke mentions instances of 'martyr *iṣṭadevatās*' [Kulke 1993b: 100-101].

9 I use italics (*khaṇḍāyat*) when referring to chiefs, and block letters beginning with a capital letter (Khaṇḍāyat) when referring to the caste name. Sometimes, however, this distinction is problematic.

10 Bisoi refers to the head of a *bisi* (county). *Daḷabeherā* refers to the leader (*beherā*) of a regiment (*daḷa*). Bisoi and *daḷabeherā* were usually the same person.

11 Stein himself, in a later paper, denied the distinction between ritual suzerainty and political sovereignty in Indian kingship [1991: 233].

12 Even today, the villagers of Saori *khaṇḍāyat* communities claim that it was the Saori *khaṇḍāyat* who distributed land (*hetā* and *jagīr*) to the people.

13 Pfeffer [1978] refers to *taṅkī* given from the individual Brahman householders of Śāsana village to the principal receiver (king's preceptor) of that village, and describes it appropriately as a token. Here, as pointed out by Pfeffer [1978: 428], the Śāsana village is a microcosm of the kingdom.

14 Berkemer says that 'the more a ruler can give of his sovereignty, the higher his status is' [1993: 319]. He argues this in the context of the pyramid of legitimisation of rulers in which the greater ruler grants privileges, that is, a part of his sovereignty, to a smaller ruler whereby the smaller ruler recognises the greater sovereignty of the overlord. His argument can be applied to the case of the king granting authority and legitimation to communal entitlements, too. The more communities to which a ruler grants entitlements, the greater his territory of rule is.

15 The patronage of local tutelary divinities by the king was not a rare phenomenon. In the king's own Khurda fort, the sister goddesses Barunei and Karunei were worshipped as the tutelary goddesses of the fort (*gaṛh ṭhākurāṇi*).

16 Sharma says in the context of Orissa, 'The significance of land grants to Brahmanas is not difficult to appreciate. The grantees brought new knowledge which improved cultivation and inculcated in the aborigines a sense of loyalty to the established order upheld by the rulers, who could therefore dispense with the service of extra staff for maintaining law and order' (Sharma 1965 p. 281, quoted by Kulke 1982: 246). Kulke reemphasised the 'constructive' aspect of the land grants to the Brāhmaṇas through which the king attempted integration of the locality *pace* the tendency of the Feudalism School to see the alienation of the central power to the intermediaries despite the important point made by Sharma. Karashima 1984 points out the importance of *brahmadeya* (the land donated to the Brāhmaṇa) as a part of the king's policy to govern the locality in the case of Chola.

17 In Orissan villages, there is 'House of Bhagavat' (*bhāgabat ghar*) where the palm leaf scripts of Oriya version of *Bhāgavataṃ* rewritten by Jagannath Das are kept and worshipped. It is also used as a meeting place for the villagers in the evening. This tax named *gaṛa bhagabāt*, (I have kept the original spellings.), may be related to this 'House of Bhagavat'.

18 There is no description in the part of the document dealing with *khañjā* about whether there was a *jagīr* of the royal general. It is possible that the *jagīr* of the royal general was further given as salary to soldiers but this is not certain.

19 '*Thānā*' means 'local.' Formal members of the local community are called *thānī* in Cuttack region.

20 This refers to the Ramachandi festival held in autumn. The sword hut is the place where the sword as the medium of the goddess's power is worshipped.

21 From this document, it is possible to know that 16 rupees was equivalent to 64 *kāhāṇa*. This means that 1 rupee was 4 *kāhāṇa* at that time. This rate matches that of the late eighteenth to early nineteenth centuries [De 1952; Heimann 1980; Perlin 1987: 367; Vogel 1991: 252].

22 The festival of Goddess Ramachandi represents most succinctly the cultural paradigm of 'the sacrificer state and sacrificial community.' For the analysis of the festival of Goddess Ramachandi from a different point of view, see Tanabe [1999].

23 It is stated in the Ewer report that: 'Under the Government of its native princes nearly the whole of Khoordah was parcelled out into jagirs, the holders of which were bound by the terms of their tenure to perform certain services, whether of a private or public nature, about the person and court of the Rajah, besides paying a light quit-rent in cowries, denominated tunkee, or to supply certain proportions of grain, cloth, &c, for his public wardrobe and household expenditure.' Thus, the 'army of paiks ..., the public and private servants of the Rajah, his religious establishments, the members of his family, and even his table cloth and wardrobe, being thus provided for, his expenses must have been extremely trifling, at the same time that he had scarcely any disposable revenue.' [From W. Ewer to W.B. Bailey: 13th May 1818, Paragraph 171-73, in *Selections from the Correspondence on the Settlement of Khoordah Estate in the District of Pooree*, vol. I. p. 59.]

24 It may be added that the Khurda king, in turn, presented a part of his income in the form of tribute of *peshkash* to the paramount power, namely the Mughals or the Marathas.

25 From W. Ewer to W.B. Bailey: 13th May 1818, Paragraph 173, in *Selections from the Correspondence on the Settlement of Khoordah Estate in the District of Pooree*, vol. I. p. 59.

26 According to *A Glossary of Colloquial Anglo-Indian Words and Phrases (Hobson-Jobson)*, '(T)he term Sayer in the 18th century was applied to

a variety of inland imposts, but especially to local and arbitrary charges levied by *zamindārs* and other individuals, with a show of authority, on all goods passing through their estate by land or water, or sold at markets (bazar, haut, gunge) established by them, charges which formed in the aggregate an enormous burden upon the trade of the country.'

27 From W. Ewer to W.B. Bailey: 13th May 1818, Paragraph 173, in *Selections from the Correspondence on the Settlement of Khoordah Estate in the District of Pooree*, vol. I. p. 59.

28 The rest were 'house and back yard' 13.3 acres (0.15%), 'rice fields' 502.43 acres (77.79%) and 'vegetables' 1.35 acres (0.21%). The figures are based on palm leaf script land records.

29 Hossain [1979: 342] gives 'the occupational structure of production' of textile in a table in which it is shown that many kinds of people (Weavers, Dhuneya, Washermen, Nurdeas, Rafugars, Kundigars, Istriwalah and others) were involved in the different works in the process of manufacturing cotton textiles. If the case was similar in Orissa, which it likely was, it means that more people than I have described here were actually involved in the manufacture and monetary transactions.

30 Hossain [1979: 340-41] says that weavers received advance payment in sicca rupees but exchanged them for cowries to shop in the market (*hat*).

31 Fishermen (Keuta) produced flattened rice in Khurda.

32 For example, Raychaudhuri says, in *Cambridge Economic History of India*, 'The collection of revenue in cash generated a pressure to sell' [1982: 327]. Fuller, citing Raychaudhuri, says 'the demand for cash revenue was a major factor serving to integrate villages into a wider economy' [1989: 45].

33 I state this in reference to rice in the hilly tract of Khurda. Textiles already, of course, were produced for the market. Production of rice for the market in the hilly tract of Khurda seems a later phenomenon probably dating from the mid-nineteenth century.

34 Sometimes entitlement-holders were themselves cultivators as in the case of service castes. Among the Khaṇḍāyats, they were sometimes cultivators for one's own entitled land, and sometimes for other's land also. Brāhmaṇas and Karaṇas had cultivators assigned to their land.

35 Menon [unpublished manuscript] also points out, 'There is a tendency to conceive of the economies of town and countryside in opposed terms in which commerce and the market are seen as independent of peasant sociology. The rural sphere is seen as characterised by a moral redistributive economy.' However, he argues, in reference to the pre-colonial situation in Malabar, 'what we have here is a situation in which both the independence offered by the market and jajmani style patronage coexisted largely on account of the volatile nature of the economy.' His line of thought represents a totalising perspective which sees the relationship between the community and the market as not necessarily opposed but interdependent.

The kind of *jajmānī* relationships that developed around the households, that Menon describes, seem quite different from the communal structure in Khurda though. His *jajmānī* relations may represent the stage when the communal structure was inflected by commercialisation and reorganised around individual households. In Khurda, the communal 'redistributive economy' in the countryside seems to have been compatible with the existence of the trade alongside. There is thus a need to investigate more seriously the conditions and contents of transformation of community in late pre-colonial period in different areas.

36 Stein, for example, sees an incompatibility between 'the relations of production self reproduced ... through caste-based relations of subsistence and non-market exchange' and 'money and market' [1989: 10].

37 Hossain mentions that weavers who received money in advance went to market to purchase cotton thread, rice, and other things. [1979: 340].

## References

Bayly, C.A.

1992 (original 1983) *Rulers, Townsmen and Bazaars: North Indian Society in the Age of British Expansion, 1770-1870*, Delhi, Oxford University Press.

Berkemer, G.

1993 'Summary and Conclusion,' *Little Kingdom in Kalinga: Ideologie, Legitimation und Politik regionaler Eliten*, Stuttgart, Franz Steitner Verlag.

Cohn, B.S.

1959 'Some Notes on Law and Change in North India,' *Economic Development and Cultural Change* 8, 1, pp. 79-93.

1987 'Political Systems in Eighteenth Century India: the Benares Region,' *An Anthropologist Among the Historians and Other Essays*, Delhi, Oxford University Press, pp. 483-99.

De, S.C. (ed.)

1952 'Cowry Currency in India,' *Orissa Historical Research Journal* no. 1 pp. 1-10.

1961a *A Guide to Orissan Records Vol. 1.* Bhubaneswar, the State Archives of Orissa.

1961b *A Guide to Orissan Records Vol. 2*, Bhubaneswar, the State Archives of Orissa.

Dirks, N.B.

1979 'The Structure and Meaning of Political Relations in a South

Indian Little Kingdom,' *Contributions to Indian Sociology* (n.s.) 13, 2, pp. 169-204.

1987 *The Hollow Crown: Ethnohistory of an Indian Little Kingdom*, Cambridge, Cambridge University Press.

Fuller, C.

1977 'British India or Traditional India?: An Anthropological Problem,' *Ethnos* 3-4, pp. 95-121.

1989 'Misconceiving the Grain Heap: A Critique of the Concept of the Indian Jajmani System,' Parry, J. and Bloch, M. eds., *Money and the Morality of Exchange*, Cambridge, Cambridge University Press, pp. 33-63.

Geertz, C.

1980 *Negara: The Theatre State in Nineteenth-century Bali*, Princeton, Princeton University Press.

Heimann, J.

1980 'Small Change and Ballast: Cowry trade and usage as an example of Indian ocean economic history,' *South Asia* (n.s.) vol. 3, no. 1, pp. 49-69

Hocart, A.

1950 *Caste: A Comparative Study*, London, Methuen.

1970 [1938] *Kings and Councillors*, Chicago, University of Chicago Press.

Hossain, H.

1979 'The Alienation of Weavers: Impact of the conflict between the revenue and commercial interests of the East India Company, 1750-1800,' *Indian Economic and Social History Review*, XVI, No. 3, pp. 323-45.

Joshi, A. (ed.)

1986 *Phiringi Kali Bharata*, Cuttack, Cuttack Trading Company.

Karashima, N.

1984 *South Indian History and Society: Studies from Inscriptions A.D. 850-1800*, Delhi, Oxford University Press

Kulke, H.

1974 'Kings Without a Kingdom: The Rajas of Khurda and the Jagannatha Cult,' *South Asia* 4, pp. 60-74.

1976 'Kshatriyaization and Social Change: A Study in Orissa Setting,' S. D. Pillai ed., *Studies in Honour of Prof. G.S. Ghurye*, Bombay, pp. 398-409.

1982 'Fragmentation and Segmentation versus Integration?: Reflections on the Concepts of the Indian Feudalism and the

Segmentary State in Indian History,' *Studies in History* vol. IV, no. 2.

1978 'The Struggle between the Rājās of Khurda and the Muslim Subahdārs of Cuttack for Dominance of the Jagannāth Cult,' A. Eschmann, H. Kulke, G. C. Tripathy eds., *The Cult of Jagannath and the Regional Tradition of Orissa*, New Delhi, Manohar, pp. 321-42.

1993a 'Ksetra and Ksatra: The Cult of Jagannath of Puri and the Royal Letters of the Rajas of Khurda,' *Kings and Cults: State Formation and Legitimation in India and Southeast Asia*, New Delhi, Manohar, pp. 51-65.

1993b 'Legitimation and Townplanning in the Feudatory States of Central Orissa,' *Kings and Cults: State Formation and Legitimation in India and Southeast Asia*, New Delhi, Manohar, pp. 93-112.

1995 'Introduction' in Kulke ed., *The State in India 1000-1700*, New Delhi, Oxford University Press.

Madan, T.N.

1997 *Modern Myths, Locked Minds: Secularism and Fundamentalism in India*, New Delhi, Oxford University Press.

Mahapatra, K.N.

1954 'Antiquity of Jagannath-Puri as a Place of Pilgrimage,' *Orissa Historical Research Journal* III, No. 1, pp. 296-306.

1969 *Khurudhā Itihāsa*, Cuttack, Granthamandir.

Mahapatra, L.K.

1977 'Gods, Kings and the Caste System in India,' David, K. ed., *The New Wind: Changing Identities in South Asia*, The Hague, Mouton, pp. 159-78.

Mayer, P.

1993 'Inventing Village Tradition: The Late 19th Century Origins of the North Indian "Jajmani System",' *Modern Asian Studies* 27, 2, pp. 357-95.

Menon, D.

1996 'Becoming "Hindu" and "Muslim": Identity and Conflict in Malabar, 1900-1936,' N. Gupta and P. Mehra eds., *Society, Religion and the State: Identity Crises in Indian History*, Madras.

[unpublished manuscript] 'Houses by the Sea: State Experimentation on the South-west Coast of India, 1760-1800.'

Mishra, K.C.
1971 (1984 second revised edition) *The Cult of Jagannatha*, Calcutta, Firma KLM.

O'Malley, L.S.
1979 (1908) *Puri: A Gazetteer. Bengal District Gazetteers*, New Delhi, Usha Jain.

Pattanaik, P.K.
1979 *A Forgotten Chapter of Orissan History (with special reference to the Rajas of Khurda and Puri) 1568-1828*, Calcutta, Punthi Pustak.

Peabody, N.
1991a 'Koṭā Mahājagat, or the Great Universe of Kota: Sovereignty and Territory in 18th Century Rajasthan,' *Contributions to Indian Sociology* (N.S.) 25, 1, pp. 29-56.
1991b 'In Whose Turban Does the Lord Reside ?: The Objectification of Charisma and the Fetishism of Objects in the Hindu Kingdom of Kota,' *Comparative Study in Society and History* vol. 35 no. 4, pp. 726-54.

Perlin, F.
1983 'Proto-industrialisation and Pre-colonial South Asia,' *Past and Present* 98, pp. 30-95.
1985 'State Formation Reconsidered,' *Modern Asian Studies* 19, 3, pp. 415-80.
1986 'Monetary Revolution and Societal Change in the Late Medieval and Early Modern Times - A Review Article,' *Journal of Asian Studies* Vol. XLV, no. 5 pp. 1037-49
1987 'Money-use in Late Pre-colonial India and the International Trade in Currency Media,' J.F. Richards ed., *The Imperial Monetary System of Mughal India*, New Delhi, Oxford University Press.

Quigley, D.
1993 *The Interpretation of Caste*, Oxford, Clarendon Press.

Raheja, G.G.
1988 *The Poison in the Gift: Ritual, Prestation and the Dominant Caste in a North Indian Village*, Chicago, University of Chicago Press.

Rajaguru, S.N.
1968/1973 *History of the Gangas*, 2 vols., Bhubaneswar, State Museum, Orissa.

Raychaudhuri, T.

1982 'Inland Trade,' T. Raychaudhuri and I. Habib eds., *The Cambridge Economic History of India*, vol. 1 (c. 1200-c. 1750), New Delhi, Orient Longman and Cambridge University Press, pp. 325-59.

Schnepel, B.

1995 'Durga and the King: Ethnohistorical Aspects of Politico-ritual Life in a South Orissan Jungle Kingdom,' *The Journal of the Royal Anthropological Institute* (N.S.) 1, 1, pp. 145-66.

*Selections from the Correspondence on the Settlement of Khoordah Estate in the District of Pooree*, vol. I, vol. II & vol. III, 1879, 1882 & 1885, Calcutta.

Sharma, R.S.

1965 *Indian Feudalism: c. 300-1200*, Calcutta.

Srinivas, M.N.

1952 *Religion and Society among the Coorgs of South India*, Oxford, Clarendon Press.

Stein, B.

1980 *Peasant, State and Society in Medieval South India*, New Delhi, Oxford University Press.

1985 'Vijayanagara and the Transition to Patrimonial Systems,' *Vijayanagara – City and Empire: New Currents of Research*, ed. by A. L. Dallapicola in collaboration with S. Zingel-Ave Lalemant, Stuttgart, Steiner Verlag Wiesbaden GMBH.

1989 'Eighteenth Century India: Another Point of View,' *Studies in History* 5, 1, pp. 1-26.

1991 'The segmentary state: interim reflections,' J. Pouchepadass and H Stern eds., *De la Royauté à l'État dans le Monde Indien*, Paris, éditions de l'école des hautes études en sciences sociales, collection *Puruṣārtha*.

1998 *A History of India*, Oxford, Blackwell.

Sterling, A.

1904 [1822] *An Account (Geographical, Statistical, and Historical) of Orissa Proper or Cuttack with Appendices*, Calcutta, Bengal Secretariat Press.

Subrahmanyam, S.

1990a 'Introduction,' S. Subrahmanyam ed., *Merchants, Markets and the State in Early Modern India*, New Delhi, Oxford University Press.

1900b 'The Portuguese, the port of Basrur, and the rice trade, 1600-

50,' S. Subrahmanyam ed., *Merchants, Markets and the State in Early Modern India*, New Delhi, Oxford University Press.

Temple, (Sir) R.C. (ed.)

1905 'A Geographical Account of Countries round the Bay of Bengal: 1669-1679,' by Capt. Thomas Bowrey (1650-1713) published in *Hakluyt Society Ser.* ii, vol. xii, found at India Office Library under 'MSS EUR D 782.'

Tanabe, A.

1998 'Ethnohistory of Land and Identity in Khurda, Orissa: From Pre-colonial Past to Post-colonial Present,' *Journal of Asian and African Studies* no. 56, Institute for the Study of Languages and Cultures of Asia and Africa (ILCAA), Tokyo University of Foreign Studies, pp. 75-112.

1999 'The Transformation of *Śakti*: Gender and Sexuality in the Festival of Goddess Ramachandi,' M. Tanaka and M. Tachikawa eds., *Living with Śakti: Gender, Sexuality and Religion in South Asia*, Senri Ethnological Series, Osaka, National Museum of Ethnology.

[forthcoming] 'The Structure of Local Community in Pre-colonial Khurda: The case of "the system of entitlements" in Garh Manitri,' (provisional title) P.K. Nayak and R. Parkin eds., *Rethinking Orissa: Society, Culture and History* (provisional title), New Delhi, Manohar.

Vogel, H.U.

1991 'Cowry trade and its role in the economy of Yunnan, the ninth to the middle of the seventeenth century,' R. Ptak and D. Rothermund ed., *Emporia, Commodities and Entrepreneurs in Asian Maritime Trade, C. 1400-1750*, Stuttgart, Franz Steiner Verlag.

# 9

# Kingship, State and Local Society in the Seventeenth-to-Nineteenth-Century Deccan with Special Reference to Ritual Functions

HIROYUKI KOTANI

## Introduction

Of late, the anthropological study of kingship in India, and a few other countries having been under the cultural influence of India, such as Sri Lanka and Nepal, is attracting more attention than the more commonly accepted historical study of kingship. It seems rather peculiar that anthropology as a discipline aiming at understanding modern society in the light of 'other cultures' is taking such an interest in kingship which has hitherto been studied principally in a historical context. Thus, anthropological studies of kingship have been inviting considerable attention by historians, though many of them, including the present writer, are more or less critical of this approach.

There are two principal problematic aspects of anthropological studies of kingship in India which can be summarised as follows:

One is the problem inherent in the essentialist approach to 'Hindu' (hereafter, simply Hindu, though with reservations) kingship which has resulted in the search for ritual Hindu kings in the marginal areas and remoter hills and forests under Muslim or British political overlordship, and even in independent India. In this approach, the so-called auspiciousness-inauspiciousness ideology pivoting around the Hindu kings, (as has been discussed, for example, in Inden [1985]), as opposed to the pureness-impureness ideology being regulated by the Brahmans [Dumont 1980], is expected to play the central role in regulating such societal systems as the caste system. Thus, Muslim kings who could not perform the Hindu rituals are to be ignored even though they were the bearers of central kingship in medieval India, and, as such, functioned as maintainers of the caste system as was formerly suggested by J.H. Hutton and will be discussed later in this essay.[1]

Second is the problem of the endless downward diffusion of the concept of Hindu kingship from the king down to local chiefs, dominant castes, village heads and even to peasants, washermen and barbers under Muslim and British overlordship where Hindu kings of substantial standing were disappearing. After the virtual disappearance of Hindu kings worthy of the name, *yajmāns* (*jajmāns*) at the village level have been observed in place of the king in anthropological studies of kingship in India (for example, [Quigley 1993: 70, 129, 130, 155 and elsewhere]). This downward diffusion of the concept of kingship seems to have made the very idea of kingship itself hollow and meaningless. Even Dirks' concept of 'sharing of the king's sovereignty' by local chiefs through the bestowal of the 'substance of kingship' to them [Dirks 1987: 86] can not counter the same tendency of downward diffusion of the concept of kingship.

Thus, the focus of this essay is, firstly, to examine the actual functions of the king in any given society in Indian history without being constrained by the presupposition of the Hindu ritual king. The most difficult theoretical problem pertaining to kingship is the distinction and relationship between the state and kingship. If kingship is merely seen as one part of the state machinery as the impersonal apparatus of physical power of compulsion, it would be useless to discuss purposefully the problem of kingship in Indian history. The problem, therefore, is how to grasp the specific, supposedly ritual, function of kingship and, in a sense, how it outgrew the state machinery. In other words, the problem to be investigated is the personal function of kingship and its inherent limitation in the historical context of the development of kingship in Indian history.[2]

The second problem to be examined in this essay is the actual relationship between the king/state and the local society such as the village and caste, and whether or not kingship or statecraft permeated down to the bottom of the local society, or conversely, whether or not the local society enjoyed a kind of local autonomy. This problem of relationship between kingship/statecraft and society in Indian history necessarily involves the problem of the role of local dignitaries like Brahmans functioning as Dharmadhikaris and Joshis in the local society.

This essay aims to approach these problems by examining kingship, state and local society in the Maratha kingdom (A.D. 1674-1818) against the background of the classical kingship theory of India, and in the outlook for social changes under the Bombay government as well. Medieval

Marathi documents ranging from the state-level, (state papers such as Royal Orders), down to the local-level, (papers such as those preserved in the families of Kulkarni and Dharmadhikari), which are quite rich in quality as well as quantity, are expected to throw ample light on every side of the state apparatus and kingship down to the local social system.[3]

## *Rājadaṇḍa*, *Pariṣaddaṇḍa* and *Jātidaṇḍa*: Kingship Theory in Classical Law Books

The classical law books of India prescribed the protection of the subject as the first duty of the king (*rājadharma*). According to the *Manu-smṛti*,[4] the Lord (*prabhū*) created the king in order to protect (*rakṣā*) the common people from the inevitable fear (*bhaya*) of chaos (*vidruta*) caused by the absence of a king (*arājaka*) [VII-3]. The king, however, without the necessary means to achieve this purpose could not provide his people with the protection they required. Therefore, the Lord created punishment (*daṇḍa*) and gave it to the king [VII-14]. Through the subsequent fear of the punishment to be inflicted by the king (*rājadaṇḍa*), people abided by their own required duties (*svadharma*) and could thus enjoy their lives [VII-15]. In principle then, the concept of punishment governed people so as to protect them [VII-18].

Referring to the *Manu-smṛti*, the seven constituent parts of the state (*saptāṅga*) were the king (*svāmi*), minister, capital, realm, treasury, army and ally [IX-294], so that the king was regarded as the first but still one of the constituent parts of the state. In spite of this, the *Manu-smṛti* laid down the protection of the subject as the first duty of the king rather than that of the state as a whole comprising its seven constituent parts, including the king. Therefore the distinction between the impersonal state apparatus with the king at its head, and kingship with the personal authority embodied in the person of the king, was not clarified sufficiently in the *Manu-smṛti*. As a result, the king was regarded as representing the entire apparatus of the state in its duty to protect the subject, with punishment by the state as well, thereby being known as *rājadaṇḍa* (the punishment of the king).

Even in the classical law books, however, the role of protection of the common people was not meant to be concentrated in or monopolised by the king. Two other institutions were laid down in the classical law books as guardians of society complementary to kingship. One was *pariṣad* or the 'assembly of learned men' who prescribed penances (*pariṣaddaṇḍa* or *daivadaṇḍa*) to be undergone by grave sinners [Kane: IV, 72]. This means that crimes to be punished by the king were, at the same time, sins to be purified and removed through penances prescribed by *pariṣad*, though it was not clearly laid down whether all of the criminals were to be penanced. *Pariṣad* thus worked as a guarantor of social order by imposition of ethical or moral obligation to the criminal as the sinner in laying down various penances for respective sins. In the *Manu-smṛti*, rules providing penances for each sin occupied a conspicuous portion [XI-43-259].

The second institution meant to be complementary to kingship in providing safety to the people was the community (*jāti*) and the penalties imposed by it (*jātidaṇḍa*) [Kane: IV, 76]. The representative form of *jātidaṇḍa* was excommunication. Community members who violated the rules laid down by the community were excommunicated through performance of a ritual known as *ghaṭasphoṭa* (the breaking of a water vessel [*Manu-smṛti*: XI-181,182]). The excommunicated were designated as *patita* and any association (*saṃsarga* [*Manu-smṛti*: XI-180]) with community members, such as conversation (*sambhāṣaṇa*) and the sitting-together (*sahāsana*) with members of the community, were outlawed and further excluded from the inheritance [*Manu-smṛti*: XI-183, 184]. This means that the community (*jāti*) itself was equipped with the function to maintain order within itself.

Thus, the classical law books of India prescribed the protection of the subject as the first duty of the king, providing *pariṣaddaṇḍa* and *jātidaṇḍa* as a guarantor of social order complementary to the punishment of the king (*rājadaṇḍa*). This triad of *rājadaṇḍa*, *pariṣaddaṇḍa* and *jātidaṇḍa* with historical changes in meaning and designation constitutes the main point of the next section.

## Kingship and Social Order in the Maratha Kingdom

### *Rājadaṇḍa and Brahmadaṇḍa*

In the seventeenth-eighteenth century Maratha kingdom, there existed concepts resembling *rājadaṇḍa* and *pariṣaddaṇḍa* as described in the classical law books. The concept of *rājadaṇḍa* in the medieval Maratha kingdom was, however, considerably different from that of *rājadaṇḍa* as outlined in the classical law books, while the word *pariṣaddaṇḍa* was substituted by the word *brahmadaṇḍa* in the Maratha kingdom. The following case of a murder committed by a Brahman helps to clarify the meaning of *rājadaṇḍa* and *brahmadaṇḍa* in the Maratha kingdom:

> Sadasiv Ganesh Kelkar appealed to the Hozur (a Persian word denoting the king: in the case of the Maratha kingdom of the eighteenth century, however, the word Hozur indicated Peshva), as follows: 'I was arrested under the suspicion of murdering the wife of Gunaji Ganesh Tiwalekar of the village Vanivade and imprisoned in the Vandan fort for 10 years. I was recently discharged from imprisonment but was not purified through the performance of *prāyaścitta* (the purification ceremony). So, I humbly petition the Hozur for ordering me to undergo *prāyaścitta* levying *rājadaṇḍa* in accordance with my means of livelihood and thus for releasing me from the sin (*doṣa*).' In response to his petition, Sadasiv Ganesh Kelkar was made to undergo *prāyaścitta* and was purified as prescribed by the assembly of Brahmans after levying *rājadaṇḍa* and *brahmadaṇḍa* from him. This deed is issued as proof.
>
> [SSRPD VIII-892. A.D. 1792-93]

In this case, the following three *daṇḍas* were inflicted upon the culprit: (1) imprisonment (within a fortress jail), (2) *rājadaṇḍa* paid to the king who sanctioned the performance of *prāyaścitta*, and (3) *brahmadaṇḍa* paid to the Brahmans who prescribed the method of *prāyaścitta* and actually performed it. Of the three *daṇḍas*, (1) imprisonment was punishment determined by the state seen as an impersonal apparatus of power resembling that of punishment of modern states today. This *daṇḍa* of imprisonment thus had no particular relationship to kingship. On the contrary, (2) *rājadaṇḍa* was closely connected to the personal authority of the king. This culprit appealed to the Hozur (Peshva) to sanction the performance of *prāyaścitta* to purify his sin after his release from jail. For a culprit who committed a grave crime (sin) such as murder, it was not sufficient to be punished by the state alone in order to be readmitted into society or a caste (*jāti*). He had to undergo the purification ceremony known as *prāyaścitta* after serving out his term of imprisonment to remove the sin from his body.

This document denotes that the authority to sanction the performance of *prāyaścitta* was embodied in the person of the king. Thus, this authority of the king is seen as a personal function of the king rather than as the impersonal function of the state as the power apparatus. *Rājadaṇḍa* in the Maratha kingdom can be understood as the reward paid to the king as a token of gratitude for his favour of sanctioning *prāyaścitta*. Thus, the meaning of *rājadaṇḍa* in the Maratha kingdom differed considerably from that of *rājadaṇḍa* prescribed in the classical law books. The historical development which brought about the change in the meaning of *rājadaṇḍa* would have been the establishment of the impersonal state apparatus (power structure), resulting in kingship itself having strengthened its personal aspect of ritual authority.

In contrast to *rājadaṇḍa* as a fine (reward) payable to the king, *brahmadaṇḍa* was a reward paid to Brahmans who prescribed the method of *prāyaścitta* and actually performed it. There is no specific account of the 'assembly of Brahmans' in the document but it might have been the assembly of Brahmans engaged by the government. It is difficult to ascertain whether this 'assembly of Brahmans' was of the same character as *pariṣad* noted in the classical law books, though it can be regarded as the medieval variety of *pariṣad*. *Brahmadaṇḍa*, likewise, can be deemed as the medieval successor of *pariṣaddaṇḍa*.

The next case referring to *rājadaṇḍa* and *brahmadaṇḍa* in the Maratha kingdom is a suicide case. In the *Manu-smṛti*, the rule regulating suicide is described in Chapter V, that is, the chapter concerning purification (pollution) as follows:

> The ceremony of water (*udakakriyā*) shall not be performed on those who have been born in vain (who neglect the prescribed), on those born in consequence of an illegal mixture of *jāti*, on those who are ascetics, and on those who have ruined themselves (who have committed suicide).
>
> [V-88]

This means suicide was regarded as an act which brought about pollution rather than as a crime (sin) which should be punished by the state and purified by *prāyaścitta* as well. In contrast to this, suicide was a kind of crime (sin) in the medieval Deccan.

In the suicide case of a daughter-in-law of a Brahman, Rangbhat Dekne, the father-in-law appealed to the Hozur as follows:

> My daughter-in-law, Tama, tried to take her six-year-old son to a river for *sparśasnāna* (the ablution of contact) on the night of a lunar eclipse in the month of Bhadrapad. I advised her not to take the boy for ablution as he was ill at that time. Becoming angry at this she went to the river alone and tried to commit suicide when women of my family stopped her and brought her back home. They continued to watch her at home but she managed to steal out of the house and went to the river for *mokṣasnāna* (the ablution of emancipation).

Since then we know nothing about her. She must have committed suicide as we could not find her though we searched after her for six months. Thus, we want to perform her funeral ceremony so as to enable us to perform *māngalya* (festive ceremonies like marriage). I humbly appeal for your sanction to do this.

In response to this petition, the following deed was issued:

Your daughter-in-law committed suicide. You have already been purified, however, by being made to undergo *prāyaścitta* in accordance with Shastra and paid *brahmadaṇḍa*. Therefore, do the business of Brahman as before and live happily. In connection with this, *rājadaṇḍa* of a hundred rupees has been levied.

[SSRPD VII-592. A.D. 1765-66]

This document denotes that suicide was a kind of crime (sin) in the Maratha kingdom, which was transmittable to the family members of a suicide victim, so that they were obliged to undergo *prāyaścitta* to purify the sin transmitted onto them. For this, however, *rājadaṇḍa* and *brahmadaṇḍa* had to be paid to the Hozur and Brahmans respectively.

Thus, the concepts of *rājadaṇḍa* and *pariṣaddaṇḍa* in the classical law books continued to exist and actually functioned in the medieval Maratha kingdom though their meanings and designations had changed in respective ways.

### *Caste Penalty and Governmental Punishment*

There is no mention in the afore-cited two documents of something similar to the counterpart of *jātidaṇḍa* in the classical law books. In the Maratha kingdom, however, the culprit and his family or kindred were excommunicated from their caste (*jāti*) and had to follow the prescribed procedure for being readmitted into the caste. This penalty of expulsion from the caste or, in the case of readmission, the payment of necessary expenses for a readmission ceremony was, in fact, *jātidaṇḍa* in the medieval Deccan, though the word *jātidaṇḍa* does not seem to be in common use in medieval Marathi documents. (As a rare example in a form of *dñyātidaṇḍa*, see SSRPD VIII-1128.)

*Jātidaṇḍa* in its original meaning must have been the expulsion from the caste, as the ceremony of *ghaṭasphoṭa* in the classical law books denotes. The following is one of the actual excommunication cases in the Maratha kingdom.

Moraji, of the Boi caste (palanquin bearers), was suspected of murdering Karoji of the same caste by using *bhūta* (a malignant spirit). The caste meeting of Bois of the Pune District was thus convened and the suspicion of Moraji was affirmed. Therefore, the caste meeting decided to excommunicate him after breaking out his two foreteeth and also making him drink the water drawn from a well of Chambhars (an untouchable caste) to disable his capacity to use *bhūta.* Against this decision of the caste meeting, Moraji threatened to attack the caste members by joining the Ramoshis (a hill tribe) and the Mangs (an untouchable caste) in case he actually be excommunicated. Anxious caste members appealed to the government for help, in response to which the government imprisoned Moraji in a jail in Kahaj Fort and decided in accordance with the decision of the caste to break out his two foreteeth and to make him drink the water of Chambhars' well [SSRPD VIII-929. A.D. 1775-76].

In this case, the government was asked to excercise its power of physical compulsion against the caste member who refused to obey the decision of the caste meeting, and actually inflicted the punishment on him according to the decision of the caste meeting. This punishment thus can be regarded as governmental punishment as well as caste punishment executed by the state on behalf of the caste.

It is thus true that the caste in the medieval Deccan could excommunicate a caste member who violated the caste rule, but permanent expulsion from the caste was rather rare. In most cases, the excommunicated were readmitted into the caste by the prescribed procedure. The procedure of readmission to the caste seems to differ according to circumstances, particularly whether the excommunicated was a Brahman or a non-Brahman. It would be proper, therefore, to examine the cases of a Brahman first.

In the medieval Deccan, as was the case with ancient India, Brahmans were, in principle, prohibited from drinking liquor and eating the meat of animals. Therefore, Brahmans who took to drinking liquor and eating meat were excommunicated as *patitas.* In one case, a Brahman, Bhikaji Keshav, accused another Brahman, Ragho Lavate, of being a lawbreaker (*adharmī*) and a drinker (*madya prāśanī*) to the Acharya Svami (the spiritual guide of Brahmans). Ragho was accordingly excluded from the commensal seat (*pankti*). Ragho complained of this treatment to a government official who conversely blamed him as follows:

> I and many other persons have been advising you not to drink liquor, saying such an act will lead to the eating of animal meat (*prāṇamāsa*).

Ragho, however, turned a deaf ear to his warning and caused trouble again. So, the official decided to make him undergo *prāyaścitta* asking Brahman communities (*brāhmaṇa-samdāya*) to prescribe the method to purify the sin of Ragho [SPD XXXXIII-159].

In another case of a similar nature, a Brahman, Baraji Dondodev, began to live with a dancer (*kaḷvantīṇa*) and took to drinking liquor (*surāpāna*) and eating meat (*māsabhakṣaṇa*). He was thus regarded as *patita*, and all of his kindred were also excluded from the commensal seat. Knowing this, the Hozur convened the assembly of Brahmans (*brahmasabhā*) where it was decided to make them undergo *prāyaścitta.* They were accordingly sent to a holy place on Ganga (Godavari) River after completing the first half of *prāyaścitta* [SPD XXXXIII-29].[5]

These cases denote that even Brahmans who violated such an important rule for the Brahmans as the prohibition of drinking liquor and eating meat could be readmitted provided they underwent *prāyaścitta*. In the case of Brahmans, however, the caste network was much wider than that of the ordinary castes so that assemblies of Brahmans in many places had to be convened to prescribe the method of *prāyaścitta.*

There is no particular mention of *jātidaṇḍa* in the above-cited two documents. This could be attributed to the circumstances that *jātidaṇḍa* in the case of Brahmans in the medieval Deccan was nothing other than *brahmadaṇḍa* though the character of the document, as an official report from an official to the government, might exclude the possible mention of *jātidaṇḍa*.

*Jātidaṇḍa* appears clearly in the case of non-Brahman castes such as the Kunbi (a peasant caste). In the medieval rural Deccan, peasants used to breed many cows, bullocks and other cattle so that the careless killing of cows (*gohatyā*) and other cattle was often unavoidable. In one case, a Kunbi,Vithuji Valekar, beat his cow one day while milking her in order to discipline her for teasing him (*nāṭhāḷpaṇa*) and unintentionally killed her. He became so frightened thinking he may suffer the curse (*abhiśrāpa* from a Sanskrit word, *abhiśāpa*) of cow killing and be made to fall into hell (*naraka*) that he came to Pune to ask an official of the government (Sarkar) to punish him in a proper manner so as to remove the sin of cow killing from him. The following order was accordingly issued to the headman of his village:

> This peasant is very poor and does not have means to pay the government fine (*sarkārdaṇḍa*). Trying to levy a fine by selling his bullocks and cattle (*baila-ḍhora*), the government lands under his cultivation

> would fall out of cultivation. The fine was thus exempted taking into consideration his poverty and honesty and the cultivation of goverment lands. This deed was issued to certify it. You should send him to a holy place on Krishna River to ask the favour of releasing him from the sin of cow killing before *devabrāhmaṇa* (God and Brahmans). After his return to the village, you should make him hold the commensal meeting (*jāti-jevaṇa*) and then readmit him into the caste body (*jāti-gota*).
>
> [Oturkar no.191][6]

This document denotes that for a grave crime (sin), such as cow killing, inflicted on the criminal was not only the levying of a government fine but also the performance of *prāyaścitta* in a holy place and the holding of the commensal meeting of the caste by inviting all members of the caste. In this case, though, the government fine was exempted and there was no mention of *rājadaṇḍa* and *brahmadaṇḍa* in connection with *prāyaścitta*. Thus, the holding of the commensal meeting of the caste (defraying its expenses) as a necessary procedure for the readmission to the caste can be regarded as the equivalent to *jātidaṇḍa* in the medieval Deccan.[7]

## Local Autonomy in the Medieval Deccan

### *Ritual Role of Dharmadhikari*

In the Maratha kingdom, as mentioned above, the following three *daṇḍas* were combined to maintain social order and control crimes (sins): (1) governmental punishment, (2) *prāyaścitta* (the ceremony for penance) and (3) caste penalty. Ethical or moral offenses not constituting criminal or penal crimes were, however, generally handled without governmental intervention. In other words, local society in the medieval Deccan was equipped with its own institution of dispensing justice in such cases, at the centre of which there was the office of Dharmadhikari (*dharma+ adhikārī*; the officer of *dharma*).

The office of Dharmadhikari was not an office of the state. It was a patrimony (*vṛtti* in Sanskrit and *mirās* or *vatan* from Persian) of specific Brahman families being inherited from generation to generation. There seem to have been two different types of Dharmadhikari. One was the Dharmadhikari of the district (*pargaṇā*). In one case of a dispute between the Mahars and Brahman Joshis of the Paudkhor District in connection with the problem of a practice of whether the Joshis of a district could be requested to officiate as the priest at a marriage ceremony of the Mahars, the Brahman Joshi family of the district claimed to possess the *vṛttis* of Joshi, Upadya and Dharmadhikari of the district [SSRPD VIII-1132]. In another case, a dispute broke out between the Brahmans and Prabhus of the Cheul District with regard to the marriage custom of the Prabhus, when the then Peshva, Bajirav, issued an order in favour of the Brahmans to the Dharmadhikari and to the other Brahmans of the district [ASS VI-66]. These documents denote that there must have been a Dharmadhikari office in each district, but their function is difficult to ascertain in detail.

The other type of Dharmadhikari office was the office that could be inherited within a Brahman family of a holy place. Though many Brahmans lived together in holy places, all of them did not hold the office of Dharmadhikari. Rather this office seems to have been inherited by a particular Brahman family but it is not certain whether the office existed in every holy place or only in specific sites.

The Dharmadhikari played the role of maintaining social order in the local society through the performance of such rituals as *prāyaścitta*. In connection with this function, two peculiar kinds of documents, *doṣa-patra* (the statement of sin) and *śuddhi-patra* (the certificate of purification), were handed down in the family of Dharmadhikari. The following description draws on *doṣa-patras* and *śuddhi-patras* being preserved in the family of Dharmadhikari of Nasik.

In one case, Gangaji, a son of Ranoji Jadhav, formerly living in Nasik submitted the following *doṣa-patra* to the Dharmadhikari of Nasik:

> My father ran mad and began to eat with persons of other castes so that our caste excommunicated my father and myself. We went to the village Gavade and lived there for two years, at which time my father died from madness. I have repented of this and decided to get *prāyaścitta* performed on my father's bones as well as on myself, and then to perform my father's funeral on Ganga (Godavari) River so that I may be released from the sin (*doṣa*) and discharge the obligation to my father, and be freed from exclusion from the commensal and marriage relationship of the caste. With this in mind, I have presented myself before you and stated my sin. So please perform *prāyaścitta* on me and remove the sin which rests on me.
>
> [ASS I-194. A.D. 1795]

In this case, the son of a man, (his caste seems to be that of the

Maratha as judged from the family name of Jadhav), who committed the crime (sin) of violating the commensal rule of his caste, tried to regain admission into the caste after his father's death by being allowed to undergo the purification ceremony (*prāyaścitta*). For this, he went directly to the Dharmadhikari of Nasik and submitted the *doṣa-patra* without appealing to the Hozur to sanction the ceremony. Thus, this procedure of removing the sin, as it were, side-stepped the king. This could be attributable to the circumstances that his father's crime was merely one of an ethical or moral character, that of eating with persons of other castes, and not one of a criminal or penal nature against which governmental punishment was mandatory.[8]

However, in the afore-cited case of a Brahman who lived and dined with a dancer, resulting in his excommunication, the Hozur intervened, ordering him to undergo *prāyaścitta*. What seems to have differentiated these two cases was that the accused party in the former case was a Brahman, whereas that in the latter was a non-Brahman (probably a Maratha) though the Brahman in the former case might be regarded as committing the very graver sin of eating meat and drinking liquor.

In the case of the crime (sin) of physical contact with an untouchable (*sparśa*), the offender could also be readmitted to his caste by merely undergoing *prāyaścitta* as prescribed by the Dharmadhikari.[9]

In one case, Vithu, the son of a barber, Mayaji of Nasik, submitted the following *doṣa-patra* to the Dharmadhikari of Nasik:

> When I was sitting on Ganga (Godavari) River waiting for a customer, a man of Budhalkar (an untouchable caste of skin vessel makers) approached and asked me to cut his hair. I did not inquire into his caste, and he, as well, did not inform me that he was a Budhalkar. So, I wetted his head and began to cut his hair, when one of the members of my caste happened to come along and said to me 'He is a Budhalkar. Why do you cut his hair? You should not cut his hair!' Thus, I (stopped and) returned home. Some days after, I went for the commensality to the house of a member of my caste where some members accused me of the *doṣa* of making contact with a Budhalkar's head. So, I walked out of the commensality while it was still going on. I have, on these grounds, come to you. The *doṣa* of touching a Budhalkar's head is on my body, from which I must be released.
>
> [ASS I-193. A.D. 1795]

This barber, by committing the crime (sin) of *sparśa* (physical contact) with an untouchable through unknowingly cutting a Budhalkar's hair, was regarded as being polluted and was excluded from the commensal seat of his caste. The barber therefore directly asked the Dharmadhikari of Nasik to purify him by performing *prāyaścitta* without having to appeal to the Hozur for the sanction.

Accepting the *doṣa-patra*, the Dharmadhikari prescribed the method of *prāyaścitta* and performed it, as proof of which he issued the *śuddhi-patra* (the certificate of purification) to the party concerned. The following case illustrates the actual procedure of issuing the *śuddhi-patra.*

The mother of Hari Jadhav and Ramachandra Jadhav, two brothers, committed suicide as the result of a quarrel with a maidservant (*kuṇbīṇa*) by throwing herself into a well. The sin of suicide being regarded as transmitted to the relatives of a suicide victim, the brothers were excommunicated by their caste. One year passed in this state, after which they performed the funeral rites for their mother. Soon thereafter, they presented themselves before the Dharmadhikari of Nasik to submit the *doṣa-patra* and asked him to order them to undergo *prāyaścitta.* Brahmans of Nasik then assembled together to prescribe the adequate method of *prāyaścitta* to remove the sin from them, and actually performed the ceremony at the confluence of Aruna. Thus, the brothers were made fit for the commensality (*panktipāvana*) of the caste after paying the necessary expenses of the ceremony. The *śuddhi-patra* to prove this was issued, the main part of which reads as follows:

> *Prāyaścitta* having been performed, you are now fit for the commensality of the caste. There remains no sin on you. Everybody should communicate with you as before in every location and in every country. You, two brothers, are now pure. Nobody should have doubt about this in every location and in every country. As proof of this, this *śuddhi-patra* is issued.
>
> [ASS I-203. A.D. 1806]

In this suicide case of a mother, the sons directly asked the Dharmadhikari of Nasik to make them undergo *prāyaścitta* without appealing to the Hozur to sanction it, while in the previously-cited case of the suicide of Tama, the father-in-law asked for the sanction from the Hozur. The procedural difference between these two cases can likewise be attributable to the circumstances that the former was a Brahman case while the latter was a non-Brahman case. (The caste of the brothers seems to be the Maratha judging from their family name of Jadhav.)

Though the circumstances of the latter case lead us to believe there was no doubt that the criminal (sinful) act was a suicide, the suicide case of Tama is less clear and might somehow contribute to the procedural difference noted.

In the case of the crime (sin) of *saṃsarga* (association, intercourse) with the untouchables also, there was a delicate problem as to whether the sin could be removed solely by the Dharmadhikari or required the intervention of the Hozur.[10]

In one case, Balajipant and others, members of the Joshi and Kulkarni family of the village Pokhali, Parner District, came to Nasik and submitted the following statement to the Brahmans there:

> We committed the crime (sin) of *saṃsarga* with a woman of Chandala, the skinners (*carmakī cāṇḍāḷī*). Therefore we have presented the *doṣa-patra* to the Dharmadhikari of Nasik. We humbly ask all of you to purify all of the members of our family.

Accordingly, *prāyaścitta* was performed and the Dharmadhikari of Nasik issued the following *śuddhi-patra*:

> All of the Brahmans assembled together at the confluence of Aruna and decided the method of *prāyaścitta* in accordance with Shastra taking into consideration their means of livelihood and then ordered them to undergo *prāyaścitta*. The prescribed ceremony of *prāyaścitta* was duly performed before all of the Brahmans so that they might become fit for the commensal seat (of the Brahmans).
>
> [ASS I-200. A.D. 1756]

There is no mention of the circumstances in which *saṃsarga* occurred to the members of this family with a 'woman of Chandala, the skinners,' (the classical name of Chandala in this document must be the Brahmanical expression of the Chambhar caste, as there did not exist a caste called Chandala in the medieval Deccan), though it was not rare that an untouchable woman was employed unnoticed at the home of a Brahman even as a maidservant.[11]

In this case also, there was no appeal to the king to sanction the performance of *prāyaścitta*, even though this was a Brahman case. In some other cases of the crime (sin) of *saṃsarga* with the untouchables, however, the king intervened in the procedure of purification of the sin. The following is one such case. A maidservant (*baṭīka*) of the Prabhu caste, working at the home of the Mamledar of Sivaner District, Balaji Mahadev, was discovered to have committed adultery with a man of the Antyaja (the untouchables). She was therefore regarded as being as degraded and polluted as the untouchables. Thus, the members of the family of the Mamledar living with her were regarded as having committed the same crime (sin) of *saṃsarga* with an untouchable. They, the Mamledar, his mother, wife, sons, wives of sons and a nephew, thus had to undergo *prāyaścitta* called *prājāpatya*. In practice, however, one *prājāpatya* was commuted for two rupees, and the money thus collected by the government was distributed among Brahmans of various places [SSRPD VIII-1125. A.D. 1781-82]. In spite of the fact that the parties of both of the above-cited cases were Brahmans, the procedure of purification differed considerably in relation to the Hozur. The exact cause of this procedural difference is difficult to ascertain but it might partly be attributable to the circumstances that the party in the latter case was a high official of the government like the Mamledar of a district.

The procedure of the purification ceremony of a sin thus differed considerably even in the cases of ethical or moral crimes (sins) without any criminal or penal nature depending on the difference of *varṇa* of the accused party, specifically Brahman or non-Brahman, as well as the difference of the political status of the party. This means that three constituent parts of the machinery for dispensing justice and maintaining social order, namely (1) governmental punishment, (2) the purification ceremony of the sin and (3) the caste penalty, worked together in very delicate ways in the medieval Deccan. In other words, there was no uniform and concrete judicial procedure for dispensing social justice disregarding circumstances such as the difference of *varṇa* and political status.

The king (Peshva) played his own role in this flexible machinery of maintaining social order, since the king possessed the personal authority somewhat outreaching its part or role within the power apparatus of the state. *Rājadaṇḍa* in the Maratha kingdom was a representation of this personal authority of Hindu kings in the medieval Deccan. Maratha kings (Peshvas) thus played an ideological role in regulating social order through its ritual function.

This ritual function was, however, not the monopoly of the king, as in the local society the Dharmadhikari could discharge the same ritual function through prescribing and performing the purification ceremony without the sanction of the king. What guaranteed this independent ritual function of the Dharmadhikari was the authority bestowed on him by the structure of the local society itself which can be characterised as the Vatan system. The Vatan system constituted the basic framework of local society in the medieval Deccan in which the full-fledged members of local society held respective *vatans*. The *vatan*-holders (*vatandārs*) included local district ofiicers like Deshmukh and Deshpande as well as such village establishment as Patil, Kulkarni and *bārā balute* (12 sorts of village servants) which comprised the Lohar (ironsmith), Sutar (carpenter), Kumbhar (potter), Nhavi (barber), Parit (washerman) and some untouchables like the Mahar and Mang. The patrimonial rights of *vatandārs* were so deeply rooted in local society that the states in the medieval Deccan utilised the Vatan system as the substitute for the state's local administration system. The independent authority of the Dharmadhikari, (the Dharmadhikari was also one of *vatandārs*), was therefore solidly sustained by this Vatan system.[12]

*Division of Labour in Village Rituals*

Various rituals and festivals similar in name at least to those held in the power centre by the king were also performed in villages of the medieval Deccan. On these occasions, all of the villagers played their respective roles assigned to them by the village system of the division of labour, that is, the Vatan system as mentioned previously. This means that the division of labour in a village of the medieval Deccan included not only the division of productive or material labour but also the division of spiritual or ritual labour. Thus, the village in the medieval Deccan was a kind of ritual community as well, in which each member had his own ritual part to play.

In the village of the medieval Deccan, there existed a body of village servants collectively known as the *bārā balute* as mentioned before. The services provided by the *bārā balute* to the village included ritual services seemingly with more relative importance in comparison with material services offered by them in the everyday life of the villagers. The following case of the Parit (washerman) serves as a good example of this. In a certificate (*dākhalepatra*) given to the Parits of the Cheul District, their duties in relation to a marriage ceremony and some festivals such as Dasara, as well as the perquisites pertaining to each duty, are denoted as follows:

1. When the Parit spread *pāighaḍyā* (the cloths at a wedding that are spread from the place at which the bridegroom's party alight to the house of the bride), they shall take four *lahārīs* (1 *lahārī* = 3 *āṇās*) with a meal.

2. When the Parit overlay *maṇḍapa* (an open hall erected temporarily for a marriage ceremony) with cloth, they shall take four *lahārīs* with a meal.
3. When the Parit give a robe and turban (cleansed by them) to the bridegroom at the marriage of the Shudra castes, they shall take two *lahārīs*.
4. When the Parit sing a song on the occasion of a marriage of the Shudra castes, they shall take one *lahārī* with a meal.
5. When the Parit wash the clothes of the bride and bridegroom, they shall take one *lahārī* from the bride and two *lahārīs* from the bridegroom.
6. On the occasion of Dasara, the zamindar shall give a turban (cleansed by the Parit) to the following persons: Deshmukh, Deshpande,....
7. When the Parit wave a burning lamp around the head of an idol on the occasion of Dasara and Navratri, they shall take one *sajgaṇī* (two *pāīs*).

[SCS X-4]

This document denotes that the Parit's services to the village were heavily inclined towards ritual services, even including the waving of a lamp on Dasara and Navratri, and singing at the marriage of the Shudra castes. Their main duty of washing also was not limited to the washing of ordinary cloth or clothes. It further included, so to speak, the ritual washing of cloth and formal dress used in the marriage ceremony.

The ritual character of the labour (duty) of the *bārā balute* is discernable in the cases of village artisans as well. In the case of Kumbhar (potter), their main duty is assumed to be the production of earthen kitchen utensils to be distributed to the villagers. But the following duties of Kumbhar gathered from various articles of a very detailed document on the village rituals show that many of the Kumbhar's duties were also closely related to village rituals:

1. On the occasion of Aksayatritiya in the month of Vaishak, the Kumbhar shall give an earthen water vessel to every villager.
2. On Pola of cattle, the Kumbhar shall give an earthen bull to every villager.
3. On Nagapanchami in the month of Shravan, an earthen *nāga* (cobra) is to be installed in the village by the Kumbhar.

4. On Gauri in the month of Bhadrapad, the Kumbhar shall give an earthen Gauri to every villager.
5. On Ganapatichathurthi in the month of Bhadrapad, the Kumbhar shall give an earthen Ganapati to the Deshmukh, Deshpande, Patil, Chaugla and Hakim.
6. On Dasara in the month of Ashvin, the Kumbhar shall give a water vessel to the village god (*grāmdeva*) and to every villager.
7. On Holi in the month of Phalgun, the Kumbhar shall dance.

[ASS III-127]

This list of the Kumbhar's ritual duties gives the impression that the ritual duty of supplying to the villagers earthen idols of gods, bulls and other figures on festive occasions was the essential part of their services to the village. Added to this ritual duty relative to his profession as a potter was the duty of dancing on the occasion of Holi which resembled the Parit's duty of singing at the marriage ceremony of Shudra castes.

As the following cases suggest, all members of the village played their own respective roles in village rituals. The articles concerning Dasara in the aforementioned document on village rituals provide a good picture of this village division of ritual labour in the medieval Deccan:

1. The Kumbhar shall give a water vessel to the village god (*grāmdeva*), and then to all of the villagers taking perquisites from them.
2. Installment of the water vessel in front of the village god.

   (1) The Mokadam Patil shall perform *pūjā*.
   (2) The village Joshi shall take *dakṣiṇā*, the eatable offered to the idol, money and *supārī* cast in the water vessel when it shall be removed.

   The water vessel shall be brought to the house of the Patil where *śidhā* (undressed rice) and *dakṣiṇā* shall be offered to it.
3. Rules relative to the water vessel and Mokadam are as follows:

   (1) The Joshi shall proceed with the water vessel in hand.
   (2) All of the villagers shall accompany him.
   (3) A goat shall be given (as a sacrifice) to the water vessel.
   (4) *Kaḍkaṇe* (a circular paper suspended over an idol) shall be put on the water-vessel.
   (5) A half-cut coconut shell shall be offered to the water vessel.

(6) The *vājantrī* shall perform music to whom the Patil shall give perquisites.

[ASS III-127]

To these articles were added the list of perquisites which each participant of the festivals of Dasara and Navratri would receive. On the left side of the list, there were names of village officials such as the Mokadam (Patil), Kulkarni, Joshi and Chaugla along with the *thal mirāsī* (*thalkarī mirāsdār*) who were the regular and full-fledged peasant members of the village community, more commonly known as the *vatandār* Kunbi, as compared to the *uparī* (a temporary-resident tenant). The right side of the list, on the other hand, included the Sonar, Nhavi, Tamboli and Gurav followed by some district officials, such as the Deshmukh and Naikvadi.

Thus, in these articles concerning Dasara and Navratri, almost all of the villagers appeared though roles of some important members of the *bārā balute* such as the Mahar and Mang were not clear in this document.

In the case of Holi in the same document, however, more members of the village including the Mahar and Mang took part in it:

1. The Koli shall prepare the festival site by sprinkling coloured powder over it.
2. *Viḍā* and *supārī* offered to *racavī* made by the Parit shall be taken by the Parit.
3. The Mali shall provide sugar cane and *eraṇḍa* (a castor oil-plant).
4. The Mahar shall bring the Holi fire. *Viḍā*, *naivedya* and a half-cut coconut shell offered to the fire shall be taken by the head of the Mahars.
5. The Mokadam Patil shall bring *poḷī* (a plain wheaten cake) to tie it to the *eraṇḍa*.
6. The Joshi shall say a prayer. *Dakṣiṇā*, *naivedya* and *viḍā-supārī* shall be taken by the Joshi.
7. The next day, a half-cut coconut shell shall be broken in every home to be distributed to *phaḍkarī* (a music player), to children who danced and to the *bārā balute* who disguised themselves at the festival. What remains shall be distributed to the villagers.
8. *Naivedya* offered to the Holi fire by the village shall be given to the Koli, Kumbhar, Sutar, Nhavi, Parit, Chambhar and Mahar.
9. The Kumbhar shall dance.

10. The Sutar, Parit, Kumbhar, Nhavi and Gurav shall disguise themselves at the festival.
11. The Chambhar shall hold *divaṭī* (a torch or lamp).
12. Cloths used in the festival shall be taken by the Parit.
13. The Nhavi shall give *guḍguḍa* (a kernel of a coconut) to the disguisers (invited from outside).

[ASS III-127]

The village division of ritual labour discussed so far illustrates that the village in the later medieval Deccan was a kind of a ritual community which organised various rituals or festivals on the communal principle of the division of labour.[13] It is difficult to ascertain the influence of the king's rituals at the power centre on these village rituals, though the names of the rituals were almost identical.[14]

One of the other important rituals in the village was one known as *śānti*. Bad omens like the appearance of a comet and the eclipse of the sun or the moon, an epidemic such as cholera and smallpox, and any calamity like an earthquake were regarded as being caused by the anger of the *devī* (the goddess of soil). On these occasions therefore a ritual called *śānti*, where the untouchables such as the Mahar and Mang played the central role, was performed in the village to pacify the anger of the *devī*. In the village ritual of *śānti*, a bull decorated with flower garlands was made to walk around the village boundary with the Mahar and Mang walking before the bull throwing *peḍhā* (a sweetmeat) from a pot they carried outside the village boundary. Afterwards, the bull was sliced at the throat by the Mahar and Mang as a sacrifice to the *devī*. The blood shed from the throat of the bull was poured on the idol of the *devī*.[15] In this manner, the untouchables such as the Mahar and Mang played a very important role in the village ritual of *śānti*. Thus, it is also difficult to detect any trace of the king's ritual of *śānti* conducted through the medium of Brahmans in the village ritual of *śānti* performed by the untouchables.[16]

## Kingship, State and Caste System

### *Religious Neutrality of the State*

It was, by nature, the function of the caste meeting (*jāti-sabhā*) to maintain order within the caste when any problems or disputes occurred among caste members. The caste, however, did not possess the compulsory power sufficient to enforce a decision of the caste meeting on a defiant member who refused to obey such a decision as the aforementioned case of the Boi caste denotes. In such cases, the state exercised its physical power of compulsion to punish such a caste member who disobeyed the decision of the caste. Thus, what guaranteed the effectiveness of caste penalty in the medieval Deccan was the actual physical power of the state.[17]

It was also the role of the state in the medieval Deccan to mediate when any disputes took place among various castes. In one case, a dispute regarding the animal on which a bridegroom was to ride in a marriage procession occurred in Khandesh between the Kumbhars as one party and the Kasars, Sutars and Lohars as the opposing party in the late 1770s. The Kasars and others accused the Kumbhars of violating the rule that prescribed the Kumbhars to make their bridegroom ride on a bull by actually making him ride a horse in the marriage procession. This type of dispute often occurred among various castes, as the animal on which a bridegroom of a caste rode indicated the caste ranking. In this case, the caste whose bridegroom rode a horse was assumed to be higher in caste ranking than the caste whose bridegroom rode on a bull. The government finally intervened and decided in favour of the Kumbhars [SSRPD VIII-1123].[18]

Another case of a similar nature occurred between the Kasars and the Lingayat Vanis in the Karad District. In the marriage procession of the Kasars, a man carrying a pot full of holy water (drawn from a holy river) would head the procession sprinkling holy water on the road. The Vanis began to object, asserting this type of marriage procession was a priviledge of the castes belonging to the Kshatriya *varṇa.* This dispute was entrusted to the judgement of a state official who decided in favour of the Kasars on the grounds that the Kasar was considered to belong to the Kshatriya of *somavaṃśa* referring to Shastras [SSRPD VII-762. A.D. 1767-68].

It was thus the state as the apparatus of physical power of compulsion rather than the authority of kingship that played the role of maintaining social order embodied in the caste system (the order within each caste and between various castes). The state, in performing this function, exercised its public power paying no heed to the religion of the subjects as well as kings or the ruling class themselves. In other words, the distinction between the Muslim state and the Hindu state made, in essence, no difference in this function of the state in maintaining social order.

The religious 'neutrality' of the state in maintaining social order appeared clearly in cases where disputes within, and between, Hindu castes were brought to the Muslim states, or where Hindu castes tried to make use of the Muslim state for their own advantage. A good example of this is the long-standing dispute among the Brahmans in Paithan, a holy place on Godavari River.

A Brahman of Paithan, Narhari Ranalekar, was taken prisoner by the Afghans in the battle of Panipat in 1761 when the Marathas suffered a complete defeat at the hands of an Afghanistan troop and was forcibly converted to Islam. After nearly 10-years' detention, Narhari Ranalekar was released and returned to the Deccan where the Brahmans of Paithan performed a ceremony to purify him. Other Brahmans, however, opposed his purification and appealed to the Hozur (Peshva) for a final decision. An assembly of Vaidiks and Pandits was thus convened by the Hozur to make a decision in accordance with Shastras. The outcome of the decision was that it was not proper to perform a purification ceremony on a man who had lived with the Muslims for more than 10 years. The Brahmans who purified him were therefore excommunicated (*bahiśkāra*) but many of them were then readmitted by undergoing *prāyaścitta*. Another 40 to 50 Brahmans, however, refused to undergo the penance and remained excommunicated.

At that time, Paithan was in a state of double-control or double-power shared by the Mughals (Moglai, but in substance under the power of the Nizams of Haydarabad), and the Marathas (Svarajya), so that Mughal officials too were stationed there. The Brahmans who were excommunicated by the order of the Peshva appealed successfully to the Mughal officials in Paithan for support. They forced other Brahmans who had undergone *prāyaścitta* to accept them on their commensal seats (*pankti*), relying on the support of Mughal officials. Knowing this, the Hozur ordered district officials of the Maratha kingdom not to allow all of the Brahmans of Paithan to sit on the commensal seat with the Brahmans of other locations [SPD XXXXIII-25. A.D. 1772].

This case denotes that even Brahmans did not hesitate to make use of the power of the Muslim state if it proved an advantageous solution in a dispute of religious character, such as reconversion to Hinduism.

It was also the case with disputes between various castes. In the aforementioned case, the Mahars of the Paudkhor District appealed to Aurangzeb, the then ruler of the northern Deccan, for a favourable decision in a dispute with the Brahman Joshis of the district. In the later seventeenth century, Aurangzeb made camp in Aurangabad for the conquest of the entire Deccan and actually put a considerable part of the

Deccan under his direct control. The dispute between the Mahars and the Brahman Joshis of the Paudkhor District began around this same time. The Mahars, several thousand in number, flocked together from mountain forts where they were posted as Naiks (guards),[19] as well as from villages where they were *vatandārs* (holders of Mahar-*vatan*), asserting that the Brahman Joshis should officiate at the marriage of the Mahars. They tried to press Aurangzeb to order the Brahman Joshis to comply with their request. Aurangzeb, however, decided that the Brahman Joshis were not obliged to officiate at the marriage of untouchables like the Mahar taking into consideration the long-standing custom of the location [SSRPD VIII-1132].

In this case, the Muslim king Aurangzeb played the role as arbitrator in the dispute between the Brahmans and the Mahars: Aurangzeb being a part of the power apparatus of the state, was in charge of maintaining social order even among Hindu castes, in which function his religious affiliation had no significance at all.

There were also the opposite cases of Muslim castes appealing to Hindu kings for arbitration in disputes among caste members. In one case, a Mhetar (headman)[20] of the Atar caste (Muslim perfumers) petitioned to the Hozur (Peshva) as follows:

> The *vatan* of the Atar Mhetar of this district is mine. When a marriage or ceremony of circumsion is performed in a home of Atars, I can take perquisites in the form of a shawl and *pāna* (betel leaves) from the party requesting the ceremony. Buwaji, an Atar of Pune, however, rejected giving perquisites to me, thereby causing trouble. I humbly request you to summon him and order him to give perquisites to me.
>
> [SSRPD I-300. A.D. 1745-46]

This petition from the headman of the Atar caste was sanctioned by the Hozur and an order of alleged purport was issued.

In this case, a Hindu king arbitrated in a dispute within a Muslim caste, as it was his duty to maintain order even within a Muslim caste living in his kingdom. Muslim castes did not feel it strange to appeal to a Hindu king to mediate in disputes among themselves, as the function of the king as an arbitrator of disputes among his subjects had no relationship whatsoever to the king's religion. The king in this function was merely a constituent part of the state without relevance to the ritual authority of the king, which went somewhat beyond the state machinery. This means that what ultimately guaranteed the caste system was rather the state as the impersonal apparatus of the physical power of compulsion than the king equipped with his personified ritual authority.

### *Upward-movement of Castes and State: Maratha Kingdom and Bombay Government*

As a corollary of the state's role in maintaining social order or social relations, the state in the medieval Deccan played the role of restraining the social upward-movement of castes by means of introducing Brahmanical practices which would have shaken the social order embodied in the caste system. (The concept of Sanskritization is not used in this essay.) One of the castes who had been trying hard to move upward in the social ranking of castes in the medieval Deccan was the Prabhu. The Prabhu in western India consist of two sub-castes, that is to say, the Chandraseniya Kayastha Prabhu and the Patane Prabhu. Both of these sub-castes showed a strong tendency of upward-movement regardless of the opposition of the Brahman and oppression by the state.

In 1736, the then Peshva, Bajirao, issued the following notice on the status of the Prabhus to Pandits, Dharmadhikaris, Pauraniks, Joshis, Upadyas and all Brahmans of the Astagar and Revadanda districts of the Cheul Province:

> Patane Prabhus residing in Cheul-Revadanda and the Mumbai Province traditionally have followed the marriage practices prevalent among lower castes, such as the Shudra castes and mixed castes (*saṃkarajāti*). It is known now that some Brahmans secretly perform *vedokta* rituals in the home of Patane Prabhus for the sake of material gain and last year a Brahman, Vishvanath Joshi Rairkar, came to Mumbai and gave a *śāstrārtha* (declaring the Patane Prabhu as Kshatriya). In the month of Shravan, Brahmans (Pandits) assembled in Pune from Varanasi, Paithan, Shringeri in Karnataka and some other sacred places. Taking advantage of this opportunity, a meeting of Pandits was convened to inquire into the state of affairs by summoning Vishvanath Joshi Rairkar, and it was decided on the grounds of all of the *nibandhas* that the Patane Prabhu are not Kshatriya but simply a *saṃkara* caste. Accordingly, Vishvanath wrote a letter addressed to all of you purporting that he had not given the *śāstrārtha* declaring the Patane Prabhu as Kshatriya after a full investigation, and that now he officially acknowledged the Patane Prabhu are not Kshatriya, so that the Patane Prabhu have no right to have *vedokta* rituals performed in their home. His letter of this intent was sent to you all.

The Brahmans who secretly performed *vedokta* rituals were made to undergo *prāyaścitta* after taking *daṇḍa* in the form of money. Brahmans who now reside in the countryside or beyond the sea are to come here and undergo *prāyaścitta*. Until then, they are put out of the caste (*dñyātibāhya*) and can not sit on the commensal seat (*apankta*). Furthermore, all of the Pandits assembled in Pune wrote a letter to you all, the gist of which was that any Brahman who performed *vedokta* rituals in the Patane Prabhu's home could not sit on the commensal seat and would be punished. Keep this strongly in mind and perform the rituals meant for the Shudra castes in the Patane Prabhu's home as you have been doing according to tradition.

[ASS VI-66]

Thus, the Patane Prabhu had been endeavouring to obtain the status of Kshatriya as early as in the first half of the eighteenth century by having *vedokta* rituals, forbidden to the Shudra castes, performed in their home by Brahmans. On this occasion, however, it was decided that the Patane Prabhu was a *saṃkarajāti* (a mixed *jāti* assumed to be formed through the marriage of different *varṇas*) by the assembly of Brahmans from Varanasi and other sacred places.

But the Patane Prabhus were not dispirited by this. In 1743, a man of Patane Prabhu was excommunicated by reason of his marriage with a widow. The Patane Prabhu had been trying to move up the social ranking of castes by adopting the practice of prohibiting widow remarriage which had been the priviledged practice allowed only to the Brahman. Brahmans, thus offended by the behaviour of the Patane Prabhu, appealed to the Peshva stating that the remarriage of a widow was an established practice of the Patane Prabhu. Accordingly, the then Peshva, Balaji Bajirao, issued an order to the Patane Prabhu not to prevent the remarriage of a widow.[21]

In the last decades of the eighteenth century, the Prabhu further strengthened the social upward-movement of its caste in spite of repeated suppression by the government. In 1789, the following order was issued by the Peshva government to the district officials of Konkan, Khandesh and Gujarat:

All of the Brahmans of the town Pen, Sakase District came to the Hozur and stated as follows: In the reign of the late Peshva, Narayanrao (A.D. 1772-73), a settlement regarding the way of conduct of the Prabhu was executed by the government. They must behave according to this settlement but they do not do so. They are behaving as they like abandoning their own *dharma* and secretly doing the business of the Brahman. So please command them in this regard and restrain them under control. In response to this appeal, an inquiry was conducted with the result that in the time of the late Peshva, an investigation regarding the conduct of the Prabhu was made and a settlement was reached. The Prabhu wrote the deed of pledge according to this settlement, the details of which were as follows:

1. We do not perform any ritual using the *mantras* of Veda.
2. We do not chant the *mantras* of Veda though we can do so.
3. We do not use the *piṇḍa* of rice.
4. We perform rituals like *devapūjā* by chanting the *mantras* of Purana: We do not offer food to Brahmans in our home.
5. We do not worship *śāligrāma* (a black stone found in Gandak River and worshiped as sacred to Vishnu).
6. We worship in a temple where the Shudra worship.
7. We use the word *daṇḍvata* as a salute to the Brahman as well as among ourselves.
8. We do not engage Vaidik Brahmans, Acharis, *pāṇkyas* (water carriers), Shagirda Brahmans and Brahman women in our home.
9. If a widow wants to remarry on her own free will, we do not prevent it.

The Prabhu wrote the above nine articles, but they secretly continued to do the business of the Brahman in their home. Therefore, the dispute between Brahmans of Pen and Prabhus worsened and all of the business of the Prabhu was suspended. The Prabhu should behave as was formerly settled but they do not do so and behave as they like. This is improper for them. What is proper is the former settlement. The Hozur thus issued an order of the above substance to Prabhus residing in Pune. Therefore, force Prabhus to behave according to the former settlement in every district. If any Prabhu behaves otherwise, punish him and take a fine.

[SSRPD VIII-1144]

As this document denotes, the Prabhu dared even to do the business of the Brahman by chanting the *mantras* of Veda. Further it is clear from the last article of this document that they did not abandon their attempt to introduce the Brahmanical practice of prohibiting widow remarriage.

This type of dispute known as *grāmaṇya* still continued to occur, and in 1796, the order of the Peshva, numbering more than 300 but having the same substance, was issued to the Brahmans of various districts purporting that the Brahmans should perform rituals like *munjī* in the home of Prabhus according to the former practice [SSRPD V-235].

In the Maratha kingdom the social upward-movement by means of introducing Brahmanical practices was thus opposed by the Brahman and oppressed by the state. Under British colonial rule, however, the Bombay government rejected any interference in this type of dispute, so that many castes, conspicuously the Maratha, Prabhu and Sonar, began to adopt, without restraint, Brahmanical practices such as the prohibition of widow remarriage and the abandonment of drinking liquor and eating meat [Wagle 1980; Wagle 1987].

This change in the govenment policy under British colonial rule in regard to the caste system contributed in great measure to allow Brahmanical practices, and subsequently pureness-impureness ideology, to become prevalent among various castes. The following extract from Baba Padmanji's autobiography, *Aruṇodaya* (Mumbai, 1879), serves to prove this tendency.

Baba Padmanji was born a Kasar (a caste of braziers commonly regarded as Shudra) in Belgaum in 1831, and was later baptised in the London Missionary Society's church in Belgaum. The following depictes his experience when he was a small boy in the 1830s:

> My family is not Brahman but used to observe firmly *sovaḷā*. Needless to say, no one took a meal without performing ablution. We were to wear clothes of *sovaḷā* such as *mugtā*, *pītambara*, *dhābalī* and so forth when we performed *sandyā* and *devapūjā* or took a meal. No Shudra servants could enter our *devakhalī* (a chamber of gods) and kitchen. We received water from the hand of Shudra only after they had purification bathing. We used to draw water for the *devapūjā* ourselves from a well. When a Parit delivered washed clothes, we touched them after sprinkling drops of water on them. We did not touch new leather footwear without brushing them first with a bundle of dried grass. After bathing we did not touch a Hajam (a barber). When we touched a Mahar in the bazar, we had to perform *sacelasnāna* (ablution in one's garments). I remember I did so several times. I took great care that the shadow of Mahars should not fall on my body [pp. 7-8].

Thus the family of Baba Padmanji, though a Kasar of Shudra *varṇa*, used to observe the very troublesome rituals resembling those of the Brahmans. In relation to this, the word *sovaḷā* as opposed to the word *ovaḷā* was often used. The word *sovaḷā* was used in other parts of *Aruṇodaya* as well:

> In front of our house were two houses of the Sonar. We were obliged to bring water from a well of one of the two houses of the Sonar as the water of our well was blackish.... We could not get water from the well of the Brahmans. Even if possible, we men of Shudra castes had to carry a drawing rope from our house as Brahmans never allowed us and our servants to touch their drawing rope. If we touched it, they did not use it until having poured water on it. Their *sovaḷā* was like this.... Women of the Brahman took great care not to touch us. On a rare occasion when women of the Brahman visited our home, we had to offer them special stools to sit on. They never sat on our carpet. Their *sovaḷā* was so [pp. 3-4].

*Sovaḷā* is a word derived from the Sanskrit word of *sa-maṅgala* while *ovaḷā* is from *a-maṅgala*, the original meanings of which must be auspiciouness-inauspiciousness. This dichotomous word of *sovaḷā-ovaḷā* was hardly used in medieval Marathi documents. Thus, the word *sovaḷā-ovaḷā* came into extensive use only in the nineteenth century with the change of meaning from auspiciousness-inauspiciousness to purity-impurity. *Sovaḷā-ovaḷā* can therfore be understood to be a popular expression of the normative or Brahmanical ideology of pureness-impureness which was becoming more and more prevalent among various castes under the rule of the Bombay government as a result of its non-interference policy to the social upward-movement by means of introducing Brahmanical practices. Thus, it can be assumed to be British colonial rule that ultimately brought about the social reality where the pureness-impureness ideology dominates in social relations.

## Conclusion

As a result of the discussion presented above, the two problems posed in the Introduction can be addressed as follows.

Firstly, as far as the king's function as a part of the state machinery for maintaining social order is concerned, the king's role was 'secular,' or impersonal, having no relevance to the religion of the king himself. There was no difference in this regard between the Mughals and the Marathas in the medieval Deccan. Kings (Peshvas) of the Maratha kingdom, however, did have the characteristic of a ritual king in sanctioning the performance of *prāyaścitta* for removing the sin from grave sinners like murderers and cow killers by taking *rājadaṇḍa* from them. This ritual function of the Maratha kings (Peshvas) could not be shared by the Mughal kings.

The Maratha kings (Peshvas) using such ritual authority played an ideological role in maintaining social order. This role, however, was not the monopoly of the king, as the Dharmadhikari played a similar role in the local society quite independently from the authority of the king. The king could not deny or intervene in this ritual authority of the Dharmadhikari which was sustained by the structure of the local society, that is, the Vatan system itself.

Secondly, the autonomous feature of local society is observable in ritual functions as well. The king's rituals in the power centre did not permeate down to the village rituals which were organized on the communal principle of the village division of labour (the Vatan system). The village ritual of *śānti*, performed by untouchables like the Mahar and the Mang, had nothing to do with the king's ritual of *śānti* performed by Brahmans. Taking into consideration the independency of these village rituals from the king's rituals in the centre, it can not be affirmed that kingship ideologically permeated down to the village level through, for example, the bestowal of gifts such as emblems, titles, honours and land [Dirks 1987: 93] in the medieval Deccan, though in the Maratha kingdom, the Patil, as an exaple, was bestowed, supposedly once a year, with *sirpāv* (turban) and *pāna* (betel leaf) being given from the *divāṇ* (the government, not the king) [SSRPD I-289].

Thirdly, with regard to the autonomous character of the caste community, it is certain that the Maratha government occasionally intervened in the procedure of excommunication from and restoration to the caste, but there were many cases also in which this procedure was completed without interference from the government. Governmental intervention in this procedure seems to have been limited to the cases of Brahmans and high government officials. In this sense, the essentiality of the autonomous character of the caste can not be denied though it had become somehow difficult for castes to maintain their order totally independently from the state power apparatus.

Fourthly, the social upward-movement of a caste set free under the rule of the Bombay government accompanied by the gradual dying out of the so-called Hindu kings has made the purity-impurity ideology popularly expressed as *sovaḷā-ovaḷā* more and more prevalent among many castes, most of which are of Shudra *varṇa* such as the Kasar. To trace minutely this process of spreading *sovaḷā-ovaḷā* ideology among various strata of Indian society is a subject yet to be pursued energetically. However, this process can be assumed to bring about the social reality that lies at the base of the Dumontian understanding of the caste system. In this sense, overemphasis of the role of ritual kingship and the auspiciousness-inauspiciousness ideology in modern India will surely lead to misunderstanding of the social changes that took place under British colonial rule and continue to do so in independent India.

## Notes

1 In his classical work on the caste system, *Caste in India*, J.H. Hutton points out as follows:

> So clearly has the principle that the secular power is the final arbiter of caste been accepted in the past, that the Mughal rulers of Bengal and their British successors have in turn found themselves in the position of judges of such matters.... In Bengal the Mughal governors retained the right to sanction readmission to caste, and O'malley quotes ... a case in which a Nawab of Bengal refused to restore a Brahman family that had been put out of caste. He goes on to quote Verelst (*View of the English Government in Bengal* [1772], p. 238) on the instructions drafted in 1769 for British officers in charge of the revenue administration there: 'When any man has naturally forfeited his cast (sic), you are to observe that he cannot be restored to it without the sanction of Government: which was a political supremacy reserved to themselves by the Mahomedans' [Third edition, 1961, p. 96].

The exact title of the book written by Verelst (Harry Verelst, the Governor of Bengal from 1767 to 1769) is *A View of the Rise, Progress, and Present State of the English Government in Bengal* (London, 1772) and the page of reference given by Hutton (p. 238) is the page of the Appendix of Verelst's book.

2 D. Quigley criticised Hutton in reference to the passage quoted in Note 1 above saying 'Hutton's characterization of traditional Indian kings as "secular" must, however, be challenged.... The secularization of the Hindu king is the converse of the assumption that "Brahmans are the highest caste" and it is not only Dumont's theory of caste which depends on this assumption' [1993: 149]. Quigley's criticism of Hutton, however, merely

reveals the fact that Quigley's concept of the state and king is not clear enough. In the cited page, Hutton deals only with the king as a part of the impersonal machinery of physical compulsion of the state. He seems to be saying that so far as this function of the king in maintaining the caste system is concerned, the religion of the king or ruling class made no difference whatsoever. In other words, the king as a part of the state compulsory machinery was 'secular' in this function. As opposed to this, Hindu kings' personal authority in ritual function was not 'secular.' Quigley does not pay due attention to this double character of the king.

3 For reference to medieval Marathi documents, the abbreviations shown in the Reference below with Roman numerals denoting the volume number and Arabic numerals indicating the document number are used. Proper nouns and names of castes and offices in Marathi are transcribed in customary forms with initial upper case letters, but without any diacritical marks, while other techinical terms in Marathi are printed in italics with diacritical marks.

4 I have consulted the English translation of the *Manu-smṛti* by G. Bühler in *The Sacred Books of the East* as well as the excellent Japanese translation by Prof. N. Watase throughout while also referring to the *Manu-smṛti* in its original text.

5 In another case of a similar nature, a Brahman who went mad and began to eat Shudra's food (*śūdranna*), including meat, was sent to Trimbak to be purified [SPD XXXXIII-113].

6 The date given to this document, that is, A.D. 1823, by the editor seems to be incorrect. Pune had been under British (East India Company) colonial rule since 1818, so that there could have been no other Sarkar than the British in A.D. 1823, while the Sarkar in this document cannot be the Company Sarkar.

7 In the case of non-Brahman castes, however, the purification ceremony (*prāyaścitta*) could be omitted, as the commensal meeting of the caste itself was regarded as the purification ceremony. In one example, a son of Sayaji, a Mali of the Sasvad District, committed adultery (*bad-amal*) with a Tamboli woman. The family members were thus excommunicated by the caste but they were readmitted as having been purified merely by holding the commensal meeting for two days at their home [Oturkar no. 167. A.D. 1748].

8 In a similar case, a Kasar began to live and dine with a maidservant (*kuṇbīṇa*) so that he and his brothers were excommunicated. In this case as well, the brothers directly asked the Dharmadhikari of Nasik to make them undergo *prāyaścitta* [ASS I-190. A.D. 1791].

9 With reference to *sparśa* with the untouchables, see Kotani [1997: 57-58].

10 With reference to *saṃsarga* with the untouchables, see Kotani [1997: 56-57].

11 In one case, a maidservant of a Joshi, Anand Gopal, was discovered to

be a woman of Chambhar, so that his family and guests were ordered to undergo *prāyaścitta* [SPD XXXXIII-92. A.D. 1795].

12 With reference to the Vatan system, see Kotani [1996].

13 One of the most difficult problems pertaining to the village system of the division of labour is the role of women. In the aforementioned document on village rituals as well, the mention of the role of women is rather sporadic. In one article related to festivals in the month of Margsirsh, women of the Parit, Mahar and Mang were assigned the role of waving a lamp around the head of an idol. In the case of Nagapanchami, the Nhavi played the role of calling for women (*bāikā*) to the worship of *nāga* installed on a hillock of ants. These are the only items relating to the role of women, with some other ambiguous mention elsewhere to women of Parit. Women in the medieval Deccan must have played various roles in the village rituals, but it is still difficult to ascertain women's role in detail.

14 In anthropological studies on kingship, the centrality of the king in organising and maintaining social relations down to the village level is too often emphasised. N.B. Dirks notes as follows:

> A.M. Hocart pointed out the myriad interconnections which linked the constituent parts of the village community together and which in turn linked the village to the state.... The relation of the village to the state was based on the development of kingship, which played an important role in organizing the complex of ritual and social services. One of the fundamental requirements of Indic kingship was that the king be a munificent provider of fertile lands for Brahmans...; for festival such as Dasara which renewed the sovereignty of the king and regenerated the kingdom, and which together with temples were central to the constitution and maintenance of the social collectives of localities, villages, castes and subcastes;....
>
> [1987: 121]

It might be possible in the case of 'little kingdom' or 'little chiefdom' that the king or chief himself was the organiser or maintainer of the whole social relations under his rule but this could not be the case with the ordinary kingdom, not to mention such great kingdoms as the Mughals and the Marathas. In regard to 'little kingdom', see Tanabe [1999].

15 With reference to *śānti*, see Kotani [1997: 67-69].

16 Inden stresses the role of the king in performing the ritual of *śānti* in ancient and medieval India when a bad omen appeared [1985: 35-36]. It is noteworthy, however, that in the medieval Deccan, the performers of *śānti* in the local society were the untouchables such as the Mahar and the Mang who could not be regarded as enjoying a share of the king's authority in

performing the *śānti* at the highest level of the state.

17 The late Prof. H. Fukazawa greatly contributed in documenting this point by utilising medieval Marathi source [1991: 199-244].

This fact, however, does not mean that the caste system was a status system established by the state, (so to say, the state status system). The caste system was essentially a type of social order or social ranking produced from within society itself (so to say, the social status system). The caste system, however, had become unsustainable simply by the society itself in the time of the Maratha kingdom so that it needed the support of the state.

18 Similar disputes occurred even among untouchable castes as shown in the dispute between the Mahars and the Mangs of the Parner District [Kotani 1997: 63-64].

19 The Mahar has been casually called an untouchable caste but at least as late as the eighteenth century a considerable portion of Mahars were still a kind of hill tribe and some of them possessed the *vatan* of Naik (guard) of hill forts [Kotani 1997: 69-74].

20 Caste groups of each district had a headman called Mhetar who was in charge of maintaining order within his own caste by convening the caste meeting when any problem arose within the caste [Kotani 1997: 62-63].

21 *Dñyanodaya*, 1846-11-2. This document can not be found in any authentic compilation of medieval Marathi documents.

## References


*Sanskrit and Marathi*

*Manu-smṛti*: *Manu-smṛti with the Manubhāṣya of Medhātithi*, ed., Ganganatha Jha, in 2 vols.

*Aruṇodaya*: Autobiography of Baba Padmanji (1831-1906), Mumbai, 1879.

*Dñyanodaya*: A Christian periodical published from Ahmadnagar and then Bombay since 1842.

SPD: G.S. Sardesai, ed., *Selections from the Peshwa Daftar*, 45 vols., 1930-34, Bombay.

SSRPD: G.C. Vad, ed., *Selections from the Satara Rajas' and the Peshvas' Diaries*, 9 vols., 1905-11, Poona and Bombay.

SCS: Bharat Itihas Samśodhak Maṇḍal, ed., *Shiva Charitra Sāhitya*, 13 vols., 1926-65, Pune.

ASS: Bharat Itihas Samśodhak Maṇḍal, ed., *Aitihāsik Saṃkīrṇa Sāhitya*, 13 vols., 1934-67, Pune.

Oturkar: R.V. Oturkar, ed., *Pesve Kālīn Sāmājik va Ārthik Patravyavahār*, 1950, Pune.

*English*

Dirks, N.B.
1987 *The Hollow Crown*, Cambridge University Press.
Dumont, Louis
1980 *Homo Hierarchicus* [1966], Revised English translation, University of Chicago Press.
Fukazawa, H.
1991 *The Medieval Deccan: Peasants, Social Systems and States, Sixteenth to Eighteenth Centuries*, Oxford University Press (India).
Hutton, J.H.
1961 *Caste in India* [1946], Third edition, Oxford University Press.
Inden, R.
1985 'Kings and Omens,' J.B. Carman and F.A. Marglin eds., *Purity and Auspiciousness in Indian Society*, Leiden, 1985.
Kane, P.V.
*History of Dharmaśāstra*, 5 vols., Bhandarkar Oriental Research Institute, Poona, Second edition, 1968-77.
Kotani, H.
1996 'The Vatan-system in the Sixteenth-Eighteenth Century Deccan,' D.N. Jha ed., *Society and Ideology in India: Essays in Honour of Professor R.S. Sharma*, New Delhi, 1996.
1997 'Ati-Śūdra Castes in the Medieval Deccan,' H. Kotani ed., *Caste System, Untouchability and the Depressed*, New Delhi, 1997.
Tanabe, A.
1999 'Kingship, Community and Commerce in Late Pre-colonial Khurda,' N. Karashima ed., *Kingship in Indian History*, New Delhi, 1999.
Quigley, D.
1993 *The Interpretation of Caste*, Oxford.
Wagle, N.K.
1980 'A Dispute between the Pancal Devajna Sonars and the Brahmans of Pune regarding Social Rank and Ritual Privilege,' N.K. Wagle ed., *Images of Maharashtra–A Regional Profile of India*, London, 1980.
1987 'Ritual and Change in Early Nineteenth Century Society in

Maharashtra: Vedokta Disputes in Baroda, Pune and Satara, 1824-1838,' Milton Israel and N.K. Wagle eds., *Religion and Society in Maharashtra*, Toronto, 1987.